P9-CQK-226

WORK
IN ORGANIZATIONS

WORK IN ORGANIZATIONS

Edited by

BARRY M. STAW
University of California, Berkeley

L.L. CUMMINGS
University of Minnesota

JAI PRESS INC.
Greenwich, Connecticut   London, England

Library of Congress Cataloging-in-Publication Data

Work in organizations / edited by Barry M. Staw, L.L. Cummings.
       p.   cm.
   ISBN 1-55938-216-3
   1. Organizational behavior. I. Staw, Barry M. II. Cummings, Larry L.
HD58.7.W67   1990
658.3—dc20

                                      90-4475
                                      CIP

Copyright © 1990 JAI PRESS INC.
55 Old Post Road, No. 2
Greenwich, Connecticut 06836

JAI PRESS LTD.
118 Pentonville Road
London N1 9JN
England

All rights reserved. No part of this publication may be reproduced,
stored on a retrieval system, or transmitted in any form or by any means, electronic,
mechanical photocopying, filming, recording or otherwise without prior
permission in writing from the publisher.

Manufactured in the United States of America

CONTENTS

LIST OF CONTRIBUTORS   vii

PREFACE   ix

MOTIVATION THEORY RECONSIDERED   1
  Frank J. Landy and Wendy S. Becker

ACTIVATION THEORY AND JOB DESIGN:
REVIEW AND RECONCEPTUALIZATION   39
  Donald G. Gardner and L.L. Cummings

TOWARD AN INTEGRATED THEORY OF TASK DESIGN   81
  Ricky M. Griffin

OF ART AND WORK: AESTHETIC EXPERIENCE
AND THE PSYCHOLOGY OF WORK FEELINGS   123
  Lloyd E. Sandelands and Georgette C. Buckner

THE EXPRESSION OF EMOTION IN
ORGANIZATIONAL LIFE   151
  Anat Rafaeli and Robert I. Sutton

"REAL FEELINGS": EMOTIONAL EXPRESSION AND
ORGANIZATIONAL CULTURE   193
  John Van Maanen and Gideon Kunda

WORK VALUES AND THE CONDUCT OF
ORGANIZATIONAL BEHAVIOR   255
  Walter R. Nord, Arthur P. Brief,
  Jennifer M. Atieh, and Elizabeth M. Doherty

LIST OF CONTRIBUTORS

Jennifer M. Atieh
Texas A&M University

Wendy S. Becker
Pennsylvania State University

Arthur P. Brief
Tulane University

Georgette C. Buckner
Columbia University

L.L. Cummings
University of Minnesota

Elizabeth M. Doherty
Washington University

Donald G. Gardner
University of Colorado

Ricky W. Griffin
Texas A&M University

Gideon Kunda
Tel Aviv University

Frank J. Landy
Pennsylvania State University

Walter R. Nord
University of South Florida

Anat Rafaeli
Hebrew University of Jerusalem

Lloyd E. Sandelands
University of Michigan

Robert I. Sutton
Stanford University

John Van Maanen
*Massachusetts Institute of
    Technology*

PREFACE

The nature of work and how people respond to it have long been of interest to organizational researchers. Therefore, we have drawn together seven essays from recent volumes of the annual series, *Research in Organizational Behavior*, to further explore this theme. The essays are diverse as well as representative of the most up-to-date thinking about work—ranging from questions of motivation to theories of job design and emotion in organizational settings.

The anthology starts with Frank Landy and Wendy Becker's essay on task motivation. They provide a strong critique of current motivation research and argue that the search for a universal theory of work behavior is quixotic. In its place, they advocate a middle-range approach in which different theories (such as equity, expectancy, and goal-setting) are used to explain separate and identifiable behaviors such as choice, performance, and satisfaction.

The next three chapters explore ways jobs are constructed and their multiple effects on individuals. Donald Gardner and L.L. Cummings review current research on activation theory to explain individuals' physiological responses to work. Ricky Griffin then outlines the debate between the job characteristics model of work and the social-information-processing approach, producing an integrated model that accounts for people's reactions to the objective nature of the job as well as the prevalence of social influences. Finally, in an unusual and provocative approach to the topic, Lloyd Sandelands and Georgette Buckner argue that work should be considered as an aesthetic experience. To learn about feelings of work we are instructed to consider the characteristics of art and how it is experienced by individuals.

The following two essays move from the way tasks influence individual behaviors and attitudes to how emotions are expressed on the job. Anat Rafaeli and Robert Sutton present a general model of variables determining the expression of emotion, ranging from individual personality traits to display rules governing the particular work situation. Through two brief ethnographies, John Van Maanen and Gideon Kunda then explore the role of organizational culture in the display of emotion. They show how organizational norms mold and channel individual feelings toward co-workers, customers, and oneself, obscuring the boundaries between real and displayed emotions at work.

The final chapter of this anthology concerns work values. Walter Nord, Arthur Brief, Jennifer Atieh, and Elizabeth Doherty critique our current view of work in light of historical and philosophical research, arguing that the common alignment of the Protestant work ethic with the desire of people for intrinsically interesting work is misconceived. They propose that work ethics should be conceived as a socially defined concept, with more attention paid to cultural and institutional variables underlying task values.

Although many of the chapters in this volume have already achieved prominence as individual contributions, it is our hope that, by pulling these essays together, further collective progress can be made. Studies of work behavior are starting to move away from traditional models of job satisfaction and performance and toward new conceptual schemes. We believe this collection of essays is both reflective and stimulative of this trend.

L.L. CUMMINGS
Minneapolis, Minnesota

BARRY M. STAW
Berkeley, California

MOTIVATION THEORY RECONSIDERED

Frank J. Landy and Wendy S. Becker

ABSTRACT

As has been the case in many areas of psychology, the history of motivation
theory and research has seen a search for the "right" theory. It has been
assumed that when such a theory was found, a wide range of behaviors
would be better understood. Many models have been examined. One of the
earliest was the need model. This was followed by the reinforcement model,
equity theory, and expectancy theory. Most recently, the goal-setting model
has received a good deal of attention.

There is one theme that seems apparent in current discussions of motivational models—the importance of cognitive processes. This is not surprising because the cognitive revolution has swept virtually all of psychology.
In the present chapter, each of the approaches to motivation is considered
from the cognitive perspective. Research that bears on the general cognitive
hypothesis is presented.

In the course of reviewing recent research on the various models, we
speculate that there has been a natural nesting of dependent variables in
particular motivational approaches. It is suggested that need and equity approaches might be best suited to exploring affective consequences of work.
Reinforcement models and goal theory seem well suited to the understanding
of specific work behaviors. Expectancy theory is philosophically, historically, and structurally suited to the prediction of choice among alternatives.

We conclude with some suggestions for future research themes. First,
we propose that particular cognitive operations be examined in the context
of motivational models. Next, we suggest that dependent variables be arranged on a temporal continuum and an attempt be made to consider the
role of time frame on choice of motivational approach. Finally, we encourage
the reader to combine the elements of various approaches to form new,
middle-range theories of behavior.

1

In preparing this chapter, we were encouraged by the editors to take the position of the essayist rather than the chronicler. Our task is to introduce some lines of speculation, to sample some recent research that gives rise to that speculation, to present specimens of new theory and research designs and, ultimately, to persuade the reader to pick up the burden of a novel idea or approach and to carry it some distance for us. In a sense, we would like to act as idea entrepreneur.

In accepting the challenge of the essay, we readily recognize and admit to some limitations. The research that we describe has been chosen because it supports or illustrates some a priori positions that we hold. The chapter was not intended to be nor should it be considered an inductive exercise in which propositions follow closely from careful reviews of limited research results. If anything, the process worked in reverse. We had some ideas and looked around for research or independent theory that agreed with those ideas. On the other hand, the propositions that we explore have been carved from many years of reading and research in the area of work and general motivation, so they are something more than the stream of consciousness overflowing its banks.

The construct of motivation is incredibly broad, a point well illustrated by the wide diversity of theories and data that we will consider. A book chapter does not present sufficient space to treat such a topic in any comprehensive manner. As a result, we have a choice. We can either deal with one limited aspect of motivation theory (e.g., the role of memory in current theories of motivation), or we can pull together a ''sampler'' of important issues. The latter strategy is the more exciting of the two for the present authors and, arguably, more valuable for the reader. As a result, our essay will be built around the sampler model. Even with this model, we have not chosen topics randomly. Instead, there are several themes that will pervade our comments. The first theme is that of cognition. To borrow and bend a quote from Tolman, behavior reeks of cognition. There is no theoretical approach that can ignore cognitive mechanisms of one kind or another, the only issue is the extent to which the theorist emphasizes those mechanisms. For example, even the ''noncognitive'' approach of the behaviorists requires a memory mechanism. How could associations be formed without such a function. The behaviorists might glibly counter with a reductionist response about the neurochemical basis for memory but we are left with the phenomenon of meta-memory, that is, the realization by individuals that they ''have'' and can ''use'' the memory function to their advantage.

A second theme that will run through the sampler is the notion that various theoretical approaches are differentially suited for explaining behavior on a continuum ranging from the broad to the specific. There is no reason to believe that the same theory that will explain career choice will also explain the absence or work-related effort of an individual. In fact, we will try to show that there is a type of inchoate realization of this differentiation obvious in the way in which various motivational researchers choose their dependent variables.

What we are really trying to say in this essay is that we have more than enough theories of motivation and more than enough data on motivational phenomena. What is needed is a new synthesis of both theory and data. We need to be more clever with what we already have.

There will be three major sections to the essay. The first section will present a rough taxonomy of motivation theory that will be used in later sections. In addition, this section will deal with the general issues relating to the development and testing of current theories of motivation. The second section will deal with the extent to which the cognitive revolution in psychology that began in the early 1960s is manifest in theories of work motivation. More to the point, we will suggest areas where cognitive mechanisms need greater representation. The third section will consider motivation theory from the perspective of the behavior it purports to explain. We have used the label *middle-range theories* to describe this section. The label was taken from a recent book by Pinder (1984) in which he argues for smaller theories of motivation. We agree and try to demonstrate that these middle-range theories can be linked to particular dependent variables.

The diversity of material to be covered in these three sections is intimidating to author and reader alike. Nevertheless, it is our feeling that this diversity also increases the probability that we can stimulate and inform the reader. Most of the points that we raise in this chapter represent "itches" that we have endured for many years now—they need to be scratched and this chapter is a good opportunity to do just that. As Karl Weick mused in a convention paper presented many years ago "How do I know what I mean until I see what I say?" We feel the same way. It is our hope that we will be able to clarify our own and the reader's thinking in the course of developing these multiple topics.

One final note of caution. We assume that the reader is generally familiar with motivational literature and will, as a result, often assume such general familiarity in our discussions of a particular point.

THE CURRENT STATUS OF MOTIVATION THEORY

Do We Need the Construct of Motivation?

Kleinginna and Kleinginna (1981) have gathered no fewer than 140 definitions of *motivation* that have appeared in the literature. Some of these definitions are hopeful and others are skeptical. For example, Vroom (1964) defines motivation as "a process governing choices made by persons or lower organisms among alternative forms of voluntary activity," an admiring definition. On the other hand, Bolles (1975) suggests that "motivation seems to be neither a fact of experience nor a fact of behavior, but rather an idea or concept we introduce when we undertake to explain behavior." This definition places the motivation construct in the role of a heuristic device, useful for communication but little else. In a decidedly more negative vein, Dewsbury (1978) proposes that the "concept of motivation tends to be used as a garbage pail for a variety of factors whose nature is not well understood." Although there has been a great deal of debate in the psychological community in general about the role of or need for the construct of motivation, this has not been an issue for much discussion in industrial and organizational psychology. It seems as if we, as a group, have accepted the role of the motivational construct in understanding behavior. Such an uncritical acceptance is dangerous and, at best, ascientific.

One of the points we will try to make in this chapter is that motivational research and theory is in a state of disorder. One reason for this disorder is the uncritical acceptance of the construct. Consider a relatively simple question: What is motivated behavior? Attempts to answer that question highlight the implicit confusion about the construct and its role. Certainly, the fact that people choose certain dependent variables to examine when testing a motivational theory must imply that these people consider the behavior chosen to be "motivated." If not, why would they risk the test of theory on such a dependent variable? Thus, effort expenditure, absenteeism, satisfaction, job choice, career choice, and performance must be considered, by some, to be motivated behaviors, because they assume the role of dependent variables in motivational research.

Let's take one more step p back from the phenomenon and ask a second question: Given that the preceding variables are considered examples of motivated behavior, are they *always* instances of motivational mechanisms? Now some squirming begins to appear. Certainly, not every instance of performance is motivated. Nor can many of us decompose our absences in strictly motivational terms. In fact, we could describe our behavior as falling on a continuum from reflex to consciously initiated patterns of behavior to overlearned and automatic patterns or habits. Few would describe a sneeze or a startle response as motivated behavior. Similarly, many of us are only vaguely aware of the route we choose to drive to work each day and even less aware of the actions involved in driving our car to the office. Thus, there must be some range between reflex and habit that is the proper domain for motivational theory. There has been precious little discussion of the size or borders of that domain.

Perhaps a realistic compromise might be to consider the *relative influence* of motivational processes on observable behavior. If only certain aspects of our behavior warrant the label "motivated," we should be more modest in our expectations. Perhaps the strength of the relationship between motivational mechanisms and behavior is a great deal more modest than we assume. Perhaps, in the course of a working day, motivated behavior is like a needle in a haystack—more prominent by its absence than by its presence. Perhaps motivation can be seen more in disordered or disoriented behavior than in "goal-directed" behavior. Many years ago, Baldamus (1952) coined the phrase *traction* to describe the tendency to continue doing what you are currently doing. This is in contrast to *distraction* or being interrupted in what you were doing. Perhaps motivational processes are only important in switching from one activity component or string to another.

The point we are attempting to make here is that many important motivational questions have been begged in past research and theory building. In the sections that follow, we will reexamine many of those questions.

A Definition

There is general agreement that motivated behavior consists of any or all of the following behavioral elements: initiation, direction, persistence, intensity, and termination. In spite of this general agreement, however, different theorists and researchers are more interested in one aspect than in others. One researcher might be interested in only the motivational foundations for employee absence (e.g., Chadwick-Jones, Nicholson, & Brown, 1982); a second might be concerned with how an individual chooses between two courses of action (e.g., Vroom, 1964), and a third might be concerned with predicting self-reported intensity or effort (e.g., DeLeo & Pritchard, 1974). By default, then, each theorist runs the risk of the blind men describing the elephant. One has it by the tail, one by the trunk, and one by the leg. In fact all are parts of the elephant but no one can describe it adequately. Motivational research has often been limited by this myopia. Thus, although all of us might agree that motivated behavior can include any of the five elements just listed, each of us cares about a very few (possibly only one) of those parameters. As we shall see below, the dependent variable that interests us may very well limit our interest to a small number of motivational approaches.

In other words, we are suggesting that there are a number of independent parameters to what we accept as motivated behavior. One of these parameters is initiation, another direction, etc. You will see that this multiple-component definition fits nicely with the notion of middle-range theories.

The implication is that some theories address the initiation and termination of behavior, other address the persistence and intensity of behavior, and still others address the direction of behavior. We will propose that no *one* theory is suited to an understanding of all of the parameters of motivated behavior.

A Working Taxonomy

Since there are literally dozens of motivation theories, a necessary first step in discussing them is to develop some clusters or groups of similar theories. We propose a five-cluster working taxonomy with the following categories: need theory, reinforcement theory, balance theory, expectancy theory, and goal-setting theory. This taxonomy has been useful in earlier reviews of motivational theory and research (Landy & Trumbo, 1976; Landy & Trumbo, 1980; Landy, 1985). These five categories are sufficient for including most of the research and theorizing that characterize modern motivation theory. It will also prove useful for later sections of this chapter by helping to illustrate trends in motivational research with respect to variables studied. We are not arguing that the taxonomy is definitive, only helpful for present purposes.

The "One Best" Theory

If one were to examine the current research or theoretical literature on motivation, the preponderance of writings would fall into one of the five categories above. Herein lies a problem. Pinder (1984) has referred to this problem as the tendency to seek universal applicability. It is generally assumed that one of these approaches is "right" and the others wrong, as if these theories were in competition with one another. This is not particularly surprising given the traditional operations of the scientific method. It is common to pit competing hypotheses against each other in investigation. Unfortunately, this tendency has not been of much benefit in the area of motivational theory and research. This is true for at least three reasons. First, there have been few truly comparative studies of theoretical positions. With the exception of Menlo, Cartledge, and Locke's (1980) comparative examination of need theory, expectancy theory, and goal-setting theory, most "comparative" tests of theoretical propositions have involved empirically testing the propositions of one approach while disparaging the logic or data supporting the alternatives approaches. A second reason for pessimism with respect to this "one best" approach to the development of motivation theories is the fact that the desire to identify the "right" model of motivation has made the advocates of one approach reluctant to consider *any* of the propositions of other "competing" approaches.

The third pitfall in the universalist approach has been the necessity to account for all "motivated behavior" from the particular theoretical perspective under consideration. Thus, every behavior from a simple one such as arriving for work on time to a complex one such as deciding to change jobs is dragged (often reluctantly) under a single motivational theory. As we suggested earlier, many of these behaviors might not be "motivated" at all. Further, some behaviors can be better understood from one theoretical perspective than another.

It appears to us that progress in determining what role motivation might play in understanding behavior will depend on reorientation of thinking and research. Until recently, the thrust in motivational research has been to find the "correct" theory. Presumably, we will know when we find it because it will be capable of describing all of the conditions that influence each of the five parameters of motivation behavior (i.e., initiation, direction, persistence, intensity, and termination). We think that this search for the holy grail will continue to frustrate students of motivation. It is time to stop designing new mousetraps and make use of the ones we have. A good place to start is with a consideration of the cognitive revolution in psychology and the extent to which it has influenced motivation theories.

COGNITIVE COMPONENTS IN THEORIES OF MOTIVATION

In the mid-1960s, a cognitive wave engulfed virtually every substantive area of psychology. Developmental psychology was captivated by Piaget; verbal learning became psycholinguistics and was heavily influenced by the notions of Chomsky. Clinical psychology moved away simultaneously from Freudian theory and behavior modification and toward cognitive diagnosis and therapy. Even radical behaviorists deserted to the cognitive camp by considering processes such as self-control, modeling, and social learning.

It is not surprising then that motivation theory was similarly transformed. The predominant motivational paradigm to that point had been need theory of one variety or another. In the area of work motivation, this meant either Herzberg's two-factor theory or Maslow's need hierarchy. It is interesting to note that in spite of the fact that Georgopolous, Mahoney, and Jones (1957) had sketched the mechanics of expectancy theory (calling it path-goal theory) some 7 years prior to the publication of Vroom's (1964) expectancy theory of work motivation, the publication precipitated no major shift toward the cognitive approach. The more general cognitive revolution was not quite underway at that point.

Prior to Vroom's book, there had been little use for words such as *planning* or *intention* in discussions of work motivation. But in the early 1960s, rational economic man had become an attractive model of human behavior. Equity theory and expectancy theory were natural extensions of that concept, proposing that individuals were capable of calculating costs and benefits and, further, that individuals used the results of those calculations to choose among alternative courses of action. To the extent that choice precedes action, this meant that behavior sequences were controlled by comparative evaluations of costs and benefits. Although equity theory relied more heavily on social comparison than did expectancy theory, both implied that cognitive processes were major determinants of motivated behavior. Since that time, a good deal of research has confirmed the importance of cognitive variables and processes in motivation. Expectancy theory became a popular framework not only in industrial and organizational psychology, but in learning theory and social psychology as well (Mitchell & Biglan, 1971). Shortly after the appearance of Vroom's book, several other books appeared on the topic of intentional behavior (Irwin, 1971; Ryan, 1970).

The point we are making here is not so much that expectancy theory replaced all other theoretical approaches, but that cognitive variables were becoming popular in most explanations of behavior. In clinical psychology, cognitive therapies (e.g., Beck, 1976) were beginning to appear. In developmental psychology, Piaget's notions of cognitive development were a major driving force. It was to be expected that the exploration of cognitive processes in motivated behavior would become popular.

In this section, we will review some of the recent research that highlights the role of cognitive variables in several of the motivational approaches in the taxonomy presented earlier. This treatment is meant to be illustrative rather than comprehensive.

Need Theory

In 1972, Alderfer suggested a revision of Maslow's need hierarchy theory. This revision involved modifications of both process and content of Maslow's theory. The process modification was an expansion from a straight satisfaction-progression mechanism (Landy, 1985) to one that also included a frustration-regression mechanism. In Maslow's model, if one is frustrated at a particular need level, one stays at that level until the need is satisfied. Once the need is satisfied, the individual progresses to the next level of the hierarchy. Unfortunately, empirical research has failed consistently to confirm this mechanism (e.g., Lawler & Suttle, 1972; Hall & Nougaim, 1968; Rauschenberger, Schmitt, & Hunter, 1980). Alderfer proposed a more complex mechanism involving both satisfaction–progression and frustration–regression components. In effect, Alderfer suggested that when an individual becomes frustrated at a particular need level, the individual might regress to a lower level and find a relief of tension in the successful satisfaction of needs that had been previously satisfied. In addition to this process modification, Alderfer also suggested that instead of Maslow's five-need level (physical, safety, love, esteem, self-actualization), a more appropriate hierarchy would be based on three need levels (existence, relatedness, and growth).

Unfortunately, Alderfer's theory has not received much more empirical support than Maslow's. From the cognitive perspective, however, Alderfer's theory was a radical step forward. In addition to compressing Maslow's five levels into three, Alderfer suggested an underlying continuum for these three levels. He suggested that the higher-level needs were more abstract and the lower-level needs more concrete. This higher level of abstraction implies uncertainty and ambiguity. This underlying cognitive continuum provided a rationale for the frustration–regression mechanism. When an individual is frustrated in satisfying a particular need, the individual moves "back" to a less cognitively demanding task. Although such an underlying cognitive continuum might have been plausible (and even implied) in the Maslovian framework, Alderfer was the first to suggest this continuum directly.

A recent study by Veroff, Reuman, and Feld (1984) provides some support for the notion of a relationship between need levels and cognitive states. In a study of the stability of motives in men and women from a life-span perspective, Veroff et al. found evidence to suggest that uncertainty in work settings might lead to an emphasis on affiliation motives. In other words, the more uncertain the environment, the more likely it was for individuals to exert effort in developing and maintaining social relationships. It may be that these relationships provide an improved opportunity to gather information via social comparison and thus reduce uncertainty. The Veroff et al. data are compatible with the frustration–regression mechanism that Alderfer suggested. Although these data do not directly address the issue of a hierarchy of motives, they do support a possible relationship between motive salience and cognitive state (i.e., uncertainty).

The second issue raised by Alderfer via his revision of Maslow's theory concerns the number of need levels. Alderfer (and others) sought to identify the "correct" number of levels, as if every individual functioned from such a hierarchy. This can be seen as another variation on the "universalist'' theme described earlier (Pinder, 1984). What if this were not true? What if different individuals have structurally different hierarchies? It is reasonable to assume that individuals group stimuli and form concepts to take the place of individual stimulus elements in their environments (Landy & Becker, 1983). To the extent that grouping does occur, it makes sense to think of ''needs.'' But rather than think of them as hard-wired biological and/or psychological mechanisms, it might be more useful to think of these groups or clusters of elements as manifestations of cognitive operations of the individuals being studied. Lawler and Suttle (1972) anticipated this revised view of needs when they suggested that needs are really just collections of similar stimulus elements. The point that might have been added to that observation is that *similar* is a judgment made by an individual. As a result, there must be some cognitive process by which individuals accomplish this grouping. Of course, there is and it has been the center of attention for both developmental and experimental psychologists for many years. It is known as concept formation and depends heavily on the cognitive abilities of inductive and deductive reasoning. Inductive reasoning permits one to identify parameters on which objects (or events) might be arranged. Deductive reasoning permits one to place new objects or events in preexisting categories. Piagetian theory relabels these processes as accommodation and assimilation.

It is reasonable to assume that there are individual differences in concept formation. No two of us use identical categories or categorization rules. It may very well be that some people use five categories for clustering potential rewards (as Maslow suggested); others might use three categories (as Alderfer suggested); still others might use only two categories (as implied by Herzberg). From a cognitive perspective, it is important to know several things: (1) How many categories (i.e., concepts) do individuals use in decomposing their reward environment? (2) How are these categories arranged on a concrete to abstract continuum? (3) To what extent do the definitions and number of categories change situationally? and (4) To what extent do the definitions and number of categories change developmentally (i.e., over the life span of a given individual)? In a combined cross-sectional and longitudinal pilot study conducted many years ago, the first author discovered that engineering students anticipated job satisfaction in very different ways as they approached graduation. A factor analysis of the responses of first-year students to anticipated satisfaction questions resulted in a small number of factors that accounted for a majority of the variance. Factor analyses of second-, third-, and fourth-year responses showed an increasing number (and, presumably, differentiation) of factors. As an example, first-year students did not distinguish between pay and promotional opportunities. Fourth-year students made a clear distinction between these two aspects of the job. This suggests that as the students got closer to the point of graduation, they were confronted with more information about prospective jobs and, as a result, found a need for more-refined categories. This is the basic mechanism proposed by Piaget. These results suggest that the categorization of stimulus elements (i.e., clusters of "need satisfiers") may be influenced by experience.

There may be some value in reexamining need theories from the cognitive perspective. An early (but unwitting) movement in this direction was made by Schaffer (1953), who discovered that overall job satisfaction could be accounted for by knowing the extent to which the two most important needs of an individual were being met. Schaffer recognized that need hierarchies are individually defined rather than being universal. Nevertheless, he was bound to Murray's trait theory and had not considered the possibility that there might be individual differences in the number or definition of need categories, although he did recognize the possible individual differences in need strength. Cognitive psychologists would be very reluctant to accept the notion that each individual works with the same number of (need) categories or that these category definitions are unaffected by development or environmental interaction. Researchers in motivation would be well advised to be equally skeptical of the fixed hierarchy notion. On the other hand, cognitive psychologists would accept the proposition n that individuals do form clusters of objects in their environments and use those clusters for forming strategies and courses of action. Thus, motivation research and theory development might very well profit from a reconsideration, and possibly a redefinition, of need theory.

Reinforcement Theory

Traditional reinforcement theory has been reluctant to admit to the value of including cognitive mechanisms in explanations of behavior. The radical behaviorism of the Skinnerians is even less enthusiastic about cognitive explanations. Nevertheless, the results of operant studies often reveal clear indications of cognitive mechanisms in operation. There are two "clues" to look for in operant results. First, when subjects are told about an impending change in a reinforcement schedule or system, behavior often changes very rapidly, more rapidly than one might expect from a straight contingency perspective. Consider the data in Figure 1. They are taken from a study by Luthans, Paul, and Baker (1981). As you can see, on the day that an attractive contingent reinforcement schedule was introduced, behavior changed dramatically, in spite of the fact that rewards would not be dispensed until several days or weeks later. A traditional reinforcement approach would imply that behavior should not change systematically until and unless a particular pattern was reinforced. Dramatic

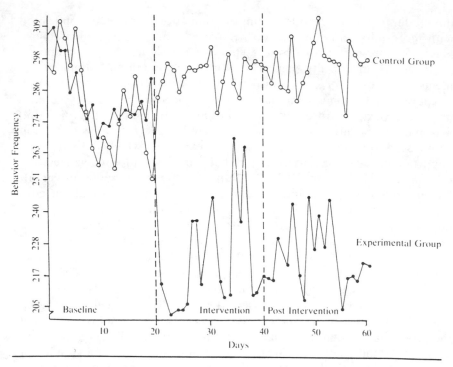

Source: Luthans, F., Paul, R., and Baker, D. An experimental analysis of the impact of contingent reinforcement on sales persons' performance behavior. *Journal of Applied Psychology.* 1981, 66, 320. Reprinted with permission.

Figure 1.   Absence from the Work Station and Idle Time

and rapid changes, such as those illustrated in Figure 1, would seem to argue rather convincingly for a broader exploration of cognitive operations in motivated behavior.

A second anomaly appears in the same figure and might also be raw material for additional cognitive analysis. Consider the post-intervention period on the right side of the graph. In spite of the fact that reinforcement has been suspended, the behavioral change remains strong. This is quite different than the situations usually encountered in behavior modification programs directed toward such activities as eating or smoking or being on time. In these latter situations, recidivism is rampant and positive behaviors disappear as soon as reinforcement is terminated. The point is that something unusual is happening here and that "something unusual" is most likely cognitive in origin. It can't be that the subjects are simply too dumb to realize that rewards have been suspended. Instead, they must now "realize" the long-term value of behaving in particular ways. This realization must be something more substantial than simply "developing a new operant."

Certainly, the growing empirical support for the mechanisms of social learning theory and modeling suggest a broad cognitive arena for research in a neo-behaviorist paradigm. But in the case of the Luthans et al. data, neither social learning nor modeling provide satisfying explanations. To some extent, social learning theory is no different from traditional reinforcement theory—the assumption is made that a behavior must occur and be reinforced before permanent change occurs. In the present case, the desired behavior occurred almost immediately. The notion of new behavior patterns being "reinforced" is strained in this situation. Similarly, any modeling that occurred must have been exclusively in the abstract. If there was a "model" of good selling behavior, it must have been a cognitive construction of the subjects. The fact is that in this and similar studies, it is reasonable to begin with the premise that the subjects have a concept of selling behavior. It is this concept (or scheme or script or heuristic) that is influencing behavior.

There is a second type of study that argues with equal eloquence for the role of cognitive variables. Recent examinations of feedback and behavior change also implicate cognition in motivated behavior. As an example, consider the data in Figure 2 taken from a study by Komaki, Heinzmann, and Lawson (1980). In this study, an attempt was made to reduce unsafe behavior by various employees of the public works department of a major city. These data demonstrate the incremental effect of feedback on behavior. When the intervention involved training *and* feedback, the change was more substantial than when training alone was the intervention. As nearly as can be determined from the description of the intervention, feedback was not confounded with rewards. The feedback consisted of posting information about safe behavior in a public location.

The point of these illustrations is that by ignoring cognitive mechanisms in the explanation of behavior, reinforcement approaches are refusing to talk about the elephant in the room. There is no doubt that when pressed, the behaviorist can find or create a series of labels for these cognitive activities that leave the behaviorist position bloody but unbowed. Historically, concepts such as stimulus-and-response generalization, vicarious trial-and-error learning, etc., have been used to dodge the cognitive bullets. Nevertheless, a less-baroque approach might be to begin using terms such as *inductive reasoning* and *deductive reasoning,* or *concept formation* or *information ordering.* This is a more dramatic step than simply talking about the facilitating role of feedback. Examination of the effect of feedback retains the "experimenter control" flavor of traditional reinforcement theory. The real point is that the information provided to the subject is

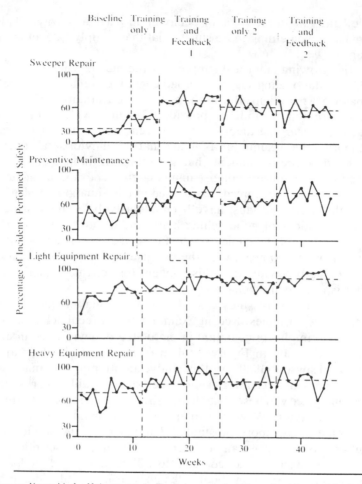

Source: Kormaki, J., Heinzmann, A. T., & Lawson, L. Effect of training and feedback: Component analysis of a safety training program. *Journal of Applied Psychology,* 1980, 65, 260–270. Copyright 1980 by the American Psychological Association. Reprinted with permission.

Figure 2. Percentage of Incidents Performed Safely by Employees in Four Vehicle Maintenance Sections under Five Experimental Conditions

incorporated into some preexisting knowledge structure and used as a self-controlling mechanism in a subsequent behavioral sequence. To say that *feedback* had a particular effect is a perpetuation of the traditional insularity with respect to cognitive behavior. As the work of Mahoney (1974) suggests, the behaviorist has much to gain by embracing rather than opposing cognitive mechanisms.

Balance Theory

Equity theory continues to be one of the more popular versions of balance theory in the area of work motivation. As we indicated earlier, its theoretical roots can be found in the cognitive dissonance propositions of Festinger. Thus, it is not surprising that cognitive mechanisms would hold the key to future development of the theoretical approach. In the last several years, three particular lines of research have suggested novel avenues for extension of the theory.

Moral maturity and equity theory. The first line of research is illustrated by the work of Vecchio (1981) on moral maturity. Equity theory implies that people are capable and willing to perceive fairness in their immediate environment. This may be an unwarranted assumption. In terms of cognitive ability, fairness calculations can be difficult. These calculations usually involve comparing two very different types of variables or metrics. Consider what is being done when an individual compares input and outcome. Input includes things such as ability, effort, and training. Outcome includes such things as monetary rewards, praise, and improved promotional opportunities. What type of transformation is necessary before inputs can be compared to outcomes? How many "units" of effort or ability are necessary to warrant praise or a promotion or a $100 bonus? In all likelihood, the rules necessary to make such transformations are quite complex (Hook & Cook, 1979). This may account for the role of "significant others" in the equity propositions. It may be that as a result of the difficulty in making complex calculations, it is common to use the experience of other individuals as a heuristic device to aid in this calculation. In other words, comparing ourselves to others might be a form of "poor man's calculus."

Both Zedeck (1977) and Stahl and Harrell (1981) have demonstrated that there are individual differences in information-processing mechanisms. These differences range along a simple to complex continuum. In fact, some recent research has shown that many equity calculations are difficult or impossible for most preadolescents. Hook and Cook (1979) specifically consider the proportional equity theory of Adams (1965) and conclude that it can only operate when cognitive ability has reached a rather high level—a level described by Piaget (1970) as that of formal operations. Because the development of abilities implied by the term *formal operations* depends on *both* environmental demand and maturation, it cannot be assumed that every adult is equally capable of applying the complex rules of equity theory. Consider Vecchio's research.

Vecchio reasoned that in order for equity predictions to hold for an individual, it would be necessary for that individual to have some appreciation of the concept of fairness. He further reasoned that this concept was more likely to have relevance for individuals who were morally mature than for those who were morally immature. As a result, he conducted research in which moral maturity was placed in the role of a moderator variable. He proposed that for morally mature subjects, equity predictions would hold but that equity theory would be less useful in predicting the behavior of morally immature subjects. The results supported Vecchio's hypotheses.

From a cognitive perspective, Vecchio's findings are very exciting. There are two predominant theories of moral development—the theories of Piaget (1965) and Kohlberg (1976). Both of these theories place heavy reliance on cognitive development in describing individual differences in moral behavior. Higher levels of cognitive development imply greater maturity in situations involving moral judgment. The point is that moral judgement often involves some rather abstract and subtle concepts. The "right" decision or the choice of the "best" strategy often involve high levels of syllogistic reasoning and rule application. Thus, it would not be surprising to find that people who have attained high levels of cognitive development are better able to apply equity propositions than are those who have not achieved these levels. In our opinion, the moderator variable that improved Vecchio's predictions was level of cognitive development rather than some social–personality construct such as conventional morality. As we indicated above, the prevailing developmental view of moral maturity is that it is a manifestation of cognitive development. Like language, it is used by the developmental psychologist as a mirror of the mind. The cognitive continuum underlying moral behavior is explicit in the theory and research of both Kohlberg and Piaget. Behaving in a normatively "moral" way is a cognitive challenge, not a social one. It follows that equity predictions would be best supported in populations of subjects who possess the prerequisite cognitive capacities. Vecchio was able to isolate those individuals. We would encourage a substantial examination of other, similar, measures of cognitive development and functioning in order to assess the extent to which such variables constrain equity predictions.

The "half-life" of equity perceptions.   The second research line that represents a novel approach to equity predictions can be found in a recent study by Greenberg and Ornstein (1983). These researchers set out to examine the effect of outcomes other than money on perceived equity. This was a reasonable avenue to pursue because it has generally been accepted that equity theory does (or should) transcend particular types of outcomes (such as money) and apply to outcomes in the generic sense. In this particular study, a title was used as a reward. Some subjects received a title as a reward for excellent work, others received a title capriciously regardless of level of performance, and others were asked to do extra work implied by the title but were never given the title. The results demonstrated clearly that titles have many of the same properties as more concrete rewards such as money. From our perspective, however, the results also demonstrated something startling with respect to equity perceptions. Greenberg and Ornstein discovered that for the group of subjects who were given a title yet were aware that they had not earned that title, there was a radical alteration of equity perceptions over a relatively brief period of time. The first reaction of the unearned-title group was one of satisfaction. They were pleased to receive the title and, as traditional equity theory would predict, increased their output as if to reduce the tension created by the "overpayment" condition. But what followed shortly after that reaction was a reversal of this effect. Satisfaction was drastically reduced and productivity similarly declined. The researchers concluded that the subjects might have felt that they were being duped into working harder by the unearned title. This might be called the "Tom Sawyer" phenomenon—tricking someone into helping you paint the fence. From this perspective, the title became an input rather than an outcome and the subjects would have resented being "fooled" into doing extra work.

There are two interesting points to derive from this study. The first, and most dramatic, is that without *any external intervention or treatment*, perceptions changed. This implies that the cognitive activity continued *after* the initial calculation of equity. This possibility has been seldom discussed in the equity literature. It is assumed that once the individual determines the relative equity of the situation, a choice is made and equity is not "recalculated." These data suggest a very different process, one much more dynamic than had been previously assumed. Additionally, these data suggest that the identification of something as an outcome or an input is relative, both between and within individuals. The first author considers the opportunity to add 5 miles on to a 10-mile run a "reward"; the second author would feel punished with the 10 mile run let alone the additional 5. Inputs and outcomes are idiosyncratic. The Greenberg and Ornstein finding implies that much more needs to be known about the time-course of equity perceptions. There has been little if any research that informs us with respect to how *long* inequity perceptions persist and what conditions influence their dissipation.

The phenomenon discovered by Greenberg and Ornstein is one that is receiving substantial attention in more-traditional cognitive research, particularly in the area of memory and concept formation. As an example, the work of Loftus (1975) on memory for events as well as the work of Bransford and Franks (1971) on memory for prose suggests that the computer analogue for describing cognitive activity may not be a good one. In the computer metaphor, information is stored and retrieved in isomorphic form. In contrast, in what might be called the "constructivist" metaphor, information goes in, is transformed and then retrieved. To this point, equity research has been oriented toward events in the external environment as explanatory mechanisms for the presence or absence of tension; that is, tension can be created or dissipated through manipulation of outcomes. This is almost behaviorist in tone. The Greenberg and Ornstein's results suggest that the search for understanding must turn to internal mental representations as well in order to understand the more dynamic aspects of equity perceptions.

   Adjustment equity.   One of the questions that has often surfaced in equity research has been the base level at which an individual starts calculating equity. For example, if you and I both work for the same organization and we both make a substantial contribution, should we both get the same dollar amount as a bonus or should we each get a bonus that is the same *percentage* of our base salary? In the former situation, if we had both done an outstanding job, we might both receive $1,000. This would be known as absolute equity. In the latter situation, assuming that my base salary was $20,000 and yours was $30,000, our bonus might be 5% of base salary, in which case I would receive $1,000 and you would receive $1,500. This is known as relative equity. Clearly, the answer to this question is at least as important as is the estimation of inputs and outcomes in determining perceived fairness. If individuals calculate equity on a percentage basis, "absolute equity" would be perceived as inequitable by some individuals. On the other hand, if equity is calculated on an absolute basis, then a system based on rewards geared toward a percentage of base salary would be perceived as inequitable.

   Recent work by Birnbaum (1983) and Mellers (1982) suggests that the truth lies somewhere in between. It appears that individuals use a much broader equity scale than either of those suggested previously. This theory has been labeled *adjustment equity* and implies that an individual has long-term parity in mind in work situations rather than short-term considerations. Adjustment equity assumes that individuals seek to place themselves in the same ordinal position on a scale of outcomes as they perceive themselves to occupy on a scale of merit. In other words, individuals have a pretty good idea of their position in the distribution of talent in their organization. They know, approximately, if they are in the 90th percentile or the 50th or the 10th. Further, they have some guess with respect to where they fall on the compensation continuum. As on the talent continuum, they see themselves in the 90th or 50th or 10th percentile. The adjustment equity mechanism assumes that these two continua are compared. If an individual feels that he or she is at the same relative position on both continua, equity is experienced. If, on the other hand, there is a discrepancy in the two ordinal positions, inequity is experienced. From this perspective, equity–inequity is a broad concept. It does not speak to the specific comparison of my inputs and outcomes vis-à-vis a significant other; instead, it speaks to the rank-order correlation between the input and the outcome continua in the subsystem that represents "my organization."

An implication of the adjustment equity mechanism is that individuals see equity as a goal to work toward over time rather than n to accomplish in one large step or adjustment. In some senses, the type of mechanism suggested in adjustment equity implies that a good deal of the earlier equity research has been looking at too short a time frame and too restricted a scale of both outcomes and inputs. As a result, the data may not have seemed particularly favorable toward equity predictions when, in fact, support might have been there all along had we only known what perspective to consider. The works of Birnbaum and Mellers strongly suggest that we need to consider alternative definitions of equity that more closely match the calculating heuristics of our subjects.

Expectancy Theory

Expectancy theory is built on a cognitive paradigm. It suggests that individuals consider alternatives, weigh costs and benefits, and choose a course of action of maximum utility. The general model proposes that the force on a person to engage in a particular action is a multiplicative function of valence, instrumentality, and expectancy. Although that model seems relatively straightforward, some recent research has suggested that we need to know a good deal more about the cognitive operations than we know presently.

Number of outcomes. One line of research that seems profitable is related to the nature of the outcomes considered. At least two aspects of these outcomes have been examined: (1) the number of alternative outcomes and (2) the extent to which the outcomes are positive or negative. In a study of the number of outcomes considered, Leon (1979) discovered that as the number of outcomes increased, the accuracy of prediction using expectancy propositions decreased. In other words, as the number of different outcomes or end states increases, the potential for predicting which outcome will be chosen decreases. This is true for ranges of outcomes from 5 through 15. Leon came to this conclusion after a meta-analysis of 31 expectancy studies. This should come as no surprise to the student of cognitive processes. Miller (1956) demonstrated long ago that effective information processing (and in particular simultaneous discrimination) occurred in the stimulus range of 7 ± 2. Thus, it should be obvious that there would be a decline in the efficiency with which individuals apply computational heuristics as the number of alternatives being considered increases beyond the range of 9. Presumably, this processing handicap could be eliminated if individuals were permitted or encouraged to chunk or cluster outcomes prior to comparison. Thus, even though the basic expectancy-theory propositions are silent with respect to the effect of number of outcomes, both theory and data suggest a limit to the effective comparison of outcomes.

Positive vs. negative outcomes. Leon also conducted research on the effect of outcome valence on predictive accuracy in the expectancy paradigm. Again, his results suggest an important limit to the efficiency of the expectancy model. In a study comparing the manner in which positive and negative outcomes are combined, Leon (1981) discovered that they have quite different effects. Positive outcomes are combined in the manner suggested by the theory. There seems to be a positive linear relationship between the (positive) valence of the outcome and the force on the individual to choose that outcome. In other words, when positive outcomes are involved, more is better. The same relationship does *not* hold, however, when negative outcomes are involved. The decision process seems to be much more primitive. When negative outcomes are involved, it does not seem to matter *how* negative they are. In other words, the extent of negativity is not related to the force to avoid that outcome—more is not worse. The case of negative outcomes seems to be all or none.

This should come as no surprise. We know from other research paradigms that negative information is treated differently than positive information. For example, in the employment interview, negative information is often given a disproportionately large weight in making final decisions (Webster, 1982). Similarly, in gambling situations it is commonly the case that individuals devote disproportionate time (and decrease final utility) by avoiding losses at any cost. Once again, Leon has demonstrated that the basic propositions of expectancy theory need to be modified to account for a unique information-processing strategy.

Combinatorial rules. The expectancy model is based on the proposition that individuals can combine information about valences and expectancies in a multiplicative manner. Multiplicative combination is a demanding operation and several researchers have examined this proposition. The results are not particularly encouraging. Stahl and Harrell (1981) discovered that some individuals do use multiplicative rules as the theory suggests, but others use additive rules. In other words, for some people, the force on them to choose a particular outcome is the simple sum of valences and expectancies. It is conceivable that, using an additive rule, an individual might choose an outcome that has a very high valence but little probability of occurrence. Such a choice would be much less likely using multiplicative rules for combining valences and expectancies. Thus, in spite of the fact that additive rules can occasionally run counter to the notion of rational economic man *(homo algebraicus)* suggested by expectancy theory, these suboptimal rules are still used *(homo heuristicus)*. Perhaps this is what March and Simon (1958) had in mind when they introduced the notion of limited rationality. In Stahl and Harrell's (1981) study, only 37% of the subjects used the multiplicative rule for making a choice; the other 63% used the additive rule.

It seems to be the case that many of the motivational models demand substantial cognitive skills on the part of the person being considered. We have already seen hints of this in the earlier discussion of equity theory in Vecchio's work on moral maturity. It seems equally plausible that expectancy theory is an appropriate motivational framework for only some subset of the population. Many studies in decision making have illustrated that interactive processing (i.e., the use of multiplicative rules of combination) is difficult for many people (Slovic, Fischoff, & Lichtenstein, 1977). Zedeck (1977) has taken this logic a step further and identified many different strategies that individuals use for combining information, suggesting that the simple multiplicative and additive models tested by Stahl and Harrell are only a subset of a larger array of strategies.

It is clear that we need to know more about how individuals combine information in assessing alternative outcomes. It is not sufficient to know that individuals are different; we need to know why they are different or under what circumstances they will act differently. Both Stahl and Harrell and Zedeck imply that there are stable individual differences in how information is combined—some people use one set of rules and some people use another. There are other possibilities as well. For example, Shiflett and Cohen (1982) have demonstrated that the role of valence, instrumentality, and expectancy changes as a function of whether you are trying to predict satisfaction, effort, or intention to act in a particular manner. This finding suggests that there are *intra*-individual differences in combination rules. Kopelman (1979) has demonstrated a similar phenomenon in examining expectancy-theory predictions of behavior vs. satisfaction. He found that although the orthodox $V \times E$ composite (multiplicative) did a good job of predicting behavior, a subtractive model, a composite $E - V$ (discrepancy) measure produced significantly higher correlations with a measure of satisfaction. He explains this by referring to the theoretical propositions of Stotland (1969) and Seligman (1975), who both suggest that the most dissatisfied individual is one who has low expectancies for a highly valued outcome. Seligman goes so far as to suggest that it is exactly this combination that leads to the circumstances of reactive depression and learned helplessness. In traditional version of expectancy theory, similar satisfaction levels are predicted for low expectancy/high valence individuals and high expectancy/low valence individuals. Kopelman (and his data) suggest otherwise. The more you want something, the more its absence hurts.

Data and argument such as those presented by Kopelman can be discouraging to those looking for a single model that applies in all situations. Those individuals might argue that there is no use for "theory" at all because a different "theory" is necessary for different behaviors. To us, this would seem to be hyperbole. Most psychologists would accept the notion that a theory of personality is only peripherally relevant for understanding skilled motor performance. Theories of personality and theories of skilled motor performance are permitted to coexist peacefully. The same may be true of effort expenditure and satisfaction—two distinct theories may be necessary for understanding the two phenomena. It does not necessarily follow that the need for two (or more) theories illustrates the uselessness of theory. On the contrary, it signals a more refined appreciation of the mechanisms involved in the two different behaviors in question. The central nervous system of the "average" adult is 1,000 times more (structurally) complex than the most complex computer currently available. This estimate can be deduced from our joint knowledge of neuroanatomy and electro-transmission in computers. Just as the computer can use multiple algorithms to analyze multiple data sets, so can the human employ varying heuristics to consider varying outcome states.

Individual differences between individuals in information processing (Slovic, Fischoff, & Lichtenstein, 1977; Zedeck, 1977; Stahl & Harrell, 1981) as well as within individuals between situations (Mischel, 1976) are to be expected. Theories of motivation must include propositions that recognize these differences. Complexity will not go away simply because it is ignored.

From the earlier discussions of outcomes (i.e., number and positive vs. negative), it occurs to us that other explanations are possible for the extent to which individuals use multiplicative vs. additive vs. other rules in assessing outcomes. For example, it is possible that as the number of outcomes increases, individuals are likely to use simpler (e.g., additive) rules. In Leon's (1979) review of the "number-of-outcomes" literature, he could not explore the possibility that although the traditional expectancy model was less accurate with more outcomes, a simpler model would have yielded increased accuracy. Similarly, with respect to the assessment of positive and negative outcomes, Leon (1981) discovered that these two types of outcomes are assessed quite differently. Negative outcomes have a more dramatic effect on decisions, functioning in what seems to be an all-or-none manner. This might be considered as a situational or moderator variable affecting observed individual differences in outcomes assessment. It may be that if only positive outcomes are being considered and if there are fewer than nine of these outcomes, we are all able to use multiplicative rules reasonably well. On the other hand, if there are negative outcomes and/or there are more than nine outcomes to consider, the cognitive demand becomes substantially greater and the predictive efficiency of the multiplicative model degenerates for some individuals.

The preceding discussion suggests that there are many different variables that need to be considered when examining the proposed multiplicative process that is fundamental to the orthodox expectancy models. These variables might include individual differences in cognitive skills, the number of outcomes, the valence of outcomes, and particular dependent variable chosen for study (i.e., choice, affect, or behavior). The key to improving the predictive efficiency of the expectancy model might lie in any or all of these variables. What is needed is a systematic program of research geared toward exploring the way in which individuals combine different types of information.

Goal-Setting Theory

Perhaps the most obviously cognitive theory of motivation available at present is goal-setting theory. Goal-setting theory has achieved a new theoretical "respectability" as a result of the introduction of cognitive mechanisms. In the early work of Locke and his colleagues (see Locke, Shaw, Saari, & Latham, 1981, for a review of this work), there was one major proposition—difficult goals that are accepted by the individual result in higher levels of performance than do easier goals accepted by the individual. For almost a decade, this proposition represented more a technology than a theory, much like behaviorism. Recently, however, an elaboration of the basic proposition has lead to a resurgence in interest among researchers and theorists. Consider the model as depicted in Figure 3 (from Landy, 1985). It is obvious that components such as *strategies, direction,*

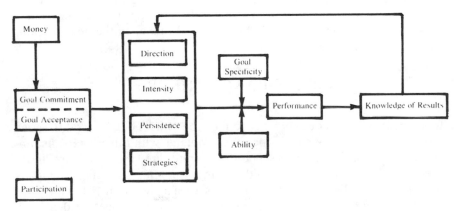

Figure 3. A Diagram of Goal Theory

ability, and the feedback loop connecting *knowledge of results* with behavioral adjustments imply cognitive activity.

It would be misleading to "call for" an increase in cognitively oriented
research in goal-setting theory. The theory has clearly taken a cognitive
turn and will continue in that direction (fruitfully, we would anticipate)
for some time. Additional momentum has been added by the recent research of (Bandura & Cervone, 1983) on the perception of self-efficacy
and the relationship of that perception to goal setting and effort expenditure. Our point is that with the introduction of cognitive variables to the
basic goal-setting model, the approach holds out new promise.

Summary

It seems clear to us that there is a substantial amount of basic work
that needs to be done in understanding how cognitive abilities and processes fit into the various motivational models. In spite of the fact that
both equity theory and expectancy theory purport to be "cognitive"
models of motivation, they do not tell us much about what cognitive processes are operating and what the boundary conditions to those processes
are. Although most need theories would not claim to be cognitive, there
is opportunity for cognitive research within the bounds of these theories
as well. Behaviorism is often embarrassed by its own data in arguing
against the value of cognitive mechanisms. Goal-setting theory provides
many opportunities for the exploration of cognitive processes. There is
not a single motivational approach currently available that could not benefit
from research dedicated to uncovering cognitive mechanisms implied by
the components or processes of the particular approach.

To this point, we have been arguing that no current theory is capable
of handling the many dependent variables examined in motivational research. Some would take this as a challenge to develop still another theory.
This may not be the most profitable avenue to take. In the next section,
we will consider an alternative.

MIDDLE-RANGE THEORIES

In a recent book, Pinder (1984) describes the pitfalls of universal theories
of work motivation. We described the problems with this universalist approach earlier in the essay. As a potential solution to this problem, Pinder
suggests the development of middle-range theories. By this, he means
that instead of developing new theories to deal with all behaviors, we
should concentrate on developing less-ambitious theories that deal with
a limited range of behavioral phenomena. This less-ambitious form of the-

ory is given the name *middle-range theory*. Pinder's notion of how these theories would be developed revolves around a matrix that combines situations with motivational types. He suggests that within a given situation, there are a limited number of styles of motivational response. These styles of response can be best understood as the parameters that define motivational subgroups of individuals. For example, in one type of situation (e.g., making decisions under time constraints), a particular motivational strategy might be adopted by members of one subgroup but not by members of a different subgroup. Similarly, one particular motivational subgroup might systematically vary their motivational strategy across a range of work contexts or situations. Pinder suggests that approaches such as those proposed by Owens and Schoenfeldt (1979) for identifying types or clusters of individuals based on biodata might be a good way to start identifying these motivational subgroups.

There is much to admire about Pinder's suggestion. It should be obvious to even the casual observer of motivational theory and research that there is little hope of identifying a universal theory of motivation. Thus, middle-range theories make perfect sense. We would like to suggest a very different type of middle-range theory, however. Instead of a type X situation matrix, we would propose that varying motivational approaches are better suited to predicting particular dependent variables. Pinder implies that it may be necessary to develop a new "set" of middle-range motivational theories. We would like to suggest that we have all of the theories that we need right now and that they have been already unwittingly developed as middle-range theories.

In this section, we will attempt to illustrate this point by looking at the dependent variables and/or designs most often employed in the tests of particular theoretical approaches. As an example, Guest (1984), in a recent review of new developments in theories of work motivation, notes that expectancy theory seems to work best in situations in which individuals are making occupational and/or organizational choices. He further suggests that expectancy theory works best in situations in which there are few constraints on the range of alternatives being considered. Thus, he proposes that expectancy theory would not do well in predicting work behavior (e.g., quality or quantity of performance) because there are often constraints on the range of this behavior, the constraints imposed by work methods, supervision methods, and work contexts.

We are in agreement with both Pinder and Guest with respect to the observation that current motivation theories are expected to do too much, to predict too wide a range of dependent variables. Our approach to this issue has been to identify the dependent variables that are typically studied in various tests of motivational approaches and assume that there is a sort of inchoate realization of the appropriate range of the particular theory.

In other words, researchers seem to recognize, almost intuitively, the type of dependent variable that makes most sense in testing a particular theory of motivation. In a sense, we are suggesting that one can almost induce the thrust of a theory by looking at what it attempts to predict or explain. Next, we will briefly review the common motivational approaches from this perspective.

Need Theory

By far, the most common dependent variable in studies of need theory has been satisfaction. This should not be particularly surprising because the very term *need theory* is often used as a shorthand reference—the more complete label (at least historically) being *need satisfaction theory*. The early work of Schaffer (1953), Herzberg, Mausner, and Snyderman (1959), and most recently Alderfer (1972) clearly emphasizes the use of reported satisfaction as the appropriate response to be predicted by their respective theories. In addition, those who apply Maslow's theory to work settings have also chosen to concentrate on reported satisfaction as the raw material for testing the need hierarchy.

Similarly, those who have attempted to refute need-type theories have typically gathered data suggesting that reported levels of satisfaction (either facet satisfaction or overall satisfaction) cannot be predicted from knowledge of individual need strength. Although the need strength–need satisfaction relationship may be debatable, there is little or no data to support a need satisfaction–behavior (e.g., productivity, absence) relationship.

Need theories seem to be poor choices for predicting these other dependent variables. This is to be expected given the loose or nonexistent connections between the major variables in these need theories and observable behavior. At best, the typical need theory assumes a hedonic mechanism that moves people toward satisfying environments and away from aversive ones. Nevertheless, little has been done in the way of articulating how these approach and avoidance mechanisms might manifest themselves in the form of varied work productivity or amount of effort expended or job choice. The recent models of absenteeism (e.g., Steers & Rhodes, 1978) or turnover (Mobley, Horner, & Hollingsworth, 1978) have little to say about need strength or satisfaction directly. In their models, need structures play an indirect role in withdrawal, influencing the process through perceived satisfaction.

The simple conclusion that one might draw from a review of need theories of motivation is that if they have any value at all, their "acceptable range" of predictability is limited to understanding or predicting affective reactions to various job characteristics. Even that proposition, however, would be difficult to support in light of theory and research that runs counter to this link. For example, Salancik and Pfeffer (1977; 1978) argue convincingly for an attributional interpretation of job attitudes. Their proposition might be labeled the "constructivist" position. It suggests that people create internal representations of external environments rather than simply monitor external environments and compare them to internal need states. Recent data (James & Jones, 1980; Caldwell & O'Reilly, 1982; Pulakos & Schmitt, 1983) support this more-dynamic cognitive view of the job-attitude domain. Nevertheless, even these newer conceptions and data do not undermine the proposition that individuals form clusters of stimulus objects and respond to those clusters (or concepts) rather than to individual stimulus elements. Thus, although the "need satisfaction" version of need theory may lack intuitive and empirical appeal, there may still be a place for the notion of "need categories" as cognitive heuristics.

The links between these reactions and other behaviors (e.g., effort, productivity, choice, or withdrawal) are complex and must be supported with alternative theoretical frameworks.

Equity Theory

Research on equity-theory propositions has usually revolved around two issues: (1) the tension or distress experienced by individuals who find themselves in inequitable situations, and (2) the strategies that individuals use to eliminate or reduce this tension or distress. Typically, dissatisfaction is the central focus of equity research. Although there has been a consistent effort to demonstrate that felt inequity has predictable consequences for performance quality and quantity, such demonstrations have been few and far between.

Goodman and Friedman (1971) chide researchers for studying anything other than perception processes. They contend that equity theory was never intended to be anything more than an account of how people assign affective meaning to individual-environment interactions. Certainly, it was never intended to predict productivity levels. Goodman and Friedman also used the framework to study choice behavior, in particular the range of choices that individuals have available to them in identifying significant or referent others.

There have been some attempts to demonstrate that inequity is related to avoidance and withdrawal behaviors. It is common to think of quitting when you discover that a co-worker received a particular benefit that you were denied (e.g., a promotion, a bonus, a special assignment). To the extent that the tension produced by inequity is aversive, it would make sense to avoid or leave the situation causing that tension. In a recent study by Croyle and Cooper (1983) it was demonstrated that dissonant cognitions produce psychophysiological arousal (as measured by galvanic skin response). If all dissonance is arousing (and aversive), we can assume that one strategy that might be employed to reduce that arousal would be avoidance (or withdrawal). Dittrich and Carrell (1979) did find that employee perceptions of equitable treatment were stronger predictions of absence and turnover than were measures of job satisfaction. On the other hand, as was the case with need theory, current models of absence and turnover place only modest emphasis on satisfaction (or dissatisfaction).

Based on the research literature surrounding tests of equity theory, we would propose that this approach carve its middle range out of the affective domain. It would seem that equity theory is best suited to explaining the affective reactions that result from perceptions of equity. There might also be some value in considering the implications of perceived equity for effort expenditure. If inequity leads to arousal and arousal leads to effort expenditure, there is reason to examine a corollary that links inequity and effort expenditure.

There seems to be little compelling logic for directly examining work performance as a dependent variable in equity research. The Porter–Lawler (1968) model of VIE theory argues persuasively that several variables intervene to turn effort into performance. Most notable among those variables are role perceptions and traits/skills/abilities. On the other hand, if these variables could be measured or held constant and if effort could be included into the prediction scheme, there may be substantial value in examining the relationship between perceived equity–inequity and performance or other behavioral outcomes. In spite of the fact that classical equity theory implies behavioral responses (e.g., withdrawal, lowered or increased performance), it is not at all clear how and why these patterns manifest themselves in conditions of inequity. This has been the continuing obstacle to a fuller acceptance of equity-theory propositions—any clear statement with respect to the conditions favoring one behavioral response rather than another in the presence of inequity. There is considerably more theory and research to suggest that affective reactions are the proper domain of equity theory (e.g., Helson, 1964; Solomon & Corbit, 1974).

Reinforcement Theory

There are a number of clear trends in research employing the behaviorist paradigm. For example, there is virtually no interest in satisfaction as a dependent variable. This makes sense because the behaviorists are uninterested in "mental events." There have been some exceptions but they have been few and far between. As an example, Latham and his associates (e.g., Latham & Dossett, 1978) were active researchers in the behaviorist paradigm prior to their shift of allegiance to goal-setting theory. During that orthodox behaviorist period, they would occasionally ask subjects about their satisfaction with various reinforcement schedules (though less often about their satisfaction with the work they were performing). The classic behaviorist study including job satisfaction as a dependent variable was conducted by Cherrington, Reitz, and Scott (1971). In that study, the fickle nature of satisfaction–performance relationships was illustrated. It was demonstrated that it was possible to have low performance and high satisfaction as a result of the reward schedule. For many researchers inclined toward the behaviorist world view, this was all the information they needed to exclude satisfaction from the domain of interesting dependent variables, because it had questionable or irrelevant implications for the control of "real" behavior.

Another clear trend in "behaviorist" research in the motivational arena is the concentration on discrete behaviors to control, predict, or understand. Favorites are absenteeism, tardiness, and accident rates. The behaviorist approach is also one of the most common for studying traditional aspects of performance. These include quality, quantity, and persistence. Typically, the behaviors to be considered are discrete parts of larger jobs rather than broad parameters of those jobs. Thus, researchers might study the number of arithmetic problems completed, the number of computer cards sorted, the accuracy of cashiers in using the cash register, the number of beavers trapped, the number of trees planted, or the number of words read per unit time. Although the behaviorist approach suggests itself as appropriate for the examination of effort expenditure, effort is seldom chosen as a dependent variable. If one were to choose a "modal" dependent variable it would most likely be the frequency of particular discrete behaviors per unit time, conceptually identical to the rate of bar pressing that so captivated Skinner in the late 1930s.

Choice behavior is seldom the dependent variable in behaviorist research. Thus, one should not expect to see among behaviorist studies studies involving occupational or organizational choice. Similarly, one is unlikely to see "intentions" as behavior to be predicted in the orthodox behaviorist paradigm, in spite of the fact that intention to quit or intention to be absent have been identified as central to actual quits or absences.

Thus, from the middle-range perspective, the behaviorist or reinforcement paradigm would seem best suited to noncognitive, discrete, and well-bounded behaviors. These behaviors must be amenable to specification (for the subject) and careful measurement (for the researcher). One is tempted to use the word "small" in describing the nature of the dependent variables of interest.

Expectancy Theory

In spite of the fact that expectancy researchers have examined a full range of dependent variables, empirical research (Wanous, Keon, & Latack, 1983) and theoretical propositions (Vroom, 1964) seem to point clearly at *choice* as the variable of interest. Behavioral intention is the operational definition of choice in many motivational studies. Nonindustrial research (see Mitchell & Biglan, 1971) as well as research in work motivation (models of absenteeism and turnover) make clear use of expectancy predictions in choice behavior (as defined by behavioral intentions).

Most theoretical statements of expectancy propositions deal with the force on an individual to *choose* one course of action over another, or to *prefer* one strategy to another, or to *intend* to behave in one way rather than another. Wanous, Keon, and Latack (1983) go so far as to suggest that expectancy theory is best at predicting *discrete* choices (e.g., which of several occupations or organizations will be chosen) rather than observed levels of some dependent continuum (e.g., eventual performance or effort-expenditure level). They seem to be saying that to the extent to which an individual has a clear choice among a number of outcomes or levels, expectancy theory can do a good job of predicting that choice. On the other hand, if there is no choice implied in the action or the choice is not clearly discrete, then expectancy theory may not be helpful in understanding the behavior in question.

Wanous et al. (1983) stress another aspect of expectancy research that might be revealing. They suggest that expectancy models work best when there is sufficient time for the individual to consider all of the alternatives from the perspective of costs and benefits. A common criticism of expectancy theory has been that it is unlikely that individuals actually carry out all of the complicated calculations implied by y most expectancy models. Wanous et al. would seem to agree. They imply that expectancy mechanisms only come into play when there is a period for reflection on the possible outcomes. Because occupational and organizational choices are usually made over a substantial period of time (days, weeks, or months), expectancy theory would seem well suited to this type of choice. On the other hand, in the midst of a conversation with a supervisor, the choice between acting in a respectful or a rude manner is unlikely to be understood using traditional expectancy propositions.

Guest (1984) makes some similar observations about the value of expectancy theory. He suggests that expectancy theory is best suited for understanding "important" decisions or, at least, those that capture the attention of the individual. This latter notion is an interesting one because it introduces a very different construct into the motivational sequence (i.e., attention), but one that has been a central part of many other psychological theories. Guest also suggests that expectancy theory will be most useful in explaining choices in situations where the nature of the task and the demands on the worker are clear. It seems fair to say that Guest is suggesting a middle-range role for expectancy theory.

There seems to be some sentiment for excluding satisfaction as a dependent variable in expectancy research as well. Kopelman (1979) and Korman (1976) both dismiss satisfaction as an inappropriate concern for expectancy research. This makes sense from a theoretical perspective as well, because Vroom (1964) among others identified *anticipated* satisfaction rather than actual satisfaction as the affective focal point of his expectancy model. As Shiflett and Cohen (1982) suggest, what you *have* may determine satisfaction but what you *want* may determine choice and ultimate behavior.

Although Wanous et al. (1983) emphasize the value of expectancy theory for making decisions with respect to pursuing occupations and joining organizations, the mirror image of that decision would also seem to be amenable to consideration from the expectancy perspective. The decision to leave an organization is equally discrete, implies generous time constraints, and is clearly a decision before it is a behavior.

It seems obvious to us that the expectancy theory finds its middle-range value in choice behavior. Circumstances that make any choice difficult would also have a distorting effect on the accuracy of expectancy predictions. Too many outcomes, anxiety caused by potentially aversive outcomes, too short a time for considering outcomes, and being required to make choices from a continuous rather than a discrete continuum all suggest less-than-efficient prediction from the expectancy framework.

Goal Theory

It is somewhat awkward to consider the appropriate role for goal theory in our middle-range framework. As we indicated earlier, goal theory is undergoing a radical transformation that is not likely to be completed for some time. Locke et al. (1981) trace the careful development of the goal-setting paradigm from the late 1960s to its present status. In some respects, until recently, goal setting and acceptance was a sterile phenomenon without any supporting theory, resting on broad philosophical statements of people such as Tolman (1932), Ryan (1970), and Irwin (1971). It was more the manifestation of a teleogical orientation than a theory of industrial behavior. Although there seemed to be little dispute that clear, difficult goals led to higher levels of performance, there was no ready explanation for the phenomenon.

An examination of goal-setting research conducted over the past 15 years suggests that the actual behaviors studied have been quite specific and bounded, much like the dependent variables in the research of the behaviorists. Typical tasks have involved solving arithmetic problems, checking columns of numbers, sorting computer cards, sorting index cards, generating ideas in a brainstorming session, and assembling toys. The tasks have been easy to present to naive subjects, performance has been easy to record, and the tasks have been amenable to laboratory settings and samples of convenience. There have also been field tests of goal-setting predictions involving tasks such as hauling logs, planting trees, and trapping beaver, but these tasks have also been simple rather than complex with the added advantage of being easy to measure. Interestingly enough, researchers initially interested in the reinforcement paradigm have become interested in goal-setting theory (e.g., Latham and Komaki). Perhaps this was the result of a disenchantment with the limitation of radical behaviorism to the role of a technology rather than that of a theory (Locke, 1980). Perhaps it was a desire to conduct research in a paradigm that allowed for cognitive events and capacities. At the very least, goal-setting theory looked into the black box by introducing the concept of *acceptance*. This clearly implied cognitive activity by the individual. In that sense, the cognitive camel snuck its nose under the behaviorist tent. In a few short years, the camel was sleeping in the tent on a regular basis.

It would appear that having made the philosophical transition from behaviorism to goal-setting theory, it is now time to make the operational switch and begin to consider "bigger" behavioral sequences than have typically been the case. Of all of the theories that we have considered, goal-setting theory has the potential for the greatest scope in the context of middle-range theories. It is likely that variables such as job performance, job satisfaction, task satisfaction, and effort expenditure are amenable to explanation from the goal-setting perspective. On the other hand, absence and turnover as well as discrete choices from ranges of outcomes (e.g., occupational or organizational choice) would seem less well explained from the goal-setting perspective than from expectancy propositions.

CONCLUDING COMMENT

This consideration of the limitations on the "universality" of current theories of work motivation is intended to have several effects on the reader. First, we are agreeing with Pinder that middle-range theories are called for. In addition, we are departing from Pinder's suggestion with respect to how those middle-range theories might be developed. It is our opinion that we have the theories we need right now. The only thing necessary is to realize the limits of those theories. The point that we have tried to make is that you might choose your theory based on the dependent variable that is of interest. In fact, we have tried to demonstrate that just such a process occurs now and is evident in the empirical research literature. Consider the 5 × 5 matrix produced by crossing dependent variables with theoretical approaches. This matrix appears in Figure 4. It is our feeling

MOTIVATIONAL APPROACH

DEPENDENT
VARIABLE

	Need	Reinforcement	Equity	Expectancy	Goal
Choice			X	XX	X
Effort	X	X	X		
Satisfaction	X		X		
Performance		X	X		X
Withdrawal		X	X	X	

Figure 4. Hypothetical approach X variable matrix

that this matrix accurately depicts the state of motivational research currently. The only thing missing has been the realization and articulation of this pattern.

Consider another matrix—one formed by combining each theory with each other theory. For example, one might combine need theory with reinforcement theory. As we suggested earlier, it is plausible that individuals form concepts to represent classes of stimulus elements (e.g., co-workers or working conditions or compensation). These concepts may correspond to the classical definitions of needs. If that is the case, there is reason to consider the effect of a wide variety of contingent rewards (i.e., different reinforcements that are conceptually similar). Similarly, expectancy theory might be profitably linked to equity theory in forming a more encompassing middle-range approach. It may be that an individual's decision to expend effort depends on examinations of the behavior of others and vicarious experiences of satisfaction or dissatisfaction. In fact, the merging of expectancy theory and goal-setting theory is already well advanced (Matsui, Okada, & Mizuguchi, 1981; Matsui, Okada, & Inoshita, 1983; Landy, 1985). It is likely that many combinations implied by Figure 5 will have the capacity to predict broader and more encompassing behavioral sequences than will either theory alone. Finally, it is possible that each of these theoretical approaches might play a role in a broad meta-theory of motivation, as we have suggested elsewhere (Landy & Becker, 1982; Landy, 1985). This is not intended to affirm the value of an even *bigger* theory of motivation (a position we oppose). Rather, we are suggesting that there may be some value in considering a framework that links various extant theories in some reasonable manner.

What have we said in this paper that would inform or stimulate future research efforts? First, we have taken a strong position with respect to

	Need	Reinforcement	Equity	Expectancy	Goal
Need	-	X			
Reinforcement	-	-			
Equity	-	-	-	X	
Expectancy	-	-	-	-	X
Goal	-	-	-	-	-

Figure 5.   Hypothetical Combinations of Motivational Approaches

the importance of cognitive variables in motivational research. Here, we can be more specific. The term *cognitive* is often used loosely in the discussions among industrial and organizational psychologists. It is time for that to stop. There are a sufficient number of taxonomies of cognitive variables available so that we can be more detailed in our discussions. As an example, Fleishman and Quaintance (1984) describe a taxonomy of cognitive abilities that includes operations such as memory, inductive and deductive reasoning, information ordering, verbal comprehension, etc. These abilities must be implicated in the motivational process. We need to know more about *how* each of these abilities is used in various components of the alternative motivational approaches. Similarly, Guilford (1967) has presented sections of his "structure of the intellect" model of cognitive operations and Sternberg (1979) has received substantial attention for his model of componential intelligence. It would be worthwhile to pursue any or all of these approaches to more clearly defining the role of cognitive variables in motivated behavior. Unless someone takes this next step, 20 years from now we will still be agreeing that the cognitive approach is the "way to go" without any firm handle on what the cognitive approach implies. Motivational researchers need to identify specific cognitive operations and explore the role of those operations in various motivational theories. We nominate memory as a process to start with because it is clearly implied by every motivational approach.

Another principle comes to mind when considering what we have said about the possible correspondence between particular theories and particular behaviors. It is possible to arrange the dependent variables of interest on a temporal continuum. There are some immediate behaviors and there are others that are longer term. Satisfaction is a spontaneous phenomenon. What we feel is what we are. Regardless of how satisfied I was yesterday, today's satisfaction will depend on what I am confronted with here and now. Turnover has a greater time frame to it. We might consider quitting a particular job for months or years before actually doing it. Performance has both a short- and a long-term perspective to it. On the one hand, it is an exaggeration to suggest that all instances of performance have conscious and articulated goals attached to them. On the other hand, it is equally unreasonable to suggest that we do not have long-term performance goals such as meeting deadlines, producing a fixed quantity, or maintaining a particular quality level. It may be possible to arrange motivational approaches along a temporal continuum, implying that certain approaches are more suited for understanding actions that take place in a short time frame whereas other theories are better suited to more extended time frames. Clear and careful calculation of the costs and benefits of a given action takes time—not milliseconds but minutes, hours, days, and sometimes months. Information must be gathered, evaluated, categorized, and applied. It may be that when the time frame is short, cognitive operations give way to heuristics, past associations, or environmental demands. When the time frame is long, we may have the luxury of behaving in that rational–economic mode so representative of the value-expectancy models.

Any advances in motivation theory in the next few decades are likely to come from a reconceptualization of basic principles rather than from a refinement of instruments, measurement procedures, or analytic strategies. What we need is divergent thinking—different ways of combining generally accepted motivational processes. What we do not need is a new theory of motivation or a new instrument to measure a parameter of motivated behavior. What we do need is a more complex system for considering antecedent–consequent variable pairings. In this chapter, we hope that we have been able to provide some avenues for developing such a system.

ACKNOWLEDGMENT

The preparation of this chapter was facilitated by a grant (N0014-81-K-0197) from the Office of Naval Research (Organizational Effectiveness Research Program), Frank J. Landy, Principal Investigator.

REFERENCES

Adams, J.S. (1965). Inequity in social exchange. In L. Berkowitz (Ed.), *Advances in experimental social psychology: Volume 2* (pp. 267–299). New York: Academic Press.

Alderfer, C.P. (1972). *Existence, relatedness and growth: Human needs in organizational settings.* New York: Free Press.

Baldamus, W. (1952). Type of work and motivation. *British Journal of Sociology, 2,* 44–58.

Bandura, A. (1969). *Principles of behavior modification.* New York: Holt, Rinehart and Winston.

Bandura, A, & Cervone, D. (1983). Self-evaluative and self-efficacy mechanisms governing the motivational effects of goal systems. *Journal of Personality and Social Psychology, 45,* 1017–1028.

Beck, A.T. (1976). *Cognitive therapy and the emotional disorders.* New York: International University Press.

Birnbaum, M.H. (1983). Perceived equity of salary policies. *Journal of Applied Psychology*, 68, 49–59.

Bolles, R.C. (1975). *Theory of Motivation* (2nd Ed.). New York: Harper & Row.

Bransford, J.D., & Franks, J.J. (1971). The abstraction of linguistic ideas. *Cognitive Psychology*, 2, 331–350.

Caldwell, D.F., & O'Reilly, C.A. (1982). Task perceptions and job satisfaction: A question of causalities. *Journal of Applied Psychology*, 67, 361–169.

Chadwick-Jones, J.K., Nicholson, N., & Brown, C. (1982). *The social psychology of absenteeism*. New York: Praeger.

Cherrington, D.J., Reitz, H.J., & Scott, W. (1971). Effect of contingent and noncontingent reward on the relationship between job satisfaction and task performance. *Journal of Applied Psychology*, 53, 531–536.

Croyle, R.T., & Cooper, J. (1983). Dissonance arousal: Physiological evidence. *Journal of Personality and Social Psychology*, 45, 782–791.

DeLeo, P.J., & Pritchard, R.D. (1974). An examination of some methodological problems in testing expectancy-valence models with survey techniques. *Organizational Behavior and Human Performance*, 12, 143–148.

Dewsbury, D.A. (1978). *Comparative animal behavior*. New York: McGraw-Hill.

Dittrich, J.E., & Carrell, M.R. (1979). Organization equity perceptions, employee job satisfaction and departmental absence and turnover rates. *Organizational Behavior and Human Performance*, 24, 29–40.

Fleishman, E.A., & Quaintance, M.K. (1984). *Taxonomies of human performance: The description of human tasks*. New York: Academic Press.

Georgopolous, B.S., Mahoney, G.M., & Jones, N.W. (1957). A path-goal approach to productivity. *Journal of Applied Psychology*, 41, 345–353.

Goodman, P.S., & Friedman, A. (1971). An examination of Adams' theory of inequity. *Administrative Science Quarterly*, 16, 271–288.

Greenberg, J., & Ornstein, S. (1983). High status job title as compensation for underpayment: A test of equity theory. *Journal of Applied Psychology*, 68, 285–297.

Guest, D. (1984, May). What's new in motivation. *Personnel Management*, pp.20–23.

Guilford, J.P. (1967). *The nature of human intelligence*. New York: McGraw-Hill.

Hall, D., & Nougaim, K.E. (1968). An examination of Maslow's need hierarchy in an organizational setting. *Organizational Behavior and Human Performance*, 3, 12–35.

Helson, H. (1964). *Adaptation-level theory: An experimental and systematic approach to behavior*. New York: Harper & Row.

Herzberg, F., Mausner, B., & Snyderman, , B. (1959). *The motivation to work*. New York: Wiley.

Hook, J.G., & Cook, T.D. (1979) Equity theory and the cognitive ability of children. *Psychological Bulletin*, 86, 429–445.

Irwin, F.W. (1971). *Intentional behavior and motivation: A cognitive theory*. Philadelphia: Lippincott.

James, L.R., & Jones, A.P. (1980). Perceived job characteristics and job satisfaction: An examination of reciprocal causation. *Personnel Psychology*, 33, 97–135.

Kleinginna, P.R., & Kleinginna, A.M. (1981). A categorized list of motivation definitions with a suggestion for a consensual definition. *Motivation and Emotion*, 5, 263–292.

Kohlberg, L. (1976). Moral stages and moralization: The cognitive developmental approach. In T. Lickona (Ed.), *Moral development and behavior: Theory, research, and social issues* (pp. 195–261). New York: Holt, Rinehart and Winston.

Komaki, J., Heinzmann, A.T., & Lawson, L. (1980). Effect of training and feedback: Component analysis of a safety training program. *Journal of Applied Psychology*, 65, 261–270.

Kopelman, R.E. (1979). Directionally different expectancy theory predictions of work motivation and job satisfaction. *Motivation and Emotion, 3,* 299–317.

Korman, A.K. (1976). Hypothesis of work behavior revisited and an extension. *Academy of Management Review, 1,* 50–63.

Landy, F.J. (1985). *The psychology of work behavior* (3rd ed.). Homewood, IL: Dorsey Press.

Landy, F.J., & Becker, W. (1982). Adaptive motivation theory. In *Annual Report to Office of Naval Research.* University Park, PA: Department of Psychology.

Landy, F.J., & Trumbo, D.A. (1976). *The psychology of work behavior.* Homewood, IL: Dorsey Press.

Landy, F.J., & Trumbo, D.A. (1980). *The psychology of work behavior* (2nd ed.). Homewood, IL: Dorsey Press.

Latham, G.P. & Dossett, D.L. (1978). Designing incentive plays for unionized employees. *Personnel Psychology, 31,* 47–61.

Lawler, E.E., & Suttle, J.L. (1972). A causal correlational test of the need hierarchy concept. *Organizational Behavior and Human Performance, 7,* 265–287.

Leon, F.R. (1979) Number of outcomes and accuracy of prediction in expectancy research. *Organizational Behavior and Human Performance, 23,* 251–267.

Leon, F.R. (1981). The role of positive and negative outcomes in the causation of motivational forces. *Journal of Applied Psychology, 66,* 45–53.

Locke, E.A. (1980). Latham vs. Komaki: A tale of two paradigms. *Journal of Applied Psychology, 65,* 16–23.

Locke, E.A., Shaw, K.N., Saari, L.M., & Latham, G.P. (1981). Goal setting and task performance: 1969–1980. *Psychological Bulletin, 90,* 125–152.

Loftus, E. (1975). *Eyewitness testimony.* Cambridge, MA: Harvard University Press.

Luthans, F., Paul, R., & Baker, D. (1981). An experimental analysis of the impact of contingent reinforcement on sales persons' performance and behavior. *Journal of Applied Psychology, 66,* 314–323.

Mahoney, M.J. (1974). *Cognition and behavior modification.* Cambridge, MA: Ballinger.

March, J.G. and Simon, H.A. (1958). *Organizations.* New York: John Wiley & Sons.

Matsui, T., Okada, A., & Inoshita, O. (1983). Mechanism of feedback affecting task performance. *Organizational Behavior and Human Performance, 31,* 114–122.

Matsui, T., Okada, A., & Mizuguchi, R. (1981). Expectancy theory prediction of the goal theory postulate "the harder the goals, the higher the performance." *Journal of Applied Psychology, 66,* 54–58.

Mellers, B.A. (1982). Equity judgment. A revision of Aristotelian views. *Journal of Experimental Psychology: General, 111,* 242 270.

Menlo, A.J., Cartledge, N.D., & Locke, E.A. (1980). Maryland vs. Michigan vs. Minnesota: Another look at the relationship of expectancy and goal difficulty to task performance. *Organizational Behavior and Human Performance, 25,* 419–440.

Miller, G.A. (1956). The magical number seven plus or minus two: Some limits on our capacity for information processing. *Psychological Review, 63,* 81–97.

Mischel, W. (1976). *Introduction to personality* (2nd ed.). New York: Holt, Rinehart and Winston.

Mitchell, T.R., & Biglan, A. (1971). Instrumentality theory: Current uses in psychology. *Psychological Bulletin, 76,* 432–454.

Mobley, W.H., Horner, S.O., & Hollingsworth, A.T. (1978). An evaluation of precursors of hospital employee turnover. *Journal of Applied Psychology, 63,* 408–414.

Owens, W.A., & Schoenfeldt, L.F. (1979). Toward a classification of persons. *Journal of Applied Psychology, 64,* 569–607.

Piaget, J. (1965). *The moral judgement of the child* (M. Gabain, Trans.). New York: Free Press.

Piaget, J. (1970). *Genetic epistemology*. New York: Norton.

Pinder, C.C. (1984). *Work motivation*. Glenview, IL: Scott, Foresman.

Porter, L.W., & Lawler, E.E. (1968). *Managerial attitudes and performance*. Homewood, IL: Dorsey.

Pulakos, E., & Schmitt, N. (1983). A longitudinal study of a valence model approach for the prediction of job satisfaction of new employees. *Journal of Applied Psychology, 68*, 307–312.

Rauschenberger, J., Schmitt, N., & Hunter, J.E. (1980). A test of the need hierarchy concept by a Markov model of change in need strength. *Administrative Science Quarterly, 25*, 654–670.

Rotter, J.B. (1955). The role of the psychological situation in determining the direction of human behavior. In M.R. Jones (Ed.), *Nebraska Symposium on Motivation*. Lincoln: University of Nebraska Press.

Ryan, T.A. (1970). *Intentional behavior*. New York: Ronald Press.

Salancik, G.R., & Pfeffer, J. (1977). An examination of need satisfaction models of job attitudes. *Administrative Science Quarterly, 22*, 427–456.

Salancik, G.R., & Pfeffer, J. (1978). A social information processing approach to job attitudes and task design. *Administrative Science Quarterly, 23*, 224–253.

Schaffer, R.H. (1953). Job satisfaction as related to need satisfaction in work. *Psychological Monographs, 67*, No. 304.

Seligman, M.P.E. (1975). *Helplessness*. San Francisco: W.H. Freeman.

Shiflett, S., & Cohen, S.L. (1982). The shifting salience of valence and instrumentality in the prediction of perceived effort, satisfaction and turnover. *Motivation and Emotion, 6*, 65–78.

Slovic, P., Fischoff, B., & Lichtenstein, S. (1977). Behavioral decision theory. *Annual Review of Psychology, 28*, 1–39.

Solomon, R.L., & Corbit, J.D. (1974). An opponent process theory of motivation: I. Temporal dynamics of affect. *Psychological Review, 81*, 119–145.

Stahl, M.J., & Harrell, A.M. (1981). Effort decisions with behavioral decision theory: Toward an individual differences model. *Organizational Behavior and Human Performance, 27*, 303–325.

Steers, R.M., & Rhodes, S.R. (1978). Major influences on employee attendance: A process model. *Journal of Applied Psychology, 63*, 391–407.

Sternberg, R. (1979). The nature of mental abilities. *American Psychologist, 34*, 214–230.

Stotland, E. (1969). *the psychology of hope*. San Francisco: Jossey-Bass, 1969.

Tolman, E.C. (1932). *Purposive Behavior in Animals and Man*. New York: Century.

Vecchio, R.P. (1981). An individual differences interpretation of the conflicting predictors generated by equity theory and expectancy theory. *Journal of Applied Psychology, 66*, 470–481.

Veroff, J., Reuman, D., & Feld, S. (1984). Motives in American men and women across the adult life span. *Developmental Psychology, 20*, 1142–1158.

Vroom, V. (1964). *Work and motivation*. New York: Wiley.

Wanous, J.P., Keon, T.L., & Latack, J.C. (1983). Expectancy theory and occupational and organizational choices: A review and test. *Organizational Behavior and Human Performance, 32*, 66–85.

Webster, E.C. (1982). *The employment interview: A social judgment process*. Schomberg, Ontario, Canada: SIP Publications.

Zedeck, S. (1977). An information processing model and approach to the study of motivation. *Organizational Behavior and Human Performance, 18*, 47–77.

ACTIVATION THEORY AND JOB DESIGN:
REVIEW AND RECONCEPTUALIZATION

Donald G. Gardner and L.L. Cummings

ABSTRACT

Activation theory predictions about the effects of variations in job design on affective, behavioral, and physiological responses of job performers are presented, and relevant empirical literature reviewed. Activation theory is modified to account for the frequent empirical finding that relatively non-stimulating jobs cause high arousal levels. Next, two individual differences, extraversion and electrodermal lability, are integrated into activation theory predictions. Activation theory is then compared and contrasted with competing theories of job design, job stress, and goal-setting. Lastly, current problems with activation theory and suggestions for future research are discussed.

Researchers have long been interested in how variations in the design of work affect indices of job satisfaction, motivation, performance, and other measures of employee effectiveness (e.g., Taylor, 1911; Herzberg, Mausner, & Snyderman, 1959). One goal of this research and theorizing has been to determine what job characteristics maximize employee effectiveness. Reviews of this literature (e.g., Hulin & Blood, 1968; Pierce & Dunham, 1976) converge on the conclusion that at the empirical level "job enlargement" and "job enrichment" result in higher levels of job satisfaction than jobs that are monotonous and nonchallenging to the performer. But at the conceptual level theories of job design have been criticized for their limited ability to explain *why* job enrichment affects the attitudes and behaviors of job incumbents (Roberts & Glick, 1981; Steers & Mowday, 1977).

One possible explanation for the effects of variations in job design on response of job performers is activation theory (Scott, 1966). Yet, activation theory has received the least amount of research attention out of the eight or more existing job design theories (cf. Steers & Mowday, 1977). This lack of interest on the part of job design researchers is not unwarranted, because activation theory is currently at a stage of refinement that offers few specific predictions about job characteristics—employee response relationships. Consistent with this position, Steers and Mowday (1977) argued that:

> Activation theory presents an intriguing explanation for the effects of job design on individual reactions. But at this time its utility in the workplace appears limited. At its present level of development . . . activation theory does not allow precise statements concerning how or when to enrich jobs in the workplace. Research is needed . . . before this theory can serve as a useful guide in organizations. (p. 650)

Thus, activation theory has been relatively ignored as a job design theory because of ambiguities in specifying how different job characteristics affect job performers.

The purpose of this chapter is to demonstrate that activation theory is a viable job design theory, capable of making precise hypotheses about how variations in job design affect job performers. The paper consists of three major sections. The first section presents the basic propositions of activation theory and briefly reviews research to support those propositions. The second section discusses how two individual differences constructs can be integrated into an activation theory nomological network. The third section differentiates activation theory from prevailing job design theories, and also offers a rationale for expanding use of activation theory to explain workplace phenomena.

At the outset it should be noted that few of the studies reviewed here were explicitly designed to test activation theory-based hypotheses. Studies are included, however, if they provide information relevant to activation theory. It should also be noted that activation theory is a comprehensive theory that allows predictions about behaviors ranging from musical preferences to drug abuse (Fiske & Maddi, 1961). As such, studies reviewed here are culled from a variety of areas of scientific inquiry, including psychophysiology, personality, clinical, and organizational psychology, organizational behavior, industrial engineering, ergonomics, and human factors. Consistent with the purposes of this chapter, though, the majority of the reviewed studies concern responses of individuals to job/task performance.[1]

ACTIVATION THEORY AND JOB DESIGN

The Concepts of Activation and Arousal

In understanding activation theory it is necessary to differentiate activation and arousal, terms that are frequently used interchangeably and inconsistently in the extant literature. Activation is defined here as the state of neural excitation in the reticular activating system (RAS) of the central nervous system (the brain and spinal cord). Activation level is defined as the degree of neural excitation in the RAS (Fiske & Maddi, 1961). The definition of activation level is restricted to the RAS in discussions of activation theory because several characteristics of the RAS ultimately form the basis for most activation theory predictions (cf. Berlyne, 1960; Eysenck, 1967; Hebb, 1955; Lindsley, 1961).

Three characteristics of the RAS are particularly important in explicating activation theory. First, because the RAS is neurally connected to external and internal sensory receptors and to the cerebral cortex, activation level increases monotonically as stimulation from internal sources (e.g., cognitions) and external sources (e.g., temperature) increase (Lindsley, 1956, 1961). Second, a major function of the RAS is to maintain an optimal level of activation for the cerebral cortex (Lindsley, 1956). The RAS accentuates and filters sensory impulses that cause too low or too high cortical excitation levels. Third, the RAS is critically involved with habituation to stimuli. Nonvarying repeated stimulation of sensory receptors over time causes declining receptor activity (adaptation) and activation level (habituation).

Direct measurement of activation level is difficult. Electrodes can be placed in the brainstem, where the RAS is located, and electrical activity is then recorded with appropriate equipment. Given that humans are averse to having such measures made upon them, only indirect measures of activation level are usually obtained in research on humans.[2] Other measures of central nervous system activation (e.g., EEGs) are usually used to index activation levels in research on humans.

Arousal, in contrast to activation, is caused by peripheral nervous system activity (viz., the sympathetic and parasympathetic nervous systems). Arousal is neither easily defined (Lacey, 1967) nor measured (Levenson, 1983). A number of measures may be used to operationalize arousal (e.g., heart rate, blood pressure, skin conductance; cf. Andreassi, 1980; Greenfield & Sternbach, 1972). Each measure represents an aspect of physiological arousal. But, because humans respond to stimulation in "stereotypical" ways (e.g., changes in heart rate versus respiration rate), and because different kinds of stimulation configurations cause "stereotypical" reactions (e.g., heart rate acceleration for some types of tasks, heart rate deceleration for other types of tasks), any given arousal measure at a given time may be deficient in indexing overall arousal (cf. Lacey, 1967; Sersen, Clausen, & Lidsky, 1978). As a result, different measures of arousal reflect different aspects of the overall arousal construct (Levenson, 1983). An operational result is that different arousal measures often do not correlate highly with one another.

Because of the complex relationship of RAS to other nervous system structures (Duffy, 1972; Weil, 1974), arousal is both a manifestation and a determinant of activation. High arousal levels cause high activation levels and/or are a result of high activation levels. It is difficult to empirically differentiate the antecedent (determinant) and consequence (manifestation) status aspects of arousal. Nevertheless, the dual role of arousal in relating to activation has important theoretical implications. It should be noted here that, for reasons discussed below, arousal is best considered a manifestation of activation levels, and can be expected to covary with activation levels as a result.

Characteristic Level of Activation and Impact-Modifying Behaviors

Perhaps the key proposition of activation theory is that humans have a characteristic level of activation. That is, there is a consistent pattern of activation (and arousal) level measured across time at the same points in the circadian cycle (Humphreys & Revelle, 1984; Kleitman, 1949). It was on the basis of this physiological research on humans that Lindsley (1951; 1956) proposed one of the earliest formulations of activation theory. Specifically, Lindsley proposed that the characteristic level of activation is that level of activation that allows the central nervous system, especially the cerebral cortex, to function most efficiently. This in turn results in enhanced behavioral (e.g., reaction time) and cerebral (i.e., information processing) performance, because they are a function of central nervous system efficiency. As the experienced activation level of an individual deviates positively or negatively from the characteristic level of activation, central nervous system efficiency is diminished (Lorente de No, 1939), as is quality of motor responses and thought processes.

The effects that experienced activation levels have on central nervous system functioning results in the hypothesis of an inverted-U relationship between experienced activation level and goal-directed behavior (Malmo, 1958). Maddi (1961) later expanded this inverted-U hypothesis when he proposed that the characteristic level of activation also causes positive affect.[3] As with behavioral efficiency, positive affect is predicted to decrease as experienced activation levels deviate from the characteristic level (see Figure 1).[4]

Activation theory further posits that individuals are motivated to maintain their characteristic levels of activation (Fiske & Maddi, 1961; Scott, 1966). That is, if the total stimulation that impacts an individual from internal and external sources (henceforth termed situation impact) results in an experienced activation level that deviates substantially from the characteristic level, an individual will initiate behaviors that alter the ex-

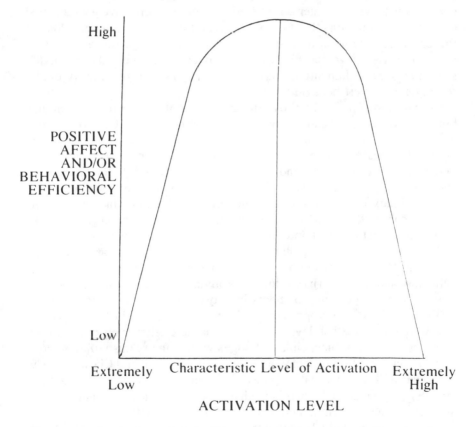

Figure 1. Illustration of the affects of experienced activation level on positive affect and behavioral efficiency.

perienced activation level in a direction towards the characteristic level. If situation impact is low, resulting in a negative deviation, an individual will initiate activation-increasing behaviors. If situation impact is high, resulting in a positive deviation, an individual will engage in activation-decreasing behaviors. Any purposeful action that modifies an individual's experienced activation level is considered an impact-modifying behavior because it is intended to affect the situation impact on the RAS. Impact-modifying behaviors can manifest themselves in a virtually unlimited number of ways. Watching television, daydreaming, and "stretching" may all be considered impact-modifying behaviors.

It is important to note that in many situations an individual will not have complete freedom to initiate impact-modifying behaviors. Work rules, personal finances, expectations of referent others, and other situational constraints all serve to restrict an individual's ability to maintain a characteristic level of activation. Nevertheless, it may be predicted that individuals will evince greater positive affect and more effective goal-directed behaviors in situations that (a) directly result in activation levels close to the characteristic level than situations that cause large deviations from the characteristic level, or (b) allow the individual some flexibility to modify situation impact than situations that severely constrain an individual's thoughts and overt behaviors.

Research to support the above-discussed hypotheses is not voluminous but does, overall, indicate support for activation theory. Corlett and Mahadeva (1970) and Salvendy and Pilitsis (1971) provide evidence for the inverted-U relationship between experienced activation levels and human body efficiency. Baschera and Grandjean (1979) found (a) linear relationships between task difficulty, which affects situation impact, and activation level (as indexed by critical fusion frequency, the rate at which a flickering light appears to "fuse" into a steady light), and (b) inverted-U relationships between activation level and positive affect (task satisfaction).

Perhaps the most compelling evidence for hypotheses about a characteristic level of activation comes from research on impact-modifying behaviors and actions. That is, there is convincing evidence that individuals react to their typical environments in ways that maintain a moderate activation level. At a neurophysiological level, Grossman (1968) summarizes research indicating that deviations from characteristic levels of activation cause neural and/or biochemical changes within an organism that precede overt impact-modifying behaviors. Relatedly, Birchall and Claridge (1979) demonstrated that cortical responses to stimulation (cortical evoked potentials) are augmented when individuals experience low activation levels, and are reduced when individuals experience high activation levels. The point at which individuals switch from augmenting to reducing could conceivably be the characteristic level of activation. This seems especially so given that the RAS is believed to regulate the augmenting/reducing phenomenon (Lukas & Siegal, 1977), and also is consistent with Lindsley's (1956) hypotheses about how the RAS relates to the cerebral cortex.

Support for the hypothesis that individuals initiate impact-modifying behaviors in response to high or low experienced activation levels comes from a number of studies. In laboratory experiments (e.g., Arkes & Clark, 1975; Avolio, Alexander, Barrett, & Sterns, 1979; Gardner, 1986a; Scott, 1969), field experiments (Suominen, Basila, Salvendy, & McCabe, 1980), and field studies (Kishida, 1973) it has been found that individuals engage in activation-increasing behaviors in low situation impact environments, and activation-decreasing behaviors when in high situation impact environments. Kishida (1973) also found that low measured levels of activation preceded activation-increasing behaviors. Much research on coping behaviors in response to stressors indicates that humans readily initiate impact-modifying behaviors in high situation impact ("stressful") environments (e.g., Bloom, Houston, Holmes, & Burish, 1977; Corum & Thurmond, 1977; Lazarus, 1966, 1968; see Thompson, 1981, for a review). All of this evidence supports the hypothesis that humans attempt to maintain a moderate, presumably characteristic, level of experienced activation.

In sum, activation theory posits an inverted-U relationship between experienced activation level and both behavioral efficiency and positive affect, through the intervening variable of central nervous system efficiency. The apex of the inverted-U is the characteristic level of activation, which individuals are motivated to maintain but that they may be unable to do because of situational constraints. Support for the inverted-U hypothesis is sparse, as most studies of the hypothesis have used measures of arousal instead of measures of activation (discussed below). In contrast, a larger number of studies indicate that individuals do initiate a variety of behaviors in response to low and high situation impact environments.

Effects of Variations in Job and Task Characteristics

Application of activation theory propositions to the area of job design is neither new (cf. Farh & Scott, 1983; Fiske & Maddi, 1961; Scott & Erskine, 1980) nor complicated. Whereas the preceding section focused on situation impact and its effects on experienced activation levels, application of activation theory to job design focuses on stimulation impact that arises from performing a task or job. These extensions of the basic activation theory hypotheses may be stated in the form of several additional hypotheses.

The first hypothesis is that jobs differ on a stimulation impact dimension, which we will term job impact. That is, jobs differ in terms of the resulting experienced activation level of the job performer. Jobs with low impact cause low activation levels, and jobs with high impact cause high activation levels. Job and task characteristics which differentiate high impact and low impact jobs include the following (more could be posited; cf. Berlyne, 1967; Scott, 1966):

1. *Intensity:* the degree to which one or a few sensory receptors of the same modality (e.g., tactile) send neural impulses to the RAS.
2. *Complexity:* the degree to which a variety of sensory receptors send impulses to the RAS; the greater the number of different sensory modalities stimulated, the greater the complexity of the job.
3. *Associativity:* the degree to which sensory impulses impact the cerebral cortex and cue off neural associations (e.g., cognitions, information processing) in the cortex.
4. *Novelty:* the degree to which job stimulation is unexpected, and/or has never been experienced before.
5. *Variation in Stimulation:* the degree to which job stimulation varies sufficiently to prevent habituation processes in the RAS. The less repetitive/monotonous a job is, the less habituation to job-based stimulation.

These five characteristics, if measured and summed, would provide a fairly comprehensive index of potential job impact. It would not be a perfect predictor of job performer activation levels because jobs vary in the degree to which they constrain impact-modifying behaviors. For example, machine-paced jobs cause lower activation levels than self-paced but otherwise identical jobs (Salvendy, 1980) because self-paced jobs allow the performer to maintain a less repetitive pace for themselves.

If jobs do differ in terms of the resulting experienced activation levels of job performers, then extension of activation theory hypotheses to the job environment is straightforward. Behavioral efficiency and positive affect is predicted to decline in proportion to the degree to which performing a job results in experienced activation levels that deviate from the performer's characteristic level. And, to the extent that behavioral efficiency is necessary for effective job performance, it is further predicted that job performance level declines as a job performers' experienced activation level deviates from the characteristic level. These hypotheses suggest inverted-U relationships between activation level, and job performance and job satisfaction (positive affect).

The predicted inverted-U relationship between activation level and performance is affected by differences in job content. Jobs with low information processing requirements (i.e., simple or easy jobs) are predicted to require a higher activation level for maximum performance than jobs with higher information processing requirements. The point on the experienced activation level continuum at which performance is maximized need not coincide with a job performer's characteristic level of activation. Simple jobs are also predicted to allow a wider range of experienced activation levels that result in effective job performance than complex jobs. These relationships are illustrated in Figure 2.

Justification for the differences illustrated in Figure 2 may be found in a number of sources (e.g., Easterbrook, 1959; Eysenck, 1985; Hockey, 1979; Humphreys & Revelle, 1984; Kahneman, 1973; Teichner, 1968). The basic proposition that can be distilled from these various reviews is that high and low activation levels impair the ability to process information, by lowering information processing capacity. If little information needs to be processed, as is the case for a simple job, extremes in activation

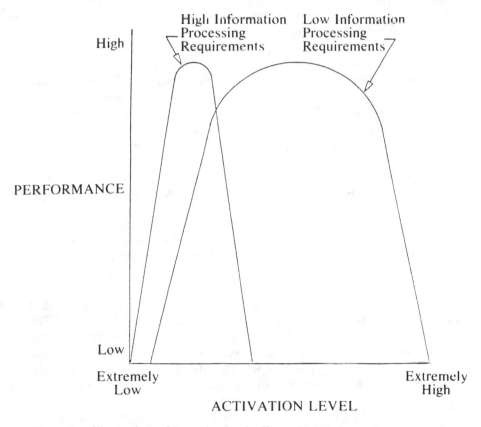

Figure 2. Illustration of hypothesized effect of job information processing requirements on the inverted-U relationship between activation level and performance.

level do not affect performance greatly because little information processing capacity is needed. On the other hand, performance on jobs that have high information processing requirements is affected by extremes in activation, because high levels of information processing capacity is needed. Empirically, these differences make it more difficult to demonstrate inverted-U relationships for simple jobs than complex jobs (Gardner, 1986a).[5]

Research on activation theory-based hypotheses about job design is scarce. There is support for an inverted-U relationship between activation level and job satisfaction (e.g., Baschera & Grandjean, 1979; Champoux, 1978, 1980). And, there is some support for an inverted-U relationship between activation levels and performance (Baschera & Grandjean, 1979; Gardner, 1986a; Grossman, 1968; Weber, Fussler, O'Hanlon, Gierer, & Grandjean, 1980). The most damaging evidence against an activation theory analysis is research related to the basic hypothesis that there is a monotonic relationship between job impact and experienced activation levels. Most of this research has focused on the effects of job impact on physiological arousal. While this line of research has not produced an entirely consistent set of results, there is considerable empirical evidence indicating that low impact jobs cause higher arousal levels than moderate impact jobs. This result has been obtained in laboratory experiments (e.g., Frankenheuser, Nordhegen, Myrsten, & Post, 1970; London, Schubert, & Washburn, 1972; Salvendy, 1980), field experiments (e.g., Timio & Gentili, 1976), field studies (e.g., Johansson, Aronsson, & Lindstrom, 1978), and epidemiological surveys (e.g., O'Hanlon, 1981). In sum, low job stimulation levels cause higher arousal than moderate job stimulation levels, an apparent contradiction to activation theory.

Two experiments in which both activation levels and arousal levels were measured found that arousal levels were higher for low impact tasks than moderate impact tasks (Baschera & Grandjean, 1979; Weber et al., 1980). But, activation levels, as indexed by critical fusion frequency, were monotonically related to task impact as hypothesized. This led Gardner (1982) to hypothesize that elevated arousal levels may be caused by deviations of experienced activation level from the characteristic level, as did Teichner (1968) in his review. In the case of negative deviations, elevated arousal levels would increase depressed RAS activation levels (a "compensatory reaction" in Teichner's terms). In the case of positive deviations, elevated arousal levels would reflect "stress," an invocation of the alarm stage of the well-documented General Adaptation Syndrome (Selye, 1976). Gardner (1982, 1986a) tested the hypothesis in an explicit examination of activation theory and found that low impact tasks cause lower activation levels and higher arousal levels than moderate impact tasks. Two other experiments that followed (Gardner, 1986b; Gardner, Krieger,

& Baker, 1987) also produced results consistent with this hypothesis about the relationship between activation and arousal levels. Thus, both high impact and low impact tasks/jobs cause elevated arousal levels, because there appears to be a U-shaped relationship between activation and arousal levels. Gardner (1986b) also found, as hypothesized, that low impact tasks cause more impact-modifying behaviors than a moderate impact task.

Figure 3 summarizes this section on the application of activation theory to job design. Essentially, Figure 3 indicates that both positive and negative deviations of activation level that result from performing a job causes high arousal, lessened performance, lowered task satisfaction, and increased motivation to engage in impact-modifying behaviors. Withdrawal behaviors are indicated separately as an outcome but are in fact a special case of impact-modifying behaviors. If performance of a job causes experienced activation levels near the characteristic level of activation, characteristic arousal levels, positive affect, and high performance is expected. Performance effects are less robust because of the effects of job information processing requirements (see Figure 2).

Methodological Issues in Activation Theory Research

Researching activation theory is hard work. Rigorous tests of activation theory hypotheses almost inevitably requires making physiological measurements on subjects, which normally can only be done individually. Equipment and time costs are high. For most organizational behavior researchers, new measurement techniques are learned. In addition, researchers must be attuned to several methodological issues that, if ignored, contribute to the lack of progress in testing activation theory propositions. These issues include:

1. Develop and use independent measures of job impact. If one cannot verify that jobs have low, high, or moderate impact, independent of effects on job performers, then one is left in the position where just about any obtained effect can be accommodated by a postieri placing jobs on the impact continuum. As Schwab and Cummings (1976) pointed out, there is a definite need in the job design area for impact measures that are less subjective than currently used measures (e.g., the Job Diagnostic Survey; Hackman & Oldham, 1975).

2. Use multiple measures of arousal. For reasons noted above, single indices of arousal often times do not capture the arousal construct. Multiple measures (e.g., heart rate, skin conductance, respiration rate) increase the probability of measuring arousal in a given job-sample combination. Self-report measures of arousal do not index physiological arousal very well (Gardner, 1986a,b; Gardner et al., 1987; Lazarus, 1966), but do cor-

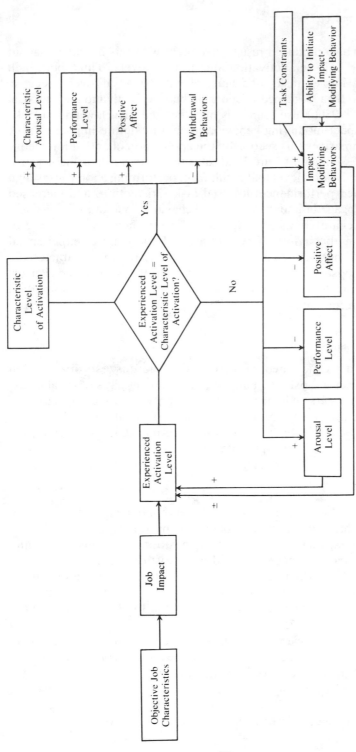

Figure 3. The hypothesized relationships between objective job characteristics, job impact, activation levels, arousal, affect, performance, and impact-modifying behaviors.

50

relate modestly with measures of activation (Baschera & Grandjean, 1979; Gardner, 1986a).

3. In testing activation-performance relationships, consider effects of information processing requirements of jobs. If only simple jobs are examined, linear and curvilinear relationships become more difficult to demonstrate. Relatedly, in experiments where job impact is manipulated, researchers must attend to potential restriction of range in the independent variable, causing restriction of range in subjects' activation levels.

4. Use within-subjects designs where possible. Between-subjects designs offer little information about activation-performance relationships (McGrath, 1976).

5. Control for knowledge of results. Unless effects of feedback are part of the research question, feedback about performance needs to be controlled to prevent confounding with job content. Knowledge of failure causes increased arousal and activation (Carriero & Fite, 1977; O'Hanlon, 1981).

INDIVIDUAL DIFFERENCES

Activation theory has been criticized as a job design theory because it fails to consider how (or which) individual differences affect relationships between job characteristics and responses of job performers (Hackman & Oldham, 1980; Hulin & Blood, 1968). This criticism is justified as all major earlier treatises on activation theory (Fiske & Maddi, 1961; Malmo, 1959; Scott, 1966; Scott & Erskine, 1980) make little or no mention of how individual differences fit into an activation theory nomological network. This is an important deficiency for at least two reasons. First, in practical terms, it leads to the assumption that variations in job design have uniform effects on all individuals. Past research has clearly shown that this is not true. Second, it precludes rigorous testing of main effects activation theory hypotheses. That is, to the extent that individual differences moderate the effects of job impact on activation levels, their systematic inclusion in activation theory research may be used to theoretically specify how individuals differentially react to jobs, and reduce what might have otherwise been sources of error variance in statistical analyses.

Two individual differences are hypothesized here to fit into an activation theory nomological network: Extraversion and Electrodermal Lability. Their selection was based on a desire to choose individual differences that reflect variation in some feature of the RAS. It appears that both variables index sensitivity to stimulation, which is to a large extent modulated by the RAS. Relevant research and resultant hypotheses are discussed next.

Extraversion

Several different approaches to the study of personality exist, but the approach of Eysenck (1953, 1967, 1976) is perhaps the most relevant to activation theory and job design. Eysenck's personality theory is based upon biological differences between individuals. He posits that extraversion is a function of individual differences in RAS sensory thresholds, and thus is directly related to activation theory.

Originally Eysenck (1957, 1967) hypothesized that extraversion was a function of individual differences in ability to generate and dissipate reactive inhibition. Reactive inhibition was conceived of as an intervening variable between stimulus-response reactions (Hull, 1943; Pavlov, 1927/1960; Teplov, 1964), which has its origins in the neurophysiological substrate of an organism. Extraverts, according to this early theorizing, had "strong" nervous systems that are dominated by inhibitory neural pathways. Introverts, on the other hand, were hypothesized to have "weak" nervous systems dominated by excitatory neural pathways. Eysenck believed that reactive inhibition was rooted in the inhibitory pathways of individuals. Differences in inhibitory pathway dominance, Eysenck further hypothesized, caused observable behavioral differences between extraverts and introverts. Extraverts would be characterized by stimulation-seeking behaviors and introverts would be characterized by stimulation-avoiding behaviors. Extraverts would require a higher level of stimulation than introverts to be optimally stimulated, on a criterion of positive affect ("hedonic tone," in Eysenck's 1963 terms).

In Eysenck's 1967 book he evaluates these early hypotheses about the extraversion variable. Research indicated that extraverts do engage in stimulation-seeking behaviors (e.g., social interactions) significantly more than introverts. However, research in physiological psychology did not confirm that the observed behavioral differences are caused by differences in inhibitory neural pathway dominance. Research did suggest that extraverts may have less sensitive RASs than introverts. This in turn led to the predictions that: (a) introverts are more physiologically arousable than extraverts, and (b) introverts, to prevent occurrence of deleteriously high arousal levels, seek relatively nonstimulating situations and avoid relatively stimulating situations, while extraverts seek the opposite.

Eysenck (1967, 1976) does not overtly tie his personality theory to activation theory. Nevertheless, his hypothesized optimal levels of stimulation imply that individuals have a range of activation levels that they seek to maintain. If this were not true, then observed differences in stimulation-seeking/-avoiding behaviors (i.e., impact modifying behaviors) between extraverts and introverts become less easily explained in biological, noncognitive terms. We do not predict that introverts and extraverts differ in their characteristic levels of activation. Rather, we predict that given identical situations, introverts experience higher activation levels than extraverts. Differences in experienced activation levels are then predicted to result in affective, arousal, and behavioral differences between introverts and extraverts through the process illustrated in Figure 3.

Extraversion and arousability. A key assumption in integrating extraversion into an activation theory nomological network is that introverts are more arousable than extraverts. Eysenck (1967) reviews most of the relevant research conducted before 1967, while Smith (1983) and Stelmack and Pflouffe (1983) review more recent research. All reviews conclude that introverts are more arousable than extraverts. For example, Smith, Wilson, and Rypma (1981) found that introverts exhibit larger skin conductance changes in response to discrete auditory stimuli. The issue that presently dominates the attention of extraversion researchers is what the exact neurophysiological reason is for the observed arousability differences. Some research indicates that the differences may be due to variability in RAS reactivity. For example, Haier, Robinson, Braden, and Williams (1984) found relationships between augmenting/reducing of evoked cortical responses and extraversion such that extraverts tend to "reduce" such responses and introverts "augment" them, consistent with results obtained by Friedman and Meares (1979). This evidence is also consistent with the hypothesis that extraversion is a function of RAS differences. Other research, however, suggests that arousability differences are caused by global differences at the sensory and motor neuron level (Stelmack & Pflouffe, 1983), and at the synapses by which neurons are interconnected (Stelmack & Wilson, 1982). Yet other research points to thalamic structures of the brain (Robinson, 1982). It is neither necessary nor possible for the present chapter to evaluate the various positions on what causes introvert/extravert arousability differences. What is important for our purposes is that there is virtually no doubt that introverts react more to external stimulation than extraverts, and that result has implications for activation theory.

Extraversion and stimulation-seeking behaviors. There also is little doubt that extraverts exhibit stimulation-seeking behaviors more than introverts, whereas introverts exhibit more stimulation–avoiding behaviors than extraverts. Indeed, this is what introverts and extraverts report on standard measures of extraversion (e.g., The Eysenck Personality Inventory, Eysenck & Eysenck, 1968). For example, Brebner and Cooper (1974) found that extraverts expose themselves to higher levels of stimulation than introverts, while Geen (1984) found that extraverts chose higher levels of noise intensity in which to perform a paired-associates learning task than introverts. In addition, Geen found that extraverts performed best under high stimulation conditions, whereas introverts performed best under conditions of low stimulation. This research is not only consistent with what introverts and extraverts report about themselves, it is consistent with the hypothesis that introverts require less stimulation to achieve their characteristic level of activation than extraverts.

Extraversion and responses to low impact jobs. One situation in which introverts and extraverts may be expected to manifest significant arousal, affective, and behavioral differences is performance on relatively non-stimulating (low impact) jobs. Because introverts are more sensitive to stimulation than extraverts, they should tolerate low impact jobs better than extraverts. The rationale for this hypothesis is illustrated in Figure 3. While both introverts and extraverts should experience negative deviations of experienced activation level from their characteristic levels while performing low impact jobs, the deviations for introverts should be smaller for introverts than extraverts because they experience higher activation levels. This, according to the process illustrated in Figure 3, would cause introverts to have lower arousal, and higher performance and job satisfaction levels than extraverts while performing a low impact job. The opposite is predicted for high impact jobs, while there should be few introvert/extravert differences for moderate impact jobs. Thus, we predict that: (a) Introverts will evince lower arousal levels, higher positive affect and performance levels, and fewer impact-modifying behaviors than extraverts while performing low impact jobs; and (b) Extraverts will evince lower arousal levels, higher positive affect and performance levels, and fewer impact-modifying behaviors than introverts while performing high impact jobs.

A considerable amount of research has been conducted on the relationship of extraversion and reactions to performance of low impact jobs. Vigilance tasks in particular have been studied extensively in this regard.[6] Vigilance tasks are low impact tasks because they provide low intensity, low variation stimulation. It can be predicted that introverts would fare much better on such tasks than extraverts, for reasons stated in the preceding paragraph. And, there is a considerable amount of research to support that hypothesis (see Mackworth, 1969; and Eysenck, 1967, for reviews), though a few exceptions have been reported (Blakeslee, 1979; Hastrup, 1979). Introvert/extravert differences appear to be more robust for performance and satisfaction than for arousal, possibly because introverts, in performing better, initiate more physical movements than extraverts, which in turn increases their arousal levels.

Several other studies have confirmed activation theory-based predictions about introvert/extravert differences with tasks and jobs that are repetitive in nature, but did not require vigilance behaviors. Scott (1969) reported an investigation that suggested that introverts performed a simple manual task (screwing nuts on bolts) better than extraverts, while Thackray, Jones, and Touchstone (1974) reported that introverts perform repetitive serial reaction tasks better than extraverts. In terms of affective reactions, Salvendy and Humphreys (1979) and Salvendy (1980) found that introverts have stronger preferences for machine-paced tasks than extraverts, while extraverts prefer self-paced tasks more than introverts. Similarly, Sterns, Alexander, Barrett, and Dambrot (1983) found that extraverts prefer jobs with high levels of cognitive demand, fast pacing, and intrinsic and extrinsic rewards more than introverts. Kim (1980) found that introverts were significantly more satisfied performing a relatively nonstimulating task than extraverts, whereas the opposite occurred for a moderately stimulating task. With respect to behaviors, Hill (1975) found that extraverts exhibited more impact-modifying behaviors (varying task procedure) while performing a repetitive manual task than did introverts, as did Gardner (1986b). Lastly, Gardner (1986a) and Gardner et al. (1987) found that extraverts were more aroused while performing low impact tasks than introverts, while the opposite occurred for a moderate impact task. All of these studies support the hypothesis that introverts experience activation levels closer to their characteristic levels than extraverts while performing low impact tasks, and also provides indirect empirical support for the process illustrated in Figure 3.

In sum, research generally supports the hypotheses that introverts are more sensitive to stimulation than extraverts, and introverts perform better, are more satisfied, and are less aroused than extraverts while performing low impact jobs. Little research has examined the other aspect of the hypothesis, that extraverts would fare better on high impact jobs than introverts. Clearly, more research needs to be conducted on introvert/extravert differences for high impact jobs. Nevertheless, extraversion shows promise as an individual difference moderator of job impact-response relationships in ways consistent with our activation theory application.

Electrodermal Lability

Much research in the Soviet Union and Europe (Gray, 1964; Pavlov, 1935/1960; Teplov, 1964) has focused on the concept of reactive inhibition and its neurophysiological substrate. In particular, researchers have searched for an explanation for an individual difference construct termed "strength of nervous system." These researchers believe that individuals with "strong" nervous systems readily generate and slowly dissipate reactive inhibition, and as a result are characterized as being relatively unreactive to stimulation, and what is currently termed stable. Individuals with "weak" nervous systems are believed to be less capable of generating and more readily dissipate reactive inhibition, and as a result are characterized as being relatively reactive to stimulation, and what is termed labile.[7] Unfortunately, for theoretical, empirical, and political reasons (Robinson, 1982) this research has failed in isolating the actual physiological substrate of reactive inhibition.

A related line of research, partly influenced by mid-century behaviorists (e.g., Hull, 1943), has focused on observed individual differences in autonomic lability (Lacey, 1956). There is little question that individuals reliably differ in their arousal responses (e.g., heart rate, respiration rate) to stimulus configurations. Labiles respond more strongly than stabiles to most types of stimulation, and take longer to habituate (regress back to tonic arousal levels). This pattern of physiological responses to stimulation strongly suggests that labiles, like introverts, are more sensitive to stimulation than stabiles and extraverts.

Autonomic lability can conceivably be measured with any arousal measure. Of the several possibilities, electrodermal measures of arousal (skin conductance, skin resistance) have emerged as perhaps the most reliable and valid. The body of research that has evolved around this skin measure of autonomic lability, termed electrodermal lability (edl), considers the measure to be a relatively pure index of individual differences in sensitivity to stimulation (cf. Katkin, 1975, for a review). Electrodermal lability is a function of epidermal eccrine (sweat) gland activity, and is measured with equipment capable of recording the degree to which a low intensity (e.g., 10 millivolt) electrical current is conducted by the epidermis. The degree to which the current is conducted, skin conductance level, is a measure of arousal. Electrodermal lability measures are taken from skin conductance data, in two different ways. First, the rate at which individuals emit nonspecific skin conductance changes in a constant and relatively stimulus-free environment (e.g., a soundproof chamber) is calculated for some period of time (usually around 10 minutes). Nonspecific skin conductance changes are changes not attributable to any known stimulus (e.g., a bodily movement). Labiles emit more changes than stabiles in such situations because they react more to whatever external stimulation is still present but not controlled, and the nerves in their sympathetic system are more likely to spontaneously discharge (Edelberg, 1972). The second way in which electrodermal lability is measured is to count the number of times a discrete stimulus must be presented before individuals habituate (do not react) to the stimulus. Labiles habituate less rapidly than stabiles, and thus require more trials to habituation.

These two methods of measuring electrodermal lability apparently index the same phenomenon, as evidenced by their consistent and high correlations within a number of experiments (e.g., Crider, 1975; Goldwater &

Lewis, 1978; Lader, 1971; Siddle, O'Gorman, & Wood, 1979). Crider and Lunn (1971) review research on the reliability of electrodermal lability and report retest reliabilities of .54 and .89 over 24- and 48-hour periods, and .62 (one month) and .50 (one year) for longer periods. Freixa i Baque (1982) reports an average retest reliability of .60 for 15 different experiments considering time intervals of 24 hours to one year. These reliabilities are typical for arousal measures, and are at least minimally acceptable for research purposes. Evidence that electrodermal lability reflects autonomic lability may be found in Crider (1975), Katkin (1975), Katkin, Morell, Goldband, Bernstein, and Wise (1982), and Siddle et al. (1979).

If labiles are more sensitive to stimulation than stabiles, then given the same situation or job labiles should experience higher activation levels than stabiles. This does not mean that labiles necessarily have lower or different characteristic levels of activation. It does imply that labiles require less situation or job impact than stabiles to achieve their characteristic level of activation. Labiles are more likely than stabiles to experience activation levels above their characteristic levels. Relating these labile/stabile differences to the process illustrated in Figure 3, we predict that, analogous to the reasoning for extraversion discussed above, that labiles will experience smaller deviations of experienced activation levels from characteristic levels than stabiles while performing low impact jobs, and that the opposite should occur for high impact jobs. This leads us to further predict that: (a) Labiles will evince lower arousal levels, higher positive affect and performance levels, and fewer impact-modifying behaviors than stabiles while performing low impact jobs; and (b) Stabiles will evince lower arousal levels, higher positive affect and performance levels, and fewer impact-modifying behaviors than labiles while performing high impact jobs.

Research to support these predictions is limited but encouraging. A number of experiments (Crider & Augenbraun, 1975; Hastrup, 1979; Sostek, 1979) have demonstrated that labiles perform low impact tasks (vigilance) better than stabiles. Gardner (1986a), in an explicit test of these hypotheses, found support for the satisfaction aspects of the hypotheses, but not arousal or performance. Lastly, Hastrup (1979) and Gardner (1986b) found that stabiles exhibit more impact-modifying behaviors than labiles while performing low impact tasks. Thus, while the research literature on electrodermal lability is much less voluminous than that for extraversion, it does show promise as a moderator of the process illustrated in Figure 3. In addition, we predict that any other individual difference variable that reflects variability in sensitivity to stimulation not discussed here will result in moderator hypotheses similar to those posited above for extraversion and electrodermal lability.

ACTIVATION THEORY AND COMPETING EMPLOYEE RESPONSE THEORIES

Job Design

The major purpose of this section is to demonstrate how activation theory, as a job design theory, differs from prevailing perspectives on how variations in job design affect job performer responses. It is generally agreed that any topic of inquiry is better understood by the empirical testing of competing hypotheses from different theories about the same observable phenomena (Hamner, Ross, & Staw, 1978; Platt, 1964). As such, it is important to discuss how activation theory leads to predictions about job design that differ from predictions based upon other theories.

This process of contrasting theories becomes complex, however, when one considers that there are at least eight different job design theories (cf. James & Jones, 1980; Steers & Mowday, 1977). Fortunately, there is a significant amount of overlap between these various job design theories. Moreover, only one of these job design theories may be considered a major job design theory, based upon the number of empirical studies to test the theory (Roberts & Glick, 1981). That theory, the job characteristics model (Hackman & Oldham, 1975, 1980), epitomizes what has been termed the "job characteristics approach" to job design (Roberts & Glick, 1981). This approach, which subsumes most recent job design theories, simply suggests that there are specifiable characteristics of jobs that reliably relate to responses of job performers. To avoid both redundant and trivial discussion, activation theory is compared and contrasted only to the job characteristics model here.

The job characteristics model. The job characteristics model has been discussed at length in a number of publications (Hackman & Oldham, 1975, 1980; Hackman, Oldham, Janson, & Purdy, 1975) and is only briefly presented here. Research to support various aspects of the model is reviewed in Hackman and Oldham (1980), Pierce and Dunham (1976), and Steers and Mowday (1977). A critique of the model and supporting research may be found in Roberts and Glick (1981).

The core hypothesis of the job characteristics model states that before workers evince such personal and work outcomes as high job satisfaction, high internal motivation to perform, and other effective work behaviors, they must experience three "critical psychological states": (a) meaningfulness of work, (b) responsibility for outcomes of work, and (c) knowledge of the actual results of the work activities. The three critical psychological states are experienced, in turn, if a worker perceives that his or her job possesses high amounts of five "core job characteristics":

1. *Skill Variety*—the opportunity to use a number of different, personally valued skills.
2. *Task Identity*—the opportunity to complete a meaningful, whole piece of work.
3. *Task Significance*—the opportunity to perform a job that affects the well-being of others.
4. *Autonomy*—the opportunity to make decisions relating to the work process.
5. *Feedback*—the opportunity to learn how well one is performing a job directly from the job itself.

Combined, the five core job characteristics define a variable that Hackman and Oldham call "motivating potential." The more that a job is perceived as being high in motivating potential, by a given worker, the more one will experience the three critical psychological states, and the more one will evince the desired outcomes noted above. Motivating potential corresponds to what has been termed job "enrichment" in the extant task design literature: Increasing motivating potential signifies increasing enrichment.

For the relationships between the components of the job characteristics model to hold, however, three conditions must be fulfilled. First, a worker must possess sufficient knowledge and skills to perform the enriched job. Second, a worker must be satisfied with the "context" in which the job exists. The job context includes such variables as compensation, job security, supervision, and co-worker relations. Third, a worker must have "strong needs for personal accomplishment, for learning, and for developing themselves beyond where they are now" (Hackman & Oldham, 1980, p. 85). These various needs are encompassed in a construct that they call "growth need strength." Individuals high on the growth need strength dimension experience the three critical psychological states if: (1) they perceive high levels of core job characteristics, (2) they have the necessary knowledge and skills to perform the job, and (3) they are satisfied with the work context. Low growth need strength individuals, on the other hand, do not experience the critical psychological states and may, in fact, be threatened if they perceive their jobs as having high levels of the core job characteristics. High perceived levels of the core job characteristics satisfy psychological needs of only high growth-need strength individuals, resulting in the critical psychological states and, ultimately, the personal and work outcomes specified by the model.

The three conditions of the job characteristics model (knowledge and skills, work context satisfaction, and growth need strength) are also called "moderator variables" because they are predicted to moderate the relationships between the three major components of the model (i.e., the core job characteristics, critical psychological states, and personal and work outcomes). Specifically, if high levels of the moderator variables are present, then positive correlations should exist between measures of all three basic components of the model. If low levels of the moderators are present, then nonsignificant or even negative correlations between components are expected.

Differences between activation theory and the job characteristics model. Activation theory and the job characteristics model represent very different interpretations of how variations in job design affect job performers. Activation theory is firmly based on the work of physiologists, physiological psychologists, and psychophysiologists (e.g., Duffy, 1972; Lindsley, 1956). Activation theory is decidedly noncognitive, though presumably cognitive processes are involved in such activities as choice of an impact-modifying behavior and determination of stimulation novelty.

The job characteristics model on the other hand is strongly based on classical personality theory (e.g., Murray, 1938) and humanistic psychology (Maslow, 1954). Individuals are assumed to have psychological needs, especially higher order needs like need for achievement, and behave in ways that satisfy those needs. The nature and even the existence of the higher order needs of the job characteristics model are much more controversial (e.g., Salancik & Pfeffer, 1977) than the nature and existence of the physiological need for stimulation encompassed in activation theory.

Overall, however, the two theories make similar predictions about the effects of variations in job design on responses of job performers. An "enriched" job in the job characteristics model corresponds to one that allows the job performer to maintain a characteristic level of activation in an activation theory analysis. There are nevertheless at least five differences between activation theory and the job characteristics model.

First, while both the job characteristics model and activation theory posit that variation in job characteristics affect job performers, they specify different types of characteristics as important determinants of job performer responses. Activation theory posits characteristics that may be ascribed to any source of stimulation (e.g., intensity, novelty, complexity) and that are important only because they contribute to job impact. The job characteristics model, on the other hand, posits characteristics specific to tasks and jobs, the core job characteristics (e.g., skill variety, autonomy). Perceptions of these different types of characteristics by job performers are highly correlated (Gardner, 1982, 1986a, 1986b). Gardner (1982) hypothesized specific, differential relationships between job characteristics from the two theories (e.g., variation of stimulation and skill variety) but was unable to support those relationships empirically with perceptions of job characteristics. It seems that these differences in describing job characteristics are caused more by theoretical differences than they are by real-world phenomena, though Farh and Scott (1983) concluded that enhanced job autonomy is rather ineffective in increasing job performance levels in the absence of more substantive changes in the stimulation impact of tasks.

A second, more fundamental difference between activation theory and the job characteristics model is the degree to which perceptions of job characteristics are assigned causal properties in determining job performer responses. Activation theory ascribes few causal properties to how a job performer describes the characteristics of a job. Clearly, these self-reported perceptions correlate with objective differences in jobs (e.g., Algera, 1983; Gardner, 1982) and provide reasonably accurate measures of the impact and/or motivating potential of jobs (though other researchers ascribe dubious value to perceptions of job characteristics; cf. Farh & Scott, 1983; Schwab & Cummings, 1976; Wells, 1982). But, according to an activation theory analysis, the primary cause of job performer responses is the interaction of job impact and characteristic level of activation. A job performer need not perceive the impact of a job accurately for it to affect one in predictable ways.

The job characteristics model, in contrast, clearly assigns causal priority to perceptions of job characteristics (though Hackman & Oldham, 1980, p. 97, vacillate somewhat on this issue). If a job is in reality enriched, but is not perceived as being enriched, then higher order psychological needs cannot be satisfied. The latter prevents experience of the critical psychological states, which in turn precludes the occurrence of desired personal and work outcomes. Hackman and Oldham do, however, unequivocally state that perceptions of job characteristics are strongly determined by objective job characteristics.

Thus, activation theory and the job characteristics model differ on whether or not perceptions of job characteristics have causal properties.[8] There is little question that cognitions can affect activation levels, and activation levels can affect cognitions (e.g., Hamilton & Warburton, 1979; Lazarus, 1966). Thus the issue of whether perceptions of job characteristics affect job performers is really an issue of whether individuals seek to satisfy higher order needs while at work. Research to support the job characteristics model has been criticized for using self-report measures that create a plausible reality for respondents (Salancik & Pfeffer, 1977). Activation theory also gives little support to the hypothesis that individuals seek to satisfy higher order needs at work. Yet, other research (James & Jones, 1980; James & Tetrick, 1986) supports the hypothesis that perceptions have causal effects on attitudes and behaviors. It would seem that this difference between activation theory and the job characteristics model represents a gray area that warrants further exploration, theoretically and empirically. But, the issue does have an important implication. If the job characteristics model is correct and perceptions of job characteristics do cause job performer responses, then organizations that wish to maximize employee effectiveness can attempt to manipulate both objective job characteristics and the perceptions of those characteristics.

A third difference between activation theory and the job characteristics model is the shape of the predicted relationships between job characteristics and responses of job performers. Activation theory predicts curvilinear relationships between job impact and job performer responses, whereas the job characteristics model predicts only linear relationships between its components. Thus, the job characteristics model does not fully acknowledge that a job might be "overenriched" to the detriment of a job performer, at least low growth–need strength performers. To the extent that perceptions of job characteristics reflect objective job characteristics, activation theory would predict curvilinear relationships between those perceptions and job performer responses. Such curvilinear relationships have in fact been obtained in some research (Champoux, 1978, 1980), in support of activation theory.

A fourth difference between activation theory and the job characteristics model relates to moderators of job characteristics–job performer response relationships. Activation theory focuses on factors that may influence the job impact-characteristic activation level interaction (e.g., extraversion, electrodermal lability). The job characteristics model posits three moderators: ability, context satisfaction, and growth need strength. Activation theory does not preclude effects of ability and context variables. No theory of performance would deny the importance of ability in determining job performance levels. In addition, job failure affects activation levels (e.g., Carriero & Fite, 1977). Context variables are also accommodated by assessing their impact on an individual's experienced activation level. The major difference regarding moderators concerns growth need strength and, as discussed above, whether a need satisfaction model accounts for the effects of job characteristics on job performers. An interesting test might be to examine whether growth need strength moderates job characteristics–job performer response relationships better than extraversion and electrodermal lability (holding such things as measurement reliability and validity constant).

A fifth major difference between activation theory and the job characteristics model is the number of different types of responses to jobs each theory is capable of predicting. Basically, the job characteristics model offers predictions about affect and behaviors. Activation theory offers predictions about affect, behavior, and arousal. Thus, activation allows predictions about more aspects of individuals than the job characteristics model. Moreover, predictions from the job characteristics model are limited to reactions of job performers to job characteristics. Activation theory is more general in that any work-related stimuli that affect experienced activation level may be included in predicting responses of individuals to their work environment. For example, a monotonous task with a difficult performance goal has more impact than the same task with an easy goal, resulting in several differential hypotheses about task performer behavior, affect, and arousal (Gardner et al., 1987). Overall, activation theory is more comprehensive and widely applicable than the job characteristics model.

In sum, there are several differences between activation theory and the job characteristics model. Some of these disparities are more empirically testable than others. Nevertheless, the above discussion allows for the possibility that activation theory may be demonstrated to be superior to the job characteristics model in explaining job characteristic–job performer responses. Should future research confirm that superiority, activation theory would present a more parsimonious explanation for the effects of variation in job designs because: (a) activation theory allows predictions about a greater number of types of worker responses, (b) activation theory may be expanded to include any work-related stimuli, and (c) activation theory posits less controversial individual differences moderators.

Activation Theory and Job Stress

Job stress is an area of research that has received a great amount of theoretical and empirical interest in the behavioral sciences. However, unlike job design, there is no dominant theory of job stress that has spurred an integrated body of research, despite the number of literature reviews (e.g., Beehr & Newman, 1978; Matteson & Ivancevich, 1979; Schuler, 1980) and books (e.g., Cooper & Payne, 1978; Levi, 1981) that have been published on the topic. Instead, job stress research has been mostly atheoretical, focusing more on the identification of causes and consequences of job stress than on explaining the process that underlies the job stress phenomenon. What has resulted from this research are taxonomies of (a) stimuli that cause job stress (job stressors), (b) responses of individuals that signify job stress (job strain indices), (c) organizational and individual strategies that may alleviate the effects of job stressors (coping strategies), and (d) individual differences that reflect ability to cope with job stressors (for examples, see Beehr & Newman, 1978; Burke & Weir, 1980; Newman & Beehr, 1979; Schuler, 1980).

These various taxonomies represent important contributions to the job stress literature. However, they fail to specify, for example, why certain stimuli cause job strain, or why certain individuals are more susceptible to job stressors than others. There are exceptions to the preceding statement (e.g., French, Rogers, & Cobb, 1974; Schuler, 1980) that do attempt to delineate the process that intervenes between job stressors and job strain. But, like the job characteristics model, these process models of job stress often posit need satisfaction as the primary determinant of job performer responses. Thus, like the job characteristics model, they may overestimate the degree to which complex cognitive processes determine the psychological, physiological, and behavioral responses of individuals.

As previously noted, activation theory is a widely applicable theory in terms of explaining organizational behavior phenomena. Job stress is one such phenomenon to which activation theory may be applied. All four major components of the job stress phenomenon are included in activation theory:

1. Job stressors are any stimuli that cause an individual's experienced activation level to deviate from one's characteristic level.
2. Job strain is decreased positive affect, increased arousal, and decreased behavioral efficiency.
3. Coping strategies are impact-modifying behaviors or organizational interventions that move an individual's experienced activation level closer to one's characteristic level.
4. Individual differences in susceptibility to job stressors is a function of differences in sensitivity to stimulation.

More importantly, activation theory provides a viable explanation for the relationships between the four job stress components: job stress occurs whenever job-related stimuli cause an individual's experienced activation level to deviate substantially from one's characteristic level of activation. An individual does not have to experience psychological need frustration to be stressed.

Though activation theory represents a comparatively simple explanation for the job stress phenomenon, it is perhaps premature to consider it a job stress theory. This is because job stressors and job strain indices identified in past research cannot be easily translated into activation theory terms. For example, while activation theory allows predictions about positive affect, it does not allow specific predictions about such psychological strain indices as irritability, paranoia, and forgetfulness. Similarly, while activation theory can precisely relate such stimulation characteristics as intensity and novelty to job performer responses, it is less specific as to why such job stressors as role ambiguity, interpersonal conflict, and poor promotional opportunities cause job strain.

This does not mean that basic activation theory propositions are incorrect. It does mean that at present activation theory is at best an heuristic for understanding the process that intervenes between job stressors and job strain. Further empirical work is needed to translate specific examples of the various components of job stress into an activation theory terminology. Only then can activation theory be fully considered a job stress theory.

Activation Theory and Goal Setting

One of the most reliable empirical relationships in organizational behavior research is that specific, difficult, accepted performance goals cause higher levels of performance than global, easy, and/or unaccepted goals (Locke, Shaw, Saari, & Latham, 1981). There have been some inconsistencies, however, particularly in studies involving self-set versus assigned goals, and those examining joint effects of individual differences (e.g., Ivancevich, 1976, 1977; Ivancevich & McMahon, 1977a, 1977b; Latham & Yukl, 1975). These empirical anomalies are believed to be caused by failure to consider how goals combine with other factors in determining performance (Locke, Frederick, Lee, & Bobko, 1984). Examples of these other factors include perceptions of self-efficacy and task strategy (Locke et al., 1984), goal information, choice, and task complexity (Earley, 1985), and content of performance feedback (Kim, 1984). Virtually all of this research assumes that intentions to perform at a given level mediates the effects of goal setting and these other factors on actual performance levels.

An alternative explanation is that physiological arousal mediates the effects of goal setting on performance, and satisfaction (Huber, 1985). It can be hypothesized that if difficult goals cause higher arousal levels than easy goals, higher performance and greater satisfaction will result by virtue of hypothesized relationships between arousal and performance (Humphreys & Revelle, 1984), and arousal and satisfaction (Maddi, 1961). Research to test the hypothesis that arousal mediates effects of goal setting on performance and satisfaction is rather sparse. Ford, Wright, and Haythornthwaite (1985) concluded that "goal valence" is linearly related to arousal, which in turn is curvilinearly related to performance. But, in that study subjects were neither assigned nor given the opportunity to choose a performance goal. In addition, Ford et al. used no physiological measures of arousal. Without arousal measures one cannot unequivocally test for mediation effects. Thus, little can be inferred from this study about arousal mediation effects. Huber (1985) explicitly tested the arousal mediation hypothesis. In her laboratory experiment, she manipulated both goal difficulty and task complexity to examine their direct and interactive effects on task performance. Huber found that arousal did not predict performance over and above effects caused by goal difficulty and task complexity.

However, Huber's hierarchical regressions did not indicate whether goal difficulty and task complexity predict performance after controlling for effects of arousal. Moreover, Huber used a self-report measure of arousal, which is an imperfect index of actual physiological arousal levels (Lazarus, 1966). Thus it is difficult to unequivocally accept her conclusion that "it is arousal caused by the task and goal setting, rather than arousal per se, that is associated with performance" (Huber, 1985, p. 499).

However, it is possible that activation level mediates effects of goal setting on job performance. Goal setting in a job environment will increase performance to the extent that the goals cause an optimal level of experienced activation for job performance. Moderately difficult goals that cause moderate levels of activation should result in high performance, high satisfaction, and low arousal. If a goal is too difficult, low performance, low satisfaction, and high arousal should result because of excessively high activation. If a goal is too easy, low performance, low satisfaction, and high arousal should result because of excessively low activation. But these processes do not occur in a vacuum. Other factors within the job environment affect activation levels of job performers. For example, to the extent that difficult goals compensate for a low stimulation environment, detrimental effects should be less severe. Similarly, if an easy goal compensates for a high stimulation environment, detrimental effects should also be less severe. Thus we hypothesize:

1.   Moderately difficult goals will cause higher activation, performance, and satisfaction, and lower arousal, than easy goals.

2.   Moderately difficult goals will cause lower activation and arousal, and higher performance and satisfaction, than very difficult goals.

3.   Moderately stimulating job environments will cause higher activation, performance, and satisfaction, and lower arousal than low stimulation job environments.

4.   Moderately stimulating job environments will cause lower activation and arousal, and higher performance and satisfaction, than high stimulation job environments.

5.   Goal difficulty and job environment stimulation will interact such that: (a) moderate levels of goal difficulty and environmental stimulation result in moderate activation, high performance and satisfaction, and low arousal, (b) low levels of goal difficulty and environmental stimulation result in low activation, performance and satisfaction, and high arousal, (c) high levels of goal difficulty and environmental stimulation result in high activation and arousal, and low performance and satisfaction, and (d) that noncongruent levels of goal difficulty and environmental stimulation (viz., low/moderate and moderate/low) result in moderate activation, performance, satisfaction, and arousal.

And, consistent with earlier discussion of moderating effects of sensitivity to stimulation, we also hypothesize:

6. Extraversion will interact with goal difficulty such that:
   a. introverts perform better, are more satisfied, and less aroused than extraverts while performing under easy goal conditions, and
   b. extraverts perform better, are more satisfied, and less aroused than introverts while performing under difficult goal conditions.
7. Extraversion will interact with environmental stimulation such that:
   a. introverts perform better, are more satisfied, and less aroused than extraverts while performing in a low stimulation environment, and
   b. extraverts perform better, are more satisfied, and less aroused than introverts while performing in a high stimulation environment.
8. Electrodermal lability will interact with goal difficulty such that:
   a. labiles perform better, are more satisfied, and less aroused than stabiles while performing under easy goal conditions, and
   b. stabiles perform better, are more satisfied, and less aroused than labiles while performing under difficult goal conditions.
9. Electrodermal lability will interact with environmental stimulation such that:
   a. labiles perform better, are more satisfied, and less aroused than stabiles while performing in a low stimulation environment, and
   b. stabiles perform better, are more satisfied, and less aroused than labiles while performing in a high stimulation environment.

Finally, we do not expect measures of physiological arousal to mediate effects of goal setting and job environment stimulation because arousal, like performance and satisfaction, is a result of deviations of experienced activation level from the characteristic level.

Gardner et al. (1987) tested most of these hypotheses about goal setting and activation theory. In a laboratory experiment they manipulated goal difficulty and environmental stimulation, and simultaneously obtained arousal measures while subjects performed a proofreading task. All hypotheses tended to be supported for performance and arousal, but not for task satisfaction. They concluded that subjects' cognitions affected their responses to task performance over and above activation level effects. These results require replication but do imply that: (a) activation theory at least partly accounts for effects of goal setting on job performers, and (b) that our knowledge of activation theory probably needs further development to account for job performer cognitions.

SUMMARY AND CRITIQUE OF ACTIVATION THEORY AS AN ORGANIZATIONAL BEHAVIOR THEORY

The purpose of this chapter was to demonstrate that activation theory is a viable explanation for the effects of variations in job design on responses of job performers, and to illustrate how the theory could be applied to other areas of organizational behavior. We accomplished this by (a) showing how activation theory may be used to make specific predictions about the effects of job characteristics on job performers, (b) suggesting how individual differences might fruitfully be integrated into an activation theory nomological network, (c) comparing and contrasting activation theory with the job characteristics model, and (d) showing how activation theory can be used to explain job stress and effects of goal setting. The process by which we hypothesize that activation level causes or mediates these effects is illustrated in Figure 4. The core of Figure 4 is the comparator that evaluates whether an individual's experienced activation level at a given time equals or approximates that individual's characteristic level of activation. If experienced activation level is in fact close to characteristic level, then we predict that the individual will exhibit characteristic (normal) arousal, positive affect, high performance, low motivation to initiate impact-modifying behaviors (including withdrawal behaviors), and low levels of other indices of job strain. If the individual's experienced activation level is substantially higher (positive deviation) or substantially lower (negative deviation) than his or her characteristic level, then we predict that the individual will exhibit high arousal, negative affect, low performance, high motivation to initiate impact-modifying behaviors, and high levels of other indices of job strain. Impact-modifying behaviors are constrained by situational demands and the individual's repertoire of behaviors. If impact-modifying behaviors are successful, the activation deviation is eliminated and levels of arousal, affect, performance, and other job strain indices are restored to characteristic levels. Performance predictions are less precise than those for arousal and affect because the information processing requirements of the job may require activation levels higher or lower than the individual's characteristic level of activation. Primary determinants of experienced activation level, as covered in this review, include objective job characteristics, goal difficulty, other work environment stimulation, and freedom to initiate impact-modifying behaviors. The combined effects of these variables on the individual result in situation impact and resulting experienced activation level. The effects of a given level of situation impact on an individual is moderated by sensitivity to stimulation such that the higher the sensitivity of an individual, the higher the resultant experienced activation level. Extraversion and electrodermal

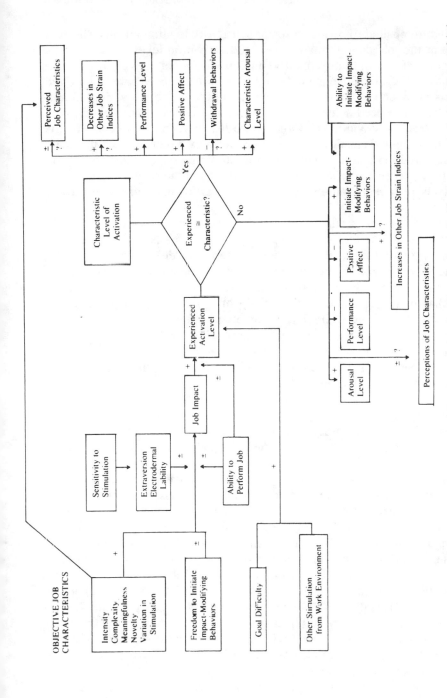

Figure 4. Summary of activation theory hypotheses about effects of work environment on responses of job performers.

lability are posited to be measures of sensitivity to stimulation. Ability to perform the job also affects experienced activation level because of the activating effects of failure. Lastly, perceptions of core job characteristics from the job characteristics model are hypothesized to be caused by direct effects of objective job characteristics, and the degree to which an individual's experienced activation level approximates his or her characteristic level. Negative deviations should cause low perception levels. Positive deviations should result in high ratings but only because most measures of perceived job characteristics do not allow the respondents to indicate that they perceive levels of the perceived job characteristics as being excessively high. Perceptions of job characteristics may affect worker responses.

Figure 4 contains a number of question marks that indicate uncertainties about some of the hypothesized relationships. This is because research has not provided sufficient evidence to support or disconfirm the validity of the hypothesized relationships. These question marks concern: (a) the determinants of perceived job characteristics, (b) the effects of perceived job characteristics, (c) the relationship of the deviation of experienced activation level from characteristic levels to other job strain indices, (d) the relationship between experienced activation level and withdrawal behaviors, and (e) the relationship between goal difficulty and situation impact. We believe that these question marks represent the primary needs for research on activation theory.

Before concluding this chapter, it is appropriate to discuss major deficiencies of activation theory. These deficiencies do not warrant rejection of activation theory. Rather, they indicate limitations of the theory as well as other aspects of the theory that need empirical clarification before the theory can be considered refined.

The first and perhaps major problem with activation theory is that it does not clearly indicate what effects cognitive processes and prior learning have on responses of job performers. For example, how does an individual choose what impact-modifying behavior one will engage in to adjust his or her activation level? It would seem that some degree of cognitive processing of information is involved in such situations, though a reinforcement explanation is possible (Scott, 1966; Scott & Erskine, 1980). Effects of emotional reactions on arousal are believed to be affected by cognitions (e.g., Foa & Kozak, 1986; Ohman, 1986) and it certainly seems that activation theory needs to better accommodate cognitions. In sum, while activation theory is incongruent with higher order need satisfaction models of work behavior, it is not clear at present the extent to which other types of information processing affect worker responses.

A second problem with activation theory is that it does not explain situations where an individual may be expected to have both high experienced activation level and high positive affect (e.g., a "happy birthday" effect). Moreover, feelings of pleasure are believed to originate in the limbic activating system, not the RAS. There is, however, some evidence that activation in the limbic system suppresses activation in the RAS (cf. Zuckerman, 1979). If such is the case, the experience of extreme pleasure (i.e., high limbic activity) is not associated with high experienced activation levels in the RAS, which resolves the apparent inconsistency. At present, though, it is not known with certainty when or why particular stimuli elicit activity in the limbic activating system (Zuckerman, 1979). Future research on the relationship of the limbic activating system to the RAS may provide more substantial support for activation theory-based predictions about affect.

A third problem with activation theory, as a theory of organizational behavior, is that little is known about how other work environment factors affect activation levels. The typical work organization contains a multitude of stimuli (e.g., social interactions) that affect activation levels. Job-based stimulation might be the primary determinant of activation level for most employees, but there are other determinants. Unlike job complexity, we know very little concerning the impact these other variables have on employee activation levels. Conceivably, a situation impact measure could be developed that would encompass all relevant sources of stimulation in a work environment. Should such a measure be developed, however, the relationships indicated in Figures 3 and 4 would not change. Thus, activation theory is more flexible than theories confined to predictions only about effects of job characteristics, but the full potential of the theory has yet to be realized.

A fourth problem with activation theory is that it does not consider what effects under- and overstimulation might have on individuals over extended periods of time. The relationships indicated in Figure 4 consider only a short period of time. To the extent that both under- and overstimulation lead to chronically high arousal levels, various physical illnesses (e.g., coronary heart disease, cancer) can be predicted to occur (Kasl, 1978; Sklar & Anisman, 1981). But it may also be that an individual's characteristic level of activation may adjust to the work environment over time. Much research has been conducted on the effects of understimulation on developing organisms (Bronson, 1968; Riesen, 1961; Thompson & Schaeffer, 1961). There can be little question that chronic understimulation early in life detrimentally affects the basic functioning of animals when they later mature, including evidence that characteristic levels of activation are lowered. Maddi (1961) and Zuckerman (1979) discuss the possibility of such effects on humans.

Longitudinal research on mature humans is scarce. One study on sensory deprivation (Zubek, 1964; in Zuckerman, 1979) found that prolonged isolation from stimulation (7 to 14 days) resulted in lowered cortical activation in some subjects more than 10 days after returning to their normal environments. Salvendy and Pilitsis (1971) found that older experienced industrial workers adapt to machine-paced work better than younger workers, as would be predicted if the former had lower characteristic levels of activation than the latter. Stagner (1975) reviews several studies on the possible effects of monotonous (low impact) work on workers over time. While none of this research was longitudinal, it does suggest that workers adapt to monotonous work, possibly by involuntarily and unconsciously lowering their characteristic levels of activation. Lastly, Cox (1980) reviews research on leisure activities of individuals who perform repetitive jobs and concludes that their non-work behaviors are remarkably similar to their work behaviors, suggesting that these workers biologically adjust to their work. Chronically overstimulated workers could conceivably raise their characteristic levels for the same reason: a better biological fit between worker and job. In sum, Figure 4 may be inadequate in representing the effects of jobs on individuals over long time periods.

A fifth problem with activation theory is that it does not specify in concrete terms how one might alter objective characteristics of the work environment to increase or decrease situation impact. That is, it offers little guidance to the practitioner-researcher who might wish to redesign work environments based upon activation theory principles. The present chapter was written with the intention of making activation theory predictions about job design more testable. The resulting model (Figure 4), however, is still primarily conceptual. It is likely, though, that procedures for effecting the desired outcomes are not radically different from those suggested by other work environment theories (e.g., Hackman et al., 1975; Trist, 1978). Activation theory potentially represents a more valid explanation for the effects of those changes.

In conclusion, this chapter presents evidence which we believe demonstrates that activation theory has sufficient empirical support to be considered a viable job design theory. Based upon past research, several new predictions about the effects of variation in work design on responses of employees are offered, including possible moderating effects of two individual differences. The theory developed in this chapter also allows for the possibility that: (a) activation theory is superior to the job characteristics model, and (b) activation theory can be fruitfully expanded to cover job stress and goal setting areas of research. At a minimum, it is hoped that past criticisms that activation theory is insufficiently precise to be of use in job design research are now less justified.

NOTES

1. The job and task terms have been used somewhat interchangeably in the job design literature. Here, jobs refer to the collection of tasks that are real and for which employees are compensated. Tasks are activities designed to emulate jobs by replicating the types of tasks that jobholders perform, but in more controlled settings (e.g., laboratory experiments).

2. Knowledge about characteristics of the RAS has come from direct measurements of RAS activity in infra-humans (Fiske & Maddi, 1961).

3. The logic underlying Maddi's extension is less compelling than that for behavioral efficiency, because feelings of pleasure are believed to originate in the limbic activating system (Eysenck, 1967; Olds & Milner, 1954; Zuckerman, 1979). The RAS and the limbic structures of the brain are neurally connected, however, and the hypothesis is viable (Weil, 1974). The present chapter is not intended to detail the physiological processes that are the bases for activation theory. Interested readers are encouraged to read the original sources.

4. Actually, there is a range in which experienced activation levels are "characteristic." Thus, experienced activation levels must deviate rather substantially from the characteristic range of activation levels before behavioral efficiency and positive affect decline, as illustrated in Figure 1. Also, momentary fluctuations of experienced activation level from the characteristic range are capable of creating increased positive affect (cf. Berlyne's, 1960, discussion of "arousal jags").

5. An additional implication is that high information processing tasks should be performed under generous time limits to enhance performance. By virtue of their complexity, high information processing tasks cause higher activation levels than low information processing tasks. This, in turn, may decrease the ability of the task performer to perform the task because of too high of an activation level (see Figure 2). Spacing out task requirements would decrease the impact of the task, causing more moderate activation levels, and better task performance.

6. Vigilance tasks require subjects to monitor a stimulus screen, usually a cathode ray tube (CRT), and report each incidence of an infrequent and barely discernible stimulus (e.g., a light flash). Examples of real-world vigilance tasks include air traffic control and military radar operation.

7. This of course is descriptive of introverts (labiles) and extraverts (stabiles) and has not gone unnoticed by researchers of the strength of nervous system construct (e.g., Gray, 1964; Robinson, 1982).

8. Interestingly, the issue of whether perceptions, cognitions, thoughts, attitudes etc. affect behavior is also controversial in other areas of psychology (e.g., Nisbett & Wilson, 1977; Quattrone, 1985; Sabini & Silver, 1981).

ACKNOWLEDGMENT

The insightful comments by Barry Staw on this chapter are greatly appreciated.

REFERENCES

Algera, J.A. (1983). "Objective" and perceived task characteristics as a determinant of reactions by task performers. *Journal of Occupational Behavior, 56*, 95–107.
Andreassi, J.L. (1980). *Psychophysiology.* New York: Oxford University Press.

Arkes, H.R., & Clark, P. (1975). Effects of task difficulty on subsequent preference for visual difficulty. *Perceptual and Motor Skills, 41,* 395–399.

Avolio, B.J., Alexander, R.A., Barrett, G.V., & Sterns, H.L. (1979). Analyzing preferences for pace as a component of task performance. *Perceptual and Motor Skills, 49,* 667–674.

Baschera, P., & Grandjean, E. (1979). Effects of repetitive tasks with different degrees of difficulty on critical fusion frequency (CFF) and subjective state. *Ergonomics, 22,* 377–385.

Beehr, T.A., & Newman, J.E. (1978). Job stress, employee health, and organizational effectiveness: Facet analysis, model, and literature review. *Personnel Psychology, 31,* 665–699.

Berlyne, D.E. (1967). Arousal and reinforcement. In D. Levine (Ed.), *Nebraska symposium on motivation* (Vol. 15). Lincoln: University of Nebraska Press.

Berlyne, D.E. (1960). *Conflict, arousal and curiosity.* New York: McGraw-Hill.

Birchall, P.M.A., & Claridge, G.S. (1979). Augmenting-reducing of the visual evoked potential as a function of changes in skin conductance levels. *Psychophysiology, 16,* 482–490.

Blakeslee, P. (1979). Attention and vigilance: Performance and skin conductance response changes. *Psychophysiology, 16,* 413–419.

Bloom, L.J., Houston, B.K., Holmes, D.S., & Burish, T.G. (1977). The effectiveness of attentional diversion and situational redefinition for reducing stress due to a nonambiguous threat. *Journal of Research in Personality, 11,* 83–94.

Brebner, J., & Cooper, C. (1974). The effect of a low rate of regular signals upon the reaction times of introverts and extraverts. *Journal of Research in Personality, 8,* 264–276.

Bronson, G.W. (1968). The fear of novelty. *Psychological Bulletin, 69,* 350–358.

Burke, R.J., & Weir, T. (1980). Coping with the stress of managerial occupations. In C.L. Cooper & R. Payne (Eds.), *Current concerns in occupational stress.* New York: Wiley.

Carriero, N.J., & Fite, J. (1977). Cardiac deceleration as an indicator of correct performance. *Perceptual and Motor Skills, 44,* 275–282.

Champoux, J.E. (1978). A serendipitous field experiment in job design. *Journal of Vocational Behavior, 12,* 364–370.

Champoux, J.E. (1980). A three sample test of some extensions to the job characteristics model of work motivation. *Academy of Management Journal, 23,* 466–478.

Cooper, C.L., & Payne, R. (1978). (Eds.). *Stress at work.* New York: Wiley.

Corlett, E.N., & Mahadeva, K. (1970). A relationship between a freely chosen working pace and energy consumption curves. *Ergonomics, 13,* 517–524.

Corum, C.R., & Thurmond, J.B. (1977). Effects of acute exposure to stress on subsequent aggression and locomotor performance. *Psychosomatic Medicine, 39,* 436–443.

Cox, T. (1980). Repetitive work. In C.L. Cooper & R. Payne (Eds.), *Current concerns in occupational stress.* New York: Wiley.

Crider, A. (1975). Tonic arousal correlates of individual differences in electrodermal lability. *JSAS Catalog of Selected Documents in Psychology, 5,* 183 (Ms. 844).

Crider, A., & Augenbraun, C.B. (1975). Auditory vigilance correlates of electrodermal response habituation speed. *Psychophysiology, 12,* 36–40.

Crider, A., & Lunn, R. (1971). Electrodermal lability as a personality dimension. *Journal of Experimental Research in Personality, 5,* 145–150.

Duffy, E. (1972). Activation. In N.S. Greenfield & R.A. Sternbach (Eds.), *Handbook of psychophysiology.* New York: Holt, Rinehart, and Winston.

Earley, P.C. (1985) Influence of information, choice, and task complexity upon goal acceptance, performance, and personal goals. *Journal of Applied Psychology, 70,* 481–490.

Easterbrook, J.A. (1959). The effect of emotion on cue utilization and the organization of behavior. *Psychological Review, 66,* 187–201.

Edelberg, R. (1972). Electrical activity of the skin: Its measurement and uses in psychophysiology. In N.S. Greenfield & R.A. Sternbach (Eds.), *Handbook of psychophysiology.* New York: Holt, Rinehart, and Winston.

Eysenck, H.J. (1953). *The structure of human personality.* New York: Wiley.

Eysenck, H.J. (1957). *The dynamics of anxiety and hysteria.* New York: Praeger.

Eysenck, H.J. (1963). *Experiments with drugs.* New York: Pergamon.

Eysenck, H.J. (1967). *The biological basis of personality.* Springfield, IL: Charles C. Thomas.

Eysenck, H.J. (1976). (Ed.). *The measurement of personality.* Baltimore: University Park Press.

Eysenck, H.J., & Eysenck, S.B.G. (1968). *Manual for the Eysenck Personality Inventory.* San Diego: Educational and Industrial Testing Service.

Eysenck, M.W. (1985). Anxiety and cognitive task performance. *Personality and Individual Differences, 6,* 579–586.

Farh, J.L., & Scott, W.E. (1983). The experimental effects of "autonomy" on performance and self-reports of satisfaction. *Organizational Behavior and Human Performance, 31,* 203–222.

Fiske, D.W., & Maddi, S.R. (1961). (Eds.). *Functions of varied experience.* Homewood, IL: Dorsey Press.

Foa, E.B., & Kozak, M.J. (1986). Emotional processing of fear: Exposure to corrective information. *Psychological Bulletin, 90,* 20–35.

Ford, C.E., Wright, R.A., & Haythornthwaite, J. (1985). Task performance and magnitude of goal valence. *Journal of Research in Personality, 19,* 253–260.

Frankenheuser, M., Nordhegen, B., Myrsten, A.L., & Post, B. (1971). Psychophysiological reactions to understimulation and overstimulation. *Acta Psychologica, 35,* 298–308.

Freixa i Baque, E. (1982). Reliability of electrodermal measures: A compilation. *Biological Psychology, 14,* 219–229.

French, J.R.P., Jr., Rogers, W., & Cobb, S. (1974). Adjustment as a person-environment fit. In G.V. Coehlo, D.A. Hamburg, & J.F. Adams (Eds.), *Coping and adaptation: Interdisciplinary perspectives.* New York: Basic Books.

Friedman, J., & Meares, R. (1979). Cortical evoked potentials and extraversion. *Psychosomatic Medicine, 41,* 279–286.

Gardner, D.G. (1986a). Activation theory and task design: An empirical test of several new predictions. *Journal of Applied Psychology, 71,* 411–418.

Gardner, D.G. (1986b, November). *Effects of task complexity on nontask-related movements: An explicit test of activation theory predictions.* Annual Meeting of the Decision Sciences Institute, Honolulu.

Gardner, D.G. (1987). *Effects of task complexity on performance and activation level.* Manuscript under review.

Gardner, D.G. (1982). Activation theory and task design: Development of a conceptual model and an empirical test. *Dissertation Abstracts International, 42,* 3477B–3478B. (University Microfilms No. 8200673).

Gardner, D.G., Krieger, K.J., Baker, D.D. (1987). *Effects of goal difficulty and environmental stimulation on task performer responses: Activation level as a mediating variable.* Manuscript under review.

Geen, R.G. (1984). Preferred stimulation levels in introverts and extraverts: Effects on arousal and performance. *Journal of Personality and Social Psychology, 46,* 1303–1312.

Goldwater, B.C., & Lewis, J. (1978). Effects of arousal on habituation of the electrodermal orienting response. *Psychophysiology, 15,* 221–225.

Gray, J.A. (1964). Strength of the nervous system and levels of arousal: A reinterpretation. In J. A. Gray (Ed.), *Pavlov's typology.* Oxford: Pergamon Press.

Greenfield, N.S., & Sternbach, R.A. (Eds.). (1972). *Handbook of psychophysiology.* New York: Holt, Rinehart, and Winston.

Grossman, S.P. (1968). The physiological basis of specific and nonspecific motivation processes. In W.J. Arnold (Ed.), *Nebraska symposium on motivation* (Vol. 16). Lincoln: University of Nebraska Press.

Hackman, J.R., & Oldham, G.R. (1975). Development of the Job Diagnostic Survey. *Journal of Applied Psychology, 60,* 159–170.

Hackman, J.R., & Oldham, G.R. (1980). *Work redesign.* Reading, MA: Addison-Wesley.

Hackman, J.R., Oldham, G.R., Janson, R., & Purdy, K. (1975, Summer). A new strategy for job enrichment. *California Management Review,* 57–71.

Haier, R.J., Robinson, D.L., Braden, W., & Williams, D. (1984). Evoked potential augmenting-reducing and personality differences. *Personality and Individual Differences, 5,* 293–301.

Hamilton, V., & Warburton, D. (1979). (Eds.). *Human stress and cognition.* London: Wiley.

Hamner, W.C., Ross, J., & Staw, B.M. (1978). Motivation in organizations: The need for a new direction. In D.W. Organ (Ed.), *The applied psychology of work behavior.* Dallas: Business Publications, Inc.

Hastrup, J.L. (1979). Effects of electrodermal lability and introversion on vigilance decrement. *Psychophysiology, 16,* 302–310.

Hebb, D.O. (1955). Drives and the C.N.S. (conceptual nervous system). *Psychological Review, 62,* 243–254.

Herzberg, F., Mausner, B., & Snyderman, B. (1959). *The motivation to work.* New York: Wiley.

Hill, A.B. (1975). Extraversion and variety seeking in a monotonous task. *British Journal of Psychology, 66,* 9–13.

Hockey, R. (1979). Stress and the cognitive components of skilled performance. In V. Hamilton & D. Warburton (Eds.), *Human stress and cognition.* London: Wiley.

Huber, V.L. (1985). Effects of task difficulty, goal setting, and strategy on performance of a heuristic task. *Journal of Applied Psychology, 70,* 492–504.

Hulin, C.L., & Blood, M.R. (1968). Job enlargement, individual differences, and worker responses. *Psychological Bulletin, 68,* 41–55.

Hull, C.L. (1943). *Principles of behavior.* New York: Appleton.

Humphreys, M.S., & Revelle, W. (1984). Personality, motivation, and performance: A theory of the relationship between individual differences and information processing. *Psychological Review, 91,* 153–184.

Ivancevich, J.M. (1976). The effects of goal setting on performance and satisfaction. *Journal of Applied Psychology, 61,* 605–612.

Ivancevich, J.M. (1977). Different goal setting treatments and their effects on performance and satisfaction. *Academy of Management Journal, 20,* 406–419.

Ivancevich, J.M., & McMahon, J.T. (1977a). Education as a moderator of goal setting effectiveness. *Journal of Vocational Behavior, 11,* 83–94.

Ivancevich, J.M., & McMahon, J.T. (1977b). A study of task-goal attributes, higher order need strength, and performance. *Academy of Management Journal, 20,* 552–563.

James, L.R., & Jones, A.P. (1980). Perceived job characteristics and job satisfaction: An examination of reciprocal causation. *Personnel Psychology, 33,* 97–136.

James, L., & Tetrick, L.E. (1986). Confirmatory analytic tests of three causal models relating job perceptions to job satisfaction. *Journal of Applied Psychology, 71,* 77–82.

Johansson, B.G., Aronsson, G., & Lindstrom, B.O. (1978). Social psychological and neuroendocrine reactions in highly mechanized work. *Ergonomics, 21,* 583–599.

Kahneman, D. (1973). *Attention and effort.* Englewood Cliffs, NJ: Prentice-Hall.

Kasl, S.V. (1978). Epidemiological contributions to the study of work stress. In C.L. Cooper & R. Payne (Eds.), *Stress at work.* New York: Wiley.

Katkin, E.S. (1975). Electrodermal lability. In I.G. Sarason & C.D. Spielberger (Eds.), *Stress and anxiety* (Vol. 2). Washington, D.C.: Hemisphere.

Katkin, E.S., Morell, M.A., Goldband, S., Bernstein, G.L., & Wise, J.A. (1982). Individual differences in heartbeat discrimination. *Psychophysiology, 19,* 160–166.

Kim, J.S. (1980). Relationship of personality to perceptual and behavioral responses in stimulating and nonstimulating environments. *Academy of Management Journal, 23,* 307–319.

Kim, J.S. (1984). Effect of behavior plus outcome goal setting and feedback on employee satisfaction and performance. *Academy of Management Journal, 27,* 139–149.

Kishida, K. (1973). Temporal change in subsidiary movement. *Journal of Human Ergology, 2,* 75–89.

Kleitman, N. (1949). Biological rhythms and cycles. *Physiology Review, 29,* 1–30.

Lacey, J.I. (1956). The evaluation of autonomic responses: Towards a general solution. *Annals of New York Academy of Sciences, 67,* 125–163.

Lacey, J.I. (1967). Somatic response patterning: Some revisions of activation theory. In M.H. Appley & R. Trumbull (Eds.), *Psychological stress.* New York: Appleton-Century-Crofts.

Lader, M.H. (1971). Responses to repetitive stimulation. In L. Levi (Ed.), *Society, stress, and disease* (Vol. 1). London: Oxford University Press.

Latham, G.P., & Yukl, G.A. (1975). Assigned versus participative goal setting with educated and uneducated woods workers. *Journal of Applied Psychology, 60,* 299–302.

Lazarus, R.S. (1966). *Psychological stress and the coping responses.* New York: McGraw-Hill.

Lazarus, R.S. (1968). Emotions and adaptation: Conceptual and empirical relations. In W.J. Arnold, *Nebraska symposium on motivation* (Vol. 16). Lincoln: University of Nebraska Press.

Levenson, R.W. (1983). Personality research and psychophysiology: General considerations. *Journal of Research in Personality, 17,* 1–21.

Levi, L. (1981). *Preventing work stress.* Reading, MA: Addison-Wesley.

Lindsley, D.B. (1951). Emotion. In S.S. Stevens (Ed.), *Handbook of experimental psychology.* New York: Wiley.

Lindsley, D.B. (1956). Psychophysiology and emotion. In M.R. Jones (Ed.), *Nebraska symposium on motivation* (Vol. 5). Lincoln: University of Nebraska Press.

Lindsley, D.B. (1961). Common factors in sensory deprivation, sensory distortion, and sensory overload. In P. Solomon, P.E. Kubansky, P.H. Leiderman, J.H. Mendelson, R. Trumball, & D. Wexler (Eds.), *Sensory deprivation.* Cambridge: Harvard University Press.

Locke, E.A., Frederick, E., Lee, C., & Bobko, P. (1984). Effects of self-efficacy, goals, and task strategies on task performance. *Journal of Applied Psychology, 69,* 241–250.

Locke, E.A., Shaw, K., Saari, L.M., & Latham, G.P. (1981). Goal-setting and performance: 1969–1980. *Psychological Bulletin, 90,* 125–152.

London, H., Schubert, D.S., & Washburn, D. (1972). Increases of autonomic arousal by boredom. *Journal of Abnormal Psychology, 80,* 28–36.

Lorente de No, R. (1939). Transmission of impulses through cranial nuclei. *Journal of Neurophysiology, 2,* 402–464.

Lukas, J.H., & Siegall, J. (1977). Cortical mechanisms that augment or reduce evoked potentials in cats. *Science, 196,* 73–75.

Mackworth, J.F. (1969). *Vigilance and habituation: A neuropsychological approach.* Middlesex: Penguin.

Maddi, S.R. (1961). Unexpectedness, affective tone, and behavior. In D.W. Fiske & S.R. Maddi (Eds.), *Functions of varied experience.* Homewood, IL: Dorsey Press.

Malmo, R.B. (1958). Measurement of drive: An unsolved problem in psychology. In M.R. Jones (Ed.), *Nebraska symposium on motivation* (Vol 7). Lincoln: University of Nebraska Press.

Malmo, R.B. (1959). Activation: A neurophysiological dimension. *Psychological Review*, *66*, 367–386.

Maslow, A.H. (1954). *Motivation and personality*. New York: Harper.

Matteson, M.I., & Ivancevich, J.M. (1979). Organizational stresses and heart disease: A research model. *Academy of Management Review*, *4*, 347–358.

McGrath, J.E. (1976). Stress in organizations. In M. Dunnette (Ed.), *Handbook of industrial and organizational psychology*. Chicago: Rand-McNally.

Murray, H.A. (1938). *Explorations in personality*. New York: Oxford University Press.

Newman, J.E., & Beehr, T.A. (1979). Personal and organizational strategies for handling job stress: A review of research and opinion. *Personnel Psychology*, *32*, 1–43.

Nisbett, R.E., & Wilson, T.D. (1977). Telling more than we know: Verbal reports on mental processes. *Psychological Review*, *84*, 231–259.

O'Hanlon, J.F. (1981). Boredom: Practical consequences and a theory. *Acta Psychologica*, *49*, 53–82.

Ohman, A. (1986). Face the beast and face the face: Animal and social fears as prototypes for evolutionary analyses of fear. *Psychophysiology*, *23*, 123–145.

Olds, J., & Milner, P. (1954). Positive reinforcement produced by electrical stimulation of septal area and other regions of rat brain. *Journal of Comparative and Physiological Psychology*, *47*, 419–427.

Pavlov, I.P. (1960). *Conditional reflexes: An investigation of the physiological activity of the cerebral cortex* G.V. Anwerp (Ed. and Trans). New York: Dover (First published 1927).

Pierce, J.L., & Dunham, R.B. (1976). Task design: A literature review. *Academy of Management Review*, *1*, 83–96.

Platt, J. (1964). Strong inference. *Science*, *146*, 347–353.

Quattrone, G.A. (1985). On the congruity between thoughts and action. *Psychological Bulletin*, *98*, 3–40.

Riesen, A.H. (1961). Stimulation as a requirement for growth and function in behavioral development. In D.W. Fiske & S.R. Maddi (Eds.), *Functions of varied experience*. Homewood, IL: Dorsey Press.

Roberts, K.H., & Glick, W. (1981). The job characteristics approach to task design: A critical review. *Journal of Applied Psychology*, *66*, 193–217.

Robinson, D.L. (1982). Properties of the diffuse thalamocortical system and human personality: A direct test of Pavlovian/Eysenckian theory. *Personality and Individual Differences*, *3*, 1–16.

Sabini, J., & Silver, M. (1981). Introspection and causal accounts. *Journal of Personality and Social Psychology*, *40*, 427–456.

Salancik, G.R., & Pfeffer, J. (1977). An examination of need satisfaction models of job attitudes. *Administration Science Quarterly*, *22*, 427–456.

Salvendy, G. (1980). *Effects of job pacing on job satisfaction, psychophysiological stress, and industrial productivity*. Paper presented at the annual conference of the American Institute of Industrial Engineers.

Salvendy, G., & Humphreys, A.P. (1979). Effects of personality, perceptual difficulty, and pacing of task on productivity, job satisfaction, and psychological stress. *Perceptual and Motor Skills*, *49*, 219–222.

Salvendy, G., & Pilitsis, J. (1971). Psychophysiological aspects of paced and unpaced performance as influenced by age. *Ergonomics*, *14*, 703–711.

Schwab, D.P., & Cummings, L.L. (1976). A theoretical analysis of the impact of task scope on employee performance. *Academy of Management Review*, *1*, 23–35.

Schuler, R.S. (1981). Definition and conceptualization of stress in organizations. *Organizational Behavior and Human Performance*, *25*, 184–215.

Scott, W.E. (1966). Activation theory and task design. *Organizational Behavior and Human Performance, 1*, 3–30.

Scott, W.E. (1969). The behavioral consequences of repetitive task design: Research and theory. In L.L. Cummings & W.E. Scott (Eds.), *Organizational behavior and human performance*. Homewood, IL: Irwin-Dorsey.

Scott, W.E., & Erskine, J.A. (1980). The effects of variations in task design and monetary reinforcers on task behavior. *Organizational Behavior and Human Performance, 25*, 311–335.

Selye, H. (1976). *The stress of life* (2nd Ed.). New York: McGraw-Hill.

Sersen, E.A., Clausen, J., & Lidsky, A. (1978). Autonomic specificity and stereotyping revisited. *Psychophysiology, 15*, 60–67.

Siddle, D.A.T., O'Gorman, J.G., & Wood, L. (1979). Effects of electrodermal lability and stimulus significance on electrodermal response amplitude to stimulus change. *Psychophysiology, 16*, 520–527.

Sklar, L.S., & Anisman, H. (1981). Stress and cancer. *Psychological Bulletin, 89*, 369–406.

Smith, B.D. (1983). Extraversion and electrodermal lability: Arousability and the inverted-U. *Personality and Individual Differences, 4*, 411–419.

Smith, B.D., Wilson, R.J., & Rypma, C.B. (1981). Overhabituation and dishabituation: Effects of extraversion and amount of training. *Journal of Research in Personality, 15*, 475–487.

Sostek, A.J. (1978). Effects of electrodermal lability and payoff instructions on vigilance performance. *Psychophysiology, 15*, 561–568.

Stagner, R. (1975). Boredom on the assembly line: Age and personality variables. *Industrial Gerontology, 2*, 23–44.

Steers, R.M., & Mowday, R.T. (1977). The motivational properties of tasks. *Academy of Management Review, 2*, 645–659.

Stelmack, R.M., & Pflouffe, L. (1983). Introversion-extraversion: The Bell-Magendie Law revisited. *Personality and Individual Differences, 4*, 421–427.

Stelmack, R.M., & Wilson, K.G. (1982). Extraversion and the effects of frequency and intensity on the auditory brainstem evoked response. *Personality and Individual Differences, 3*, 373–380.

Sterns, L., Alexander, R.A., Barrett, G.V., & Dambrot, F.H. (1983). The relationship of extraversion and neuroticism with job preferences and job satisfaction for clerical employees. *Journal of Occupational Psychology, 56*, 145–153.

Suominen, S., Basila, B., Salvendy, G., & McCabe, G.P. (1980). *Nonwork-related movement in machine-paced and in self-paced work*. Unpublished manuscript, Department of Industrial Engineering, Purdue University.

Taylor, F.W. (1911). *The principles of scientific management*. New York: Harper and Row.

Teichner, W.H. (1968). Interaction of behavioral and physiological stress reactions. *Psychological Review, 75*, 271–291.

Teplov, B.M. (1964). Problems in the study of general types of higher nervous activity in men and animals. In J.A. Gray (Ed.), *Pavlov's typology*. New York: Macmillan.

Thackray, R.D., Jones, K.N., & Touchstone, R.M. (1974). Personality and physiological correlates of performance decrements on a monotonous task requiring sustained effort. *British Journal of Psychology, 65*, 351–358.

Thompson, S.C. (1981). Will it hurt less if I can control it? A complex answer to a simple question. *Psychological Bulletin, 90*, 89–101.

Thompson, W.R., & Schaefer, T. (1961). Early environmental stimulation. In D.W. Fiske & S.R. Maddi (Eds.), *Functions of varied experience*. Homewood, IL: Dorsey Press.

Timio, M., & Gentili, S. (1976). Adrenosympathetic overactivity under conditions of work stress. *British Journal of Preventative and Social Medicine, 3*, 262–265.

Trist, E.L. (1978). On socio-technical systems. In W.A. Pasmore & J.J. Sherwood (Eds.), *Sociotechnical systems: A sourcebook.* La Jolla, CA: University Associates.

Weber, A., Fussler, C., O'Hanlon, J.F., Gierer, R., & Grandjean, E. (1980). Psychophysiological effects of repetitive tasks. *Ergonomics, 23,* 1033–1046.

Weil, J.L. (1974). *A neurophysiological model of emotional and intentional behavior.* Springfield, IL: Charles C Thomas.

Wells, J.A. (1982). Objective job conditions, social support, and perceived stress among blue collar workers. *Journal of Occupational Behaviour, 3,* 79–94.

Zubek, J.P. (1964). Behavioral and EEG changes after 14 days of perceptual deprivation. *Psychonomic Science, 1,* 57–58.

Zuckerman, M. (1979). *Sensation seeking: Beyond the optimal level of arousal.* Hillsdale, NJ: Erlbaum.

TOWARD AN INTEGRATED THEORY OF TASK DESIGN

Ricky W. Griffin

ABSTRACT

At present, the study of task design lacks a clear and demonstrable focus. The reasons for this condition relate to controversies and contradictions surrounding the dominant models and theories in the area. Yet, task design remains an important topic for scientific inquiry. In an effort to reestablish focus and direction, an integrated theory of task design is proposed. The theory is not viewed as an alternative for existing models, but instead as a natural extension of each. After a brief review of the literature, several emerging questions and issues about the current viewpoints are explicated and discussed. The integrated theory is then presented. First, its major concepts are identified and defined. Next, the boundaries of the theory are delineated. System state dynamics are summarized and the nomological network among three central concepts of the theory is discussed. Each broad category of related variables is then introduced and appropriate interrelationships noted. The major elements of the theory are summarized as propositional statements. An overview of implications for future theory and research concludes the presentation.

The study of individual tasks in organizational settings has long been of interest to organizational scientists (cf. Taylor, 1911; Walker & Guest, 1952; Herzberg, Mausner, & Snyderman, 1959; Hackman & Oldham, 1976, 1980). Frequently subsumed under the labels of *task design* or *job design,* theory and research in the area have attempted to describe strategies for changing or refining jobs so as to enhance such organizationally relevant criterion variables as performance, motivation, satisfaction, absenteeism, and so forth. Academic and practitioner journals continue to publish articles dealing with task/job design with regular frequency. One recent article (Evans, Kiggundu, & House, 1979) has even compared the study of jobs to the quest for the alchemist's stone.

Over the years, the area of task design has been characterized by shifts from one theoretical perspective to another. The primary shifts have been from job specialization (e.g., Taylor, 1911) to job enlargement (e.g., Walker & Guest, 1952) to job enrichment (e.g., Herzberg et al., 1959) to job characteristics theory (e.g., Hackman & Oldham, 1976) to the social information processing perspective (Salancik & Pfeffer, 1977, 1978). This latter viewpoint initially cast such apparently insightful questions on the earlier models that they have fallen from favor, but has itself not been widely accepted as a viable alternative (see Thomas & Griffin, 1983).

At present, then, the study of task design lacks a clear and demonstrable focus. From the most pessimistic vantage point, task design suffers from a theory, measurement, and operational vacuum (cf. Roberts & Glick, 1981). More optimistically, there is simply not a shared consensus as to what directions need to be taken. Of course, this state of affairs is not altogether bad, and may, in fact, be a logical and natural step in the progression toward greater understanding of task-design issues and processes. Most areas of study in organizational science, including motivation and leadership, have evolved from perspective to perspective and have occasionally fallen into temporary periods of stagnation (cf. Pinder, 1984; Yukl, 1981). Such periods, however, can provide an opportunity for reflection, assessment, and integration (Kuhn, 1970). In many ways, the study of task design has reached an intellectual plateau (optimistically) or has fallen into a state of stagnation (pessimistically). In any event, this paper will attempt to assess and integrate current and emerging issues in task design with the goal of focusing and facilitating future theory and research.

First, the importance of task design as a topic of study will be addressed. Historical perspectives and background will then be summarized. Next, emerging controversies and issues will be noted. Finally, an integrated model of task design will be discussed in detail. This model draws from existing and related theories to provide an integrated perspective. As a part of this presentation, key components of the model are defined and their boundaries delineated. Relationships and processes among components of the model are then described. Implications for research conclude the presentation of the integrated model.

THE IMPORTANCE OF TASK DESIGN

Task design is clearly an important topic for theory and research for a variety of reasons. Perhaps foremost among these is the fact that an individual's task represents one of his or her most basic and fundamental points of contact with the organization. People come into contact with the reward system, their leader, the performance appraisal system, and other facets of the organization on a regular basis, yet they no doubt spend much of their time doing the job for which they were hired. Hence, it follows that the nature of this job will greatly influence actions, interactions, reactions, perceptions, and attitudes of employees in and toward the organization.

A second reason for the importance of task design is its potential role in various change interventions. Given that such interventions can potentially enhance various criterion variables (such as motivation, satisfaction, and/or performance) and given the primacy of the task in the individual's work experience, it follows that the task is simultaneously a likely focal point for introducing many behavioral science interventions and an element that must be considered when introducing other changes. That is, some changes, like changes in technology, work flow, work schedules, robotics, and the adoption of autonomous work groups might begin with targeted modifications in jobs. Likewise, changes in other areas, such as the reward system, the performance appraisal system, and selection criteria may require supplemental changes in tasks as well. Of course, such interventions and changes involve a variety of complex and interrelated issues (Oldham & Hackman, 1980; Pierce, Dunham, & Cummings, 1984).

A third reason for studying task design relates to employee well-being. General concerns for quality of work life for employees have been repeatedly voiced over the years (cf. Walton, 1974). More specific concerns about such things as employee mental health (Kornhauser, 1965) and employee stress (Ivancevich & Matteson, 1978) have also arisen. Task design has often been identified as a key part of most quality of work life programs (Griffin, 1982) and has recently been suggested as a stress-management technique (Quick & Quick, 1984). To the extent that such considerations become more important in the future, it follows that the study of task design will remain central to the field.

Finally, the study of task design is important for reasons of scientific curiosity. Stated in basic terms, it would seem almost trivial to learn how people perceive and respond to their jobs. However, anything beyond more-than-rudimentary understanding of the processes involved has eluded social scientists for decades. What seems to be a simple and predictable phenomenon must, therefore, actually be a complex and unpredictable phenomenon. Although this understanding itself is of some interest (Davis, 1971), more sophisticated theory development and research are needed to better grasp the intricacies of task-design concepts and processes.

THEORETICAL BACKGROUND

Because of its centrality to the field of organizational behavior, numerous theories, models, and perspectives on task design have been developed. Given the existence of several exhaustive reviews (cf. Aldag & Brief, 1979; Griffin, 1982; Hackman & Oldham, 1980), this section will briefly summarize only the two most recent models: the task attributes model and the social information processing model.

The task attributes model (Hackman & Lawler, 1971) was in many ways the catalyst for the current interest in task design. Hackman and Lawler (1971) argue that tasks can be described in terms of certain attributes which, in turn, influence employee motivation. In order for a job to be motivating, they suggest that it must (1) allow workers to feel personally responsible for a meaningful portion of the work, (2) provide outcomes that are intrinsically meaningful, and (3) provide feedback about what is accomplished. Specific attributes of the job that were presumed to affect these characteristics include autonomy, identity, variety, and feedback. As the framework was more fully refined into the job characteristics theory (Hackman & Oldham, 1976, 1980), an additional attribute, significance, was added and a diagnostic survey instrument, the Job Diagnostic Survey (Hackman & Oldham, 1975), was developed. The model suggests that perceptions of these attributes will be positively correlated with motivation, satisfaction, and performance, and that individual differences will moderate the relationships.

The job characteristics theory was one of the most widely studied and debated models in the entire field during the late 1970s. Perhaps the reasons behind its widespread popularity are that it provided an academically sound model (Hackman & Oldham, 1976), a packaged and easily used diagnostic instrument (Hackman & Oldham, 1975), a set of practitioner-oriented implementation guidelines (Hackman, Oldham, Janson, & Purdy, 1975), and an initial body of empirical support (cf. Hackman & Oldham, 1976; Hackman, Pearce, & Wolfe, 1978; Evans et al., 1979; Oldham, Hackman, & Pearce, 1976), all within a relatively narrow span of time. Interpretations of the empirical research pertaining to the theory have ranged from inferring positive (Aldag & Brief, 1979) to mixed (Griffin, 1982) to little (Roberts & Glick, 1981) support for its validity.

In the most critical review to date, Roberts and Glick (1981) highlight numerous deficiencies in the literature. They note several problems: (1) the statement of the theory is occasionally ambiguous and unclear, (2) empirical research has often failed to actually test predictions of the theory, (3) multimethod measures have seldom been used, and (4) within-person, person-situation, and situational relationships have often been confused. In light of these points, recent studies developed from a task attributes perspective have attempted to broaden, extend, or integrate the theory's basic concepts and processes (cf. Algera, 1983; Terborg & Davis, 1982; Taber, Beehr, & Walsh, 1985; Campion & Thayer, 1985; Kemp & Cook, 1983; Kiggundu, 1983; Griffeth, 1985; Pierce, 1984; Clegg, 1984). Algera (1983) and Taber et al. (1985), for example, focus on the relationship between objective and perceived job characteristics. Kemp and Cook (1983) examine the role of job longevity in task design. Campion and Thayer (1985) attempt to relate the job characteristics theory to work physiology, biomechanics, perceptual/motor concepts from experimental psychology, and mechanistic job-design techniques from industrial engineering. Finally, Pierce (1984) and Clegg (1984) focus on the relationships between job characteristics and technology. Still, a unified integration has failed to emerge.

A different set of criticisms about need satisfaction models in general and the task attributes framework in particular have been raised by Salancik and Pfeffer (1977, 1978). With respect to need satisfaction models, they argue that such models are formulated as to be virtually impossible to refute, have been assessed by research characterized by priming and consistency artifacts, and fail to capture the full spectrum of complexities embodied in employee attitudes and behaviors (Salancik & Pfeffer, 1977). Regarding the task attributes model, they note its basis in a need-satisfaction-model heritage and, therefore, question its efficacy (Salancik & Pfeffer, 1978).

As an alternative, Salancik and Pfeffer propose a social information processing (SIP) approach to job attitudes and task design. Pfeffer (1981) provides the following summary of the SIP model:

> First, the individual's social environment may provide cues as to which dimensions might be used to characterize the work environment. . . . Second, the social environment may provide information concerning how the individual should weight the

various dimensions—whether autonomy is more or less important than variety of skill, whether pay is more or less important than social usefulness or worth. Third, the social context provides cues concerning how others have come to evaluate the work environment on each of the selected dimensions. . . . And fourth, it is possible that the social context provides direct evaluation of the work setting along positive or negative dimensions, leaving it to the individual to construct a rationale to make sense of the generally shared affective reactions. (p. 10).

Thus, Salancik and Pfeffer believe that task perceptions and attitudes are largely socially constructed realities derived from social information available to the individual in the workplace.

Another important source of information used in reality construction processes, according to Salancik and Pfeffer (1978), is the individual's own present and past behaviors. Drawing from the work of Bem (1972) and Weick (1977), this idea suggests that causal attributions of the reasons for past behaviors play a role in how the individual interprets his or her present circumstances. Further, the attributional process is presumed to be affected by the person's commitment to the behavior, information about the past behaviors that is salient at the time, and social norms and expectations about what might be considered rational or legitimate explanations for past behaviors.

The logic of Salancik and Pfeffer, combined with critical assessments from other fronts (cf. Roberts & Glick, 1981), caused the task attributes framework in general and the job characteristics theory in particular to become less accepted. Simultaneously, several studies were published, most of them conducted in the laboratory, that provided support for at least some facets of the SIP model (cf. O'Reilly & Caldwell, 1979; Weiss & Shaw, 1979). These studies found support for the idea that social information does, in fact, influence task perceptions and attitudes. Subsequent research in field settings, including both cross-sectional studies (cf. Oldham & Miller, 1979; O'Reilly, Parlette, & Bloom, 1980) and one field experiment (Griffin, 1983), also provided at least partial support for a SIP perspective.

This body of research itself, however, as well as the SIP model, was not without its own problems. In terms of the model, Salancik and Pfeffer (1978) do not appropriately define all of their terms and processes and do not clearly describe all of the interrelationships among them. For example, much of the research they cite in developing the model relates fairly well to attitudes, but not to perceptions. Similarly, some of their criticisms of the job characteristics theory appear to be overstated.

The corresponding research is also characterized by problems and weaknesses. Thomas and Griffin (1983) recently reviewed 10 studies directly or indirectly designed to test various SIP effects. They conclude that social information does appear to play a role in shaping task perceptions and attitudes, but that several sets of questions remain to be answered. These questions center on the roles and relative importance of objective and social information in the formation of task perceptions and reactions and the processes used by individuals in perceiving, evaluating, and reacting to social cues in the work place. Thomas and Griffin (1983, p. 679) also note that "none of the 10 studies serves even minimally to refute the task attributes view. Further, none of the 10 studies provides specific and exact support for the SIP framework. In fact, [most of the research] offers more support for an overlapping viewpoint than for either of the other models."

Using this argument as a point of departure, Griffin, Bateman, Wayne, and Head (1984) recently conducted a complex laboratory study designed to test both main and interactive effects of objective task attributes and social cues. Subjects worked at either an enriched or unenriched task for one hour while simultaneously being exposed to either positive or negative social cues. Measures of task perceptions and attitudes were then taken. Next, the subjects were exposed to either a change or no change in task conditions and/or social cues. After working for another hour, subjects again provided measures of task perceptions and satisfaction. Thus, it was possible to assess the effects of consistent and inconsistent task conditions and social cues as well as the effects of changes in both. Results provided reasonable support for a pure task-attributes approach, modest support for a pure SIP approach, and strong support for a view suggesting main effects for both task attributes and social information.

Thus, as noted earlier, there is at present considerable ambiguity in the study of task design. Some researchers (cf. Kiggundu, 1983) continue to work from a task attributes framework, while others (cf. Dean & Brass, in press) maintain the SIP perspective. The SIP model, while raising interesting concerns about the task attributes approach, is itself characterized by ambiguity and inconclusive research findings. In the following section, several critical questions and issues about the current state of affairs will be delineated.

EMERGING QUESTIONS AND ISSUES

In light of the present ambiguities in the area, it is instructive to focus specific attention on emerging questions and issues that characterize current theory and research in task design. The most basic questions and issues are scope, objectivity, focus, construct independence, patterns of causality, measurement, the role of time, and construct formation process. The following sections will highlight each of these questions and issues and relate them to the two dominant models.

Scope

There is considerable variation in contemporary perspectives as to the level of scope presumed to be inherent in tasks. The task attributes approach takes a fairly narrow view of task scope, usually operationalized as the level of certain dimensions or attributes that characterize a job, such as task variety, autonomy, feedback, identity, and significance. Although there has been considerable debate as to how these various dimensions might be most appropriately combined (Brief, Wallace, & Aldag, 1976; Dunham, 1976), the focus has remained at a relatively narrow level in that these attributes are implicitly assumed to be collectively exhaustive.

In contrast, Salancik and Pfeffer (1978) explicitly take a broader view of task scope. For example, they refer to both the style of supervision and working conditions as examples of task characteristics (p. 227). Thus, the SIP view actually considers a complex array of factors in the workplace as elements of the task, whereas the task attributes model is more narrowly focused on the specific task being performed.

This disparity in conceptualization of scope becomes quite important when the two models are compared. Because the task is the central construct of each, it follows that their relative conceptualizations of tasks must be somewhat comparable if, indeed, they are addressing the same phenomenon. Because this does not appear to be the case, it follows that the two models evidently are focusing on different concepts. The task attributes model appears to be more appropriately focused on the task itself, as well as perceptions of and attitudes toward it. The SIP model, on the other hand, takes a broader view and is perhaps best considered to be a model of task-related attitudes, rather than a model of task perceptions. To the extent that this is an accurate view, the need to critically pit one model against the other becomes less imperative.

Objectivity

A second issue that characterizes contemporary task-design theory is whether task attributes and dimensions are objective or perceptual phenomenon. In the original monograph, Hackman and Lawler (1971, p. 264) clearly presume that perceptual elements of the task are central:

> It should be emphasized that, for all the job characteristics . . . it is not their objective state which affects employee attitudes and behavior, but rather how they are experienced by the employees. Regardless of the amount of feedback . . . a worker really has in his work, it is how much *he perceives that he has* [emphasis in the original] which will affect his reactions to the job. Objective job characteristics are important because they do affect the perceptions and experiences of employees. But there are often *substantial differences between objective job characteristics and how they are*

perceived by employees [emphasis added], and it is dangerous to assume that simply because the objective characteristics of a job have been measured (or changed) that the way that job is experienced by employees has been dealt with as well.

Over the years, however, the implicit assumptions about task objectivity made by task attributes theorists have become blurred. Hackman and Oldham (1976, p. 254) refer to "objective characteristics of jobs" and Hackman and Oldham (1980, p. 77) note that the job characteristics represent "reasonably objective, measurable, changeable properties of the work itself." Roberts and Glick (1981) repeatedly refer to objective jobs and job characteristics, and at one point (p. 196) note that "with the exception of some minor variation, task perceptions are assumed to be equivalent to objectively defined tasks." Clearly, the original position taken by Hackman and Lawler has undergone substantial modification as a result of its various translations.

In similar fashion, the SIP model's view of task objectivity has also not been uniformly interpreted. Salancik and Pfeffer (1978) freely acknowledge that some objective elements of the workplace are readily perceived (p. 228) and that jobs can be objectively changed (pp. 247–248). They also believe, however, that standard measures of task perceptions serve to artificially prime thinking, and thus responses, along rigid and not necessarily generalizable dimensions. However, virtually all of the studies identified by Thomas and Griffin (1983) purporting to test the SIP model used a variant of a standard task-attributes measure of job perceptions. Such a practice, of course, allows one to question some of the theoretical underpinnings of the task attributes model, or at least its more contemporary versions, but does not really provide a test of the SIP perspective as an alternative. In fact, it could be argued that no study to date has completely operationalized the full SIP model, at least in terms of its conceptual approach to the perceptions of tasks.

Research directed at testing the relationships between objective and perceived task attributes has also provided mixed results (Kiggundu, 1980; Taber, Beehr, & Walsh, 1985; Pokorney, Gilmore, & Beehr, 1980). These and similar studies generally suggest partial but not total overlap between perceptual and objective measures. Campion and Thayer (1985) report a promising effort at developing an interdisciplinary measure of job design that presumably taps both perceptual and objective facets of jobs. In summary, then, perhaps the task attributes model and the SIP model are not as divergent as it might initially appear, at least in terms of their views on the objectivity of tasks. Both viewpoints acknowledge that objective dimensions of the task affect perceptions, but that there is also some other set of factors that affects perceptions as well. On the other hand, they are sufficiently different as to again raise the possibility that they are actually addressing such different sets of questions as to make comparisons misleading. This stems from the emerging pattern of some similarity but greater disparity between the two models along critical dimensions of comparison.

Focus

The task attributes and SIP models also vary somewhat in their focus. As noted earlier, the original task attributes view assumes that people form perceptions of their tasks and then, in turn, develop attitudinal and behavioral responses to those perceptions. Although much attention is directed at conceptualizing and measuring task perceptions, the true focus of the model is on how those perceptions are translated into attitudes and behaviors. Operationally, for example, one of the goals of the job characteristics theory is to instruct managers in how to change task perceptions in order to enhance satisfaction, motivation, and performance (Hackman & Oldham, 1980).

The SIP model, in slight contrast, has a different focus: more attention is directed at how social and individual factors combine to affect perceptions and attitudes. Further, as discussed in the next section, perceptions and attitudes are implicitly presumed to be co-determined by these two sets of factors, as opposed to being directly linked to one another.

Hence, it can be concluded that the focus of the task attributes models is how objective and other unexplored factors affect task perceptions, and how those perceptions subsequently affect attitudes and behaviors. The focus of the SIP view is how social and individual factors affect task perceptions and attitudes. Although this difference in focus is perhaps subtle, it is also quite clear and warrants additional theoretical clarification.

Unfortunately, such clarification is difficult to explicate from the existing models. The task attributes model is a tight, narrow, and fully bounded model, whereas the SIP model is loose, broad, and ambiguous in many areas. This ambiguity at least partially explains the different interpretations and operationalizations associated with the SIP model and the confusion in the literature as to whether it is a model of task perceptions or task attitudes. Whether theorists agree or disagree with the job characteristics theory, they at least understand and accept its boundaries. With the SIP model, there is no such understanding or acceptance. The integrated model developed later in this chapter attempts to overcome these problems.

Construct Independence

The related issue noted previously is the extent to which the key constructs in the two dominant models are independent. The task attributes model clearly assumes that task perceptions, attitudes, and behaviors are orthogonal constructs. In similar fashion, the critical psychological states detailed most fully by Hackman and Oldham (1976, 1980) and the individual-difference variable-growth need strength are likewise assumed to be independent constructs. Although the various constructs in the model are assumed to be causally related, the underlying assumption of the model is that each individual construct can be measured independently and that each represents a unique and bounded entity.

In contrast, the SIP model makes no such assumption of construct independence. In fact, there are several instances where the various elements of the model are presumed to overlap. Salancik and Pfeffer (1978) do not draw sharp distinctions between task perceptions and task attitudes. In many instances they use the terms virtually interchangeably. They even go so far as to assert, based on the work of Calder and Ross (1973), that because attitude and need statements are expressions, they are also behaviors. Although perceptions, attitudes, and behaviors are generally discussed by Salancik and Pfeffer as separate entities, they are just as often discussed as though they were the same thing. Of course, this imprecision makes a normal scientific test of the SIP model impossible. Because the constructs are not carefully defined, their boundaries are not identified, and their interrelationships are not clearly specified, it would be extremely difficult to operationalize causal relationships as suggested by the complete model.

Research into this issue has produced ambiguous results. One study (Ferratt, Dunham, & Pierce, 1981) found that job satisfaction as measured by two common scales could not be adequately discriminated from task perceptions as also measured by two common scales, but that satisfaction as measured by two other scales did adequately discriminate between task attitudes and task perceptions. Unfortunately, it is unknown whether this pattern is best explained by a lack of construct independence or simply a deficiency in measures.

Patterns of Causality

Still another related issue that can be extracted from contemporary thinking is the presumed pattern of causality among variables. The general interpretation of the task attributes model is that task perceptions cause critical psychological states which, in turn, cause attitudes and behaviors (cf. Orpen, 1979; Kiggundu, 1980). In reality, Hackman and Oldham make no such claims. They state, for example:

> It should be emphasized that the objective "motivating potential" of a job does not *cause* [emphasis in the original] employees who work on that job to be internally motivated, to perform well, or to experience job satisfaction. Instead, a job that is

high in motivating potential merely creates conditions such that if the jobholder performs well he or she is likely to experience a reinforcing state of affairs as a consequence. Job characteristics, then, serve only to set the stage for internal motivation.
The *behavior* [emphasis in the original] of people who work on a job determines the
action that unfolds on the stage. (1980, p. 82)

The original statement of the SIP model is equally vague in terms of
its stated patterns of causality among variables. Although the model is
presented in terms of conventional "boxes and arrows," many of the arrows go in both directions in a complex and ambiguous pattern. For example, social information is assumed to cause job characteristics and at-
titudes-needs, although the linkages are mediated by social reality
construction processes. Job characteristics are also assumed to cause at-
titudes-needs, mediated by perceptual-judgment processes. Similarly, at-
titudes-needs and behaviors are assumed to be reciprocally related, with
each arrow mediated by a different set of processes. Hence, patterns of
causality are presumed to exist in the model, although they are only
vaguely defined (in defense of Salancik and Pfeffer, they note early on
that their model is incompletely formulated).

Other SIP theorists have taken steps to be more explicit in their consideration of causality. For example, on the basis of a laboratory study
and a field survey, Caldwell and O'Reilly (1982) argue that different levels
of satisfaction cause variations in task perceptions. On balance, though,
patterns of causality among key variables are not clearly related in a causal
sense at either a theoretic or empirical level.

Measurement

The issue of measurement is somewhat of a paradox when considered
in the task-design area. The existence of measures such as the Job Diagnostic Survey (JDS) (Hackman & Oldham, 1975), as noted earlier, can
be argued to be a major reason for the continued enthusiasm for task-
design research. These scales have been subjected to several critical assessments (cf. Roberts & Glick, 1981; Aldag, Barr, & Brief, 1981). Moreover, as also noted earlier, there are considerable differences in the presumed relationship, if any, between objective facets of the job and task
perceptions as assessed by these instruments. Nevertheless, job characteristics scales like the JDS continue to be used perhaps more frequently
than any other scale in the field, with the exception of the common satisfaction measures.

In contrast, there have been no published attempts to develop or validate
scales for measuring the central constructs in the SIP model. In all likelihood, this is attributable to the vagueness with which the central con-

structs of the model are defined, the breadth of those constructs, and the fact that their meaning is not consistent from one use to another. Research in the SIP area has generally involved manipulating objective task characteristics, social cues from others and/or other kinds of information, and then observing the effects of the different manipulations on perceived task attributes and/or satisfaction measures.

Thus, inferences regarding measurement issues are problematic and are subject to the exact nature of the question being asked. Perhaps the answer is again one of convenience. Measuring the array of constructs in the full SIP model would be difficult, if not impossible. Still, it is surprising that no attempts have been made to even measure the central parts of the model, or to otherwise empirically assess such areas as social-reality construction processes, external priming, and commitment.

The Role of Time

A crucial issue noticeably absent in the two dominant models is the role of time. In the job characteristics model, for example, several interesting time-related questions might be asked: how long does it take for task perceptions to develop, how long does it take for task changes to affect attitudes and motivation, and if no objective task changes are introduced, will task perceptions and attitudes also remain constant? A few isolated studies have considered time. For example, Griffin (1981) found that task perceptions were relatively stable across a 3-month period, but that job satisfaction was less stable. Katz (1978) found that relationships between job satisfaction and task perceptions vary as a function of job longevity. In particular, he found different patterns of correlation between task attributes and job satisfaction for groups differentiated according to time on the job. For example, only task significance was positively correlated with satisfaction for new employees, whereas the correlation between autonomy and satisfaction increased, then decreased, as longevity increased. On balance, however, the role of time has been neglected in the task attributes literature.

Similarly, time is not explicitly considered in the SIP model. Does social information bring about stable perceptions and attitudes, or are they unstable and subject to variation? Is social information itself stable over time? Although these and similar derivative questions are not dealt with in the model itself, research is beginning to address them. For example, Vance and Biddle (in press) found that increased experience, a logical element of time, decreased the effects of social cues on attitudes and behavioral intentions. Still, as with the task attributes model, much more work is needed to more completely integrate the impact of time.

Construct Formation Processes

A final issue that can be derived from current task-design literature is the attention paid to the formation of the key constructs in each model. The job characteristics model acknowledges that a variety of processes are inherent in the formation of task perceptions and attitudes. Similarly, the SIP model explicitly includes five processes and implicitly includes as many as four others. The five explicit processes are social reality construction, enactment, attribution, perception/judgment, and evaluation/choice. Implicit processes include rationalization/legitimation and, perhaps, social influence, priming, and commitment (the qualifier is necessary because at various places they are described as processes but in other places they are treated as attributes or attitudes).

Neither model, however, adequately addresses how these processes operate. For example, neither theory adequately characterizes its associated processes as being cognitive, affective, or emotional. In reality, of course, it is likely that cognitions, affect, and emotion all play a role. People are likely to perceive and learn about objective elements of their jobs (cognitions), have that learning affect and be affected by their attitudes (affect), as well as also be influenced by temporal mood and state of mind (emotion). More care should have been taken by the original theorists in describing the mechanics involved in each process as one construct influences or is influenced by another. Fortunately, useful insights into these processes are being developed in other areas. For example, Berman, Read, and Kenny (1983) found that initial expectations may influence the extent to which social information is perceived, processed, and translated into attitudes. In another area, Lord (1985) explicates in great detail how social information may be processed in the context of leadership. Although much clearly remains to be done, these efforts represent potentially useful first steps that may be of considerable value if translated into a task-design framework.

Summary

This section has identified and discussed several emerging issues and themes that can be used to characterize the existing theory and research pertaining to the job characteristics theory and the SIP model. Each of these models has been the subject of considerable research, analysis, and speculation. If nothing else, the preceding discussion has perhaps shown that the two models are more alike than different along some dimensions, and more different than alike in others. They clearly differ in their views and conceptualizations of task scope, task objectivity, focus, and construct independence. They both have implicit patterns of causality and common (even if not appropriate) methods of measurement, and each ignores the role of time and fails to adequately consider construct formation processes. Each has something to offer, but perhaps together they can offer even more. The next section outlines an integrated theory of task design that draws from both of the current dominant views. Hopefully, the aspects of each that are retained are their respective strengths, and the aspects that are modified or omitted their weaknesses.

AN INTEGRATED THEORY OF TASK DESIGN

As detailed in the previous sections, the area of task design has been the topic of considerable speculation and research for decades. There is much that scholars in the area have learned, yet at the present time many questions remain unanswered. This section will describe an integrated theory of task design presented in an effort to refocus theory and research in the area. The primary goal in presenting such a theory is to attempt to bring together the best of existing models and theories, while simultaneously addressing many of their deficiencies. The theory draws from the major emerging questions and issues cited earlier. Moreover, it follows the general guidelines for social science theory presented by Dubin (1978).

In the first section that follows, the major concepts and variables of the theory are identified and defined. The next section outlines the boundaries of the theory, focusing specifically on those matters about which the theory does and does not make predictions. System state dynamics are then explored. Next, the nomological network among three central concepts of the theory is described. Subsequent sections discuss each broad set of related variables and concepts—antecedent factors, internal/stable states, direct and indirect mediating factors, external/expressed states, and stimuli for assessment. The basic foundational elements of the theory are presented in the form of propositions that specify the presumed laws of interaction.

Key Concepts and Variables

This section will identify and define two sets of key concepts and variables that are central to the integrated theory. The first set consists of the variables of task, role, and job. The second set is comprised of the concepts of perception, attitude, and behavior.

Task, role, and job are considered to be dimensions or characteristics of the organization within which the individual functions. This is not to suggest that they are presumed to be purely objective (and thus measureable) phenomena, just that they exist independently of the person who occupies them. A *task* is defined as the set of prescribed activities a person normally performs during a typical work period. The task of a sales representative, for example, may consist of driving from customer to customer, describing the firm's products to relevant parties, and writing up orders for transmission back to headquarters. The task of an assembly line worker, similarly, could involve standing by a moving conveyor belt and attaching three modular components to in-process subassemblies as they pass down the line.

In contrast to a task, a role is somewhat broader in scope. Clegg (1984) has recently delineated the differences between task and role. He defines a *role* as the decision-making rights of the person performing the task. Basically, work roles are seen as being a function of local control, whereas tasks are more technologically derived. If tasks are rigidly controlled and structured via close supervision, routinization, and prescribed performance procedures, the individual's role has little or no latitude for individual self-regulation. Clegg (1984) defines this as a simple work role. The worker is simply an extension of the technology. In contrast, if the worker has some degree of control and discretion over decisions and procedures pertinent to his or her task, the work role is seen as being more complex.

Finally, the individual's *job* is defined here as the array of elements and dimensions of the organization with which the individual comes into contact. Thus, the job includes both the task and the role. In addition, however, it also includes the nature of the supervision received, the level of compensation received, the organization's assessment of the individual's contributions (i.e., performance appraisals, etc.), working conditions, required and optional social interactions with co-workers, and so forth. Task, role, and job, then, fall along a continuum of scope, or breadth. Tasks are the narrowest of the three concepts in scope and breadth, jobs are the broadest, and roles are typified by an intermediate level of scope and breadth. Of course, task, role, and job are not independent constructs. Indeed, as will be seen in a later section, there is a complex network of interdependencies among the three.

It is also necessary to define and delineate the related concepts of perceptions, attitudes, and behaviors. In general, as used in the integrated theory, they follow their traditional and generally accepted meanings. It is necessary to define them, however, because of the ambiguities associated with the issues of focus, construct independence, and patterns of causality described earlier. *Perception* refers simply to the processes by which people become aware of, interpret, and assimilate information obtained by their senses. Thus, perception is nonevaluative. It does, however, play a key role in the other two related variables, attitudes and behaviors.

The concept of *attitude* is viewed from a somewhat more complex perspective by scholars in the area. Calder and Schurr (1981), for example, cite three alternative models of attitudes. The dispositional view assumes a stable positive or negative disposition learned through experience. The situational view is basically Salancik and Pfeffer's (1978) SIP model. As summarized earlier, this model argues that attitudes (as well as perceptions) are socially constructed. Finally, the third model, which Calder and Schurr (1981) call the information processing view, incorporates the concepts of memory and cognitive schema. They hold that its primary advantage, relative to the other models, is that it provides a theoretical mechanism for linking organizational variables to the individual-level concept. The integrated model of task design will take a slightly modified version of the Calder and Schurr (1981) model as the most accurate representation of individual attitudes. That is, the model conceptualizes an attitude as a generalized feeling people have toward an object or referent, in this case their tasks, roles, and jobs. The determination of such attitudes is a result of ongoing information processing in the mind of the individual.

Finally, behaviors will be taken to mean the complete spectrum of organizationally relevant behaviors from which employees may choose. Prominent among these are performance, absenteeism, and turnover. By spectrum, the theory assumes that individuals can choose, within boundaries imposed by technology, organizational policies, and so forth, a range of performance levels, a range of attendance levels, and whether to leave or to stay. No attempt is made with the integrated theory to reconcile the long-standing controversies surrounding attitude–behavior relationships— both attitudes and behaviors (as well as perceptions) are seen as independent elements.

Boundaries of the Theory

Besides those noted earlier, another distinction that can be drawn between the job characteristics theory and the social information-processing model is that they vary dramatically in their breadth. The job characteristics theory is relatively narrow, focusing specifically on how perceptions of five concepts impact certain outcomes, with the relationships moderated by a limited set of other variables. In contrast, the boundaries of the SIP model are quite broad and ambiguous (and, arguably, more a theory of task attitudes than task perceptions). Numerous processes and concepts are included, and others implied, that span different levels of analysis and orientation. To avoid some of the uncertainties that have come to characterize these two views, the following paragraphs will delineate the boundaries of the integrated theory, couched in terms of the theory's purposes.

The first purpose of the theory is to predict the determinants of perceived task dynamics. *Perceived task dynamics* refer to the individual's perceptions of the relevant attributes, dimensions, and processes that characterize her or his task. Consistent with the job characteristics theory, such attributes, dimensions, and processes might include variety, autonomy, and feedback. However, they might also include routineness, predictability, social interaction, and/or other dimensions. Consistent with the SIP model, the exact set of relevant attributes, dimensions, and processes is presumed to vary from setting to setting. Four sets of variables are presumed to be the primary determinants of such perceptions. The second purpose of the theory is to specify interrelationships among perceived task, role, and job dynamics. Next, the theory identifies how these perceptions affect four sets of internal/stable states. Several other factors are identified that are presumed to mediate these relationships. Finally, attention is directed at how these internal/stable states are translated into external/expressed states.

The theory is broader than the job characteristics theory, in that it includes more than a precise conceptualization of task attributes or dimensions. It does, however, retain the assumption that relevant attributes, dimensions, and processes are adequate descriptors of tasks. It also includes a broader array of variables and concepts. At the same time, however, it is narrower and more specific than the SIP model. The elements of the theory are clearly identified and the nature of their interrelationships specified.

System State Dynamics

The integrated theory presumes that task, role, job, perceptions, attitudes, and behaviors are simultaneously interrelated and dynamic. Each affects the other, each changes over time, and the relationship between each also changes over time. Thus, the theory is basically a process model of task design. Such a perspective has both strengths and weaknesses.

The primary strength of a process approach is that it presents a more realistic view of the complexities and intricacies of behavioral relationships in organizational settings. In many ways, the job characteristics theory is a very simple model—A, B, and C are related in a linear fashion. This very simplicity, however, is also its greatest weakness. When mapped onto organizational reality, it invariably fails to capture the complete picture. By taking a more realistic process view, however, the integrated theory provides an avenue for a broader explanation of workplace phenomena.

On the other hand, the greatest weakness of a process view is that it does not easily lend itself to empirical investigation. If A leads to B, B to C, but C leads back to A, the point at which the researcher intervenes into the situation will affect the nature of the observed relationships. Nonetheless, this approach is seen as being preferable in that it allows a more complete representation of the complex network of variables that no doubt operate in work settings.

Task/Job/Role Dynamics Network

A critical element of the model is the network comprised of task, job, and role dynamics. As mentioned earlier, the three constructs are presumed to be overlapping but unique phenomena. Because the model is primarily concerned with task-design considerations, perceived task dynamics are of central importance. Perceived job and role dynamics are of secondary importance in the model; their importance is seen as being a function of the extent to which they overlap or otherwise interact with perceived task dynamics in a given situation.

The view taken by the model is that people do not form perceptions of and reactions to the workplace in a compartmentalized fashion. Although an individual might perceive his or her pay (a part of the job), role complexity (a part of the role), and task demands (perhaps a part of the task) independently and form attitudes about each, both perceptions and attitudes are likely to be a primary function of the salient referent object but also a secondary function of other referent objects. For example, when asked about his job, a worker might offer that he likes his job because his salary is good, his boss leaves him alone, and the demands are not too great. This response, then, blurs the perception of the job with perceptions of the role and task as well. Similarly, the expressed attitude toward the job also makes reference to elements of not only the job but also the role and task. Thus,

P1: Task perceptions affect and are affected by role and job perceptions.

This proposition states that the three sets of perceptions are interrelated. By the definitions presented earlier, however, they are also unique constructs. In operational terms, then, the three sets of perceptions will have some degree of shared variance but each will also have some degree of unique variance. They will be correlated but each will also be a valid independent construct. This notion of overlapping independence is shown in Figure 1 as two overlapping circles. (Because the theory has as its focus the task, job and role dynamics are superimposed as one circle for the sake of parsimony. A more complete representation would consist of three overlapping circles.)

Antecedent   Task/Job/Role
Factors   Network

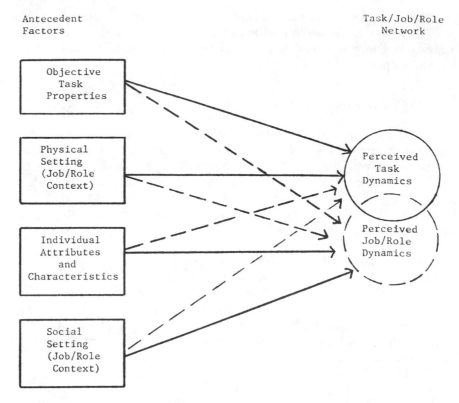

Figure 1. The Task/Job/Role Dynamics Network

Antecedent Factors

The theory presumes that there are four sets of antecedent factors that largely determine task, role, and job perceptions. As also shown in Figure 1, these factors are objective task properties, the physical setting (couched in terms of the job and role context), individual attributes and characteristics, and the social setting (also couched in terms of the job and role context).

Objective task properties. Objective task properties are those elements of the task that exist independently of any perceptual variation on the part of job incumbents. For the most part, objective task properties are a function of technology and organization structure. Several theoretical (cf. Slocum & Sims, 1980) and empirical (cf. Pierce, 1984; Rousseau, 1977) papers have linked technology with task perceptions. Similarly, structural characteristics of organizations have also been related to task design from both theoretical (cf. Griffin, 1982) and empirical (Pierce & Dunham, 1978; Moorhead, 1981; Vecchio & Keon, 1981; Zierden, 1980) perspectives. Moreover, objective task properties have been empirically linked to task perceptions both cross-sectionally (Terborg & Davis, 1982; Algera, 1983; Kiggundu, 1980) and experimentally (Orpen, 1979; Bhagat & Chassie, 1980). Therefore,

> **P2:** Objective task properties are a primary determinant of task perceptions.

This relationship is shown in Figure 1 as a solid line between objective task perceptions and perceived task dynamics. Also shown in the figure is a secondary linkage between objective task properties and perceived job and role dynamics. That is, objective task properties will have a lesser impact on perceptions of the job and the role.

Physical setting. The physical setting is the objective surroundings in which the task is performed. The role of physical setting has been, with few exceptions (cf. Steele, 1973; Davis, 1984), virtually ignored in organizational science. Yet, the physical setting of the task should logically affect how people perceive that task. In some ways, the task and its setting must be accomodated simultaneously. For example, physically demanding job settings, such as oil, coal, and diamond extraction, all require that tasks be specified in as precise a fashion as possible. Similarly, many tasks, such as that of a teacher, secretary, or machinist, require a certain setting.

In other ways, however, tasks and physical settings may be less precisely interrelated. A consultant, for example, might work out of a university office, a professional office, or off of the kitchen table at home. And, of course, the quality of the physical setting can vary dramatically from one task to another—some machinists labor in sweat-shop, dirty surroundings whereas others perform the same tasks in air conditioned, clean, modern plants. Clearly, then, the nature of the physical setting should have an impact on how task incumbents perceive those tasks. Thus,

> **P3:** The physical setting is a primary determinant of task perceptions.

This relationship is also shown in Figure 1 as a solid line to indicate the presumed primacy of the relationship. Also, as with objective task properties, the physical setting of the task is presumed to have a secondary relationship with perceived job and role demands. That is, the physical setting will influence how people perceive their jobs and role, but the magnitude of the effect will not be as great as for the physical setting–task perceptions relationship.

Individual attributes and characteristics. The third set of antecedent factors in the integrated theory consists of individual attributes and characteristics. This premise is drawn from the SIP model (Salancik & Pfeffer, 1978). The original job characteristics theory (Hackman & Oldham, 1976) predicts that individual differences will affect the relationships between task perceptions and attitudes and behaviors. However research generally has not supported this view (cf. White, 1978). Although not precisely couched in the vernacular of individual differences, the SIP model suggests that differences in people will also affect task perceptions and attitudes. The manner in which this is predicted to occur is through an interpretation of past behaviors on the part of individuals. Research has suggested that individual attitudes (Caldwell & O'Reilly, 1982) and frames of reference (O'Reilly, Parlette, & Bloom, 1980) may affect perceptions. However, these effects have not been found to explain large amounts of variance in perception. Indeed, it seems more logical to expect such individual attributes and characteristics to have a greater impact on perceptions of role and job than of the task, because such factors will generally be somewhat broader in focus. Therefore,

P4: Individual attributes and characteristics are a secondary determinant of task perceptions.

This proposition is consistent with Figure 1, which indicates a strong relationship between individual attributes and characteristics and job and role perceptions, and a weaker relationship, albeit one with considerable theoretic significance, between those attributes and characteristics and task perceptions.

Social setting. Finally, the fourth antecedent factor to influence task perceptions is the social setting. This element of the integrated theory is closest in character to Salancik and Pfeffer's original SIP model. Although there have been documented theoretical and operational problems with the model (Thomas & Griffin, 1983), social cues have been shown to affect task perceptions and attitudes in both laboratory (cf. O'Reilly & Caldwell, 1979) and field (cf. Griffin, 1983) settings. However, as shown by Griffin, et al. (1984) objective task properties tend to be more salient than do social cues. This follows from the likely role of experience, an individual characteristic but also one that affects the impact of social cues. Katz (1978) suggests that job longevity will affect task perception–attitude relationships. Vance and Biddle (in press) further document this assumption. For example, an employee with 30 years experience doing the same job will not likely have her or his perceptions or attitudes toward the job changed because of social cues in the workplace. On the other hand, a new employee confronted with an ambiguous task may lean more heavily on social information, at least in the early stages of forming perceptions and attitudes about the task. Another aspect of the social setting essentially ignored in the literature of task design is group dynamics and processes (Griffin, 1982). Factors such as group norms, cohesiveness, and roles will all likely affect how people perceive the work environment. Social cues may play a greater role in a highly cohesive group than in a less cohesive group, for example. Similarly, if role ambiguity is high, social cues may be seen as a viable mechanism for increasing clarity. Again, however, these effects are most likely to be more on the level of the role and job and less on the level of the task. Therefore,

P5: The social setting is a secondary determinant of task perceptions.

This proposition acknowledges the importance of social information in the workplace, but also puts it in its proper context, focused more on broader levels of workplace perceptions consistent with the original presentation of the SIP model (Salancik & Pfeffer, 1978) and empirical research designed to test the efficacy of the model relative to the task attributes approach (cf. Griffin et al., 1984).

Internal/Stable States

Another central component of the integrated theory is what are termed *internal/stable states*. Their relationship to the model is illustrated in Figure 2. These states coincide with common outcome variables included in many organizational science theories and models, including both the job characteristics theory (Hackman & Oldham, 1976) and the social information processing model (Salancik & Pfeffer, 1978). An important distinction made by the integrated theory, however, is the concept of internality, or stability. Before describing exactly what this is intended to convey, however, the outcome states themselves will be briefly discussed.

Cognitive impressions of task/job/role network. One basic internal/stable state resulting from the network of task/job/role dynamics network is the individual's cognitive impression of that network. That is, this set of impressions is what the person "knows" about his or her task, job, and role. Individual "beliefs" about such things as the levels of task importance, role complexity, and job-related pay, for example, are cognitive impressions.

The view of task taken by the integrated theory draws from both of the earlier dominant models. The integrated theory agrees with Hackman and Oldham (1976) in assuming that tasks in a given setting can be described in terms of a set of attributes, dimensions, or characteristics. At the same time, however, the integrated theory takes the position that the relevant

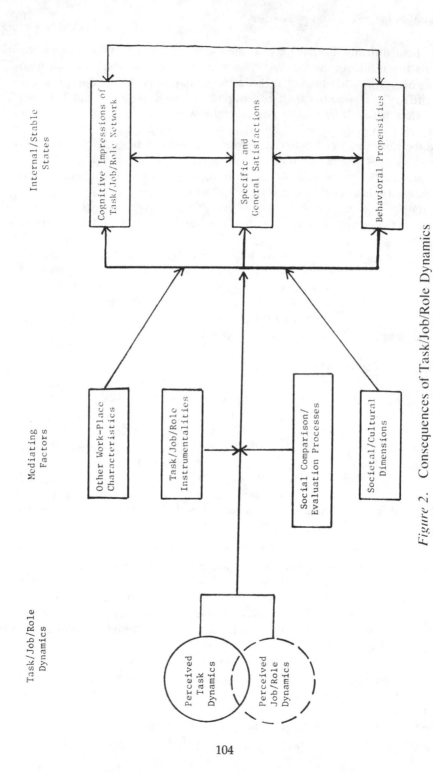

Figure 2. Consequences of Task/Job/Role Dynamics

104

set of attributes varies from one setting to another, similar to the stance taken by Salancik and Pfeffer (1978), and within the same setting over time. Moreover, even when different tasks can be essentially "captured" by the same set of attributes, their relative weightings can still vary.

A second set of internal or stable impressions is perceptions of the job and role. As noted previously, the role is conceptualized as simple or complex, depending on the degree of local control possessed by incumbents, and the job is a broader network of workplace stimuli salient for any given situation. Because perceived task, job, and role dynamics form an interdependent set of factors, it follows that perceptions of one set influences the other sets. As indicated in Figure 2, then, cognitive impressions of the task/job/role network necessarily follow the initial perceptions of relevant task/job/role dynamics.

Specific and general satisfactions. In the integrated theory, both specific and general satisfactions are also considered to be relevant internal–stable outcomes. Specific satisfactions are attitudes about specific and defineable dimensions of the organizational setting. For example, following the traditional literature on job satisfaction (cf. Locke, 1976), people may be satisfied about any number of stimuli, such as their task, pay, benefits, supervisor, co-workers, promotion opportunities, and so forth. They may also have attitudinal orientations of higher levels of aggregation or abstraction. Thus, an employee may have an overall level of job satisfaction that is some sort of a composite of all relevant specific satisfactions. Alternatively, he or she may have an intermediate number of satisfactions, each comprised of more than one but less than the total set of specific satisfactions relevant to the situation. A point made earlier, and one especially germane to this discussion, is that even when multiple attitudes exist, they are unlikely to be independent. Moreover, negative attitudes may tend to dominate neutral or positive ones. When describing feelings about a job, employees will usually express several different attitudes in the same evaluation. Hence, people will say that they do or do not like their jobs because of several different factors.

Given that multiple attitudes exist and that they tend to be interrelated, the integrated theory does not attempt to precisely distinguish between them. Rather, the view taken by the theory is that the magnitude of the relationship between perceived task dynamics and satisfaction will vary as a function of the precision of the relationship between the relevant attributes of the task and the specificity of the attitude toward that attribute. For example, the relationship between perceived task routineness and the individual's attitude toward task routineness should be quite high. Similarly, the relationship between perceived task routineness and attitudes toward the task may be moderately strong, while the relationship between task routineness and overall job satisfaction may be very low. Finally, the relationship between the perception and the attitude may be further influenced by the importance of that attitude relative to other attitudes. A worker who is extremely dissatisfied with his or her pay may express a negative attitude toward all other facets of the workplace, including task routineness, simply because of the severity of an extremely central attitude, that toward his or her pay.

Behavioral propensities. The final set of internal/stable outcomes included in the integrated theory is behavioral propensities. This set includes the complete array of relevant potential behaviors, such as productivity, performance, attendance, retention, helping, and other indicators of good organizational citizenship, and such negative behaviors (from the organization's standpoint) as theft or union activity. As with attitudes, the nature of the relationships will be at least partially determined by the specificity of the relationship in question. The relationship between perceptions of task routineness and behavioral propensities relevant to routineness should be quite strong, whereas the relationship between routineness and overall job performance may be considerably weaker. It is also useful to highlight the concept of behavioral propensities in the integrated theory. Thus, perceptions do not always have to lead to behaviors in order for the perception–behavior relationship to be pertinent. That is, if an employee with a tendency toward high levels of absenteeism is more inclined to come to work on one task than on another, there is at least a practical relationship between task perceptions and behavioral propensities.

As also noted in Figure 2, the various outcome variables are also presumed to have interrelationships among themselves. However, a detailed consideration of these interrelationships is beyond the scope of the integrated theory. Even though they are presumed to be interrelated, they are likewise presumed to be independently affected by perceptions of task dynamics. Therefore,

P6:   The task/job/role dynamics network determines cognitive impressions of that network, specific and general satisfactions, and behavioral propensities.

Internality/stability.   Although the relationships noted in P6 are expected to exist in organizational settings with varying degrees of magnitude, they are also presumed to exist, at least most of the time, in an internal or stable state. An employee is likely to build up over time a repository of feelings about his or her job. After some point, each subsequent feeling is likely to have a diminishing impact on the cumulative set of feelings. For example, if such a thing could be quantified, over a 1-year period an employee might accumulate 300 good feelings about his or her job and 40 bad feelings. The next feeling added to either set will have a minimal impact on their relative proportions. For a new employee with only 2 good and 2 bad feelings, however, the next feeling encountered may play a critical role in future attitude formations.

In general, as the repository of feelings grows, the total set takes on a generally positive, a generally neutral, or a generally negative orientation. As the set begins to take shape, it also tends to become more stable (except in cases of extreme negativism, when the employee is more likely to leave the setting). After the first day at work, the individual's spouse may ask how the day went and the individual might respond, "I think I'm going to like this job because. . . ." After several months, the question may become less frequent and the individual gradually stops forming systematic perceptions of and responses to the work setting. The reactions become internal and stable—without a stimuli for assessment (discussed later), people do not update their cognitive impressions, attitudes, and behavioral propensities on a regular basis. Hence, although *internal* and *stable* are not necessarily the same thing, in the context used here they denote states that exist within the individual (internal) on a fairly consistent (stable) basis.

As a consequence, all three sets of outcomes eventually come to take the form of internal or stable states. People have cognitive impressions of their tasks, job, and role, have both specific and general satisfactions, and tend to behave in certain ways. Yet, these outcomes are not expressed except in certain situations. These situations are described more fully later.

Mediating Factors

The integrated theory, as also shown in Figure 2, suggests that several factors mediate the relationship between perceived task–job–role dynamics and the three internal/stable states. Two sets of factors, task/job/role instrumentalities and social comparison/evaluation processes, are assumed to play a strong role in determining the relationship. Two other sets of factors, other workplace characteristics and societal–cultural dimensions, are predicted to play a less significant role.

Task/job/role instrumentalities. People work for a variety of reasons. Salancik and Pfeffer (1977) point out that models such as the job characteristics theory are based on need-satisfaction models of motivation. They take issue with this body of literature for several reasons, and subsequently propose their social information processing model (Salancik & Pfeffer, 1978) as an alternative. Yet, regardless of whether people work to satisfy a uniform and precise set of needs, there is nevertheless some reason or reasons for them to work. Consider, for example, three common but quite different kinds of workers. A manual worker who has been at the same job for 20 years and who is now counting the years until retirement will likely say that he works to earn enough money to live a reasonable kind of life. A highly trained and skilled professional may argue that she works because of the intrinsic rewards and challenges her job offers. Finally, a secretary in a department of management might work to support her husband while he finishes school, and be planning to complete her own education later. Why do these people work? They work for very clear but quite different reasons. These reasons, in turn, will affect the nature of the relationship between the task and the internal/passive outcomes.

To the extent that the manual laborer's job continues to provide him with a reasonable income and a secure outlook for the future, he will likely respond favorably to a stable and predictable set of task/job/role dynamics. If these dynamics change (for example, if he were to be assigned to a much more strenuous job) or if his reasons for working change (for example, if he were to come into a large inheritance), the relationship between perceptions and states will also change. Similarly, for the professional, if the job becomes less challenging and fulfilling or if her aspirations change or if her reasons for working change (for example, if a parent became financially dependent on her), the relationship between perceptions and states will change. Finally, if the perceived task/job/role dynamics network for the secretary were to change (for example, if the job were to become considerably more demanding) or if her reasons for working were to change (for example, if her husband dropped out of school or graduated), the relationship would again change. Essentially, these relationships will change because of the cognitive nature of people's awareness of their tasks/jobs/roles. The manual laborer "knows" his job and how it satisfies his needs. If the match between his "knowledge" of the job and how it satisfies his needs changes, his cognitive impressions, attitudes, and behavioral impressions may also be affected. Therefore,

P7:   Task/job/role instrumentalities strongly mediate the relationships between perceived task/job/role dynamics and the internal/stable states.

Social comparison–evaluation processes.   Processes of social comparison and evaluation will also mediate the relationships. Oldham and Miller (1979) reason that people would compare their jobs with the jobs of comparison others and that the results of such comparisons would bias how they view and respond to their own tasks. The argument is based on equity theory (Adams, 1965) and assumes that job quality is an important outcome that people receive in return for their inputs to the organization. Thus, from a classical equity theory perspective, people in better quality jobs than their comparison others may experience an over-reward condition, evaluate this as inequity, and subsequently be less satisfied but higher performing. Alternatively, a worker who experiences an under-reward condition due to a lesser quality task will also be less satisfied and will attempt to decrease his or her inputs by performing at a lower level. Of course, any given individual may develop multiple explanations for why he or she has a better job or earns more money (such as self-attributed experience, performance, and so forth). Yet, equity theory does provide a theoretical rationale for expecting some people to view job quality as an outcome, and the work of Oldham and Miller (1979) does provide limited support for the same notion.

In a direct extension of this idea, Slusher and Griffin (1985) recently proposed a model of comparison processes in task design. Drawing from the social comparison theories of Festinger (1954), Albert (1977), and Goodman (1977), this model describes task perceptions as a three-stage process. The first stage is task understanding at an informational level and is essentially nonevaluative. Here, the employee simply seeks as much relevant information as possible to help understand the dynamics of the task. This would be analogous to the concept of cognitive impressions as described here. In the second stage, she or he begins to make comparative evaluations as to the true nature of the task. Using the social comparison processes described by the three models referenced earlier, the person comes to believe that the dynamics of his or her task are "good" or "bad," with the evaluation usually determined as a result of comparing input–outcome ratios with relevant others. Finally, in the third stage, the person experiences varying levels of intrinsic reward as a function of over-, equitably, or under-rewarding conditions. Using the ideas presented by Oldham and Miller (1979) and refined by Slusher and Griffin (1985),

P8: Social comparison/evaluation processes strongly mediate the relationships between perceived task/job/role dynamics and the internal/passive states.

Other mediating factors. Although task–job–role instrumentalities and social comparison–evaluation processes are the primary mediating factors in the integrated theory, two secondary sets of mediating factors are also likely to be operative. First, other workplace characteristics may influence the primary relationships in the model. Examples of these characteristics could include the performance feedback processes used by the organization, the style of supervision received by the employee, and the relationship between the individual's work and nonwork activities (cf. Champoux, 1980).

Second, societal/cultural dimensions may also influence the task dynamics–outcome relationships. Examples of such dimensions might include the occupational status associated with the task, the image of the organization, and so forth. Consider, for example, differences in task perceptions for a physician and a garbage collector. Because the societal view of a physician is one of high value and prestige, the physician him- or herself is inclined to view the task in a positive way, regardless of its objective character. Similarly, the job of garbage collector is viewed as being of low value and little prestige. Thus, the jobholder is predisposed to have a negative impression of the task. Therefore,

> **P9:** Other workplace characteristics and societal/cultural dimensions also mediate the relationships between perceived task/job/role dynamics and internal/stable states.

External/expressed States and Stimuli for Assessment

The final major components of the integrated theory are external/expressed states and stimuli for assessment. As with the notions of internal/stable states, *external* and *expressed* states are not necessarily synonymous concepts. As used here, the terms refer to joint conditions of externally recognizable (i.e., actual behaviors, spoken words, etc.) and expressed perceptions, attitudes, and behaviors in response to workplace stimuli. The relationships between the internal stable and external/expressed states are depicted in Figure 3.

External/expressed states. The external or expressed states included in the integrated theory parallel the internal or stable states: emotive expressions of task/job/role network evaluations and perceptions (a function of cognitive impressions), affective expressions of feelings toward task/job/role elements (a function of specific and general satisfactions), and actual behaviors relative to the task/job/role (a function of behavioral propensities). Although there should be some degree of consistency between each external/expressed state and its analogous internal/stable state, there will also be some degree of variation as well. This variation stems from a variety of reasons. For one thing, it is difficult to fully express many feelings, moods, and emotions about the job. For another, the expressed condition may vary as a function those same moods and emotions, as well as by stress, fatigue, and so forth. For example, a worker who is caught in traffic on the way to work, has a flat tire, and arrives two hours late may express considerably more negative views of all facets of the workplace the rest of that day than will a worker whose day got off to a smoother start. Therefore,

> **P10:** Whereas internal/stable states remain relatively constant for any given individual, external/expressed states will vary as a function of mood, emotions, and other salient experiences.

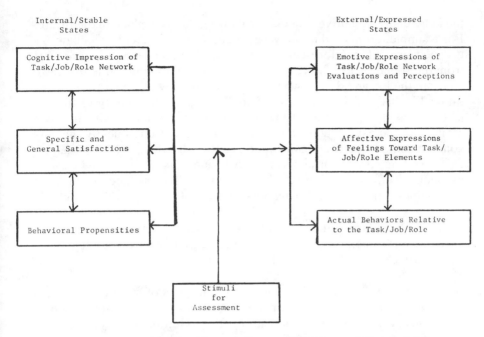

Figure 3. The Internal/Stable and External/Expressed States Linkages

As shown in Figure 3, there will also be variation between internal–stable states and external–expressed states as a function of the stimuli for assessment.

Stimuli for assessment. By *stimuli for assessment*, the theory refers to the cause or causes for the internal or stable state being translated into an external or expressed statement or observation. Numerous stimuli for assessment can be identified: an external prompt (such as a question about how the person likes his or her job or a questionnaire designed to measure task perceptions), an extreme experience (such as a very poor performance evaluation or an unexpectedly large pay increase), change (such as the adoption of a new set of work procedures or a move toward greater automation), recurring transition (such as a systematic rotation from one department to another as a part of a training program), the presence or absence of alternative opportunities (such as being offered another job or being told that one may be laid off), or an intrusive assessment made by others (such as a co-worker verbally proclaiming the virtues of the organization or a close associate leaving the organization after a disagreement with the boss). Each of these stimuli may serve to directly or indirectly elicit an evaluation, in the form of an external or expressed state, by the employee. The expression itself, of course, may then become a part of the individual's cognitive schema for viewing the workplace in the future. For example, an individual may be forced to unexpectedly evaluate his task because of the unforeseen termination of a good friend and a request from the friend that he leave as well. In essence, the person is forced to evaluate the job and decide whether to leave or stay. If he stays, he must rationalize his decision in terms of such things as the quality of the objective task, the physical setting, the tasks's congruence with his own aspirations and expectations, and the social setting. Consequently, he may come to believe that the organization is better than he originally thought. Less extreme stimuli for assessment will, in all likelihood, produce less pronounced effects but should still, over time, affect the accumulation of perceptions, attitudes, and behaviors that people compile. Therefore,

P11: The nature of the stimuli for assessment affects the nature of the external/expressed state and the degree of correspondence between it and its internal/stable analog.

As described previously, different forms and types of stimuli for assessment will shape the form of the response. Although not as integral a part of the theory as the earlier propositions, this assertion is nonetheless important because of its implications for operationalization. This point will be more completely dealt with later. First, however, it is appropriate at this point to summarize and pull together the complete model.

THE INTEGRATED THEORY: A RECAPITULATION

The preceding section detailed the various constructs and processes included in the integrated theory. Figures 1, 2, and 3 and Propositions 1 through 11 capture the basic nature and character of the theory. However, to conclude the presentation of the model, it is instructive to combine the various components and processes into one overall framework. This framework is illustrated in Figure 4.

The integrated theory identifies five sets of constructs linked through a network of interrelated processes. Four sets of antecedent factors (objective task properties, the physical setting, individual attributes and characteristics, and the social setting) determine task/job/role dynamics. This set of dynamics, in turn, is comprised of perceived dimensions, or dynamics, of the task, job, and role.

The network of task/job/role dynamics then determines three internal/stable states. These states are cognitive impressions of the task/job/role network, specific and general satisfactions, and behavioral propensities. The relationships between the network of task/job/role dynamics and the

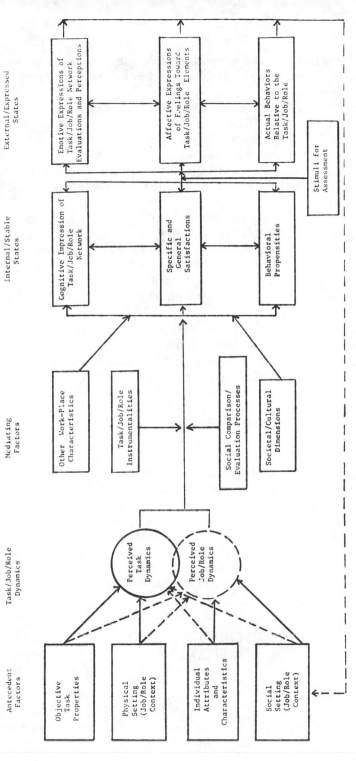

Figure 4. The Complete Integrated Model

113

internal/stable states is mediated by task/job/role instrumentalities, social comparison/evaluation processes, societal/cultural dimensions, and other workplace characteristics.

The internal/stable states then potentially lead to a set of corresponding external/expressed states. These states are emotive expressions of task/ job/role network evaluations and perceptions (a function of cognitive impressions of the task/job/role network), affective expressions of feelings toward task/job/role elements (a function of specific and general satisfactions), and actual behaviors relative to the task/job/role (a function of behavioral propensities).

The degree of correspondence between external/expressed states and their analogous internal/stable states will be affected by mood, emotion, and other salient experiences, and the relationship will be mediated by the nature of the stimuli that elicits the expressed state to be made public. Finally, the act of public expression will itself affect the initial antecedent factors, especially individual attributes and characteristics and the social setting, as the set of processes repeat themselves.

In contrast to the job characteristics theory, the integrated model represents a more comprehensive conceptualization of the workplace dynamics involved in task-design processes. Its boundaries are broader, its range of constructs and processes wider, and its ability to explain workplace phenomenon greater. On the other hand, it is at a much less advanced stage in terms of its operational properties and characteristics.

In contrast to the SIP model, on the other hand, the integrated theory is considerably more precise and focused in its approach to task perceptions and attitudes. Its constructs and processes are more carefully defined and their interrelationships more completely delineated.

Yet, as noted at the beginning of this chapter, the integrated theory is not intended to serve as a replacement for either of the other models. Instead, it represents an attempt to demonstate how the two dominant models, with appropriate supplementation from other areas, can be merged in such a way as to capitalize on their relative strengths and perhaps overcome at least some of their relative weaknesses. The next section will explore implications of the integrated model for future theory and research.

IMPLICATIONS FOR FUTURE THEORY AND RESEARCH

Numerous implications for future theory and research can be drawn from the integrated theory. This section will explicate several of the more significant implications in detail. Attention will first be focused on implications for theory. Research implications will then be addressed.

Implications for Theory

As noted earlier, the integrated theory is perhaps best viewed as a midrange theory, somewhat broader and more comprehensive than the job characteristics theory but narrower and more clearly bounded than the social information processing theory. The five areas that may provide the greatest avenues for theoretical refinement are the link between antecedent factors and perceived task dynamics, the appropriate conceptualization of perceived task dynamics, the role of social comparison/evaluation processes, the role of societal/cultural dimensions, and the link between the internal/stable states and the external/expressed states.

Researchers and theorists have already begun to address the antecedent factors–perceived task linkage, although the work to date has taken more of a competitive, rather than integrative, perspective. For example, Slocum and Sims (1980) describe in considerable detail one framework for linking dimensions of technology (clearly a determinant of objective task properties) to perceived task attributes. Similarly, O'Reilly et al. (1980) investigated how certain individual attributes and characteristics influenced task perceptions. However, Slocum and Sims (1980) used the job characteristics theory as a point of departure, whereas O'Reilly et al. (1980) were explicitly using a SIP-based theoretical framework. Because it stands to reason that such theory-specific approaches may have overlooked critical linkages between other constructs and the relationships under discussion, a broader, more integrative analysis could perhaps yield greater insights. For example, one potential starting point could be a reconceptualization of the Slocum and Sims (1980) framework, systematically incorporating critical variables from the physical and social settings as well as individual attributes and characteristics. Of course, other frameworks might be equally appropriate as starting points, but, regardless, efforts are clearly needed to develop a comprehensive understanding of the determinants of perceived task dynamics.

Perhaps of even greater importance, however, is a better understanding of exactly what constitutes perceived task dynamics. That is, there is a need for a new conceptualization of task. The job characteristics theory uses a set of imposed and prescribed dimensions to conceptualize the task. The major advantages of this approach are that it facilitates measurement and promotes generalizability and comparability between investigations. It suffers, however, from the likelihood that the dimensions are not necessarily mutually exclusive, collectively exhaustive, nor universally salient. The SIP model implicitly suggests that relevant task dimensions will vary across settings, perhaps even within settings. Although this approach might have greater conceptual power, it greatly constrains measurement and virtually eliminates the ability to generalize and compare across studies.

Two different paths toward greater theoretical understanding might be fruitful. One approach would call for the development of an inventory of task dimensions or attributes, conceptually similar to those in the job characteristics theory, but in greater numbers, diversity, and scope. Researchers would then follow some systematic procedure, such as pretesting, structured observation, or similar method to determine the most relevant dimensions for each particular research setting. This approach would allow a common frame of reference for research but would also facilitate tailoring research to specific settings. The other approach could be to follow the lead of Campion and Thayer (1985) and continue to systematically incorporate interdisciplinary views of tasks and jobs into one overarching theoretical framework. Their taxonomy of job-design approaches and outcomes, in particular, holds considerable promise in this regard.

The third area within the integrated model that may provide a foundation for theoretical refinement is the role of social comparison–evaluation processes in task perceptions and attitudes. The work of Oldham and Miller (1979) and Slusher and Griffin (1985) suggests that people do indeed compare their jobs with the jobs of comparison others and that such comparisons may influence how they subsequently perceive and respond to their own tasks. Because most jobs are performed in social settings (i.e., in locations such that an individual can see what others are doing and others can see what she or he is doing), it follows that if such arrangements do, in fact, lead to awareness and observations of others, and if such awareness and observations lead to comparisons and evaluations, greater attention should be devoted to a more refined theoretical articulation of how social comparison/evaluation processes work. The most likely path for theoretical refinement would be to build on the existing work of Festinger (1954), Albert (1977), and Goodman (1977), but with an objective of tailoring it more specifically to task comparisons and evaluations.

A fourth area, related in some ways to the preceding one, is a better appreciation of the role of societal/cultural dimensions in task-design processes. As noted earlier in the chapter, relevant societal/cultural dimensions might include occupational status and organizational image. Status is likely to be a factor both within and between organizations. For example, within a department store like Sears, an employee in the jewelry department is likely to have more status than someone who works in the hardware department who, in turn, may have more status than someone in the coffee shop (Griffin, 1982). Even more obvious examples relate to occupational-status differences, for example, between occupational groups such as doctors, lawyers, executives, and priests, as compared with groups such as cab drivers, garbage collectors, and dishwashers. Such status differentials are likely to affect how people perceive themselves and their jobs.

Similarly, the public image of the organization may also impact individual perceptions of and responses to their jobs. For example, following a major air disaster, employees of the airline involved may have their perceptions of and attitudes toward their jobs changed either temporarily or permanently.

A fifth area in need of theoretical attention is the link between internal/ stable states and external/expressed states. As detailed in the chapter, these states may be quite similar, or quite different, depending on such things as mood and emotion, and as mediated by stimuli for assessment. Perhaps a starting point in this area might be the development of a taxonomy of situations in which people are prompted to express or otherwise externally demonstrate their perceptions, attitudes, and/or behaviors toward their jobs. Next, it might be possible to extract from such a taxonomy how each prompt or stimuli will affect the degree of correspondence between the internal and external states. Finally, the concepts of mood and emotion need to be more systematically integrated into not just the integrated theory, but into other models of organizational behavior as well. In addition to these theoretical implications explicated from the integrated model, several research implications can also be drawn.

Implications for Research

In contrast to the implications for theory, research implications drawn from the integrated model are fairly obvious and straightforward. The five implications to be described in the following paragraphs relate to task measurement; appropriate consideration of the organizational context; distinctions between objective phenomena; perceptions, attitudes, and behaviors; explainable variance; and generalizability trade-offs.

Attention to task measurement should most appropriately follow refined theoretical development, as outlined earlier. It is perhaps best to move away from standard measures of task perceptions and to move toward measures that take a broader conceptualization of task dynamics. For example, to the extent that the interdisciplinary approach of Campion and Thayer (1985) becomes widely used, it follows that their Multimethod Job Design Questionnaire (MJDQ) might also be used more frequently.

Such measures also partially address the second research need suggested by the integrated model, namely, a more systematic consideration of the organizational context of the jobs and jobholders being studied. Simply measuring and then correlating task perceptions and job satisfaction, for example, ignores the complete spectrum of antecedent and mediating factors that are likely to be important. It is incumbent upon researchers to measure as many of these constructs as possible, and to learn as much as they can about the others so as to be better able to assess the likely impact of these other variables on the more narrow linkages being studied. A failure to do so results in an incomplete understanding of task-design processes.

Third, it is incumbent upon researchers to make sure that they themselves understand whether they are interested in objective phenomena, perceptions, attitudes, and/or behaviors when studying task-design issues and processes and to then use appropriate measures. If someone is interested in objective attributes of the job, then objective measures should be used. If perceptions are what are of interest, then perceptual measures are apprpriate. It is not appropriate, however, to measure objective constructs with perceptual techniques and to then assume that they reflect objective reality. Similarly, objective measures should not be taken to represent perceptions. Care should also be taken to not confuse task perceptions with task attitudes, the mistake made by the SIP model.

Researchers should also recognize and confront the trade-offs they make between specificity and generalizability. When studying task design in one organization, they must make several decisions as to what levels of analysis to use, what variables to study, what measures to use, how to sample, and so forth. Each decision affects the extent to which the knowledge gained will be of value to other researchers. The goal, then, should be to optimize the degree of specificity incorporated into any one study. The researcher should take appropriate steps to insure that the study fits the setting. Beyond that, however, she or he might also consider what other researchers are most likely to do and take whatever steps are appropriate to facilitate the aggregation of knowledge and understanding across studies. Of course, experimental, longitudinal, multisample research developed from a well-conceived theoretical foundation should always be the goal.

Finally, theorists, researchers, and practitioners alike should all recognize the constraints that exist regarding explained variance. People's perceptions, attitudes, and behaviors are joint functions of a variety of individual, social, cultural, workplace, and nonworkplace stimuli. Thus, the extent to which meaningful variance in any of the field's "standard" dependent variables can ever be explained by one set of constructs, even an extremely salient one, is limited. Whether the set of independent variables relates primarily to motivation, leadership, task design, or other areas, this fact should always be considered when assessing the significance of one's findings.

In summary, this chapter has attempted to assess current theory and research in the area of task design. An integrated theory drawing from the current dominant models, with appropriate supplementation from other areas, has been presented. Hopefully, this integrated view can serve as a framework for future theory and research as organizational scholars continue to study this important set of constructs.

ACKNOWLEDGMENT

This work was partially supported by the Office of Naval Research, Contract Number N0001483-C-0025.

REFERENCES

Adams, J.S. (1965). Inequity in social exchange. In L. Berkowitz (Ed.), *Advances in experimental social psychology: Vol. 2* (pp. 267–299). New York: Academic Press.

Albert, S. (1977). Temporal comparison theory. *Psychological Review, 84,* 485–503.

Aldag, R.J., Barr, S.H., & Brief, A.P. (1981). Measurement of perceived task characteristics. *Psychological Bulletin, 90,* 415–431.

Aldag, R.J., & Brief, A.P. (1979). *Task design and employee motivation.* Glenview, IL: Scott, Foresman.

Algera, J.A. (1983).'Objective' and perceived task characteristics as a determinant of reactions by task performers. *Journal of Occupational Psychology, 56,* 95–107.

Bem, D.J. (1972). Self-perception theory. In L. Berkowitz (Ed.), *Advances in experimental social psychology: Vol. 6* (pp. 1–62). New York: Academic Press.

Berman, J.S., Read, S.J., & Kenny, D.A. (1983). Processing inconsistent social information. *Journal of Personality and Social Psychology, 45,* 1211–1224.

Bhagat, R.S., & Chassie, M.B. (1980). Effects of changes in job characteristics on some theory-specific attitudinal outcomes: Results from a naturally occurring quasi-experiment. *Human Relations, 33,* 297–313.

Brief, A.P., Wallace, M.J., & Aldag, R.J. (1976). Linear vs. non-linear models of the formation of affective reactions: The case of job enlargement. *Decision Sciences, 7,* 1–9.

Calder, B.J., & Ross, M. (1973). *Attitudes and behavior.* Morristown, NJ: General Learning Press.

Calder, B.J., & Schurr, P.H. (1981). Attitudinal processes in organizations. In L.L. Cummings and B.M. Staw (Eds.), *Research in organizational behavior: Vol. 3* . Greenwich, CT: JAI Press.

Caldwell, D.F., & O'Reilly, C.A. (1982). Task perceptions eand job satisfaction: A question of causality. *Journal of Applied Psychology, 67,* 361–369.

Campion, M.A., & Thayer, P.W. (1985). Development and field evaluation of an interdisciplinary measure of job design. *Journal of Applied Psychology, 70,* 29–43.

Champoux, J.E. (1980). The world of nonwork: Some implications for job re-design efforts. *Personnel Psychology, 33,* 61–75.

Clegg, C.W. (1984). The derivation of job designs. *Journal of Occupational Behaviour, 5,* 131–146.

Davis, M.S. (1971). That's interesting: Toward a phenomenology of sociology and a sociology of phenomenology. *Philosophy of Social Science, 1,* 309–344.

Davis, T.R.V. (1984). The influence of the physical environment in offices. *Academy of Management Review, 9,* 271–283.

Dean, J.W. Jr., & Brass, D.J. (in press). Social interaction and the perception of job characteristics in an organization. *Human Relations*.

Dubin, R. (1978). *Theory building*. New York: Free Press.

Dunham, R.B. (1976). The measurement and dimensionality of job characteristics. *Journal of Applied Psychology*, 61, 404–409.

Evans, M.G., Kiggundu, M.N., & House, R.J. (1979). A partial test and extension of the job characteristic model of motivation. *Organizational Behavior and Human Performance*, 24, 354–381.

Ferratt, T.W., Dunham, R.B. & Pierce, J.L. (1981). Self-report measures of job characteristics and affective responses: An examination of discriminant validity. *Academy of Management Journal*, 24, 780–794.

Festinger, L. (1954). A theory of social comparison processes. *Human Relations*, 7, 117–140.

Goodman, P.S. (1977). Social comparison processes. In G.R. Salancik and B.M. Staw (Eds.), *New directions in organizational behavior*. (pp. 97–132). Chicago: St. Clair Press.

Griffeth, R.W. (1985). Moderation of the effects of job enrichment by participation: A longitudinal field experiment. *Organizational Behavior and Human Decision Processes*, 35, 73–93.

Griffin, R.W. (1981). A longitudinal investigation of task characteristics relationships. *The Academy of Management Journal*, 24, 99–113.

Griffin, R.W. (1982). *Task design: An integrative approach*. Glenview, IL: Scott, Foresman.

Griffin, R.W. (1983). Objective and social sources of information in task redesign: A field experiment. *Administrative Science Quarterly*, 28, 184–200.

Griffin, R.W., Bateman, T.S., Wayne, S.J., & Head, T. (1984, November). *Objective and social factors as determinants of task perceptions and responses: An integrative framework and empirical investigation* (Technical Report TR-ONR-DG-09, Contract Number N00014-83-C-0025). Washington, D.C.: Office of Naval Research.

Hackman, J.R., & Lawler, E. (1971). Employee reactions to job characteristics. *Journal of Applied Psychology*, 55, 259–286.

Hackman, J.R., & Oldham, G.R. (1975). Development of the Job Diagnostic Survey. *Journal of Applied Psychology*, 60, 159–170.

Hackman, J.R., & Oldham, G.R. (1976). Motivation through the design of work: Test of a theory. *Organizational Behavior and Human Performance*, 16, 250–279.

Hackman, J.R., & Oldham, G.R. (1980). *Work redesign*. Reading, MA: Addison-Wesley.

Hackman, J.R., Oldham, G.R., Janson, R., & Purdy, K. (1975, Summer). A new strategy for job enrichment. *California Management Review*, pp. 57–71.

Hackman, J.R., Pearce, J.L., & Wolfe, J.C. (1978). Effects of changes in job characteristics on work attitudes and behaviors: A naturally occurring quasi-experiment. *Organizational Behavior and Human Performance*, 21, 289–304.

Herzberg, F., Mausner, B., & Snyderman, B. (1959). *The motivation to work*. New York: Wiley.

Ivancevich, J.M., & Matteson, M.T. (1978, October). Managing for a healthier heart. *Management Review*, pp. 14–19.

Katz, R. (1978). Job longevity as a situational factor in job satisfaction. *Administrative Science Quarterly*, 23, 204–223.

Kemp, N.J., & Cook, J.D. (1983). Job longevity and growth need strength as joint moderators of the task design-job satisfaction relationship. *Human Relations*, 36, 883–898.

Kiggundu, M.N. (1980). An empirical test of the theory of job design using multiple job ratings. *Human Relations*, 33, 339–351.

Kiggundu, M.N. (1983). Task interdependence and job design: Test of a theory. *Organizational Behavior and Human Performance*, 31, 145–172.

Kornhauser, A. (1965). *Mental health of the industrial worker*. New York: Wiley.

Kuhn, T. (1970). *The structure of scientific revolutions* (2nd Ed.). Chicago: The University of Chicago Press.

Locke, E.A. (1976). The nature and causes of job satisfaction. In M. Dunnette (Ed.), *Handbook of industrial and organizational psychology.* (pp. 1297–1350). Chicago: Rand McNally.

Lord, R.G. (1985). An information processing approach to social perceptions, leadership and behavioral measurement in organizations. In L.L. Cummings and B.M. Staw (Eds.), *Research in organizational behavior: Vol. 7* (pp. 87–128). Greenwich, CT: JAI Press.

Moorhead, G. (1981). Organizational analysis: An integration of the macro and micro approaches. *Journal of Management Studies, 18,* 191–218.

Oldham, G., Hackman J., & Pearce, J. (1976). Conditions under which employees respond positively to enriched work. *Journal of Applied Psychology, 61,* 395–403.

Oldham, G.R., & Hackman, J.R. (1980). Work design in the organizational concept. In B.M. Staw and L.L. Cummings (Eds.), *Research in Organizational Behavior: Vol. 2* (pp. 247–278). Greenwich, CT: JAI Press.

Oldham, G.R., & Miller, H.E. (1979). The effect of significant other's job complexity on employee reactions to work. *Human Relations, 32,* 247–260.

O'Reilly, C.A., & Caldwell, D.F. (1979). Informational influence as a determinant of perceived task characteristics and job satisfaction. *Journal of Applied Psychology, 64,* 157–165.

O'Reilly, C., Parlette, G., & Bloom, J. (1980). Perceptual measures of task characteristics: The biasing effects of differing frames of reference and job attitudes. *Academy of Management Journal, 23,* 118–131.

Orpen, C. (1979). The effect of job enrichment on employee satisfaction, motivation, involvement, and performance: A field experiment. *Human Relations, 32,* 189–217.

Pfeffer, J.L. (1981). *Power in organizations.* Marshfield, MA: Pitman.

Pierce, J.L. (1984). Job design and technology: A sociotechnical systems perspective. *Journal of Occupational Behaviour, 5,* 147–154.

Pierce, J.L., & Dunham, R.B. (1978). An empirical demonstration of the convergence of common macro- and micro-organization measures. *Academy of Management Journal, 21,* 410–418.

Pierce, J.L., Dunham, R.B., & Cummings, L.L. (1984). Sources of environmental structuring and participant responses. *Organizational Behaviour and Human Performance, 33,* 214–242.

Pinder, C.C. (1984). *Work motivation.* Glenview, IL: Scott, Foresman.

Pokorney, J.J., Gilmore, D.C., & Beehr, T.A. (1980). Job diagnostic survey dimensions: Moderating effect of growth needs and correspondence with dimensions of job rating form. *Organizational Behavior and Human Performance, 26,* 222–237.

Quick, J.C., & Quick, J.D. (1984). *Organizational stress and preventive management.* New York: McGraw-Hill.

Roberts, K.H., & Glick, W. (1981). The job characteristics approach to task design: A critical review. *Journal of Applied Psychology, 66,* 193–217.

Rousseau, D.M. (1977). Technological differences in job characteristics, employee satisfaction, and motivation: A synthesis of job design research and sociotechnical systems theory. *Organizational Behavior and Human Performance, 19,* 18–42.

Salancik, G., & Pfeffer, J. (1977). An examination of need-satisfaction models of job attitudes. *Administrative Science Quarterly, 22,* 427–456.

Salancik, G., & Pfeffer, J. (1978). A social information processing approach to job attitudes and task design. *Administrative Science Quarterly, 23,* 224–253.

Slocum, J.W. Jr., & Sims, H.P. Jr., (1980). A typology for integrating technology, organization and job design. *Human Relations, 33,* 193–211.

Slusher, E.A., & Griffin, R.W. (1985). Comparison processes in task perceptions, evaluations, and reactions. *Journal of Business Research, 13,* 287–299.

Steele, F.I. (1973). *Physical settings and organizational development.* Reading, MA: Addison-Wesley.

Taber, T.D., Beehr, T.A., & Walsh, J.T. (1985). Relationships between job evaluation ratings and self-ratings of job characteristics. *Organizational Behavior and Human Decision Processes, 35,* 27–45.

Taylor, F.W. (1911). *The principles of scientific management.* New York: Harper & Row.

Terborg, J.R., & Davis, G.A. (1982). Evaluation of a new method for assessing change to planned job redesign as applied to Hackman and Oldham's job characteristics model. *Organizational Behavior and Human Performance, 29,* 112–128.

Thomas, J., & Griffin, R. (1983). The social information processing model of task design: A review of the literature. *Academy of Management Review, 8,* 672–682.

Vance, R.J., & Biddle, T.F. (in press). Task experience and social cues: Interaction effects on attitudinal reactions. *Organizational Behavior and Human Decision Processes.*

Vecchio, R.P., & Keon, T.L. (1981) Predicting employee satisfaction from congruency among individual need, job design, and system structure. *Journal of Occupational Behaviour, 2,* 283–292.

Walker, C.R., & Guest, R. (1952). *The man on the assembly line.* Cambridge, MA: Harvard University Press.

Walton, R.E. (1974). Improving the quality of work life. *Harvard Business Review, 52,* 12ff.

Weick, K.E. (1977). Enactment processes in organizations. In B.M. Staw and G.R. Salancik (Eds.), *New directions in organizational behavior.* (pp. 267–300). Chicago: St. Clair Press.

Weiss, H.M., & Shaw, J.B. (1979). Social influences on judgements about tasks. *Organizational Behavior and Human Performance, 24,* 126–140.

White, J.K. (1978). Individual differences and the job quality–worker response relationship: Review, integration, and comments. *Academy of Management Review, 3,* 267–280.

Yukl, G.A. (1981). *Leadership in organizations.* Englewood Cliffs, NJ: Prentice-Hall.

Zierden, W.E. (1980). Congruence in the work situation: Effects of growth needs, management style, and job structure on job-related satisfactions. *Journal of Occupational Behaviour, 1,* 297–310.

OF ART AND WORK:
AESTHETIC EXPERIENCE AND THE
PSYCHOLOGY OF WORK FEELINGS

Lloyd E. Sandelands and Georgette C. Buckner

ABSTRACT

This paper investigates a broad class of work feelings that has not yet received adequate consideration in the literature. These are feelings associated with aesthetic experience. Based on a study of art, the nature of these feelings and the conditions of their occurrence in work are proposed. The paper concludes with a discussion of how study of aesthetic experiences of work can contribute to a broader understanding of the psychology of feelings of work.

INTRODUCTION

There is a lot to learn about work feelings. Despite a reconnaissance by literally thousands of studies (see Locke, 1976, for a representative review), the territory of work feelings remains largely uncharted, beyond the frontier. Questions about why people feel as they do when working find superficial answers. It is said that the work is interesting, or challenging, or stressful, or dehumanizing. Or it is said that the match between worker and work is a good or a bad one. Such answers betray little of the subtle texture and dynamisms of the work itself, and even less of the intricate psychology of its apprehension and appreciation.

What is missing is a conceptual vocabulary adequate to describe the psychology of work feelings. Although there are good reasons for this, they are small comfort. One is that the study of feelings has not gone on for long. It is only since the industrial revolution, with its coincident regard for the efficiency of work and disregard for the humanity of workers, that the question of how work feels has drawn considered attention. More important, the research thus far has been limited almost exclusively to studies of worker feelings *about* their work (i.e., global satisfaction with the job). Few studies have considered worker feelings *of* their work (i.e., how the worker feels on the job). Yet, the latter question speaks more directly to the core issue of work feeling (Sandelands, 1988).[1] Finally, studies of work satisfaction have relied almost exclusively on worker self-reports. While this practice is appealing in its directness, it restricts inquiry to feelings about which workers are willing and able to speak (thereby excluding those below the limen of awareness or too vague or fleeting to be captured in the pale of discursive report).[2]

The purpose of this paper is to begin to describe a broad class of work feelings that are *of* work, not *about* work. These are the feelings associated with the aesthetic in work, with its beauty and good. Although aesthetic feelings typically are associated with art, it is argued that they are an important basis of feeling in work as well. Investigation of these feelings promises a rare glimpse into the ongoing emotionality of work. It promises also progress toward a conceptual vocabulary better suited to describe the psychology of work feelings.

The paper starts by making an oblique approach to the topic. It begins with a study of aesthetic experience in art. Art is examined because its activities (of art making and appreciation) are uniquely revealing of the psychology of aesthetic experience. Four questions are examined: (1) Does the concept of "aesthetic experience" make sense theoretically? (2) How does aesthetic experience feel, and why? (3) What characteristics of art works make aesthetic experience possible? and (4) What is the role of the perceiver in aesthetic experience? The answers to these four questions establish a general backdrop against which the aesthetics of work can be considered. The paper continues with a discussion of the place of aesthetic experience in work—arguing against the idea that work cannot be aesthetic because it is practical. This argument is supported by examples of aesthetic experiences of work drawn both from academic writers and from the popular business press. The paper ends with a discussion of how study of aesthetic experiences can contribute to an understanding of the psychology of feeling at work.

AN APPEAL TO ART

Any turn to art confronts the inveterate doubt that art has anything to teach psychology. Supposedly art can offer little to psychology because its aims and methods are so unlike those of science. As Bronowski (1978) points out, whereas the scientist seeks to mean the same thing to everybody who listens, the artist is content to say something universal and yet mean different things to everybody who listens.[3] This doubt about art, however, is irrelevant to the concerns of this paper, which are more substantive than methodological. We appeal to art because its activities (of art making and art appreciation) are especially indicative of the psychology of aesthetic experience. Works of art are created expressly to engage the beholder in this experience. Art works are unique also in that the conditions of their success are made objective in the work itself.

The Concept of Aesthetic Experience

For the concept of aesthetic experience to be of scientific value, the adjective *aesthetic* must mark its predicate as unique and theoretically important. To paraphrase James, it must be a difference that makes a difference.

Usually the aesthetic experience is identified by its contents or consequences. Bronowski (1978), for example, describes the aesthetic experience as a journey of discovery—as an act of mind whereby a person comes to know in a richer or deeper way some aspect or essence of experienced life. Urmson (1962) identifies the aesthetic experience with use of particular criteria of value (e.g., harmony, balance, integrity). Others remark of its phenomenology. Maslow (1971) calls attention to its peculiar, almost paradoxical, unself-consciousness, noting (seemingly with exasperation) that the experience vanishes with any attempt to corner it for inspection. More commonly, the aesthetic experience is identified by its pleasure. Bronowski (1978, p. 11) speaks of the pleasure of perceiving in a new way, of "trying out and exploring imaginary situations." Henri (1923, p. 102) adds that though the aesthetic experience is a pleasurable pastime, it is not simply so: "To apprehend beauty is to work for it. It is a mighty and entrancing effort, and the enjoyment of a picture is not only in the pleasure it inspires, but in the comprehension of the new order of construction used in its making." And, for Dewey (1934): "There is . . . an element of undergoing, of suffering in its large sense, in every experience. . . . It involves reconstruction which may be painful."[4]

Although illuminating of aesthetic experience, these distinctions prove on closer examination to be indecisive. Each admits experiences into the category "aesthetic" that do not belong and forbids others that do. Not every journey of discovery is an aesthetic experience. Unself-consciousness can occur also in highly stressful activities. And not every pleasure is an aesthetic pleasure. What distinguishes aesthetic experience is its signature process; it is a particular species of mental activity (Dewey, 1934; Gombrich, 1960; Langer, 1967). This process is marked by its relationship to purpose. Unlike other kinds of thinking, aesthetic experience is detached from purpose (Arnheim, 1966; Dewey, 1934). Bruner (1962) describes aesthetic thinking aptly as a "play of impulses at the fringe of awareness." This is in contrast to purposeful thinking that occurs at the center of awareness. According to Bruner, purpose preempts aesthetic experience by calling on the mind to search for efficient means to its satisfaction, thereby crowding out the frivolity that makes for aesthetic discovery. For aesthetic experience to occur, the demands of life that ordinarily are the reason for thinking must be set aside; the person must be on "vacation from reality" (Dewey, 1934). This is why art succeeds only when the person "gives in" to it and lets it motivate and guide imagination. Writes Bruner (1962, p. 25): "To be dominated by an object . . . is to be free of the defenses that keep us hidden from ourselves."

This detachment of aesthetic thinking from purpose remains despite the fact that purposes can be (and often are) found in it. As an example, it is sometimes observed that aesthetic thinking evolves by stages—from initial conditions of disorganization and conflict to later conditions of organization and equilibrium—and on this basis concluded that its purpose is to organize perceptions or resolve tensions (cf. Arnheim, 1971). This, however, is a very different idea of purpose from that identified with other kinds of thinking. This purpose does not come before thinking but emerges from it as a kind of consequence. It is not the reason for the thinking taking place. Whereas ordinary thinking serves a purpose, aesthetic thinking only assumes one.

Although Bruner's description of aesthetic thinking—as a play of impulses at the fringe of awareness—has much to recommend it, two of its details bear scrutiny. First, the phrase "at the fringe of awareness" must be understood not to refer to an actual place in the mind or brain (e.g., the left hemisphere) but instead to a particular kind of thinking. James (1890, p. 249) used this very phrase to describe thought processes whose dynamics are fugitive from introspection. According to James, all that can be reported about these processes are the thoughts they produce—nothing of the steps in their making. Russell (1921) called this kind of thinking "knowing by acquaintance." In contemporary writing, this thinking has been called "pattern recognition," "image-based thought," and "syncretic cognition" (see, e.g., Buck, 1985).

Second, to say that aesthetic experience exists as a play of impulses is to say neither that it is wholly spontaneous nor that it is completely free. It must have coherence and direction of some kind; otherwise it would be meaningless. In the main, the coherence and direction of aesthetic thinking come from the object being contemplated (e.g., the work of art). Indeed, it is the magic of art that it can routinely function in this way. The mind plays but on a playground of dimensions and activities determined by the art work.

Aesthetic Experiences, Art Experiences. Although the aesthetic experience is characteristic of art (some say definitive of art), it is not the only experience of art. A work of art can be appreciated not only for its beauty but also for its technical virtuosity or for the messages it conveys about social or moral life. The latter are not aesthetic experiences, though sometimes they are mistaken for such. The aesthetic experience makes no exclusive claim upon art but shares this territory with a multiplicity of others.

Although art can be experienced in many ways, each experience is singular. It is uniquely aesthetic or technical or moral or something else (see Urmson, 1962). This logical property of art experiences is built into the idea of experience types. Without it, there could be no such thing as aesthetic experiences, only experiences that have more or less of some aesthetic quality.

Feeling and Form in Art

The aesthetic experience has been shown to be a unique species of activity— one marked by features of content and form. One of these features is its characteristic pleasure. What more can be said about this pleasure? And, more important, where does it come from?

A closer look finds that aesthetic experiences are not simply pleasurable. The pleasures of art vary considerably. Arguably some are not really pleasures at all but more like trials of some kind. Mozart's piano concertos are each affecting in a different way (e.g., compare No. 21 in C-major with No. 24 in D-minor). More generally, Mozart's music has a different feeling from that of Bach or the Rolling Stones. Similarly, Van Gogh's canvasses are each felt in a different way but none in quite the same way as those of Rothko or Warhol. There are differences also between art forms. The feeling possibilities of music are different from those of painting or sculpture, which are different again from those of poetry or theater. Finally, the pleasure in any given art work may differ from one person to the next and even for the same person from one occasion to the next. Aesthetic pleasures are notoriously individual.

The subtle emotionality of aesthetic experience perplexes any attempt to explain it. Why are aesthetic experiences generally (if not unexceptionably) pleasurable? And why are these pleasures so varied? Any simple answer to the first question seems almost to condemn the answer to the second. Bronowski (1978) argues that pleasure comes from making discoveries. Urmson (1962) contends that pleasure results from meeting specific criteria of beauty (e.g., proportion, balance, harmony). More commonly, however, aesthetic feelings are explained by the process of aesthetic experience itself (see, e.g., Arnheim, 1969; Dewey, 1934; Hoffman, 1948; Langer, 1967). Feeling is said to be a quality of this process, one of its manifestations or phases. For Dewey (1934, p. 602): "All the emotions are qualifications of a drama, and they change as the drama develops." For Langer (1967), feeling emerges from the play of aesthetic thinking in much the same way that the red glow of superheated iron emerges from the play of iron molecules. Feeling is the way aesthetic thinking appears to consciousness.

The idea that aesthetic feeling is a quality of process affords a simple yet compelling account of both its generality and individuality. On one hand, the pleasure taken in aesthetic experience generally can be attributed to its characteristic process—that is, the play of impulses at the fringe of awareness. It is a kind of recreation. On the other hand, the specific cast of this pleasure in the individual case can be attributed to the particular form taken by this process. Aesthetic thinking never takes precisely the same course, nor does it wind up in the same place.

Yet the question remains: *Why* is the play of impulses at the fringe of awareness pleasing and in so many different ways? The answer usually given is that this process is lifelike—that it is alive and an exemplification of experienced life. Langer (1967) calls this "living form" and argues that it is definitive of aesthetic feeling. For Dewey (1934), feeling derives from an organic dynamism of "forces that carry the experience of an event, object, scene, and situation to its own integral fulfillment." The aesthetic experience, he contends, is a life unto itself. This is the key to its pleasure. This is the key also to its peculiar individuality. What is felt is *a* life—a life having its own dynamics and form.

What is perhaps most baffling about aesthetic feelings is that they can be pleasurable despite being about things that are unpleasant or even horrifying (e.g., death, pathos, loss, despair, guilt). For example, it is possible to feel a writer's pain (and in some fashion enjoy the feeling) without actually being pained. This is an important characteristic of aesthetic feeling: what is pleasurably felt is sometimes a figuration of a real feeling (that is not felt). This point has been made before by Campbell-Fisher (1951, p. 266) in connection with the feeling of sadness:

> My grasp of the essence of sadness . . . comes not from moments in which I have been sad, but from moments when I have seen sadness before me released from entanglements with contingency. . . . we have seen this in great beauty, in the works of our great artists.

Characteristics of Art

Talk about art can hardly begin before encountering the question of what it is. As it happens, talk about art also can hardly end on this question because it can never be answered decisively.

Art cannot be described in terms of necessary and sufficient attributes (Weitz, 1962). Works of art resemble one another as members of a family (see Wittgenstein, 1953). They share attributes with one another but have no attributes completely in common. One searches in vain for definitive properties of art.

Further, it is no help to define art by how it is experienced—for example, in terms of its feeling or sense of beauty. Art works have no imperative feeling qualities. They are vehicles for experience, opportunities for feeling or perceiving beauty. A sober view of art finds only an object (the "art work") and a thinking and perceiving person. Feeling, or a perception of beauty, is simply one way the person's experience of the object can turn out.[5] Plainly, there is something about art that encourages such experiences (just as there is something about the attitude of the person that does likewise). This something is not causal or definitive but rather facilitative.

The question better asked of art is, What properties of art works make them likely to function as vehicles of aesthetic experience? As Goodman (1978) puts it, the question is not "What is art?" but rather "When is art?" In what follows, four such properties are identified: (1) boundaries (2) dynamic tensions (3) a record of growth, and (4) unresolved possibility. Although there is no logical basis for saying so, these properties seem almost sine qua nons of the aesthetic experience. Where they find each other's company, whether by design or accident, in a defined work of art or something else—aesthetic experience is more likely to occur. Later it will be argued that properties like these also make it possible to experience work aesthetically.

Definite Boundaries. Art works have definite boundaries, which identify the work apart from other objects of the world. More important, they make it possible to regard the work openly—free to explore whatever impulses or ideas it might suggest. Secure in the knowledge that the work is finite in both space and time, the beholder is enabled to commit the otherwise dangerous act of relinquishing conscious control over his or her thinking, an act that Bronowski (1978, p. 18) describes as suspending one's "sense of judgement." The perceiver knows that whatever its course, the experience is temporary and that control can and will be reestablished. This is essential to the free play of mind that is the aesthetic experience.

According to the painter Hans Hoffman, boundaries are important not only for aesthetic appreciation but also for the creation of the art object. Boundaries, he says, present not a limiting prospect but a means for suggesting the limitless (1948, p. 42–43):

> From the beginning, your paper is limited, as all geometrical figures are limited. Within the confines is the complete creative message. Everything you do is definitely related to the paper. The outline becomes an essential part of your composition. . . . A consciousness of limitation is paramount for an expression of the Infinite. Beethoven creates Eternity in the physical limitation of his symphonies.

Whereas Hoffman notes the artistic importance of spatial and temporal boundaries, Dewey (1934) calls attention to boundaries inherent in the particular medium of the work. Art, he asserts, is defined always by its medium. It is uniquely contained by a medium and could not exist as that art in any other medium. The medium, he argues, forces a centering of the attention on a particular sense or senses and thereby makes possible the act of "intensified expression" that is art.

On reflection, the boundaries of art works can be seen to be of two kinds. There are obvious physical boundaries in space and time; for example, paintings take up only so much space (often with the contrivance of a frame to mark where they leave off and where the outside world begins); dances, dramas, operas, and symphonies have duration (often beginning and ending with the raising and lowering of curtains). There are also more subtle boundaries set up by the internal integrity of the work. Art works find coherence in the interrelations of their parts. The art work is a unity, complete and whole unto itself. This unity is not guaranteed by the physical boundaries of the work; it depends also on how the work is internally constituted. The physical boundaries of art works are not merely cessations; they also are consummations.

There is, finally, an imperative quality to the boundaries of art. Their very presence indicates that what is contained inside is something special, something to be regarded unto itself and apart from the prejudices of purpose or vanities of ego. In this sense, the boundaries of art works are social. They call for a definition of the work as art and thereby for a particular orientation to the work by the perceiver.

Dynamic Tensions. Art holds the viewer in its thrall by presenting a condition not of completion but of tension. This tension is created by the arrangement of artistic materials to produce an impression of forces operating one against another. In painting, for example, tension is created by what Hoffman (1948, pp. 44–45) calls the opposing forces of *push and pull*:

> Depth, in a pictorial, plastic sense, is not created by the arrangement of objects one after another toward a vanishing point, in the sense of the Renaissance perspective, but on the contrary (and in absolute denial of this doctrine) by the creation of forces in the sense of PUSH AND PULL. . . . To create the phenomenon of PUSH AND PULL on a flat surface, one has to understand that by nature the picture plane reacts automatically in the opposite direction to the stimulus received; thus action continues as long as it receives stimulus in the creative process. . . . The function of PUSH AND PULL in respect to form contains the secret of Michelangelo's monumentality or of Rembrandt's universality.

One form that tension often takes in art is rhythm—for example, meter in poetry, measures in music, patterning on the surface of a painting. Rhythm is given by a dialectical patterning of forces; first one is dominant, then the other. Dewey (1934, p. 631) has said that "the *first* characteristic of the environing world that makes possible the existence of artistic form is rhythm. There is rhythm in nature before poetry, painting, architecture and music exist." He argues that rhythms provide structure and stability to all life processes. Langer (1967) adds that rhythm is primary in securing the unity of art works and in identifying them as living forms.

The property of tension is important for two reasons. First, it gives the art work an arresting vitality. The work is made to seem alive and individual (though there may be many literal copies of the work available). These are characteristics of the aesthetic experience itself. Second, it calls the perceiver to action and brings to aesthetic thinking a purpose of its own—something it would not otherwise have. Tension cries to be resolved. This property of art is captured nicely by Arnheim (1971), who describes art as "disorder striving toward harmony."

Record of Growth. Art does not just present a condition of tension; it presents also a basis for its resolution (though not the resolution itself). By its very constitution, art projects a course of development—what is here called a "record of growth." Dewey (1934, p. 633) regards this aspect as essential to art:

> The structure of an object must be such that its force interacts happily (but not easily) with the energies that issue from the experience itself; when their mutual affinities and antagonisms work together to bring about a substance that develops cumulatively and surely (but not too steadily) toward a fulfilling of impulsions and tensions, then indeed there is art.

Although difficult to see in the finished product, this property of art nevertheless can be detected in the course of its creation. When laid bare, the process of artistic creation exhibits a progressive, cumulative development of order. Writes Henri (1923, p. 67):

> Art is the inevitable consequence of growth and is the manifestation of the principles of its origin. The work of art is a result; is the output of a progress in development and stands as a record and marks the degree of development. It is not an end in itself, but the work indicates the course taken and the progress made.

The record of growth is illustrated by the legacy of Matisse's series paintings and the painter's commentaries about them. In his series "Nu Bleu," he starts form a point of capturing a great deal of information about his subject and moves subsequently toward a more simplified and expressive generalization of the forms.

> The reaction of each stage is as important as the subject. For this reaction comes from me and not from the subject. It is from the basis of my interpretation that I continually react until my work comes into harmony with me. Like someone writing a sentence, I rewrite and make new discoveries. At each stage, I reach a balance, a conclusion. At the next sitting if I find a weakness—I re-enter through the breach—and reconceive the whole (Matisse, 1936).

Unresolved Possibility. By its record of growth, art asserts the prospect of resolving its created tension. Yet the art work itself does not provide resolution;

it leaves this to its beholder. In the best works, resolution is not singular but can be achieved in different ways each time it is encountered. Great art poses subtle, interesting tensions that have no simple or final resolution. They persist in challenging the perceiver, never letting matters rest. Their beauty, as Hulme (in Dewey, 1934, p. 613) puts it, is "the marking time, the stationary vibration, the feigned ecstasy, of an arrested impulse unable to reach its natural end." It is this unresolved and unresolvable possibility that makes for beauty in art and raises it above mere prettiness.

Bruner has called this property of art its "category of possibility." The name is apt; art is all about possibility. It is about tension and the possibilities of its resolution. Yet these possibilities are not unbounded; they are decidedly categorical. Only those resolutions that work, that relate meaningfully to the problem or tension posed by the work, can be accepted. As Justi (quoted in Arnheim, 1951, p. 266) makes clear, the artist "will not leave free play to phantasy, but fasten it to the spell of his creation." Henri (1923, p. 67) says about the art work that it "is not an end in itself, but the work indicates the course taken and the progress made. The work is not a finality. It promises more, and from it projection can be made."

Summary

Although these four properties are in no way definitive of art, they are common to many art works and seem signally encouraging of aesthetic experience. Together these properties define an object that begs for aesthetic contemplation. *Boundaries* allow thinking to proceed freely at the fringes of awareness, in temporary disregard of real world demands. The object can be experienced on its terms—the beholder free to be pulled along, to be dominated by the work. *Tension* brings life to the thinking process by calling upon the beholder to provide a resolution. Otherwise purposeless, thinking is able to find a purpose of its own. The *record of growth* offers a way of proceeding, a way to organize thinking toward resolution. Finally, *unresolved possibility* challenges the beholder to find a resolution, and perhaps a new one with each appraisal.

An object having these properties would seem to have a good chance of evoking and sustaining aesthetic experience. Nevertheless, it would be a chance only. As noted, the properties of art works do not cause aesthetic experience; they present conditions for its appearance. It is necessary also that the beholder be ready and interested to see the object in this way.

The Aesthetic Attitude

Aesthetic experience arises as a kind of compact between an appropriately endowed object and an appropriately inclined beholder. From the beholder, it requires openness and involvement:

You cannot look at a picture and find it beautiful by a merely passive act of seeing. The internal relations that make it beautiful to you have to be discovered and in some way have to be put in by you. The artist provides a skeleton; he provides guiding lines; he provides enough to engage your interest and touch you emotionally. But there is no picture and no poem unless you yourself enter it and fill it out (Bronowski, 1978, p. 14).

Since Bosanquet (1892), the participation of the perceiver in aesthetic experience has been recognized by postulating an "aesthetic attitude." This attitude is defined by a readiness to explore an object, to see what it might suggest. This attitude contrasts with the more familiar "instrumental attitude" whereby objects are considered more narrowly in terms of the desires they satisfy or the uses to which they can be put.

The necessity of the aesthetic attitude makes bold the point that art does not evoke or cause aesthetic experience. No matter how compelling the art object, there can be no aesthetic experience without a willing and able beholder. At the same time, it is clear that attitude by itself is not enough. There is still a need for the right kind of object to support aesthetic experience. Both the art object and aesthetic attitude are facilitating conditions for aesthetic experience; they are necessary and encouraging but not sufficient.

Is it to be concluded that aesthetic experiences do not have efficient causes? Leaving aside metaphysical arguments against the very idea of causes (e.g., Hume, 1748) and the fact that not one has yet been identified, this conclusion cannot be escaped. Aesthetic experiences could not have their own causes because they are part of an already caused stream of experience. As James (1890) made clear nearly a century ago, thinking occurs as a single continuous stream (see also Dewey, 1934). Although this stream can be analyzed into episodes according to need or interest, this in no way changes its essential unity and integrity. No matter how they are defined, episodes are not separate and independent things. Rather, they are as Dewey (1934, p. 598) describes them: "shadings of a pervading and developing hue." It follows that if aesthetic experiences are not separate and independent things, they cannot have separate and independent causes.

Insofar as aesthetic experience can be explained at all, it must be by mention of those conditions that make it more likely that the stream of experience will take this particular form. It is minimally necessary that the person have the right (aesthetic) attitude and be confronted by an object of the right nature. Under these conditions, it can be said only that aesthetic thinking is likely. Again, it must be recognized that even under these conditions, aesthetic experience need not occur. It seems there is a basic (incluctable?) indeterminancy associated with the aesthetic experience.

Conclusion

As even this brief appeal to art makes plain, there is much to learn from art about the psychology of aesthetic experience. Above, observations were made of the content and process of this experience; of the relationship of form to feeling in aesthetic experience; of the properties of art works that contribute to their functioning as vehicles of aesthetic experience; and finally, of the importance of aesthetic attitude and its implications for explaining aesthetic experience. This appeal to art makes plain also how much there is left to see. How does aesthetic experience take place? What are its features? How is this experience related to others before and after it? How long can it last? Is it easily disrupted, and if so by what? If interrupted, can it pick up where it left off, or must it begin anew? And which forms of aesthetic experience are associated with which feelings?

THE AESTHETIC IN WORK

To this point, the reader could be forgiven for thinking that the discussion has gone far afield of the problem of work feelings. Quite the contrary. What has been discussed as a psychology of art is no less a psychology of work. Aesthetic experience is not confined to art but is potential in any kind of activity. This section considers the place of aesthetic experience in the psychology of work.

The Aesthetic and the Practical

Perhaps the greatest objection to an aesthetics of work is that work celebrates practical values that are at odds with aesthetic values. In modern times, the idea of an aesthetics of work almost seems quaint. The jungle law is efficiency, and this is to be engineered by "scientific" methods of time and motion study.

A longer view of history, however, suggests a certain unity between aesthetic and practical concerns. The early cave paintings, for example, were not done as mere decorations. By depicting the hunt on the walls of the cave, the hunter "rehearsed" the event about to occur, as well as drew upon magical conjuring spirits to assist him. The art was part of his struggle for survival. What is exhibited as "primitive" art in museums today is commonly a variety of tools and objects that were used in daily life: pottery, spear handles, baskets, a beautifully carved bark canoe. All these objects could be analyzed in terms of their functionality alone, but this would leave unexplained the extraneous craftsmanship that does not increase efficiency. Dewey finds the root of early man's urge to include the aesthetic in his daily experience in his connection to the earth's rhythms:

> The participation of man in nature's rhythms, a partnership much more intimate than is any observation of them for purposes of knowledge, induced him to impose rhythm on changes where they did not appear. The apportioned reed, the stretched string and taut skin rendered the measures of action conscious through song and dance. Experiences of war, of hunt, of sowing and reaping, of the death and resurrection of vegetation, of stars circling over watchful shepherds, of constant return of the inconstant moon, were undergone to be reproduced in pantomime and generated the sense of life as drama. The mysterious movement of serpent,

elk, boar, fell into rhythms that brought the very essence of the lives of these animals to realization as they were enacted in dance, chiseled in stone, wrought in silver, of limned on the
walls of caves. The formative arts that shaped things of use were wedded to the rhythms of
voice and the self-contained movements of the body, and out of the union technical arts
gained the quality of fine art (pp. 631–632).

Hamilton's (1942) history of Hellenistic Greece makes it clear that few of the
boundaries that segment contemporary life existed for the Greeks. Scientific theories were written in verse; learning and leisure were considered synonymous,
athletes and statesmen shared a common status. Hamilton's thesis is that it was
this integration of aesthetic and practical values that occasioned a flourishing of
civilization never before (and perhaps never since) attained.[6]

Finally, the integration of practical and aesthetic values can be seen also in the
Renaissance and epochal idea of humanism. So intimate were the enterprises of
art and science during this period that it is difficult to separate the two. Artistic
advances in anatomy, perspective and construction of the great dome of the Flor-
ence Cathedral were occasions for advances in medicine, science, and engineering. The artist was a respected member of a professional class and was accorded
the same stature as the doctor and pharmacist—indeed, they were often members
of the same professional guild.

The weight of history thus gives lie to the modern idea that aesthetic and practical values are distinct. Even so, it must be admitted that it is more difficult
today than ever before to see the connection between the two. In the workplace,
the industrial revolution (with its irrepressible logic of the division of labor and
substitution of machines for people) brought more jobs with fewer opportunities
for aesthetic fulfillment (see, e.g., Braverman, 1974). Work offers fewer opportunities for the free play of impulses. Work activity is fastened more tightly to
external, rational control. In the arts, the movement has been away from making
usable things and toward making things that are aesthetic only.

These trends obscure the essential unity between aesthetic and practical concerns. Artistry is possible even in the most prosaic doings and makings of modern life. Dewey (1934) describes the by now familiar phenomenon of the average
person's finding more *genuine* aesthetic enjoyment in popular culture and the objects and events of daily life than in the highly reverenced and distant art of the
museum.[7] Dewey's case, however, rests on more than appearances. His analysis
finds no important differences between "the refined and intensified forms of experience that are works of art and the everyday events, doings, and sufferings
that are universally recognized to constitute experience" (Dewey, 1934, p. 580).
For Dewey, as for others (e.g., Hamilton, 1942; Henri, 1923; Langer, 1967;
Levin, 1957), linguistic distinctions between such concepts as work and play, art
and science, or whimsical and practical do not reflect natural divisions for people. These are misleading ways of talking about human activity that owe mainly
to Protestantism and the industrial revolution. For these authors, aesthetic expe-

rience is not divorced from everyday life but integral to it. Henri (1923, p. 15) puts the point simply:

> *Art*, when really understood, is the province of every human being. It is simply a question of doing things, anything, well. It is not an outside, extra thing. When the artist is alive in any person, whatever his kind of work may be, he becomes an inventive, searching, daring, self-expressing creature. . . . He does not have to be a painter or sculptor to be an artist. He can work in any medium. He simply has to find the gain in the work itself, not outside it.

Examples of the Aesthetic in Work

The aesthetic possibilities of work are more than a theoretical abstraction or sentimental ideal. Consider this account of the work of an engineer, taken from Kidder's (1981) chronicle of the birth of a new computer, *The Soul of the New Machine*:

> The first three bits of the address would contain the segment number of a memory compartment—in the telephone analogy, a given compartment's area code. The other bits would define the rest of the address. But Wallach wasn't interested in them just now. He was pondering the first three bits. Suddenly, without thinking about it, he was drawing another box below the first box. . . . After he had drawn the diagram he stared at it, wondering for a moment, ''Where did that come from?''

Wallach was delighted with his design for addressing memory and protecting its security, but

> the idea of placing that neat, clean structure on top of the outdated structure of the Eclipse repelled him. It was as if he had invented a particularly nice kind of arch for the doorway of a supermarket.

Later, after more design work,

> He was getting to like the looks of this architecture. He was starting to think of it not as a wart on a wart, but as a clean design with a wart on it. The wart was the Eclipse instruction set, virtually every part of which Eagle would have to contain, for the sake of compatibility. But there were some other empty corners of this canvas, aside from memory management and protection.

Wallach's design work is an embodiment of aesthetic experience. It is a creative play of mind at the fringe of awareness. The job itself even resembles art; it is a project with definite boundaries, dynamic tensions, a cumulative record of growth, and finally, a triumphant sense of possibility in the ''remaining corners of this canvas.''

The work of managing, too, has definite aesthetic possibilities. According to Peters and Waterman (1982, p. 83), leadership requires the manager to be the ''true artist, the true pathfinder. After all, he is both calling forth and exemplifying the urge for transcendence that unites us all." For Selznick (1957, pp. 152–153) leadership is art: "The art of the creative leader is the art of institution building, the reworking of human and technological materials to fashion an organism that embodies new and enduring values." This concept of the leader's job as calling for the creation of an organism embodying values makes the leader very much the artist. Like the artist, or his or her aim becomes to create "living forms" that involve others in some aspect of feeling (e.g., commitment, pride, love of product).

The aesthetic possibilities of the leader's job are perhaps nowhere more thoughtfully laid out than by Kuhn (1982, pp. 12–13). in his essay "Managing as an Art Form: The Aesthetics of Management." He points out that managing becomes art as managers create meaning and bring it to life through their actions on the job:

> In dealing with their own and other people's wisdom and follies, through the changing circumstances of organizational life, freighted with emotions and laden with reasonings, managers must sustain a point of view—an image of who they are and a vision of both what is—the complex network of interrelations that make up the organization—and what it can become. To borrow from Virginia Woolf a definition of managing as an art form, the manager continually affirms a point of view that is constructed and sustained through creative, aesthetic affirmation. Managing becomes art as managers create meaning, construct form, recognize patterns and place values on their relationships with others, both within and outside the organization. They affirm the structures of their perceptions in the face of the chaotic elements of daily life and the contradictions in nature and even the negations in themselves and in others. The meanings of their affirmations are as fleeting and fragile as the vital, creative part of the organization itself; it is art that exists only in process. It is in fact processional art.

Kidder, Peters, and Waterman, Selznick, and Kuhn leave little doubt about the presence and importance of aesthetic feeling in work. Echoing Bruner, Kidder describes computer design as a living play of the mind—a thought process that proceeds largely outside the pale of awareness. Peters and Waterman, Selznick, and Kuhn describe leadership as an essentially artistic process—a process aimed at making something that involves people in a vital and feelable play of mind. The leader is artist. He or she creates a living form, what Selznick calls an "organism."

More generally, it is perhaps this idea of aesthetic experience that lies behind the much ballyhooed and perhaps incompletely understood idea of "excellence" in organizations (see Peters and Waterman, 1982). Excellence is a kind of beauty, a kind of aesthetic. The excellent organization engages its members in transcendent values, values that rise above worldly concerns, values that can play freely at the fringe of awareness and bring aesthetic pleasure. Indeed, it is more than passing interest to note that the so-called excellent companies share many of the properties identified earlier with art works. These companies have clear and well-maintained boundaries. They are marked off from their surroundings as something special, heroic even. They also are alive with tensions of various kinds. Peters and Waterman speak of the tensions between quality and cost, service and efficiency, passion and reason. Kuhn speaks more generically of the contradictions, negations, and chaos of organized life. These companies also are records of growth. They are living histories. They celebrate the past with stories, in many cases stories about founding fathers and the values they stood for. As Peters and Waterman point out, these stories do more than recount a dead past; they are a basis and direction for the future. Last, these companies are suffused with a definite and unique sense of unresolved possibility. Always there is a vision of what the company can be, an image of a possible future not yet attained. In view of these characteristics, it is hardly surprising that these companies are able to keep their members enthralled.

From even this brief and unsystematic look at work, it is apparent that aesthetic experience is not confined to art but can be an integral part of work life as well. Further, it seems unlikely to be an isolated phenomenon peculiar to high levels of management or certain kinds of work activities (e.g., Kidder's design engineer). Rather, it is potential in any kind of work or in any kind of work organization that encourages the aesthetic turn of mind. The empirical question is thus not whether there are aesthetic experiences of work but when and how often. This question remains for further investigation.

WORK FEELINGS REVISITED

This paper began by noting that understanding of the complex emotionality of work is limited by an impoverished conceptual vocabulary. It is time now to make good the claim that study of aesthetic experiences of work can improve upon this vocabulary. How are work feelings now to be conceptualized? What might be desiderata for future research?

Aesthetic Feelings of Work

This chapter leads first to the conclusion that one source of feeling in work is aesthetic experience. Aesthetic experience is a definite kind, marked by specific contents (e.g., feeling, unself-consciousness) and a characteristic process (of thinking detached from purpose). Feeling emerges in this process and is intrinsic to it. What is felt is a play of the mind at the fringe of awareness.

This suggests that there is an aesthetics of work as surely as there is one of art. However obvious this conclusion may seem in retrospect, these aesthetics find little voice in the literature on work. Perhaps this is because aesthetic experiences are assumed not to be part of practically oriented activity. Or perhaps this is because the origins of aesthetic feeling are unobvious. Whereas it seems plain that work feelings could result from satisfactions or frustrations of values (Locke, 1976) or from social processes of interpreting and labeling work (Salanick &

Pfeffer, 1977), it is less obvious that they could "emerge" as a manifestation of the work itself. Finally, it could be that aesthetic experiences have not actually been ignored but have been understood as something else. Perhaps they have been masquerading in different dress, a prospect taken up presently.

Related Concepts of Work Feeling. How are aesthetic experiences related to other work feelings that are said to inhere in the work itself—for example, "intrinsic satisfaction" (Koch, 1956; Staw, 1976), "flow" (Csikszentmihalyi, 1975), "motivator factors" (Herzberg, Mausner, and Snyderman, 1959), and "peak experiences" (Maslow, 1971)? Consider, for example, how aesthetic experience compares to what Csikszentmihalyi (1975, p. 43) calls the "flow experience":

> 'Flow' denotes the wholistic sensation present when we act with total involvement. It is the kind of feeling after which one nostalgically says: 'that was fun,' or 'that was enjoyable.' It is the state in which action follows upon action according to an internal logic which seems to need no conscious intervention on our part. We experience it as a unified flowing from one moment to the next, in which we feel in control of our actions, and in which there is little distinction between self and environment; between stimulus and response; or between past, present, and future.

Reinforcing this similarity between aesthetic experience and flow is the further fact that "flow" arises in activities that are artlike. Obvious examples are games. Games also have definite boundaries (often defined explicitly by a set of rules), dynamic tensions (in the form of built-in challenges and organized suspense), a record of growth (as marked by a score, or by ordering of opponents), and unresolved possibility (typically guaranteed by a structure that results either in success or failure, winning or losing). Also, and as any child knows, games are not fun unless the players want to play. A certain receptive attitude is required—a kind of "aesthetic attitude."

Consider also the affinity between aesthetic experience and "intrinsically motivated" activity. Koch (1956, p. 71) defines the latter as activity that occurs outside the ken of need or conscious purpose. This activity is "intrinsically determined within the conditions of its own context . . . self-regulated, self-determining, self-motivated, self-energizing, and unfortunately, self-liquidating." More striking still is Koch's description of how thinking goes on in this kind of activity. Thoughts

> seem to well up with no apparent effort. They merely present themselves. The spontaneity and fluency of ideation and the freedom from customary blockages seem similar to certain characteristics of the dream or certain states of near dissociation. As in these latter conditions, it is often difficult to "fix," hold in mind, the thoughts which occur (67–68).

If Koch seems to be describing aesthetic experience, perhaps it is because he is. He offers the aesthetic experience as a particularly sterling example of intrinsically motivated activity. The overlap of these two kinds of activity raises intriguing theoretical questions. Are they the same thing? Does intrinsic motivation "emerge" in work activity in the same way as aesthetic feeling? If so, what sense can be made of theories that root intrinsic motivation in rational processes of causal attribution or categorization (see, e.g., Deci & Ryan, 1980; Sandelands, Ashford, & Dutton, 1983)? Does intrinsic motivation require an appropriately inclined perceiver, one with the right "aesthetic" attitude? Attention to questions such as these could lead to broader understanding of both aesthetic experience and intrinsic motivation.

Work as Art.   The prospect that work may be experienced aesthetically suggests that something can be learned about work by comparing it to art. It has been suggested here that work can have properties similar to art and that these properties can function similarly to encourage aesthetic experience. Specifically, it has been suggested that aesthetic experiences of work are made more likely by the four properties of boundaries, dynamic tensions, a record of growth, and unresolved possibility.

This particular parallel between art and work is offered more as hypothesis than conclusion. It requires testing. Even so, it seems almost commonsensical. If work did not have definite boundaries, it would be literally interminable. If it did not have dynamic tension, it would be lifeless and dull, perhaps insufficiently disquieting to arouse more than minimal interest. Without a record of growth, it would be directionless and afford no glimpse of progress. And without unresolved possibility, it would offer little cause to get involved. Looked at the other way, more positively, it is easy to see how work having these characteristics could enjoin the vital play of mind identified as aesthetic experience. With boundaries, it is possible to commit the otherwise dangerous act of relinquishing conscious control over perception and thought. With dynamic tensions, there is available a motive for involvement. With a record of growth, it is possible to glimpse movement toward resolution of tensions. And finally, with an unresolved possibility, there is reason to believe that something can be accomplished, that meaning can be found in the work.

More important than any specific parallel drawn between work and art is the very idea that work can be thought of in terms of its prospects for aesthetic experience. This is a novel and potentially illuminating way to look at work. This view centers on the characteristics of work that can evoke and sustain a play of mind at the fringe of awareness. It identifies as pleasurable work that can be experienced in this way. This view of work contrasts sharply with those taken by contemporary theories of work feeling (see, e.g., Griffin, 1987). These theories center on the characteristics of work that lead to specific interpretations of meaning. They identify as pleasurable work that is perceived as "challenging" or rewarding" (Locke, 1976) or to lead to "a feeling of being responsible for success in a meaningful job" (Hackman & Oldham, 1976). Comparing the two views, it can be seen that the former proceeds from an interest in the syntactic qualities of work (whether thinking in work assumes the aesthetic form), whereas the latter proceeds from an interest in the semantic qualities of work (what the work means). This difference in viewpoint is important and is taken up in greater detail in a moment.

Interesting though the parallels between work and art may be, it cannot be denied that there are important differences between them. Art exists for aesthetic contemplation; work does not. If work is experienced aesthetically, it is in spite of its other possibilities. Moreover, the evocative qualities of art are put there on purpose. This is not the case in work. For these reasons, art is bound to be a more rarefied and aesthetically more refined form. Still, and as argued above, these differences are not decisive. There is nothing in work that prevents it from being experienced aesthetically. As it is, the differences between art objects and work activities seem no more dramatic than those between disparate art forms such as paintings and stage plays.

Whatever differences exist between art objects and work activities, it is almost certainly true that just as there are no definitive properties of art, there are no definitive properties of aesthetically experienced work. Between aesthetically experienced work activities are resemblances that are again no stricter than those between family members. This suggests the important and sobering conclusion that there is no more hope of completely understanding aesthetic experiences of work than there is of completely understanding aesthetic experiences of art.

Aesthetic Attitude. It can also be concluded of aesthetic experiences of work that they too are likely to depend mightily on the person's attitude. The work must be regarded in a way that allows thinking to play freely within it. This means that conscious wants or desires that would otherwise direct thinking must temporarily be set aside. This aesthetic attitude contrasts with the instrumental attitude.

An important implication of this is that it is not possible to experience work aesthetically and instrumentally at the same time. To be in one frame of mind is not to be in the other. This incompatibility is a logical property of experience types. An experience of work must be aesthetic, or instrumental, or social, or something else. This is not to suggest, however, that a particular work activity cannot be experienced one way on one occasion and a different way on another occasion. Indeed it may be common for work experiences to alternate between types, perhaps even in rapid succession.

This logical incompatibility of aesthetic and instrumental experiences of work finds an interesting (and again suggestive) parallel in the incompatibility between intrinsic and extrinsic work feelings (cf. Staw, 1976). It is a well-established finding that feelings for a task can be crowded out by feelings about its rewards. Less well established, however, is the reason why this happens (see Sandelands, Ashford, & Dutton, 1983). Without putting too fine a point on it, perhaps the reason has to do with the impossibility of experiencing an activity aesthetically and instrumentally at the same time. Thinking is either detached from purpose or it is not. Which of these states prevails on any given occasion no doubt depends on the (probably subtle) interplay between task conditions and attitude.

Research Issues. Although it is beyond our scope here to make the case definitively, a few words are needed at least to make plausible the claim that aesthetic experiences of work can be studied scientifically. Can aesthetic experiences be measured? What about the conditions of work that promote these experiences? And what about the aesthetic attitude?

Because aesthetic experience takes place mainly outside awareness, it can be observed only indirectly. Self-reports might be used to determine if and when aesthetic experience has taken place. Although aesthetic experience cannot be reported as it occurs, it can be reported after the fact. If the report is made soon enough after the experience (before its trace disappears from memory), it might even include details about what the experience felt like and how long it lasted. Alternatively, aesthetic experience could be betrayed by its detachment from purpose. Where thinking is observed to occur without purpose, aesthetic experience can be inferred. This procedure is limited to kinds of thinking that leave observable traces (e.g., doing arithmetic, writing, puzzle solving). It is limited more fundamentally by being based on induction (there is no proving that thinking actually occurred without a reason). Finally, aesthetic experiences might be detected by their insusceptibility to interruption. This possibility is suggested by the fact that unlike other kinds of experiences, aesthetic experiences are self-determining, self-motivating, and self-closing. This being the case, they could be revealed by patterns of interruptibility over time—reflected, for example, in the number of interruptions reported or the amount of incidental learning during the activity (see, e.g., Sandelands & Calder, 1987). The prediction is that interruptibility would be lower during aesthetic experience and higher at other times. This kind of measure would, of course, have to be carefully calibrated and take into account other factors that also could affect interruptibility (e.g., time pressure, stress, task demands).

Probably less severe are the problems associated with identifying and measuring properties of work that promote aesthetic experience. Such properties as hypothesized above—boundaries, tensions, record of growth, and unresolved possibility—are in varying degrees subjective and thus may be measured best by self-report. Other work properties bearing on aesthetic functioning may be more objective—for example, duration, or physical demands—and may be measured better in other ways.

Finally, although there does not yet exist a validated measure of aesthetic attitude, such a measure seems practicable. What is to be measured is a kind of openness, a readiness to concede control over thinking to an outside object. Very likely this attitude is partly reflected in a variety of existing personality measures—positively in the cases of playfulness, creativity, sense of humor, ego strength, and self-actualization and negatively in the cases of dogmatism, authoritarianism, and self-consciousness. Assuming that a valid measure of aesthetic attitude can be devised, an interesting question is whether and to what extent this attitude is characterological or more narrowly situational. Very likely it is both.

The Concept of Work Feelings

As implied at the outset of this paper, this investigation was conducted only partly to show that aesthetic experiences are potentially an important basis of feeling at work. This investigation was conducted also to probe more deeply into feelings *of* work (as opposed to feelings *about* work), in the hope of moving toward a conceptual vocabulary better suited to deal with them.

Feelings of Work versus Feelings about Work. The aesthetic experience exists as a kind of thinking process. Its feeling exists as an emergent property of this process. Aesthetic feeling is *of* work, not *about* work. Aesthetic feeling is thus recognizably different from the mill run of work feelings described in the literature. Typically, work feelings are described as responses to the job or as judgments about the job. This can be seen in two well-known examples:

> Feelings are closely tied to how well [a person] performs on the job. Good performance is an occasion for self-reward, which serves as an incentive for continuing to do well. And because poor performance prompts unhappy feelings, the person may elect to try harder in the future so as to avoid those unpleasant outcomes (Hackman and Oldham, 1980:71–72).

> Job satisfaction may be viewed as the pleasurable emotional state resulting from the perception of one's job as fulfilling or allowing the fulfillment of one's important job values, providing these values are compatible with one's needs (Locke, 1976:1342).

These examples proceed from the view that work feelings results from perceptions about whether and to what extent a job gratifies job-related values or needs. They identify work feeling as an outcome of information processing the person takes stock of the job and forms an impression accordingly. Feeling is *about* work, not *of* work.

The distinction between feelings *of* work versus feelings *about* work parallels the ancient distinction between feeling and judgment and its counterpart in modern psychology between affect and attitude. It would not be worth spilling ink over were it not that these latter, more "classic" distinctions have been trampled almost beyond recognition (see Sandelands, 1988). Today it is not uncommon to find affect treated as if it were a kind of judgment, like an attitude. Indeed, sharp distinctions are rarely made between affect and attitude. Most typically, affect is regarded as a component of attitude, as part of a judgment (as for example in tripartite models of attitude). The problem is that affect is nothing like an attitude and could in no way be part of one. Affect is noncognitive. It does not result from judgment or information processing of any kind (no matter how nascent or subliminal). Rather, it emerges as a quality of ongoing activity—as a feeling *of*.[8]

The unfortunate result of confusing these feeling types has been an almost complete neglect of the nature and provenance of feelings *of* work. Ignored are the ongoing dynamics of work feeling. This problem is described by Landy (1978, p. 535) as follows:

> If one accepts the proposition that job satisfaction represents some affective state that is an important component of most theories of work motivation, it is distressing to recognize that attention has been paid almost exclusively to the conditions *antecedent* to that state. Little or no attention has been paid to the characteristics of the state itself or to the intra-individual past history of that state.

Landy, however, states the problem in a way that obscures its solution. In this case the difficulty is in the idea that job satisfaction represents an affective state. Once again, this identifies affect with a kind of judgment. In effect, it leaves no room for affect to have a dynamic life of its own. Whereas affect or "feelings of" are continuous, judgments are discrete. There simply is no room for the former in descriptions of the latter.[9]

Thus, there is much to be gained by keeping separate the concepts "feeling of" (e.g., affect, feeling) and "feeling about" (e.g., attitude, judgment). Most important, this brings to light the need to study feelings *of* work and the need for a conceptual vocabulary to talk about these wayward feelings. It is clear that it will not do to talk about these feelings in terms of information processing. Feelings *of* work are not perceptions or judgments and cannot be traced to antecedent acts of perceiving or judgment making. What is needed instead is a language that better reflects the emergent and processual nature of work feelings.

Although this paper focuses specifically on aesthetic feelings of work, it trades in concepts that are useful for describing feelings *of* work more generally. One important concept is that feelings emerge as manifestations of ongoing work activity. Feeling is a phase of doing. Related to this is the idea that work feelings are caused neither by work activity nor by the worker's attitude. Activity and attitude present only an occasion for feeling. Feelings of work do not have efficient causes. Last but not least, there is the idea that work feelings are bound inextricably to the *form* of work activity.

Feeling and Form.   Investigation of the aesthetics of work calls attention to the intimate connection between the form of work activity and the way it feels. What is felt as aesthetic experience is thinking that has the form property of being detached from purpose—a play of mind at the fringe of awareness. This suggests that there may be other coincidences between feeling and form in work—

associations that do not depend on assessments of meaning or any other sort of information processing.

This idea is foreign and undeveloped in the theory of work feeling. Where form characteristics of work are mentioned (e.g., in models of job design), they usually are lumped with characteristics of content and linked to feelings through assessments of meaning. For example, Hackman and Oldham (1976) explain the relationship between job satisfaction and form properties such as "task identity" and "feedback" with the hypothesis that incumbents use information about these properties to see whether they are "personally responsible for performing well on a meaningful job." This way of explaining feelings follows naturally from the view that feeling is a kind of judgment.

The idea that forms of work activity can be felt directly implies that it is unnecessary to know what work means to know how it feels. Work feelings can be understood simply as forms of work activity. Also, it indicates clear *how* a feeling could legitimately be said to be intrinsic to the work itself. A person with a positive feeling *of* work would neither accept nor even understand an offer of the feeling without doing the work. The feeling is of the doing; there is no cleavage between the two. Perhaps this is a clue to the longstanding mystery of intrinsic motivation. This idea raises a host of new research questions. Can forms of work activity be felt one way and yet have meanings that are felt in some other way? How are the syntax and semantics of work related? How do answers to these questions bear upon the distinction between feelings *of* work and feelings *about* work. Do these kinds of feelings intersect, and, if so, how? Other questions concern the possibilities of social influence. It is well known that feelings *about* tasks (work attitudes) can be influenced by the judgments of others (see Salancik & Pfeffer, 1978. Are feelings *of* work similarly influenceable? And, if so, how?

Although associations between feeling and form in work remain to be established, there are indications that they exist and that they can be studied systematically. For example, a recent paper (Sandelands, 1987) compared the grammatical forms and feelings of two tasks: writing poetry and grading exams.

> In poetry writing STATES and EVENTS are strongly linked. Where and how one begins affects where and how one proceeds which further affects how the task unfolds to completion. In exam-grading, STATES and EVENTS are joined more tenuously. Grading one exam has little to do with grading other exams. Associated with this difference in micro-structure . . . is a difference in continuity or "flow." . . . In poetry-writing there is a feeling of being pulled along by the task. In exam-grading there is a feeling that without constant effort, the task would never get done (pp. 132–133).

Thus it is suggested that the tasks of writing poetry and grading exams have different forms and different feelings. The flowing form of poetry writing comes with a feeling of being pulled along by the task, of being captivated. The disjointed form of the grading task comes with a feeling that constant effort and attention are needed to complete the task—a feeling that the task is hard work. Although such observations as these by no means prove the connection between feeling and form, they are consistent with the thesis that what is felt is a process having a particular form.

The study of task grammar in general promises greater understanding of the formal basis of feelings of work. The signal challenge for future research is to identify which work forms are associated with which work feelings. What are the forms of joy, amusement, frustration, disappointment? A theoretical language of some kind is needed to describe these forms.

Reclaiming the Aesthetic in Work

Such revisions as detailed above in our understanding of work feelings are important beyond what they indicate for theory and research. Although not the intention of this paper, it is scarcely possible to resist the temptation to give at least some measure of the practical significance of a serious concern for the aesthetics of work.

Obviously, and not unimportantly, attention is drawn to the aesthetic possibilities of work—to the many and various ways work can be beautiful. Although it remains for careful research to determine, a typical workday may contain several aesthetic experiences. Some of these no doubt are of short duration—lasting perhaps no more than a few seconds. Others may be of longer duration—lasting perhaps several minutes. Whatever the ecology of these experiences, they surely are an important aspect of work feeling.

Concern for the aesthetics of work leads also to suggestions about how to make work more appealing. In this chapter it has been argued that aesthetic experiences of work are more likely when work has boundaries, dynamic tensions, a record of growth and unresolved possibility. Although its shape and promise cannot now be anticipated, there is an art of job design yet to be developed.

Finally, concern for the aesthetics of work leads to the insight that the aesthetic appeal of work cannot be guaranteed merely by tinkering with its design. It is necessary also to prepare and encourage those doing the work to appreciate its aesthetic possibilities—to assume an aesthetic rather than instrumental attitude toward the work. One way to do this is by drawing attention to these possibilities. Perhaps it is not so silly to suggest that if there can be courses on art appreciation, then why not courses on work appreciation. Another way to do this is by protecting the worker from concerns that interfere with aesthetic experience (e.g., ego-related concerns, concerns about safety, security). By alleviating these concerns—such as by employment practices or reward systems—it may be possible to encourage rather than discourage aesthetic experiences of work.

ACKNOWLEDGMENTS

The authors gratefully acknowledge the helpful comments of Ellen Auster, Jeanne Brett, Art Brief, Larry Cummings, Jane Dutton, Mary Ann Glynn, David Hoy, Sid Levy, Walt Nord, Len Sayles, Barry Staw, Alice Tybout, and Jim Walsh on earlier drafts of this manuscript. This research was supported in part by a faculty grant from the General Motors Fellowship, Columbia University.

NOTES

1.   However innocent, this limitation in the scope of study may reflect an unwitting scientism that confines inquiry to feelings and feeling dynamics that can be rigorously operationalized and quantified. If understanding is to advance, chances must be taken also on concepts that are not yet amenable to such treatment.

2.   It is ironic that feeling, the most immediate and pervasive aspect of human being, should be difficult for people to talk about. Langer (1967, p. 57) suggests that this is because feelings are known without symbolic mediation and thereby without conceptual form: "To turn this knowledge by acquaintance into knowledge by description is not a simple procedure of reporting private experience, because the formal possibilities of language are not great enough to reflect the fluid structure of cerebral acts in psychical phase."

3.   This is not to say that there are not important similarities between art and science. Both are interested in human life and experience, to get it to "stand still to be looked at, and in principle, to be looked at by everybody" (Bosanquet, quoted in Langer, 1967, p. 115). Moreover, both traffic in the constructive use of metaphor. The artist's image or symbol, just like the scientist's concept or theory, functions to unite ideas or experiences not previously joined.

4.   It is interesting that aesthetic experience is often described as a kind of "work." It is said to be a kind of labor. It is said also to have wages—new and deeper understandings of the experienced world. This linguistic parallel hints of deeper affinities between these disparate-seeming activities.

5.   This contrasts with the idea that feeling or beauty is somehow contained in the art work—that the art work is a kind of symbol. This confuses the functioning of art with the way it sometimes turns out. Art functions only as a circumstance. Its beholder may "discover" in it a feeling or idea, but this feeling or idea is not actually in the work. It is in a sense "put there" by the beholder. After the fact, it only seems that the art work symbolizes that feeling or idea. Failure to recognize this has led to a number of gratuitous puzzles in aesthetic philosophy—for example, how can a work be interpreted in different ways? How can the artist's intent for a work be reconciled with the different interpretations given to it by critics? How can the significance of a work change over time? How is the "language of art" the same or different from natural language?

6.   She remarks:

> It is clear that in Greece the values were different from our own today. Indeed we are not able really to bring into one consistent whole their outlook upon life; from our point of view it seems to involve a self-contradiction. People so devoted to poetry as to make it a matter of practical importance must have been, we feel, deficient in the sense for what is practically important, dreamers, not alive to life's hard facts. Nothing could be further from the truth. The Greeks were pre-eminently realists. The temper of mind that made them carve their statues and paint their pictures from the living human beings around them, that kept their poetry within the sober limits of the possible, made them hard-headed men in the world of every-day affairs (p. 67).

7. Ironically, contemporary art also has discovered the popular movements, from comics to graffitti. But when these works are also given museum status, it seems their spontaneity vanishes, and all that is left is an idea, a "movement" in art.

8. It is easy to see how this confusion could come about. A feeling *of* can always be made to seem a feeling *about*. One simply attributes it to the satisfaction or frustration of some need—for example, a need for beauty. On logical grounds, however, it makes just as much sense (if not more) to suppose the opposite—that feelings alleged to result from satisfactions or frustrations of needs are actually misattributed feelings *of*. Satisfaction statements (feelings about) may not be feelings at all but rather just what a note-taking and rationalizing consciousness makes out to be the reasons for feeling.

9. This is a point of some confusion. Often it is assumed that judgment does explain ongoing feeling. For example, it is said that, once made, feeling judgments persist—as if by inertia. Or else it is said that feeling judgments are made continually—that what is felt at one moment is the result of a judgment made the moment before. But these explanations raise even greater difficulties than they solve. *How* could judgments persist, if not abetted by some process behind the scenes? And if feeling is not inertial, how and why does the mind make the same judgment over and over again? And why does feeling seem to be continuous?

REFERENCES

Arnheim, R. (1951). Perceptual and aesthetic aspects of the movement response. *Journal of Person-ality, 9,* 265–281.

Arnheim, R. (1966). *Towards a psychology of art.* Berkeley, CA: University of California Press.

Arnheim, R. (1969). *Visual thinking.* Berkeley, CA: University of California Press.

Arnheim, R. (1971). *Entropy and art.* Berkeley, CA: University of California Press.

Bosanquet, B. (1892). *History of aesthetic.* New York: Macmillan

Braverman, H. (1974). *Labor and monopoly capital.* New York: Monthly Review Press.

Bronowski, J. (1978). *The visionary eye.* Cambridge, MA: MIT Press.

Bruner, J. (1962). *Essays for the left hand.* Cambridge, MA: Harvard University Press.

Buck, R. (1985). Prime theory: An integrated view of motivation and emotion. *Psychological Re-view, 92:* 389–413.

Campbell-Fisher, I. G. (1951). Intrinsic expressiveness. *Journal of General Psychology 45,* 3–24.

Csikszentmihalyi, M. (1975). Play. *Journal of Humanistic Psychology, 15,* 41–63.

Deci, E. L., & Ryan, R. M. (1980). The empirical exploration of intrinsic motivational processes. In L. Berkowitz (Ed.), *Advances in experimental social psychology,* (Vol. 13, pp. 39–80). New York: Academic Press.

Dewey, J. (1934). Art as experience. Reprinted in A. Hofstadter and R. Kuhns (Eds.), (1964) *Philos-ophies of art and beauty.* Chicago: University of Chicago Press.

Gombrich, E. (1960). *Art and illusion.* New York: Pantheon.

Goodman, N. (1978). *Ways of worldmaking.* Indianapolis, IN: Hackett.

Griffin, R. (1987). Toward an integrated theory of task design. In L. L. Cummings & B. M. Staw (Eds.), *Research in organizational behavior, Vol. 9.* Greenwich, CT: JAI Press.

Hackman, J. R. & Oldham, G. R. (1976). Motivation through the design of work: Test of a theory. *Organizational Behavior and Human Performance, 16,* 250–279.

Hackman, J. R. & Oldham, G. R. (1980). *Work redesign.* Reading, MA: Addison-Wesley.

Hamilton, E. (1942). *The Greek way.* New York: Norton.

Henri, R. (1923). *The art spirit.* Philadelphia: J. B. Lippincott.

Herzberg, F.; Mausner, B. & Snyderman, B. (1959). *The motivation to work.* New York: John Wiley.

Hoffman, H. (1948). *Search for the real.* Cambridge, MA: MIT Press.

Hume, D. (1748/1955). *An inquiry concerning human understanding*. Indianapolis, IN: Bobbs-Merrill.

James, W. (1890). *The principles of psychology*. New York: Holt.

Kidder, T. (1981). *The soul of the new machine*. Boston: Little, Brown.

Koch, S. (1956). Worknotes on a pretheory of a phenomena called motivational. In D. Levine (Ed.), *Nebraska symposium on motivation*. Lincoln, NE: University of Nebraska Press.

Kuhn, J. (1982). Managing as an art form: The aesthetics of management. *Proceedings of the General Education Seminar, Vol. 11*. New York: Columbia University Press.

Landy, F. J. (1978). An opponent-process theory of job satisfaction. *Journal of Applied Psychology, 63*, 533–547.

Langer, S. K. (1967). *Mind: An essay on human feeling*. Baltimore, MD: Johns Hopkins University Press.

Levin, H. (1957). *Contexts of criticism*. Cambridge, MA: Harvard.

Locke, E. A. (1976). Job satisfaction. In M. Dunnette (Ed.), *Handbook of Industrial and Organizational Psychology*. Chicago: Rand McNally.

Maslow, A. (1971). *The farther reaches of human nature*. New York: Viking.

Matisse, H. (1936). *Matisse on art*. New York:

Peters, T. J. & Waterman, R. (1982). *In search of excellence*. New York: Harper & Row.

Russell, B. (1921). *The analysis of mind*. London: George Allen & Unwin

Salancik, G. R. & Pfeffer, J. (1978). A social information processing approach to job attitudes and task design. *Administrative Science Quarterly, 22*, 427–456.

Sandelands, L. E. (1987). Task grammar and attitude. *Motivation and Emotion, 11(2)*, 224–243.

Sandelands, L. E. (1988). The concept of work feeling. *Journal for the Theory of Social Behavior*, (in press).

Sandelands, L. E.; Ashford, S. J. & Dutton, J. E. (1983). Reconceptualizing the overjustification effect: A template matching approach. *Motivation and Emotion, 7*, 229–255.

Sandelands, L. E. & Calder, B. J. (1987). Perceptual organization in task performance. *Organizational Behavior and Human Decision Processes, 40*, 287–306.

Selznick, P. (1957). *Leadership in administration*. New York: Harper & Row.

Staw, B. M. (1976). Motivation. In B. M. Staw & G. R. Salancik (Eds.), *New Directions in Organizational Behavior*. Chicago: St. Clair Press.

Urmson, J. O. (1962). Aesthetics. In J. Margolis (Ed.), *Philosophy looks at the arts*. New York: Scribner,

Weitz, M. (1962). The work of art. In J. Margolis (Ed.), *Philosophy looks at the arts*. New York: Scribner

Wittgenstein, L. (1953). *Philosophical investigations*. Translated by G. E. M. Anscombe. London: Blackwell.

THE EXPRESSION OF EMOTION IN ORGANIZATIONAL LIFE

Anat Rafaeli and Robert I. Sutton

ABSTRACT

This chapter discusses the dimensions, antecedents, and consequences of organizational members' expressed emotions. We consider expressive behaviors that serve as a form of communication between senders ("role occupants") and receivers ("target persons"). First, we introduce a framework that specifies how norms and characteristics of role occupants influence the content, intensity, and diversity of displayed emotions at the role occupant level of analysis. Second, we propose that the emotions expressed by a role occupant in a given transaction may be refined in response to two other—more transient—influences: transaction-defining cues and feedback from the target person. Transaction-defining cues are features of the target person (e.g., gender) and of the setting (e.g., pace) that influence emotions displayed at the outset of a transaction. Feedback from the target person that emerges during the transaction can cause the role occupant further to modify his or her expressive behavior. Third, we consider how expressed emotions influence the behavior of target persons. We demonstrate how role occupants' displayed emotions can bring about both preferred and unwanted changes in others.

INTRODUCTION

This chapter is not about how people feel on the job. Nor is it about how they say they feel. Organizational researchers have considered such topics extensively, especially in studies of job satisfaction and the effects of job stress. We examine, rather, the feelings that people display on the job. Why is it important to distinguish between experienced and expressed emotions? Because there is no simple match between the emotions that organizational members feel and the emotions they learn to express (Gordon, 1981). When a food server at McDonald's smiles at you, is it because he or she likes you? Not necessarily. Experimental psychologists have confirmed that people can present facial expressions that are inconsistent with their internal feelings (Ekman & Oster, 1979; Mehrabian, 1971). This ability to exercise cognitive control means that organizational members can follow formal and informal expectations that they display certain emotions and that the sentiments they express may be unrelated to, or even in conflict with, their so-called true feelings.

Some people have jobs in which explicit organizational rules require them to express certain emotions no matter how they "really" feel. Mary Kay Ash, the founder of Mary Kay Cosmetics, expects her beauty consultants to take a "Vow of Enthusiasm" and to sing a company song, "I've got that Mary Kay Enthusiasm." Indeed, Mary Kay teaches her beauty consultants to offer fake enthusiasm to customers when they don't feel genuine enthusiasm (Ash, 1984). In contrast, other jobs require people to express nasty feelings, even if they don't feel nasty. For example, an investigator whose work entailed interrogating suspected felons told us, "They pay me to be mean."

Clients or customers may influence which emotions are expressed by people in service jobs. Rafaeli (1988), for example, carried out a participant-observation study in which she worked as a cashier in an Israeli supermarket. Customers taught her—inadvertently—about the presence of norms against acting friendly, even if she felt friendly; her good cheer was interpreted as a sign of inexperience. One customer told her, "I can tell that you are new. No one here smiles or is as friendly as you."

Studying the expression of emotion in organizational life is important because such behaviors may have potent effects on other people. In Frijda's (1986) words, an expressive behavior can be defined as an act that "establishes or enhances, weakens or breaks, some form of contact with some aspect of the environment or that aims at doing so or is accessory in doing so" (p. 13). Along these lines, we have argued elsewhere (Rafaeli & Sutton, 1987) that emotions expressed by employees may act as "control moves" (Goffman, 1959) that influence the behavior of people who are the targets of displayed feelings. This view is consistent with recent popular writings, including Peters and Austin's (1985) *Passion for Excellence*; they argue that friendly employees can attract customers and encourage them to spend more money. Such writings also suggest that employees who are rude, surely, or unenthusiastic can drive customers away.

The Southland Corporation, which owns or franchises approximately 7,500 7/Eleven stores in North America, has followed strongly in the spirit of such writings. In 1986, the corporation sponsored the ''Thanks a Million'' contest. Owners and managers of 7/Eleven stores could qualify to enter a drawing for a million dollars if their subordinates consistently offered good cheer to customers.

In other settings, the display of negative emotions by employees may bring about organizational gains. Police interrogators glare at suspects and shout at them in order to stimulate confessions (Arther & Caputo, 1959). Bill collectors use negative and esteem-degrading emotions in order to coerce debtors into paying their bills (Hochschild, 1983).

Furthermore, emotions expressed between members of the same organization may influence one another. Employees who want to maintain good relations with each other know that they must at least feign friendliness. Howe (1977) interviewed a waitress who described some ways in which such friendliness may enable employees to get what they want:

> The waitresses have to be nice to the bartenders because we need our drinks fast. The bartender has to be nice to us because if our customers complain it is his fault. The cooks are the least dependent on others, but they have to be nice to the waitresses to get the secret drinks we bring them from the bar (p. 100).

In short, the expression of emotion in organizational life is important to study because there is no simple relationship between employees' real feelings on the job and the feelings they present to others. Moreover, expressed emotions may have potent effects on the behavior, as well as the cognitions and attitudes, of people who are the targets of such expressions.

The power of expressed emotions to bring about organizational gains is also important to study because some common managerial assumptions may not be supported by empirical evidence. To illustrate, our recent study of 576 convenience stores revealed weak but significant negative relationships between the display of good cheer by sales clerks (greeting, smiling, eye contact, and saying ''thank you'') and store sales (Sutton & Rafaeli, 1988). Better theory and research are needed to help us understand the consequences, as well as the causes, of the emotions expressed by organizations members.

This chapter considers the emotions that people express at work from three perspectives. First, when comparisons are made among role occupants, there is considerable variation in expressed emotions. We introduce a framework proposing that norms and characteristics of role occupants are the primary influences on the emotions that they express to target persons. Second, although these influences form the ground rules for the emotions expressed within transactions, we propose that two other—more transient—factors further influence how each transaction unfolds: cues present at the outset of the transaction and feedback from the target person. Third, we explore how the emotions expressed by organizational members influence target persons. We conclude with a discussion of the hazards and opportunities associated with studying expressed emotions in organizational settings.

EXPLAINING VARIATION IN EMOTIONS
EXPRESSED BY ROLE OCCUPANTS

The framework in Figure 1 summarizes the factors that are proposed to influence and constrain the emotions expressed at the role-occupant level of analysis. the model predicts variation in the content, intensity, and diversity of displayed feelings. We propose that variation in these three dimensions is influenced by societal, occupational, and organizational norms concerning which emotions ought to be displayed and that variation in displayed feelings is further influenced by role occupants' enduring characteristics and inner feelings on the job. The framework also proposes that discretion about displayed emotions moderates the relationship between the two sets of influences and displayed emotions.

Dimensions of Role Occupants' Emotional Behavior

The tasks of defining, sorting, and interpreting emotions have intrigued and puzzled intellectuals for a long time. Darwin's (1965) *The Expression of Emotion in Man and Animals* was first published in 1872. William James posed the question "What is an emotion?" in 1884. More than 100 years later, this question remains unanswered: "the phenomena to which *emotion* or *emotional* is attached appear to be diverse. Also, there is no agreement about which phenomena there are" (Frijda, 1986, p. 1, emphasis in original). Describing the range of human emotion is beyond the scope of this chapter. Our focus is on expressed emotions that may, or may not, reflect a person's inner feelings. We consider displayed emotions (or expressive behavior) that serve as a form of communication between a sender and receiver. Specifically, we seek to predict variation in content, intensity, and diversity of emotions expressed by role occupants (the senders) to target persons (the receivers) whom they encounter in organizational life.

Content. The content of displayed emotions is manifested in facial expressions, bodily gestures, tone of voice, and language. These are complex behaviors. Indeed, many of the problems associated with naming, grouping, and sorting felt emotions also arise in the study of displayed emotions (Davitz, 1969; Hochschild, 1983). In comparison to felt emotions, however, there is greater consensus about the content of displayed emotions, especially facial expressions.

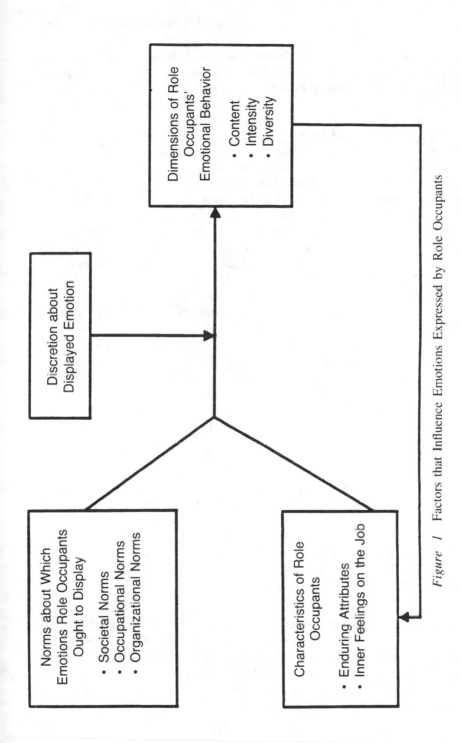

Figure 1 Factors that Influence Emotions Expressed by Role Occupants

Greater consensus arises because studying felt emotions requires making inferences about internal states from behavior; in contrast, emotional expressions are
behaviors that can be studied directly.

Psychological research on expressed emotions suggests that pleasant and unpleasant (or positive and negative) displayed feelings can be reliably distinguished by observers. Reviews of empirical research by Ekman, Friesen, and
Ellsworth (1972) and by Ekman and Oster (1979) conclude that both expert raters and untrained subjects can accurately distinguish between the display of
pleasant and unpleasant emotions. Moreover, the simple pleasant-unpleasant dimensions appears to be useful for characterizing and measuring emotions expressed across all cultures (Ekman & Oster, 1979).

Much less work has focused on whether the positive-negative continuum is
useful for studying the emotions displayed by organizational members. But some
evidence suggests that observers can reliably identify pleasant emotions expressed by employees who are working in natural settings. We found satisfactory
interrater reliabilities in a pair of studies where observers were trained to code
whether sales clerks smiled, greeted, thanked, or maintained eye contact with
customers (Sutton & Rafaeli, 1988; Rafaeli 1987).

Specific studies may also benefit from using more precise categories of expressed emotions, especially when the focus is on variation within cultures.
Kemper (1985) argues that any given culture or subculture can socialize its members to feel, convey, and identify in others as many emotions as there are social
situations that a member may encounter: "Where social patterns are very complex, emotional life differentiates into more finely shaded nuances in order to
accommodate their greater variety of socially differentiated conditions" (pp.
43–44). Geertz's (1959) ethnographic study of the Javanese culture, for example, indicated that Javanese were socialized to distinguish among three varieties
of expressed respect: *wedi*, *isin*, and *sungkan*. Although these sentiments are related to emotions expressed in other cultures, Geertz asserted that the nuances of
these three emotions were uniquely Javanese. Moreover, studies conducted
across different occupations and organizations may lead to different categorization schemes of expressed emotions even within the same culture. We expect,
for example, that professional actors and clinical psychologists will recognize
finer distinctions among expressed emotions than will engineers and airplane pilots.

Intensity.   This second dimension refers to the strength or magnitude of the
emotion expressed, regardless of its content. Laboratory research suggests that
trained raters can reliably distinguish whether expressed pleasant and unpleasant
emotions are strong or weak. Ekman and his colleagues, for example, report that
raters can reliably determine the magnitude of expressed emotions, including
happiness, disgust, and sadness, regardless of whether such displayed feelings

are contrived (Ekman & Friesen, 1975) or spontaneous (Ekman, Friesen, & Ancoli, 1980).

Organizational research has not focused directly on the intensity of expressed emotion. But ratings of intensity are likely to be reliable and valid, especially when the relatively simple positive-negative dimension is used. We contend, for example, that differences in the intensity of the positive emotions expressed by receptionists in dentist offices, people who deliver Domino's pizzas, and the beauty consultants who sell Mary Kay Cosmetics could reliably be distinguished by researchers or others.

Receptionists in dentists' offices typically respond to patients with mildly positive emotions. People who deliver Domino's pizzas are likely to display more intense positive emotions (at least to patrons), in part because they want to earn tips. In comparison to receptionists, they are more likely to offer broader smiles and to utter social pleasantries. Beauty consultants who sell Mary Kay Cosmetics display far more intense positive emotions than receptionists or pizza delivery persons. The television program "60 Minutes," for example, showed portions of the annual national convention held for these beauty consultants. They responded to one another with giant grins and streams of superlatives ("This is the best thing that ever happened in my life!"). They also sang "I've got that Mary Kay Enthusiasm," danced, and clapped their hands in a wild frenzy of normative enthusiasm.

Diversity.   The third dimension proposed in Figure 1 refers to variation in the content and intensity of expressed emotions: When multiple observations are made of a given role occupant, the range of displayed feelings may be large or small. We believe that laboratory research has not considered this dimension explicitly because, such experiments usually involve only brief observations of subjects' emotional behavior. But diversity is an analytically useful dimension in natural settings because the emotional behavior displayed by some organizational members varies relatively little, while the emotional behavior of others varies greatly in both content and diversity.

All organizational members—indeed all human beings—do display some diversity in expressive behavior (Frijda, 1986). Roy's (1959) classic study of "Banana Time" suggests that, even when a task requires or evokes little variation in expressed emotion, a wide range of emotions may be expressed during informal interaction.

But some role occupants do convey a wider range of emotions than others. Denison and Sutton (forthcoming) encountered evidence of extreme diversity in their observational study of a team of surgical nurses. They were intrigued, and occasionally a bit frightened, by the number of different emotions expressed by one nurse during the first day of the study. They discerned that the feelings she displayed included empathy and compassion (when talking with patients and their families), solemnity and respect (when working with physicians in the operating room), irritation and disgust (when talking about physicians behind their backs), surliness and laughter (when joking with physicians during break), and contempt and anger (when reprimanding the researchers for taking so much of her time).

Factors That Influence Emotions Expressed by Role Occupants

Figure 1 proposes two sets of influences on the content, intensity, and diversity of role occupants' displayed feelings: social system norms and characteristics of role occupants.

Norms.   This section focuses on display rules (Ekman, 1973), or behavioral expectations about which emotions ought to be expressed and which ought to be hidden. Display rules are distinct from feeling rules (Hochschild, 1979, 1983). Display rules refer to norms about which emotions members of a social system ought to *express*; feeling rules "define what we should feel in various circumstances" (Hochschild, 1979, p. 289); thus they refer to to emotions members ought to *experience*.

Societal norms guide interpersonal behavior in all cultures. Societal norms include display rules. The expression of emotion in organizational roles is influenced by general norms that govern which emotions should be expressed and which should be hidden in exchanges between members of a given culture (see Figure 1). Frijda (1986) reports that such widely held expectations influence both the intensity and the interpreted content of displayed emotions. He notes, for example, that the Chinese culture prescribes the amount of weeping (i.e., intensity of expressed sadness) that is appropriate at a funeral according to the relationship between the grieving person and the dead. The same emotional expression can also convey different messages in different cultures. Labarre reports that the Japanese smile when reprimanded because "Smiles should be seen as the social signal saying 'Thank you master for putting me right' " (1947, cited by Frijda, 1986, p. 62).

Norms about the expression of anger also vary across cultures. For example, temper tantrums and violence against parents are encouraged among children of the Yanomano Indians of Brazil because they are viewed as signs of bravery. But such behavior is strongly reprimanded by American parents, and chronic aggression is viewed as a sign of mental illness (Gordon, 1981).

Overarching norms of this kind also determine the content, intensity, and meaning of the emotions conveyed in organizational life. Consider the example of smiling at customers by members of three cultures. There is a strong norm in American service organizations that employees should smile at customers and act friendly; such social niceties are part of the job. The Lucky Stores supermarket chain, for example, instructs checkout clerks that "a friendly smile is a must.'' In contrast, as Rafaeli (1988) reports, such a norm does not exist in Israel. Customers there viewed smiling by a supermarket cashier as a sign of inexperience. Furthermore, in the Moslem culture smiling can be a sign of sexual attraction, and therefore women are socialized not to smile at men. Indeed, executives of a New York bank recently discovered that female tellers from Moslem countries would not smile at male customers—despite corporate rules that they should—because it signaled sexual attraction in their culture.

Occupational and organizational norms about expressed emotions are also primary influences on the content, intensity, and diversity of emotions that role occupants perceive that they ought to display on the job (see Figure 1). Occupational and organizational norms are sometimes easily distinguished. For example, a physician may learn the appropriate professional demeanor during medical school and may display that demeanor in the next seven hospitals at which he or she practices medicine. But these two sets of norms are difficult to separate; moreover, the means used to maintain such norms are similar for both occupations and organizations. Thus occupational and organizational display rules are discussed here together.

We have proposed elsewhere (Rafaeli & Sutton, 1987) that occupations and organizations use three means to maintain formal and informal norms about expressed emotions: recruitment and selection, socialization, and rewards and punishments.

Organizations use formal and informal practices in their efforts to select new members who will convey expected emotions. For instance, members of the team that designed Apple's Macintosh computer sought new employees who shared their wild enthusiasm for the product. The film *In Search of Excellence* (Tyler & Nathan, 1985) reports that a key part of the selection interview was "introducing" potential newcomers to a prototype of the machine. If an applicant did not react to the machine with the normative exaggerated enthusiasm, he or she was not invited to join the design team.

Organizations may also use interviews to emulate a job setting that calls for skilled emotion work. Hochschild (1983), for example, describes a procedure used by Pan American Airlines to select flight attendants who are able to display the good cheer required for the job:

> The recruiter called in a group of six applicants, three men and three women. She smiled at all of them and then said: "While I'm looking over your files here, I'd like to ask you to turn to your neighbor and get to know him or her. We'll take about three or four minutes, and then I'll get back to you." Immediately there was bubbly conversation, nodding of heads, expansion of posture, and overlapping ripples of laughter. After three minutes the recruiter put down the files and called the group to order. There was immediate total silence. All six looked expectantly at the recruiter: how had they done on their animation test? (pp. 96–97).

Socialization practices are among the most powerful means for inducing behavior that is consistent with organizational display rules. Organizational handbooks, training manuals, and training programs frequently include segments about emotional demeanor. Bank tellers, for example, are explicitly told that they should smile and be friendly toward customers. Along similar lines, Komaki, Blood, and Holder (1980) reported that they used behavior modification to "foster friendliness in a fast food franchise."

Socialization in some jobs entails learning to express both positive and negative emotions to others and learning how intense such affect should be. A woman who manages bill collectors told us that her subordinates learn to be pleasant to clients who are a month or two late on their Visa and MasterCard payments, to express firm disapproval to clients who are three or four months late, and to use nasty insults (e.g., "Why do you keep lying to me?") when speaking with clients who are five or six months late.

Occupational socialization conducted by agencies outside the employing organization may also include lessons about which emotions should and should not be expressed on the job. Aspiring department store Santa Clauses, for example, sometimes attend special training programs. The "University of Santa Claus" in Oakland, California, teaches future Santas to smile and be jolly "even when a kid who isn't quite potty trained has an accident" (Rules for Santas, 1984).

Socialization about the expression of emotion also occurs informally. A medical intern described in the *Journal of the American Medical Association* how she learned the display rules of the medical profession:

> In my first months as a medical student I was called a "softie" when I cried about patients.
> . . . Classmates and physicians told me "you get too emotionally involved with patients. You will never be a good doctor" (Bell, 1984, p. 2684).

Once display rules have been learned, organizations may use a variety of formal and informal practices to maintain employees' displayed rage, stoicism, friendliness, joy, or whatever other expressive behaviors are expected. We have mentioned Southland Corporation's "Thanks a Million" contest that was used to encourage friendliness among its sales clerks. Other programs that have been used in 7/Eleven stores include $25 gifts and new cars to clerks who are "caught" being friendly to mystery shoppers; in addition, large bonuses were awarded to regional managers when a high percentage of sales clerks in the stores they managed were observed thanking, greeting, and smiling at customers.

Management may even invite target persons to help enforce display rules for employees. For example, the Food and Liquor store in Hayward, California, posts a sign above the cash register that informs customers:

We Guarantee To Give You:

—A Friendly Greeting
—A Cheerful Smile
—A Register Receipt

If we fail at one of these, we will send you a $5.00 gift certificate. Please ask the clerk for a postage paid card. If you have any questions call our 24 hour toll free Hotline (800) 862-4672

Occupations also use a variety of practices to maintain display rules. Ethnographic research on poker players indicates that they use jokes, insults, and playful teasing to remind one another which emotions ought to be expressed and which ought to be hidden. An experienced player who routinely expressed too much joy and arrogance after winning a big pot (and who held up the game too much) was reprimanded as follows:

Man, you are way out of line. You ought to see yourself when you're winning. You're jerking off and telling jokes and holding up the game to your own speed. . . . You ought to play with a mirror in front of your face so you can see what you're doing (Hayano, 1982 p. 37).

Characteristics of Role Occupants.   Norms provide strong guidance about which emotions should and should not be expressed by role occupants. Figure 1 proposes. however, that expressed emotions are further shaped by a role occupant's enduring attributes and the emotions that he or she feels. Figure 1 also proposes a reciprocal causation between expressed emotions and characteristics of role occupants: felt emotions both affect and are affected by displayed emotions.

Psychologists who study individual differences have identified literally hundreds of *enduring attributes* that may influence which emotions people are predisposed to feel and express.[1] We cannot provide a complete review of this massive literature here. Instead, we consider three individual differences that are especially promising points of departure for research on the expression of emotion in organization life: gender, self-monitoring of expressive behavior, and emotional stamina.

First, gender has been found to be a consistent influence over which emotions people are likely to express. Gender differences in all facets of nonverbal behavior are well documented (Deaux, 1985). Findings suggest that women are more likely than men of display warmth and liking during transactions with others (Bem, 1974; Freize & Wicklund, 1976; Siegler & Siegler, 1976). And a similar pattern of differences appears to characterize verbal behavior (Putnam & McCallister, 1980). Moreover, gender appears to influence the content of emotions expressed by organizational members as they carry out their work roles. Rafaeli's (1989) study of transactions between approximately 1,300 clerks and 11,000 customers found that female clerks were more likely than male clerks to smile at both male and female customers.

Second, Snyder (1974) proposed that individuals vary in the extent to which they monitor their own expressive behavior. He found that a self-report measure of individual differences in self-monitoring predicted the extent to which subjects could control facial and vocal expressive behavior. He also found that people who scored higher on the measure of self monitoring attended more closely to situational cues about which emotions should and should not be displayed. Moreover, Snyder argues that people who hold jobs that require control of expressive behavior are likely to learn or be predisposed to monitor their expressive behavior more closely. Support for this argument is indicated by his finding that, in comparison to other subjects, professional stage actors engage in more self-monitoring. This work suggests that role occupants who engage in higher levels of self-monitoring are likely to have more control over the emotions that they express and likely to follow display rules more closely.

Third, we expect that emotional stamina will predict the content, intensity, and diversity of expressed emotions. Hochschild (1983) coined the term *emotional stamina*, which refers to the ability to express certain feelings over an extended period of time. She focused on the staying power of employees who are required to express emotions in accordance with corporate display rules over long periods of time.

Hochschild demonstrates that flight attendants are expected to display smiles and warmth as part of their job. The job of a flight attendant illustrates how emotional stamina influences the feelings that a role occupant will display. Flight attendants with great emotional stamina will have the ability to maintain required cheer over long periods. We expect that such stamina will enable them to maintain the expression of more intense pleasant emotions for long periods of time and that when they do "lose control," the intensity of their unpleasant emotions will be weaker. In contrast, flight attendants with low emotional stamina will stray from organizational display rules more often and thus display a lower proportion of positive feelings, display less intense positive feelings, and "lose control" and express negative emotions such as irritation more frequently.

Inner feelings on the job also influence which emotions will be expressed by organizational members (see Figure 1). Indeed, although there is no one-to-one match between expressed and felt emotions, a series of experimental studies by Ekman and his colleagues indicates that emotions conveyed through facial expressions are positively correlated with self-reported feelings. For example, Ekman, Friesen, and Ancoli (1980) found consistent positive relationships between expressed and reported happiness, as well as expressed and reported disgust. Moreover, Ekman (1981) asserts that even when people try to display emotions they do not feel, they may provide target persons with "deception clues" that lead to "leakage" of their true feelings. For example, a nurse who tries to act concerned and warm toward a patient whom he actually dislikes may betray his true feelings by tapping his foot and wringing his hands.

Although display rules may constrain emotions expressed by role occupants, we argue later that many people have jobs in which they have sufficient autonomy to express their inner feelings. Furthermore, some people may express their true feelings because they cannot suppress them. Snyder's (1974) work suggests that people who engage in low levels of self-monitoring will be less skilled at presenting false feelings and less likely to notice social cues that they should present false feelings.

Even people who work in organizations with rigid display rules may be allowed to display their true feelings on some occasions. Their jobs may include "time-outs" (Van Maanen, 1986) during which they have an opportunity for "role release" (Goffman, 1961, pp. 96–99), specifically release from formal display rules. Van Maanen implies that—as with all other social encounters—time-outs have display rules. But norms during time-outs typically support a wider range of expressive behavior and more frequent display of so-called true feelings than during times in which organization members are "on the job."

Denison and Sutton (forthcoming) observed such a time-out when the surgical nurses they studied took refuge from doctors in the nurses' lounge; during this time, the nurses felt free to complain about doctors and hospital administrators. Van Maanen's ethnographic study of Scotland Yard detectives suggests that the use of alcohol is a powerful sign that a time-out has begun; independent of the physiological effects of alcohol, the presence of wine, beer, or liquor is a sign that norms, including display rules, are relaxed, and people can feel freer to display their inner feelings. Similarly, Mars and Nicod (1984) report that when a staff party is held for restaurant employees, they are released form the display rules that govern their behavior when they are carrying out their formal roles. Indeed, some employees use these opportunities for revenge: "A few people will always seize the opportunity for role release to criticize, abuse, ridicule, humiliate, or otherwise behave offensively towards management" (p. 100).

Thus, although role occupants are socialized to present false feelings on some occasions, their inner feelings also appear to be a strong influence on the content, intensity, and diversity of feelings that they express in organizational life. This relationship between internal states and expressive behavior means that research on display of emotion in organizational life can be linked to the large body of research on variables that determine inner feelings associated with the job.

Thousands of studies have examined job satisfaction, which is a pleasurable or positive emotional state resulting from the appraisal of the job (Locke, 1976). Variables that have been found to predict satisfaction such as job design (Hackman & Oldham, 1980), supervision (Fleishman, 1973), and job stress (Kahn, 1981) may thus have indirect effects on expressive behavior in organizations. In addition to satisfaction, research on job stress has examined an array of internal feelings associated with job experiences. For example, a study by Caplan et al. (1975) suggests that role demands may evoke affective states, including depression, anxiety, irritation, and boredom. As with satisfaction, such inner feelings may also influence expressive behavior.

Finally, Figure 1 suggests a feedback loop, in which *expressed emotions influence felt emotions*. In other words, we propose that there is a reciprocal relationship between expressed and felt emotion. Our general argument is that if one offers false emotions (in response to display rules), inner feelings may change and become consistent with expressed feelings. There appear to be at least two mechanisms through which such reciprocal causation occurs, one psychological and the other physiological.

First, research on cognitive consistency suggests that if a person is induced to express an opinion that he or she does not believe, he or she will become uncomfortable. The discomfort can be resolved by changing attitudes so that they are consistent with behaviors (Festinger, 1957). A similar kind of discomfort caused by dissonance between private and displayed self may be experienced by a person who, say, has a job that requires expressing enthusiasm that he or she does not feel. Such a role occupant may eventually become enthusiastic, since expressing enthusiasm would enhance consistency between private and displayed selves, and thus eliminate the discomfort. Indeed, Mary Kay Ash (1984) offers advice to her beauty consultants that reflects this view: "We often tell our beauty consultants: You've got to fake it until you make it—that is—act enthusiastic and you will become enthusiastic" (p. 61).

Second, Zajonc's efforts to reclaim Wynbaum's 1906 theory of "facial efference" suggest another mechanism through which expressed emotions can influence experienced emotions. Zajonc (1985) proposes that smiling and laughing increase blood flow to the brain, which increases the level of oxygen in the brain, which in turn causes a feeling of exuberance. He argues:

> The proof is simple. Pull the corners of your mouth apart by contracting the major zygomatic muscle, as if in an intense exaggerated smile. After several seconds, the frontal vein will be gorged with blood. The zygomatic muscle acts as a ligature on the branches of the external cartoid *and* the slave action of the corrugator blocks the return blood. Cerebral blood is thus momentarily retained causing temporary intracerebral hyperemia, which in turn leads to a surge of subjectively felt positive affect (pp. 9–10).

Zajonc argues that frowning has converse effects; it reduces the flow of blood to the brain, which in turn leads to subjectively felt negative affect.

This theory that smiling makes one happy and frowning makes one sad has interesting—and untested—implications for the effects of organizational display rules on internal feelings. It suggests that people in jobs where they must smile will experience constant (physiologically induced) positive affect and that people who must act nasty on the job will often experience physiologically based negative affect. A long-term implication of this argument is that people who are required to act pleasant on the job may report higher levels of job satisfaction, and people in jobs where they are required to act unpleasant will report lower levels of job satisfaction.

This hypothesis could be tested by comparing "happy" and "sad" circus clowns.[2] Evidence for Wynbaum's theory would be found if clowns who work displaying happy faces reported greater job satisfaction than clowns who work displaying sad faces. Moreover, even stronger evidence would be found if a longitudinal field experiment was done in which happy and sad clowns reversed roles at several points during the study. Wynbaum's theory suggests that the switch from the sad to the happy role would lead to an increase in reported job satisfaction and that the switch from the happy to the sad role would lead to a decrease in reported job satisfaction.

Discretion about Displayed Emotions as a Constraint

What has a stronger influence over expressed emotions: norms or characteristics of role occupants? Certainly, hundreds of factors influence the relative weighting of these two sets of influences. We propose, however, that discretion about displayed emotion is among the most powerful influences on this relative weighting (Figure 1).

Discretion over expressed emotions has not been studied specifically. Much research indicates, however, that roles vary widely in the amount of overall autonomy granted to occupants (Hackman and Oldham, 1980). Our underlying assumption is that as people are allowed greater personal control over expressive behavior, they will exercise their power. Societal, occupational, and organizational norms will be heeded less, and thus enduring personal attributes and inner feelings will have a stronger influence. For instance, waiters and waitresses in restaurants are generally expected to act pleasant. But some restaurants provide waiters and waitresses very precise guidelines about expressive behavior. They may be required always to smile, or always to be enthusiastic, or never to be nasty to a customer even if her or she is deeply obnoxious. In other words, role occupants' expressive behavior is narrowly constrained. But other restaurants may allow waiters or waitresses to "be themselves" as long as they are friendly and may implicitly condone (or at least not punish) waiters and waitresses who occasionally show their true nasty feelings to obnoxious customers. In the latter example, enduring attributes and internal feelings will likely have a stronger influence than norms over emotions expressed by role occupants.

The example of Disney World employees highlights how role occupants' enduring characteristics and inner feelings can have little influence when they have low discretion over expressed emotions. These employees are trained to follow organizational display rules no matter how they feel, particularly when they are "onstage" with Disney "guests." We recently spoke with a new Disney World employee who had attended an employee orientation session known as "Traditions 1," which is required for all new Disney employees.[3] The trainer made a point of telling newcomers that when they are onstage with Disney guests, they must be nice no matter how nasty the guest happens to be and no matter how angry they feel. The trainer told an elaborate and funny story about why a nice customer might be nasty. He told the newcomers: "Everyone treats the guests as VIPs. The only reason we are here is that the guests come to see us and our show. 99% of the guests are nice, but it's that tiny 1% that you can't let get to you.'' Indeed, Disney employees learn that if they do let the "tiny 1%" get to them, it is grounds for dismissal. In short, Disney allows employees very little discretion about which emotions they convey and which they hide when they are in contact with guests.

EXPRESSED EMOTIONS BETWEEN AND WITHIN TRANSACTIONS

The previous section discussed factors that influence and constrain the emotions displayed by role occupants. We proposed a variety of factors that affect role occupants' perceptions of what emotions they ought to display. These factors include societal, occupational, and organizational norms and role occupants' enduring attributes and inner feelings on the job. The relative influence of these two sets of forces is moderated by the amount of discretion an employee has about displayed emotions. These factors have a strong influence over the feelings a role occupant conveys to the others. But specific features of the target person and the setting may help role occupants make more refined judgments about which emotions should be expressed during a particular transaction. Thus, we propose that characteristics of the target person and the setting lead to variation between individual transactions that occur within roles. Moreover, emotions expressed in a transaction may vary as the sequence of communication unfolds. Feedback from a target person may determine whether the emotions expressed initially are abandoned, revised, or maintained (Mars & Nicod, 1984; Rafaeli & Sutton, 1987). Thus variation also exists within transactions.

Figure 2 summarizes our view of the factors that determine variation in conveyed emotions between roles, between transactions, and within transactions. *Role ground rules* influence variation in emotional behavior between roles; these ground rules are the norms and characteristics of the role occupant. *Transaction-defining cues* refer to attributes of the target person and of the setting that educate the role occupant about which emotions should be expressed in a particular transaction. Cues from the target person include age, sex, race, or dress; cues from the setting include temporal features (e.g., night or day), atmospheric conditions (e.g., temperature), and the interpersonal context of the transaction (e.g., is it crowded?).

Transaction-defining cues enable the role occupant to categorize the transaction. Waiters, for example, may distinguish between "good" and "poor" tippers; flight attendants may categorize a customer as the "nagging" type; and dentists may categorize a patient as "sensitive" or "vain." Knowledge about these categories, which is based on prior experience, enables the role occupant to make more precise judgments about which emotions to express in the forthcoming interaction.

But neither role ground rules nor transaction-defining cues can govern the exact nature of the emotions displayed by a role occupant through the course of a

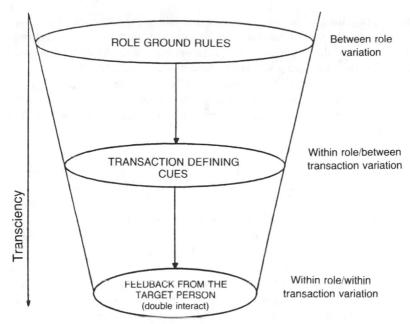

Figure 2 Expressed Emotions Between and Within Transactions

transaction. Rather, this pattern is further constrained by *feedback from the target person* as the transaction unfolds (Figure 2). We propose that this level involves mutual negotiation between the role occupant and the target person. Indeed, the give and take between sender and receiver is composed of a series of double interacts (Weick, 1979). The initial emotions conveyed by a role occupant are an "act"; this act stimulates the target person to respond with implicit or explicit feedback (an "interact"). The role occupant relies on this feedback to determine his or her "next round" of emotional behavior, hence completing a double interact. Thus, as the transaction unfolds, the role occupant and target person may subtly negotiate through a series of double interacts about which emotions the role occupant should continue to express, which to modify, and which to abandon.

The three levels in Figure 2 vary in degree of transiency. Ground rules are most stable since they vary only between roles. Transaction-defining cues are more transient; within any role these cues will vary to the extent that different target persons or settings are encountered. The negotiated aspects of an interaction are most transient; this category refers to the feedback that emerges as an interaction evolves.

Figure 2 suggests that each level sets the stage for the next level down. The first level, role ground rules, is the point of departure for each transaction. The second level, transaction-defining cues, leads to a further refinement of the emotions displayed at the outset of a transaction. The third level, feedback that emerges during the transaction, can cause the role occupant to adjust her or his behavior as the transaction unfolds. For example, waiters in a restaurant might be expected to exude enthusiasm and laughter. But a party of older diners who wear formal attire may cue a waiter to "tone down his act." If, however, members of the party drink a lot of beer and start joking with the waiter, he may view this new information as a signal to resume his usual exuberance. We explore transaction-defining cues and feedback from the target person in greater detail in the following sections.

Transaction-Defining Cues

Goffman (1955) proposed in his analysis of "face work" that "it is the rules of the group and the definition of the situation which determine how much feeling one is to have for face and how this feeling is to be distributed among the faces involved" (p. 214). Goffman's rules of the group are similar to role ground rules. We propose further that two categories of information help a role occupant "define the situation": *cues from the target person or persons* and *cues from the setting* of the transaction. These two sets of cues help a role occupant fine tune the emotions that he or she expresses at the outset of a transaction.

Cues from the Target Person.   These cues comprise the traits of target persons that can be assessed before a transaction begins, usually through only brief observation. These cues typically have the strongest influence on transactions between strangers since, as the relationship between role occupant and target continues, information is likely to emerge that causes the role occupant to modify his or her expressive behavior.

Cues from the target person include demographic variables such as age, sex, and national origin. They also include dress, jewelry, cosmetics, and flagrant mannerisms, which are akin to Goffman's (1971) "body gloss." Indeed, Goffman suggested that body gloss provides useful cues in the appraisal and categorization of others.

Imagine, for example, a professor standing in front of a new class. She observes the class and considers the students. Are they bright? How many are women? How many are foreigners? Who is smiling? Who is talking? Who is looking at me, and who is reading the newspaper? She may tell herself, "The guy in the blue shirt in the front row looks nice; but I'd better stay away from that redhead in the third row who is smirking." Such cues influence which emotional tactics she will use with the class and with individual members. Should she be harsh? Informal? Friendly? Authoritarian? In short, she seeks information that will help her determine the demeanor she should present to a group of people who are about to become the targets of her expressed emotions.

Cues from target persons are even more salient in transactions between a role occupant and a single target person or only a few target persons; the small number of target persons and their physical proximity enable the role occupant to discern relevant cues more easily. To illustrate, Mars and Nicod's ethnographic study of "The World of Waiters" (1984) led them to conclude that "what every waiter certainly must know, from the beginning of their first encounter, is into which kind of *transaction* the customer prefers to enter" (p.55). Mars and Nicod found that waiters distinguish between "boundary-open" and "boundary-closed" transactions with restaurant patrons. In boundary-open transactions, the encounter between a waiter and a diner is a kind of meeting of friends in which the waiter is an active participant. In contrast, boundary-closed transactions "put a frame around the participants, who are more concerned with exclusion" (p. 56).

According to Mars and Nicod (1984), there are rigid rules about emotional expression in boundary-closed transactions; waiters know that they must be pleasant and formal but not friendly. They also know that jokes are unacceptable. But these rules may be broken or modified if diners want a boundary-open transaction. Diners who seek a boundary-open transaction expect the waiter to be informal and friendly and to reveal his so-called real feelings. Thus, waiters look for cues from new diners to decide whether they are expecting a boundary-open or boundary-closed transaction:

> The waiter must learn the meanings attached to the cues and signals which people transmit so that he can distinguish the different types of diners and develop an appropriate set of responses. Learning how to classify and deal with the unknown diner by interpreting cues and signals has to be learned over time. With experience the waiter can distinguish various types of customers according to the kinds of transactions that they would probably involve him in (p.60).

Mars and Nicod observed that waiters rely on two sets of cues in the classification process: primary traits of a diner's appearance such as gender, race, class, and state of health, and secondary traits of appearance, such as manner of dress, gesture, posture, and bodily movement. When a waiter approaches a party of people—rather than an individual diner—he tends to use the host as the main source of transaction-defining cues.

Similar to waiters, bus drivers are also faced with the need to assess their customers with relatively little information. Richman (1969) reports that informal conversations among bus drivers often concern the analysis and classification of passenger types. Passengers may be classified as "sympathizers" or "the enemy," and this latter category is further divided into "bosses," "the awkward ones," and "fare dodgers." Passengers who check their watches as they board the bus, for example, are likely to be labeled as "bosses." Richman asserts that the behavior of a bus driver toward a passenger, particularly expressive behavior, is influenced heavily by the category in which the passenger is placed.

Members of higher-status occupations also use cues from target persons to determine which emotions they should express and which they should hide in a transaction. A pediatrician recently told Rafaeli that she always tries to spend a few minutes doing "paperwork" while the patients (parents and child) are in the office:

> That way I can learn a little more about them. Are the parents anxious? Do I need to support and console them before I deal with the child? How do they deal with the child? Is the kid spoiled? If they "baby talk" the child, I figure I should probably do the same. If not, I can be my professional self with them.

For this professional, a few seconds of observation—all the waiter and bus driver are allocated—are not sufficient. She has learned to create a longer opportunity for herself to assess the nature, needs, and expectations of the targets of her expressed emotions.

Transaction-defining cues may include information that is less obvious than that discussed above but equally important. An angry, fuming, red-faced customer, for example, is likely to trigger a different set of emotional behaviors from the role occupant than a pleasant, smiling, and patient client. To illustrate, one supermarket cashier Rafaeli (1988) interviewed reported:

> Some customers are always complaining. They do it loud, too. And you can see it on their face that they are angry about something. Usually it is about the fact that they have to stand in line. So we try to work real quick with them. We pass them through quickly without any nonsense. No jokes with them. Otherwise they will raise hell.

Target persons may also send cues indicating that they expect the forthcoming transaction to be devoid of any expressive behavior by either party. Indeed, Goffman (1971) observes that when strangers come into contact with one another, they may be careful to avoid any indication that they know each other or want to know each other ("tie-signs" in his words). When no tie-signs are made at the outset of a transaction, Goffman asserts that it will be characterized by "civil inattention"; in other words, the parties will carefully ignore each other. The omission of tie-signs may also characterize relations between people who see each other every day (e.g., people who ride a commuter train together).

Some quantitative research supports our contention that cues from target persons influence expressed emotions. Rafaeli (1989), for example, examined more than 11,000 transactions between clerks and customers in a national chain of convenience stores. She found that the gender of the customer—a transaction-defining cue that clerks can recognize immediately—influenced the emotions displayed by clerks. Rafaeli did not find a main effect for customer sex. But she did observe a significant clerk sex–customer sex interaction. Clerks of either sex offered more smiling, greeting, and eye contact to customers of the opposite sex. Rafaeli concludes that some form of social (perhaps courting) behavior spills over into on-the-job emotional behavior.

Goodsell (1976) conducted a field experiment in which he manipulated the status cues of customers who interacted with postal clerks. Goodsell reports that status symbols associated with manner of dress were significantly related to the courtesy of service and the emotional front presented by postal clerks. In a similar vein, Rafaeli (1987) found that customer status cues were significantly related to supermarket cashiers' emotional behavior: Well-dressed customers (those wearing jackets, jewelry, and accessories such as hats and ties) were more likely to receive greetings, thanks, and eye contact from cashiers.

These transaction-defining cues have powerful effects on expressive behavior. But the characteristics of target persons may mislead a role occupant about which emotions are appropriate for the transaction. The appearance or behavior of a target person may be inconsistent with what is expected of someone of his or her role and status. Mars and Nicod (1984) for example, described folklore of the restaurant industry about

> eccentrics who have none of the defining traits—either primary or secondary—that is appropriate to their particularly high status. Stories are told of well known lords, politicians and actors who appear in restaurants ragged, dirty, drunk or using crude language. These, which are impossible to authenticate, point up the anxiety that waiters experience in making their assessments on relatively little evidence (p. 61).

In sum, both the initial appearance and the behavior of target persons are important sources of information for a role occupant about which emotions he or she should present at the outset of a transaction. The power of such cues to evoke emotional expressions is so strong that role occupants may even ask target persons to deliver certain cues. Maister (1985) tells of a flight attendant on a delayed flight, where customers often feel and express anger, who encouraged passengers to set the tone for forthcoming transactions by making the following announcement: "Please pay us the courtesy of being polite to us so that we can reciprocate in kind" (p. 119).

Cues from the Setting. The second set of cues includes transient features of the context in which the transaction occurs. We discuss three sets of such cues: temporal context (e.g., day or night), atmospheric conditions (e.g., lighting and temperature), and the interpersonal context, or the number and attributes of people who are in the setting but external to the transaction (e.g., pace and density).

The temporal context, or timing of a transaction, offers cues about which emotions should be expressed and which should be hidden. Melbin (1978), for example, discusses "Night as Frontier"; he argues that different social norms govern human behavior at night than during the day. Although night is more relaxed, it is also more crime ridden and dangerous. Thus, cab drivers told Henslin (1973) that they feel more trust and are therefore friendlier toward daytime passengers because they are less likely to be robbed during the day. Cab drivers also reported that they could "get a better look" at the passengers during the day and thus could be more confident about the social status and intentions of the passenger (p. 344).

Time of year is a potentially important setting cue. Christmas and holiday time, for example, "tis the season to be jolly." But this espoused norm is threatened because everyone is so busy. For example, while Rafaeli was planning a participant observation study among supermarket cashiers, an executive told her: "I don't think that you should start until after the holiday rush. It is crazy before the holidays. There is so much work that no one really pays any attention to customers."

Along similar lines, bus drivers learn how to adjust their expressed emotions to the time of year. An American bus driver told us that she learned to be especially rude and surly to her passengers and to drivers in automobiles during the Christmas rush. She also reported that she warned new bus drivers about the emotional demands of the Christmas rush by telling them: "Remember, you get three accidents a year. Be sure to save one for the Christmas rush; people in cars are just crazy that time of year. You will want to ram at least one of them."

The difference between the scheduled and actual timing of a meeting or an event may also serve as a cue about which emotions should be expressed in a given transaction. When an employee arrives later than promised, for example, he or she is expected to convey regret to the target person. Richman (1969) suggests that even if a person is not responsible for the delay, he or she is expected to act sorry and accept some responsibility for the delay. Richman studied bus drivers in Manchester, England. He reports that a bus driver who is running late will try to:

> transmit the message that he had been moving heaven and earth to arrive at all. This he does by accelerating near the stop, then pulling up with brakes screeching loudly. If the conductor is also experienced, he will reinforce the drama by positioning himself on the platform to greet passengers with a facial expression which is a mixture of harassment and apology (p. 244).

A second category of setting cues comprises atmospheric conditions where the transaction takes place. For example, researchers have documented the negative effects that extreme temperatures have on subjective fatigue and mood (e.g., Nelson, Nillson, & Johnson, 1984). And Griffitt (1970) documented the social-psychological effects of uncomfortable temperatures, reporting that interpersonal attraction was lower among subjects exposed to high temperatures than among subjects exposed to moderate temperatures. When people are grouchy because they are hot, they are less likely to act friendly and may be less likely to expect pleasant emotions from others. Thus it may be legitimate to convey neutral or even negative affect when it is very hot.

A third set of setting cues includes the interpersonal context,—that is, the number and attributes of people who are in the setting but external to the transaction. The extent to which a setting is busy or slow can have a powerful effect on which emotions a role occupant conveys to others. To illustrate, Sutton worked as a clerk for a day at a convenience store. He noticed that the customers expected him to be friendly during slow times. In contrast, customers expected him to be fast and businesslike during busy times (Sutton & Rafaeli, 1988). He also found that he was nice to customers during slow times because, as his field notes reveal:

> [When] there weren't a lot of customers, I was bored with the jobs they were giving me. When no customers were around I'd spend my time putting prices on things, putting cans on shelves, and doing thrilling jobs such as cleaning the nacho machine. I'd get excited when a customer entered the store because talking to customers was the only vaguely interesting thing to do.

Indeed, Sutton was genuinely happy to see customers enter the store when it was slow and would act especially friendly in an effort to prolong the transaction. He engaged in a fifteen-minute conversation with one teenage customer, for example, about how to play one of the video games in the store.

When a store is busy and other customers are in a rush, clerks and target persons are less likely to display pleasant feelings to one another. Indeed, under busy conditions, occasional negative affect by either clerk or customer may be legitimate. Our research in both the United States (Sutton & Rafaeli, 1988) and Israel (Rafaeli, 1988) suggests that customers and clerks do not need to negotiate about the pace of a particular store or about the norms of emotional behavior under various pace conditions. Rather, clerks and customers reach instant, tacit agreement about whether "busy store norms" (where customers are to be treated as items for rapid processing) or "slow store norms" (where customers are a source of entertainment) apply to a transaction.

Interpersonal cues may also be provided in the behavior of the previous targets of the role occupant's expressed emotions. Helson's (1964) theory of adaptation level posits that prior exposure to a stimulus sets a reference point, or a baseline, that influences subsequent judgments. This theory is supported by experimental research by Thayer (1980) and Manstead, Wagner, and MacDonald (1983).

The theory of adaptation level suggests that interactions with prior target persons serve as a frame of reference for the role occupant about which emotions he or she should display in subsequent encounters. Thus, if a bill collector's first debtor of the day is polite and immediately agrees to pay her bill, the collector might use that prior transaction as a point of departure for the next transaction. He or she might then be especially friendly toward the next debtor. Conversely, if the first client responds with a stream of expletives and slams down the phone, then our hypothetical bill collector might be expected to be rude, or at least less pleasant, to the next debtor.

Feedback from the Target Person as the Transaction Unfolds

Transaction-defining cues set the stage for the opening of the transaction. These cues determine the emotional demeanor that will be presented during the first few moments of an interaction. But as the sequence of communication continues, feedback will be sent from the target person to the role occupant. A series of double interacts (Weick, 1979) will occur that instruct the role occupant about which emotions should and should not be displayed as the transaction unfolds. This view—that the give and take between the sender and receiver of expressed emotions is composed of a series of double interacts—highlights the active role that the target person plays in shaping the emotions expressed during a transaction. A story told to Van Maanen during his ethnographic research on police officers illustrates how new information that emerges after a transaction has started can shape the emotional behavior of a traffic cop:

> Policeman to motorist stopped for speeding: "May I see your driver's license please?"
> Motorist: "Why the hell are you picking on me and not somewhere else looking for some real criminals?"
> Policeman: "Cause you're an asshole, that's why . . . but I didn't know that until you opened your mouth" (Van Maanen, 1978 p. 234).

The policeman in this story began the transaction by expressing neutral emotions or no emotions at all. He encountered new information from the motorist that encouraged him to begin conveying negative and esteem-degrading feelings. The content and intensity of emotions may ebb and flow through the course of any transaction. But we propose that the overall effect of feedback that emerges during a transaction can be to maintain, alter the intensity, or shift the content of emotions expressed by a role occupant at the outset.

Maintaining Displayed Emotions.   Feedback may simply confirm that the role occupant's initial emotional expressions are consistent with the expectations of the target person. The feedback may be verbal or nonverbal. In either case, the message conveyed by the target person is that the role occupant should maintain the original emotional front. Clark and La Beef (1982), for example, studied the tactics used by physicians, nurses, police officers, and clergy in delivering messages about a person's death. They report that "death tellers" first deliver the news about the death in a somber manner. The behavior of the recipients of the news offers guidance about consequent emotion work. If friends or relatives react by crying or grieving, the messengers typically maintain their original somber demeanor.

Altering the Intensity of Displayed Emotions. Feedback that emerges during a transaction may also directly or indirectly encourage a role occupant to increase the intensity of emotions displayed at the outset of the transaction. In other words, the target person's behavior may encourage the role occupant to amplify his or her original expressive behavior. Komaki, Blood, and Holder (1980) suggest that smiling target persons (in the case, customers in a fast food restaurant) may reinforce role occupants who display positive emotions. Such reinforcement can lead to the amplification of the pleasant emotions displayed at the outset of a transaction.

Conversely, a vicious cycle can emerge when a role occupant acts angry at the outset of a transaction, causing the target to act angry, in turn leading to increased anger by the role occupant. To illustrate, Sutton and Callahan's (1987) study of the stigma evoked by Chapter 11 of the Federal Bankruptcy Code revealed that creditors used insults as part of their (typically futile) efforts to collect debts from the leaders of bankrupt firms. One particularly nasty interchange they observed began when a creditor ("a big fellow, with a red and angry face") started glaring and sneering at the president of a bankrupt firm. The president responded by saying that he did not deserve such treatment; he argued that the bankruptcy was not his fault and that it should blamed on the landlord. This remark made the creditor even angrier; he then told the president to "quit making excuses for your incompetence" (p. 19).

Shifting Displayed Emotions. Feedback from a target person may also lead the role occupant to change the content of the emotions he or she expresses at the outset of a transaction (e.g., from positive to negative or from negative to neutral). For example, Clark and LaBeef's (1982) work on death telling revealed that friends and relatives sometimes respond to news of the death by becoming angry at the messenger. In such cases, nurses, doctors, police officers, and clergy report that they typically shift from a warm and somber demeanor to a neutral emotional front and withdraw from the transaction as quickly as possible.

Feedback from target persons may also induce a role occupant to shift his or her emotional behavior, even though the target person may not have intended to stimulate such a shift. Rafaeli experienced such feedback during her participant-observation as a supermarket cashier. She tried to smile during initial transactions with customers, but customer feedback led to a shift in her behavior from a friendly to a neutral demeanor.

The first two examples describe situations in which the feedback from the target persons led indirectly to a shift in the emotions expressed by role occupants. Unterman and Sesser (1984), two San Francisco restaurant reviewers, offer an example of a direct form of feedback designed to cause role occupants to abandon obviously phony good cheer:

> Nothing can put a damper on a meal quicker than having a waiter bug you with "Hi, my name's Bruce" and continuing with "Is everything satisfactory" about twenty times. When

you see this sort of behavior going on at other tables, bring out a good put-down line. We've found one that works: as soon as the waiter walks up, stick out your hand and say in as cheerful a voice you can manage, "Hi, my name's Dave, and I'm your customer tonight." That's guaranteed to stop them speechless (p.vi).

We have also discovered—in several field stimulations of our own—that such obviously fake good cheer can be eliminated by asking the waiter or waitress, "What is the worst thing on the menu?"[4]

On the other hand, some target persons may use direct feedback to encourage the role occupant to convey fake friendliness rather than genuine indifference. Consider the following (somewhat disgusting) example reported by Hochschild (1983): "On a 15-hour flight from Hong Kong to New York, a young businessman puts down his drink, leans back, and takes in a flight attendant. . . . 'Hey honey,' he calls out, 'Give me a smile' " (p. 35).

EFFECTS OF EXPRESSED EMOTIONS ON OTHERS: THE CASE OF FINANCIAL OUTCOMES

Why do role occupants go through so much trouble to express emotions to others? One reason is that displayed feelings can be a potent means for influencing other people. Figure 3 summarizes our view of the effects of expressed emotions on others. It focuses on the relationship between expressed emotions and financial outcomes. Figure 3 indicates that such effects can be studied from both the perspective of individual role occupants and that of the organization in which they are embedded. It also indicates that conveyed feelings may change the behavior of a target person or persons in ways that are both preferred and unwanted. We explore below the nuances of how expressed emotions can influence financial outcomes associated with target persons.

The Individual's Perspective

Figure 3 proposes that expressed emotions can cause a role occupant to influence the behavior of others in ways that can lead to both preferred and unwanted financial outcomes. In other words, expressive behavior can either enhance or decrease a role occupant's control over a target person.

Control over forthcoming events is important to all human beings. Control can be defined as the existence of a contingent relationship between a person's actions and the subsequent occurrence of outcomes that he or she prefers (Seligman, 1975). Adler stated in 1930 that the need to control one's relevant environment is "an intrinsic necessity of life itself" (cited by Langer & Rodin, 1976, p. 398). This theme is repeated in Seligman's (1975) work on learned helplessness, Lazarus's (1966) writings on coping and stress, and Bandura's (1977a) work on

	Expressed Emotions That Lead to Preferred Outcomes	Expressed Emotions That Lead to Unwanted Outcomes
From Individual's Perspective	A poker player taunts an opponent about being "a rock"; the opponent then bets freely and loses to his tormentor.	A fake smile by a waiter alienates a customer who insults the waiter and doesn't leave a tip.
From Organization's Perspective	A TV station makes a decision to abandon the "happy talk" among the news staff and subsequently increases its market share of television viewers.	A bill collection agency revises its policy and instructs collectors not to be nasty to debtors who are less than 90 days late. Subsequently, the proportion of uncollected bills increases.

Figure 3 Effects of Expressed Emotions on Others: The Case of Financial Outcomes

self-efficacy. Despite differences in jargon, all of these writings emphasize that dependence between behavioral responses and preferred outcomes in one's environment is essential for human well-being.

This view that expressive behavior can be an instrumental act is reflected in Edinger and Patterson's (1983) discussion of the influence of nonverbal behavior, which includes nonverbal affective behavior, on social control. They summarize:

> In contrast to the common assumption that nonverbal behavior usually reflects a spontaneous and consistent affective reaction, this research strongly suggests that in many instances nonverbal behavior may be managed to influence the behavior of others (p. 30).

The effects that Edinger and Patterson attribute to nonverbal displays are not limited to situations where one person is more powerful or more dominant than the one he or she wishes to influence. Mars and Nicod note that although waiters tend to be of lower status than their customers, they can nonetheless "seize and hold the initiative by skillful manipulation and by using subtle aggression" (1984 p. 65).

A limited body of quantitative research has documented that emotional expressions can increase the amount of influence that a role occupant has over a target person. Most of this work has focused on eye contact and gaze. Hamlet, Axelrod, and Kuerschner (1984), for example, explicitly demanded eye contact from junior high school students (e.g., "Jessica, look at me") (p. 555). Their subjects were asked to do tasks such as hanging up their coats, turning around, and putting down their pencils. Explicit demands for eye contact from students "resulted in levels of compliance that were double and triple those of baseline" (p. 553). Along similar lines, Kleinke and Singer (1979) report that pedestrians who were gazed at by researchers were significantly more likely to accept a pamphlet than pedestrians who were not gazed at.

In organizational settings, the ability to use emotional expressions to control target persons can bring about financial gains for role occupants. Mars and Nicod (1984), for example, describe a control-enhancing tactic used by a waitress when she served families with young children. The waitress would knock over the child's drink but make it appear as if the child was the culprit. She would then offer pleasant emotions to the parents through comments such as, "Don't worry; he is only a baby," along with enthusiastic assistance in cleaning up the mess (p. 80). Mars and Nicod report that the continuous good cheer of this waitress, in spite of the discomfort that her customers had "caused," created a sense of obligation in the customers that was usually reflected in their attitude toward the waitress and in the size of their tip. The extra effort to increase her control was especially important to the waitress in such transactions because, as Mars and Nicod note, families with young children are reputed to be notoriously poor tippers.

The display of emotions can bring about a variety of desirable outcomes. Among waiters, waitresses, salespersons, and many other service employees, the most important outcome is immediate financial gain, such as a tip or sales commission. Some quantitative research has documented the positive consequences of skilled emotion work by restaurant employees. Tidd and Lockard (1978) examined the influence of smiling by a cocktail waitress over the tips she received from 96 customers. The 48 patrons who received broad smiles offered larger tips ($23.20 in total) than the other 48 patrons, who were victims of weak, or "minimal" smiles ($9.40 in total).

Skilled emotion work that includes physical contract has also been shown to generate higher tips. To illustrate, Crusco and Wetzel (1984) describe how touching by a waitress had a positive effect on the tips she collected. The touch manipulation is described as follows:

Participants [diners] were randomly assigned to one of three levels of touch. In the Fleeting Touch condition, the waitress twice touched the diner's palm with her fingers for one half second as she returned the diner's change. In the Shoulder Touch condition, she placed her hand on the diner's shoulder for one to one and one half seconds. In the No-Touch condition, there was no physical contact with the customer. The waitresses were carefully trained to behave consistently during the change-returning transaction (p. 514).

The authors report that touch had a main effect, although the difference between the two touch manipulations was not statistically significant. Customers in the no-touch condition tipped an average of 12.2%; customers who received a fleeting touch tipped an average of 16.7%; and the shoulder touch yielded an average tip of 14.4%.

The financial effects of displaying positive emotions are not limited to service employees. Bradshaw (1980, reported in Webb et al, 1981), for example, found that people who solicit contributions may also benefit from the use of smiles and good cheer. Bradshaw posed as a nun soliciting alms in Grand Central Terminal in New York City. The first day, she wore a glum expression and garnered $143 in alms. The second day, she wore a broad smile and collected $186.

The expression of negative affect can also lead to significant financial gains. Hayano's (1982) ethnographic research on poker players indicates that players use emotional expressions of aggression and hostility to weaken an opponent, and hence increase their personal gains:

> Players in aggressive games express much of their table talk in the idioms of power and dominance. They threaten to "punish" or "take care of" others. To punish another player means to beat him out of future pots or to "burn up" his money by excessive raising. Among some of the more vibrant players, splashing chips and money around, pressing an aggressive front, and talking a game indeed act as effective symbols of power. These players can "buy" pots by frightening and intimidating opponents who are too confused to defend themselves (p. 57).

So far we have emphasized how the expression of positive or negative emotions may increase the control that a role occupant holds over a target person. Nonetheless, as shown in Figure 3, the expression of inappropriate emotions, or emotions that are construed as insincere by the target person, may cause unwanted effects on the target person, and such effects can have undesirable financial consequences for the role occupant. Customers in restaurants frequently have negative reactions toward what they believe to be "phony" smiles. For example, we observed an incident in which a customer told his waiter, "Its OK. You don't have to smile. I'll give you a tip anyway." In such cases, the customer has expressed a negative reaction to what he or she construes as false good cheer. Customers who have expressed such sentiments are indicating to the waiter that they will not be controlled; in Whyte's (1946) term, such customers have "gotten the jump." The role occupant's emotional display has caused him or her to lose control of the transaction. Such feedback from the target person also implies that if the waiter continues to present his usual emotional facade, the tip will be small.

Along similar lines, Hayano (1982) described how professional poker players—whose livelihood depends on other people who lose money—have an unwritten rule that such "feeders" should never be made to feel bad about their losses. Perhaps the worst sin in this regard is expressing too much joy and arrogance about winning money from a feeder. One of the players Hayano gambled with chastised his fellow players for such potentially costly behavior:

> You guys better tone down on all your yelling and fooling around during the game. You're going to lose all the feeders, and then who're you going to be left with? Just yourselves jerkin' off as usual. Whose going to support you then? (p. 57).

Our discussion here, along with Figure 3, emphasizes how expressed emotions influence financial outcomes associated with a target person or persons. Such outcomes are important to organizational members because money is among the most flexible, universally exchangeable, and symbolically powerful resources. But the emotions expressed in organizational life also bring about numerous nonfinancial outcomes, some of which may also be instrumental from the target person's perspective. To illustrate, in a qualitative study of emotional behavior in slow versus busy settings, we found that when business is slow and there are few customers, convenience store employees often seek the entertainment that a new customer can provide (Sutton & Rafaeli, 1988). Thus clerks in slow stores are likely to offer customers positive emotions such as smiling, greeting, and eye contact because it introduces variety in an otherwise boring job. These clerks genuinely enjoy the interaction with the customer, and they believe that the display of positive emotion will cause the customer to stay longer. In this case, the display of positive affect has enhanced the clerk's control because such expressive behavior has increased the chances that he or she will be entertained by customers, a preferred outcome.

Control over the emotional reactions of target persons is another outcome that role occupants may prefer. U.S. deputy marshals who have the task of informing others about the death of friends or relatives, for example, told McClenahen and Lofland (1976) that an important part of delivering bad news was "shoring up or using interaction tactics to mitigate the 'badness' of the news, as well as to control the emotional reactions of the receivers" (in Clark & LaBeef, 1982 p. 367). Furthermore, many of the emotions displayed in organizational life may be expressed for altruistic rather than instrumental purposes. The death tellers may offer kind words because they care about other human beings. Or a supervisor may offer social support to a distressed subordinate out of compassion rather than an instrumental desire to increase the subordinate's productivity.

The Organization's Perspective

Figure 3 indicates that the emotions displayed by role occupants may also increase or decrease the chances that goals will be reached that are desirable from the organization's perspective. The emotions encountered by target persons are displayed by individual employees. But people typically develop an overall image of the emotions that will be displayed in a given organization. Such overall images arise because, after repeated encounters, stimuli generalization takes place. One may hear comments such as "people in the marketing department are really nasty." Similarly, as a result of stimulus generalization, authors of guidebooks publish overall judgments about the level of friendliness and good cheer that can be expected at hotels and restaurants (e.g., Unterman & Sesser, 1984; Birnbaum, 1987).

The contingent relationship between the expression of emotion by organizational members and various organizational outcomes is especially salient in service organizations. Customers can discern differences in the quality of the emotional front associated with different organizations. And managerial folklore suggests that organizational profits can be increased by employees who display positive and esteem-enhancing emotions to customers (Ash, 1984; Peters & Waterman, 1982; Peters & Austin, 1985). Such writings suggest that if all other factors are held equal, the display of positive emotions by organizational members can increase organizational sales and profits. A training program developed by a national chain of convenience stores teaches managers and clerks that friendly employees create regular customers. The underlying assumption is that clerks' expressive behavior influences the buying behavior of customers. The "S-M-I-L-E System for Increased Sales" module instructs trainees: "Smile!! Service with a smile will make them loyal and make them keep coming back."

Theories of human memory and learning may explain why, in the aggregate, service organizations that employ people who display pleasant emotions that at least appear to be genuine may promote organizational goals. Customers often have considerable degrees of freedom in deciding which organization to patronize for products and services. The emotional front that patrons associate with a particular organization may influence such decisions. Evidence from laboratory studies indicates that positive feelings about an event make it more accessible to memory and more likely to come to mind (Bruner & Postman, 1947; Isen & Shalker, 1982; Teasdale & Fogarty, 1979). Westbrook's research (1980) suggests that these findings may be generalized to organizational settings. Westbrook reports that customers who have felt good about a particular product (that is, their mood was better, they were optimistic, and they expressed general life satisfaction) are more likely to remember the store the next time they consider where to shop.

Moreover, pleasant or unpleasant emotions displayed by organization members may be positively or negatively reinforcing for target persons. To the extent that a customer encounters positive emotions when interacting with an organizational member, he or she will be more likely to seek further interaction with the organization. In the case of customers who are doing their shopping, for example, initial encounters with friendly employees may mark the start of an operant conditioning cycle (Skinner, 1953); the emotions displayed by store employees are the reinforcers, and patronizing the organization is the reinforced behavior. The probability that a given customer will visit a store a second time is increased following the display of positive emotions by salespeople.

A similar cycle may operate when debtors want to avoid the negative emotions previously displayed by bill collectors or when suspects do not want to experience the hostile attitude of interrogators. In both cases, the unpleasant emotional behavior of role occupants may act as a negative reinforcement. Target persons display negatively reinforced behaviors (i.e., they pay their debts or provide information) in order to avoid the role occupant's esteem-deflating emotions.

An organization's emotional front may also influence a target person's behavior through vicarious learning (Bandura, 1977b; Tolman, 1949). The target person does not have to experience the positive or negative reinforcement personally. He or she may watch other target persons encounter such emotions or may decide on a pattern of behavior after hearing or reading that employees of an organization are either nice or surly. For example, diners may select a certain restaurant after reading a review describing it as filled with fun and friendly waiters and waitresses.

But expressing socially desirable emotions may not always increase sales, despite case examples that support these conceptual arguments, including Nordstrom's (Peters & Austin, 1985) and McDonald's (Boas & Chain, 1976). We conducted a study of the relationship between displays of positive emotion (greeting, smiling, thanking, and offering eye contact to customers) and store sales in a national sample of urban convenience stores (Sutton & Rafaeli, 1988) and found—to our surprise—that there were weak but significant negative relationships between the expression of positive emotion by clerks and store sales. This finding contradicted the assumption held by executives of this corporation that more smiles led to more sales. We concluded eventually, on the basis of qualitative evidence, that the expression of positive emotion by clerks did not influence customers' shopping behavior because the service ideal associated with these stores (i.e., what customers expected to get from a visit to the store) has traditionally emphasized speed rather than friendliness. Thus, we contend that although extremely rude clerks may reduce sales, most customers who visit these stores don't care whether the clerk acts friendly.

The weak negative relationship was observed because of the differences in the norms between slow and busy stores. Stores that have greater sales are busier with customers standing in line, asking questions, and wandering around. Such busy stores provide little or no support for the expression of positive emotion because people are in a hurry, and they are irritated because of time pressure. In contrast, norms in slow stores support the expression of positive emotion because clerks and customers are not irritated by such pressures, they have time to be friendly, and clerks in slow stores view customers as an important source of entertainment in their boring jobs.

Finally, as Figure 3 indicates, emotions expressed by employees—rather than having no effect or financial performance—may backfire completely and reduce the organization's control over clients or customers. Figure 3 offers the hypothetical example of a bill collection agency that makes less money because of a change in display rules: bill collectors are instructed to be less nasty to some debtors. We also presented several examples earlier of restaurants whose customers were offended by phony good cheer; when such false cheerfulness is presented by any or all employees, it may become part of the organization's image and may drive customers away.

DISCUSSION

We urge the field to devote more effort to building and testing theory about the dimensions, causes, and consequences of the emotions expressed in organizational life. Indeed, a primary aim of this chapter is to generate interest in this topic. Yet our optimism about studying expressive behavior in organizational settings occasionally wavers; while writing this and other papers on this topic, we have been haunted by several nagging doubts about the proposed perspective and its implications for empirical research. We describe three of the most troublesome of these concerns below, along with arguments why they do not pose a severe threat to this stream of research.

1. Are We Really Proposing Anything New?

We have argued here and elsewhere (Rafaeli & Sutton, 1987) that although organizational researchers have paid much attention to the internal feelings of organizational members, they have paid relatively little attention to the expression of emotion in organizational life. Nonetheless we have, on occasion, been concerned that we are simply disguising old topics under new labels. In particular, research on leadership and on social support has, at least implicitly, considered the expression of emotion. Three frequently cited dimensions of leadership are "consideration" (Fleishman, 1973), "concern for people" (Blake & Mouton, 1968), and the extent to which leaders are employee centered (Likert, 1967). Each dimension refers in part to the intensity of the positive emotions that leaders convey to their subordinates.

Similarly, social support theorists have identified the specific dimension of "emotional support" or "affective support," which is defined as "expressions of liking, admiration, respect or love" (House, 1981 p. 16). Both leadership and social support researchers have developed survey methods that measure the intensity and frequency with which positive affect is conveyed by organizational members. In the language used here, these survey questions may measure the expressive behavior of role occupants from the perspective of target persons.

These streams of research are clearly related to work on expressed emotions. Nonetheless, neither stream has been viewed by investigators as the explicit study of expressed emotions. "Consideration" and "social support" are usually conceived of and measured in ways that confound them with phenomena other than expressive behavior. For example, although Fleishman's measure of consideration (see Cook et al., 1981, p. 238) does include items that imply expressed positive emotions (e.g., "He is friendly and easily approached"), many other items in this scale measure aspects of consideration that have nothing to do with expressed emotion, such as flexibility (e.g., "He is willing to make changes") and communication skills (e.g., "He is easy to understand").

In a similar vein, survey research on social support has used items that do not distinguish between emotional and nonemotional forms of help from others. Caplan and his colleagues' (1975) measure of social support, for example, asks respondents if supervisors and other people at work "do things to make your work life easier for you" and "can be relied on when things get tough at work." In short, existing studies of leadership and social support measure a set of behaviors that is much broader, and therefore more vague, than expressed emotion.

2. Can Expressive Behavior Be Studied with Rigor?

We have also had concerns about whether emotions can be studied with rigor. Research on emotions has historically relied on self-report data, especially introspection, which often suffer from measurement error and response bias. Establishing the reliability and validity of introspective data is especially difficult. When a person reports feeling happy or sad, we cannot send another observer into the respondent's head to confirm such feelings.

Nonetheless, although methodological problems do arise, expressed emotions are easier to study than internal feelings. Such behaviors can be observed directly. And expressed emotions are present wherever there are human beings. We do not assert that our perspective eliminates the problems associated with studying internal feelings. Indeed, the framework presented in Figure 1 encompasses internal feelings; thus researchers who study the effects of internal feelings on expressive behavior will face the methodological problems associated with introspective data. But at least the primary variable described here, expressive behavior, can be observed and measured directly.

Our efforts to study expressive behavior have also led us to develop a pair of suggestions about how colleagues who join this stream of research can make the best use of their efforts; (1) If you want to do quantitative research, focus on categories of expressive behaviors that are simple and observable, and (2) use qualitative research to capture the complexities of expressive behavior and to develop new theory.

Simple and readily observable expressive behaviors are especially amenable to structured observation. Our research has taught us that behaviors including smiling, greeting, thanking, and maintaining eye contact can be reliably assessed in natural settings. To illustrate this point, one study revealed satisfactory interrater reliability among eight observers of these behaviors; reliability coefficients for each behavior ranged from .94 to .67. The mean correlation was .82, and the median correlation was .85 (Sutton & Rafaeli, 1988). Moreover, when the four behaviors (greeting, smiling, eye contact, and thanking) were combined into an index, we obtained a Cronbach's alpha of .76 at the store level of analysis (Sutton & Rafaeli, 1988) and .92 at the clerk level of analysis (Rafaeli, 1989).

We believe that this form of structured observation, and related methods, are useful for capturing the basic pleasant and unpleasant emotions conveyed by employees. But we may be looking where the light shines brightest. We worry about this problem because smiling, greeting, and eye contact are only a small subset of the emotions that people express in organizational life. Given current knowledge, we believe that these simple behaviors are a valuable point of departure for quantitative research. Yet for understanding the shades of emotion expressed by organizational members—and for generating new theory—qualitative evidence is more useful.

The apparent precision of quantitative evidence can lead to a shallow and inaccurate picture of the role of expressive behavior in organizational life. Fine distinctions between emotions are difficult to make if one uses structured observations, even if the precise methods developed by Ekman and his colleagues are employed. In contrast, qualitative evidence allows researchers to identify more nuances in expressive behavior. For example, Geertz (1959) was able to distinguish between three slightly different kinds of expressed respect in his ethnographic work with the Javanese. Existing quantitative methods would be of little use for distinguishing among these subtle shades of respect.

Even when expressive behaviors are relatively simple, qualitative evidence is especially well suited for induction, for discovering new things. When we embarked on our quantitative study of the impact of clerk emotional behavior on store performance, it never occurred to us that customers might be a source of entertainment for bored clerks. Nor did we anticipate that displayed emotions are used by clerks use to prolong interactions with their customers. Our hypothesis—that in slow stores customers are an important source of entertainment for bored clerks—was discovered only after we began gathering qualitative data (Sutton & Rafaeli, 1988).

3. So What? Isn't It a Trivial Topic?

We are haunted by this concern most strongly when one of us was invited to give a seminar at a prestigious management school. The invited speaker suggested a talk on expressed emotions, which evoked a cool and unenthusiastic response from the professor who made the invitation. Another professor from the management school later called to tell the invited speaker (for "your own good") that "we don't care whether people smile or frown at work." In particular, the second professor asserted that management theorists at his school didn't care whether clerks in convenience stores were friendly or rude since it "didn't have anything to do" with managing a Fortune 500 company. These arguments were intimidating, and the topic of talk was changed. But, in retrospect, this decision was wrong. We believe that the study of expressed emotions has important implications for management, even for executives in Fortune 500 companies.

Our conversations with executives who manage chains of convenience stores and the empirical research on such organizations that we described earlier are telling. The Southland Corporation, a Fortune 500 company, recently spent over $11 million on the Thanks a Million contest, which was designed to increase the portion of 7/Eleven clerks who offered good cheer to customers. Southland executives thought that the contest was a good investment since they believed that friendly clerks encourage customers to spend more during each visit and to return more frequently. They reasoned that increasing employee courtesy might be a relatively inexpensive way to increase sales 1 to 2%; a 2% increase in sales would bring in more than $100 million in additional revenues to the corporation.

Our cross-sectional research on convenience stores contradicts this assumption (Sutton & Rafaeli, 1988), but it is not conclusive. Unfortunately, theory and research on the power of expressed emotions are not sufficiently well developed to discover if indeed smiling clerks do increase sales in other types of stores. One task for organizational researchers is to provide an answer to questions of this kind.

Southland executives are not alone in needing the answer to such empirical questions. Our economy is shifting away from manufacturing and toward service industries. As a result, leaders of an increasing number of Fortune 500 firms need to understand the nuances of the relationship between the expression of positive emotions and customer behavior. Other executives, such as those who manage the collection of overdue Visa and MasterCard bills, need to understand the relationship between expressed negative emotions and the behavior of debtors. And all leaders could benefit from knowledge about the influence of emotions expressed between members of the organizations that they manage. For example, some firms encourage laughter and giggles during conversations, while such behavior is viewed as unprofessional and may lead to sanctions in other firms. It would be useful to know if employees who are encouraged to laugh and giggle are more creative and more loyal, as some managers claim, or if they generate silly ideas and don't take their work seriously, as other managers claim.

The shift to a service economy (Heskett, 1986), which has occurred in tandem with popular writings on the importance of employees' expressive behavior in service organizations (e.g. Ash, 1984; Peters & Austin, 1985), also means that an increasing number of employees hold jobs in which they are expected to follow carefully specified display rules about which emotions they should and should not display. The impact of such norms on employee well-being is another aspect of the so-what question that executives should be concerned with, for both humanistic and financial reasons. The humanistic considerations are obvious. But employee well-being also has financial impact because physically and mentally ill employees may lead to costly increases in health insurance premiums, turnovers, and absenteeism.

Hochschild (1983) offers qualitative evidence that emotional dissonance has negative effects on the well-being of flight attendants. Emotional dissonance occurs when employees express emotions that satisfy display rules but clash with their inner feelings. We have qualified Hochschild's argument (see Rafaeli & Sutton, 1987) and proposed that the impact of emotional dissonance depends on whether an employee has internalized organizational display rules. If employees believe that offering false emotions should not be part of the job, then they are *faking in bad faith*. But if employees offer false emotions and believe that offering them should be part of their job, then they are *faking in good faith*. We contend that emotional dissonance will be most strongly related to strain among people who fake in bad faith since their level of psychological discomfort will be much higher than people who fake in good faith.

Hochschild's (1983) predictions about the negative effects of emotional dissonance, along with our refinements, are only speculation at this point. Occupational stress researchers have yet to examine systematically the consequences of expressing fake emotions for the mental and physical health of organizational members. Moreover, they have yet to examine how emotional deviance, or expressing emotions that violate display rules (Rafaeli & Sutton, 1987; Thoits, 1985), can influence the mental and physical well-being of role occupants.

Recognizing the role that emotions play in organizational life also has important implications for a wide range of organizational practices. If managers believe that employees should smile and be cheerful on the job, then tools for assessing and predicting the occurrence of such behaviors need to be developed. The literature on personnel selection at present offers very little help in determining whether a flight attendant or a salesperson will be friendly to their clients, especially during interactions with the 100th or 1000th client encountered. Knowledge about teaching, monitoring, and maintaining a given set of expressive behaviors is also limited. We are still unsure, for example, what to tell a manager who wants to ensure that all receptionists in his or her company will act friendly to customers. Along similar lines, it is equally difficult to determine what a manager at a bill collection agency can do to incite subordinates to act nasty toward delinquent debtors.

We believe that these are difficult and important questions for future research. We also believe that organizational researchers can answer them. If emotional dissonance and deviance prove to have little or no effect on well-being, then leaders need not worry about the damage wrought by implementing narrowly defined display rules and by giving employees little discretion over their expressive behavior. If so, "only" the questions of selection, socialization, and maintaining such behaviors over long periods of time need to be addressed.

In contrast, however, if Hochschild is right, then enforcing such norms may come back to haunt leaders when employees experience mental and physical illness and when organizations pay the direct and indirect costs of the damage to individual well-being. Furthermore, managers and organizational researchers will have to scramble to detect which display rules can cause such damage and which do not.

CONCLUDING REMARKS

Our hope is that this chapter will guide and inspire additional theory building and testing on the expression of emotion in organizational life. We have sought to encourage such efforts through typical scholarly means. We argued that the topic was important. We defined the dimensions of expressive behavior. We described how this dependent variable is shaped by phenomena at three levels of analysis. We made proposals about the effects of such behavior on others. And in the discussion, we raised three of our most haunting doubts about the hazards of studying this subject and then offered (perhaps self-serving) arguments about why these are not severe threats to the study of expressed emotions in organizational settings.

In closing, we offer a less common reason why our colleagues—you, dear reader—might consider studying expressed emotions: IT IS INTERESTING. Studying this interesting topic has offered us some sweet rewards that other researchers may find appealing. We have taken so much pleasure from studying, writing, talking, and arguing about expressed emotions that we often forget that we were "working." We have also found that our colleagues and our students seem especially interested in hearing about research on expressed emotion. Frankly, they seem far more interested in hearing about expressed emotions than about our other research. And it is not only fun to talk about a topic that generates smiles and laughs. If Weick (1979) is right about the virtues of generating interest, then researchers who work on this topic may be rewarded by having their work remembered and used.

ACKNOWLEDGMENTS

We wish to thank Larry Cummings. Larry Ford, Debra Meyerson, Kathleen Much, Barry Staw, and John Van Maanen for their good suggestions and encouragement. Anat Rafaeli received financial support for writing this paper form the Reccanati Fund of the School of Business at the Hebrew University of Jerusalem and the Mutual Fund of the Center for Research and Development of the Hebrew University of Jerusalem. Robert Sutton wrote this paper while he was a fellow at the Center for Advanced Study in the Behavioral Sciences. He is grateful for the financial support provided by the Carnegie Corporation of New York and the William and Flora Hewlett Foundation.

NOTES

1.   It would be possible to develop literally hundreds of other proposals about the links between individual personality and demographic characteristics and expressed emotions. Examples include: (1) role occupants with high self-esteem are more likely to express positive emotions than those with low self-esteem (Rosenberg, 1965); (2) role occupants with authoritarian personalities are more likely to be pleasant to superiors and unpleasant to subordinates than those who lack authoritarian personalities (Adorno, Frenkel-Brunswik, Levinson, & Sanford, 1950); and (3) role occupants with a high need for social desirability are more likely to express positive emotions to all target persons than are role occupants with a low need for social desirability (Edwards, 1957). Indeed, it would be possible to develop one or more specific hypotheses for almost all of the hundreds of personality characteristics identified in the psychological literature. But our aim here is simply to illustrate that enduring attributes do influence emotions expressed in organizational life and to identify a few attributes that may be especially useful for subsequent research. We do not to seek to propose a complete theory of the relationship between expressed emotions and enduring attributes of persons. Moreover, we would hesitate to embark on such an endeavor because it would probably result in an unparsimonious—and dreary—conceptual perspective.

2.   We wish to thank Larry Cummings for suggesting this research strategy.

3.   The new employee was generous enough to describe "Traditions I" in detail and to share her extensive notes. In addition, interested readers may wish to see Tyler and Nathan's (1985) film version of *In Search of Excellence*, which includes some entertaining and enlightening footage of "Traditions I." These norms are also spelled out in detail in the written training materials used by Disney (see Walt Disney Productions, 1982).

4.   We wish to thank Gerald Ledford for suggesting this field stimulation.

REFERENCES

Adorno, T. W., Frenkel-Brunswik, E., Levenson, D. J., & Sanford, R. N. (1950) *The authoritarian personality*. New York: Harper.

Arther, R. O., & Caputo, R. R. (1959). *Interrogation for investigators*. New York: William C. Copp & Associates.

Ash, M. K. (1984). *Mary Kay on people management*. New York: Warner Books.

Bandura, A. (1977a). Self efficacy: Toward a unifying theory of behavioral change. *Psychological Review, 54*, 191–215.

Bandura, A. (1977b). *Social learning theory*. Englewood Cliffs, N.J.: Prentice-Hall.

Bell, M. (1984). Teachings of the heart. *Journal of the American Medical Association, 252*; 2684.

Bem. S. L. (1974). The measurement of psychological androgyny. *Journal of Consulting and Clinical Psychology, 42*, 155–162.

Birnbaum, S. (1987). *Brinbaum's Italy*. Boston: Houghton Mifflin.

Blake, R. R., & Mouton, J. S. (1968). *Corporate excellence through grid organizational development*. Houston TX: Gulf Publishing

Boas, M., & Chain, S. (1976). *Big Mac: The unauthorized story of McDonald's*. New York: Dutton.

Bruner, J. S., & Postman, L. (1947). Emotional selectivity in perception and reaction. *Journal of Personality, 16*, 69–77.

Caplan, R. D., Cobb, S., French, J. R. P., Harrison, R. V., & Pinneau, S. R. (1975). *Job demands and worker health*. Report No. 75-160. Washington, D.C.: Department of Health, Education & Welfare.

Clark, R. E., & LaBeef, E. E. (1982). Death telling: Managing the delivery of bad news. *Journal of Health and Social Behavior, 23*, 366–380.

Cook, J. D., Hepworth, S. J., Wall, T. D., & Warr, P. B. (1981). *The experience of work.* London: Academic Press.

Crusco, A. H., & Wetzel, C. G. (1984). The Midas touch: The effects of interpersonal touch on restaurant tipping. *Personality and Social Psychology Bulletin, 10*, 512–517.

Darwin, C. (1965). *The expression of emotions in man and animals.* Chicago: University of Chicago Press.

Davitz, J. R. (1969). *The language of emotion.* New York: Academic Press.

Deaux, K. (1985). Sex differences. *Annual Review of Psychology, 36*, 49–82.

Denison, D. R., & Sutton, R. I. (Forthcoming). Work design and social regions in the operating suite: Lessons from a team of surgical nurses. In J. R. Hackman (Ed.), *Groups that work.* San Francisco: Jossey-Bass.

Edinger, J. A., & Patterson, M. L. (1983). Nonverbal involvement and social control. *Psychological Bulletin, 93*, 30–56.

Edwards, A. (1957). *The social desirability variable in personality assessment and research.* New York: Dryden.

Ekman, P. (1973). Cross culture studies of facial expression. In P. Ekman (Ed.), *Darwin and facial expression: A century of research in review*, (pp. 169–222). NY: Academic Press.

Ekman, P. (1981). Mistakes when deceiving. *Annals of the New York Academy of Sciences 364*; 269–278.

Ekman, P., & Friesen, W. V. (1975). *Unmasking the face.* Englewood Cliffs, N.J.: Prentice-Hall.

Ekman, P., Friesen, W. V., & Ancoli, S. (1980). Facial signs of emotional experience. *Journal of Personality and Social Psychology, 39*, 1125–1134.

Ekman, P., Friesen, W. V., & Ellsworth, P. (1972). *Emotion in the human face: Guidelines for research and a review of findings.* New York: Pergamon.

Ekman, P., & Oster, H. (1979). Facial expression of emotion. *Annual Review of Psychology, 30*; 527–554.

Festinger, L. (1957). *A theory of cognitive dissonance.* Evanston, ILL: Row, Peterson.

Fleishman, E. A. (1973). Twenty years of consideration and structure. In E. A. Fleishman & J. G. Hunt (Eds.), *Current developments in the study of leadership, 53*, 65–72.

Freize, I. H. & Wicklund, R. A. (1972). Nonverbal maintenance of traditional sex roles. *Journal of Social Issues, 32*; 133–141.

Frijda, N. H. (1986). *The emotions.* Cambridge MA: Cambridge University Press.

Geertz, H. (1959). The vocabulary of emotion. *Psychiatry, 22*, 225–237.

Goffman, E. (1955). On face work: An analysis of ritual elements in social interactions. *Psychiatry, 18*, 213–231.

Goffman, E. (1959). *The presentation of self in everyday life.* New York: Doubleday Anchor.

Goffman, E. (1961). *Asylums: Essays on the social situation of mental patients and other inmates.* Garden City, N.Y.: Doubleday Anchor

Goffman, E. (1971). *Relations in public.* New York: Harper & Row.

Goodsell, C. T. (1976). Cross cultural comparisons of behavior of postal clerks toward clients. *Administrative Science Quarterly, 21*, 140–150.

Gordon, S. (1981). The sociology of sentiment and emotions. In M. Rosenberg & R. H. Turner (Eds.), *Social psychology: Sociological perspectives*, (pp. 261–278). New York: Basic Books.

Griffitt, W. (1970). Environmental effects on interpersonal affective behavior: Ambient-effective temperature and attraction. *Journal of Personality and Social Psychology, 15*, 240–244.

Hackman, J. G. & Oldham, G. R. (1980). *Work redesign.* Reading MA: Addison-Welsey.

Hamlet, C. C., Axelrod, S., & Kuerschner, S. (1984). Eye contact as an antecedent to compliant behavior. *Journal of Applied Behavior Analysis, 17*, 553–557.

Hayano, D. M. (1982). *Poker faces*. Berkeley: University of California Press.

Helson, H. (1964). *Adaptation-level theory*. New York: Harper & Row.

Henslin, J. M. (1973). Trust and the cab dirver. In E. Katz & B. Danet (Eds.), *Burearcracy and the public*, (pp. 338–356). New York: Basic Books.

Heskett, J. L. (1986). *Managing in the service economy*. Boston: Harvard Business School Press.

Hochschild, A. R. (1979). Emotion work, feeling rules, and social structure. *American Journal of Sociology, 85*, 551–575.

Hochschild, A. R. (1983). *The managed heart*. Berkeley & Los Angeles, CA: University of California Press.

House, J. S. (1981). *Work stress and social support*. Reading, MA: Addison-Wesley.

Howe, L. P. (1977). *Pink collar workers*. New York: Putnam.

Isen, A. M., & Shalker, T. E. (1982). The effect of feeling state on evaluation of positive neutral and negative stimuli: When you "accentuate the positive" do you "eliminate the negative"? *Social Psychology Quarterly, 45*, 58–63.

James, W. (1884). What is an emotion? *Mind, 9*, 188–205.

Kahn, R. L. (1981). *Work and health*. New York: Wiley.

Kemper, T. D. (1985). How many emotions are there? Wedding the social and the autonomic components. Paper presented at the 80th Annual Meeting of the American Sociological Association, Washington D.C.

Kleinke, C. L., & Singer, D. A. (1979). Influence of gaze on compliance with demanding and conciliatroy requests in a field setting. *Personality and Social Psychology Bulletin, 5*, 386–390.

Komaki, J., Blood, M. R., & Holder, D. (1980). Fostering friendliness in a fast food franchise. *Journal of Organizational Behavior Management, 2*, 151–164.

Langer, E. J., & Rodin, J. (1976). The effects of choice and enhanced personal responsibility for the aged: A field experiment in an institutional setting. *Journal of Personality and Social Psychology, 34*, 191–198.

Lazarus, R. S. (1966). *Psychological stress and the coping process. New York: McGraw-Hill*.

Likert, R. (1967). *The human organization*. New York: McGraw-Hill.

Locke, E. A. (1976). The nature and causes of job satisfaction. In M. D. Dunnette (Ed.), *Handbook of industrial and organizational psychology*, (pp. 1297–1350) Chicago: Rand McNally

McClenahen, L. & Lofland, J. (1976). Bearing bad news: Tactics of the Deputy U. S. Marshal. *Sociology of Work and Occupations, 3*, 251–272.

Maister, D. H. (1985). The psychology of waiting in lines. In J. A. Cziepiel, M. R. Solomon, & C. F. Surprenant (Eds.), *The service encounter*, (pp. 113–123). Lexington: Lexington Books.

Manstead, A. S. R., Wagner, H. L., & MacDonald, C. J. (1983). A contrast effect in judgments of our emotional state. *Motivation and Emotion, 7*, 279–290.

Mars, G., & Nicod, M. (1984). *The world of waiters*. London: George Allen & Unwin.

Mehrabian, A. (1971). Non-verbal betrayal of feeling. *Journal of Experimantal Research. Personality 5*: 64–73.

Melbin, M. (1978). Night as frontier. *American Sociological Review 43*, 3–22.

Nelson, T. M., Nillson, T. H., & Johnson, M. (1984). Interaction of temperature, illuminance, and apparent time of sedentary work fatigue. *Ergonomics, 27*, 89–101.

Peters, T. J., & Austin, N. (1985). *A passion for excellence*. New York: Harper & Row.

Peters, T. J., & Waterman, R. H., Jr. (1982). *In search of excellence*. New York: Harper & Row.

Putnam, L., & McCallister, L. (1983). Situational effects of task and gender on nonverbal display. In D. Nimmo (Ed.), *Communications Yearbook*, (pp. 679–692).

Rafaeli, A. (1989). When clerks meet customers: A test of variables related to emotional expressons on the job. *Journal of Applied Psychology*, in press.

Rafaeli, A. (1988). When cashiers meet customers: An analysis of the supermarket cashiers. Paper under review.

Rafaeli, A. (1987). The relationship of customer attributes and situational variables to service employees' emotional behavior. Paper in progress.

Rafaeli, A. & Sutton, R. I. (1987). Expression of emotion as part of the work role. *Academy of Management Review, 12*, 23–37.

Richman, J. (1969). Busmen vs. the public. *New Society 14*, 243–245.

Rosenberg, M. (1965). *Society and the adolescent self-image.* Princeton, N.J.: Princeton University Press.

Roy, D. F. (1959). "Banana time": Job satisfaction and informal interaction. *Human Organization, 18*, 158–168.

Rules for Santas—Don't say "ho, ho, ho" (1984, November 15). *San Francisco Chronicle*, p. 3.

Seligman, M. E. P. (1975). *Helplessness* San Francisco: W. H. Freeman.

Siegler, D. M. & Siegler, R. S. (1976). Stereotypes of males' and females' speech. *Psychological Reports, 39*, 167–170.

Skinner, B. F. (1953). *Science and human behavior.* New York: Macmillan

Snyder, M. (1974). Self monitoring of expressive behavior. *Journal of Personality and Social Psychology, 30*, 526–537.

Sutton, R. I., & Callahan, A. L. (1987). The stigma of bankruptcy: Spoiled organizational image and its management. *Academy of Management Journal, 30*, 405–436.

Sutton, R. I., & Rafaeli, A. (1988). Untangling the relationship between displayed emotions and organizational sales: The case of convenience stores. *Academy of Management Journal, 31*, 461–487.

Teasdale, J. D., & Fogarty, S. J. (1979). Differential effects of induced mood on retrieval of pleasant and unpleasant events from episodic memory. *Journal of Abnormal Psychology 88*, 248–257.

Thayer, S. (1980). The effect of expression sequence and expressor identity on judgments fo the intensity of facial expression. *Journal of Nonverbal Behavoir, 5*, 71–79.

Thoits, P. A. (1985). Self-labelling processes in mental illnesses: The role of emotional deviance. *American Journal of Sociology, 19*, 221–247.

Tidd, K. L. & Lockard, J. S. (1978). Monetary significance of the affiliative smile: A case for reciprocal altruism. *Bulletin of the Psychonomic Society, 11*, 344–346.

Tolman, E. C. (1949). There is more than one kind of learning. *Psychological Review 56*, 144–155.

Tyler, S., & Nathan, J. (1985) *In search of excellence.* New York: Public Broadcast System (film).

Unterman, P., & Sesser, S. (1984). *Restaurants of San Francisco.* San Francisco: Chronicle Books.

Van Maanen, J. (1978). The asshole. In P. K. Manning & J. Van Mannen (Eds.), *Policing,* (pp. 231–238). Santa Monica, CA: Goodyear Press.

Van Maanen, J. (1986). Power in the bottle: Informal interacton and formal authority. In S. Srivastva and Associates (Eds.), *Executive power,* (pp. 204–238). San Francisco: Jossey-Bass.

Walt Disney Productions (1982). *Your role in the Walt Disney World show.* Orlando, FL: Walt Disney Productions.

Webb, E. J., Campbell, D. T., Schwartz, D. S., Sechrest, L., & Grove, J. B. (1981). *Nonreactaive measures in the social sciences.* Boston: Houghton Mifflin.

Weick, K. (1979). *The social psychology of organizing.* (2d ed.) Reading MA: Addison-Wesley.

Westbrook, R. A. (1980). Intrapersonal affective influences on consumer satisfaction with products. *Journal of Consumer Research, 7*, 49–54.

Whyte, W. F. (1946). *Human relations in the restaurant industry.* New York: McGraw-Hill.

Zajonc, R. B. (1985). Emotion and facial efference: An ignored theory reclaimed. *Science*, April 5, 15–21.

"REAL FEELINGS":
EMOTIONAL EXPRESSION AND ORGANIZATIONAL CULTURE

John Van Maanen and Gideon Kunda

ABSTRACT

The display of emotion at work is the concern of this paper. An argument is developed that links the rules that govern emotional expression to the cultural understandings organizational members hold as to what is proper and improper behavior in the workplace. The paper begins with some examples of emotional display at work and notes the ritualized form of such display. The following sections provide working definitions for culture and emotion and tie the two together conceptually. The main body of the paper presents two brief ethnographies detailing how organizational life is structured to channel, mold, enhance, sustain, challenge, and otherwise influence the feeling or organizational members—toward the organization itself, others in the organization, customers of the organization, and, crucially, themselves. Disneyland and High Technology Incorporated (a pseudonym) are the two organizations studied. The paper concludes by considering how these two organizational cultures are built and maintained, as well as the emotional costs and benefits membership within them provides.

TANDEM IN PARADISE

It is a day like all other days in paradise.[1] Soft tradewinds blow across a golden beach ringed with tropical plants, coco palms, and expensive hotels. Bronzed locals gather under the available shade, lounging about drinking beer, smoking dope, and gambling. Red tourists bake in the sun by the sea, occasionally dropping into the warm waters to inspect life-forms of the coral reef that shelters the beach. Slowly, however, the interest of both these nominal groups is drawn toward a pale third group emerging from one of the hotels and marching up the street that borders the beach toward a private park where elaborate preparations have been made for some sort of festivity. Attention on the beach is rapt as perhaps two or three hundred similarly dressed men and women of middle age approach the park. All wear tennis shoes, bermuda shorts, white polo shirts emblazoned with a corporate insignia and nameplate, and odd white sailor caps turned down as something of a sun shield.

Apparently oblivious of the gawking locals and tourists, this hearty crew arrives at their destination and breaks rank to mingle and circulate about several well-stocked refreshment tables behind which stand formally attired waiters serving drinks. Soon, in the midst of this relaxed socializing, several sporty red-shirted fellows take center stage and begin to organize a series of activities that pit one seemingly identical group against another. There are sack races, spoon relays, lavacious balloon-passing games, and several varieties of drinking contests. All are accompanied by lots of cheering and raucous laughter. Songs are sung loudly, if not musically. A temporary fence is in place surrounding the occasion, and several tourists wonder aloud whether the fence is in place to keep the onlookers out or the merrymakers in.

The games and songs go on for perhaps three hours. Chants and cheers fill the air. Speeches are given to urge on the competitors. Trophies and ribbons are dispensed and, seemingly, everyone wins something. Above the tables fly corporate flags bearing the Tandem Computer emblem. Promptly at five o'clock, the racket stops, the tables are cleared, the drinking ceases, and the gathering begins to lurch back to the hotel from where it first emerged. Tourists and locals again fix their gaze on the incongruous parade as the Tandem throng departs from their ceremonial grounds. The march back is marked again by the bemused attention the beachgoers place on this mobile crowd, although those in the Tandem bunch appear to have eyes and ears for only each other. Throughout the afternoon, in fact, those eyes and ears were firmly committed to one another, for only a few strays could be spotted wandering beyond the fence. Two strays who happened to pause on the beach during the recessional stroll were asked by one curious tourist with perverse interests: "What are you folks up to?" One of the strays responded promptly, if somewhat defensively, as if worried about the social impact of being an adult caught engaged in childish merriment: "Oh, we're just working on our culture."

EMOTIONAL MOBILIZATION

What is going on here? Several hundred well-paid employees of a more or less high high-technology firm jet in from around the globe at company expense to a lush, remote, and distant Shangri-la. On arrival, their activities are carefully planned and organized around various events seemingly without enduring purpose other than to celebrate being with one another. The affair lasts three days, whereupon all but a few return to their ordinary roles in the office and at home. During this respite— an organizational time-out of sorts—they drink, chatter, gossip, and party with others in the company, many of whom they've never met before, and generally enjoy what they can of the scenic pleasures paradise offers. To some participants, this little adventure may represent a well-deserved reward for hard work; to others, a sign that more rewards are to come; to still others, a mild diversion in an otherwise nose-to-the-grindstone world. Most participants can work up many rationales to ascribe rhyme and reason for this somewhat frivolous gobbling of organizational slack.

To observers, the *Cynic* might make such of the silliness of the little corporate games being played by these Tandem holidayers. Doubt would be cast on the sincerity of those singing corporate songs and otherwise participating in the worked-up warmth and summer camp roles of the occasion. A kind of contract theory would be alluded to whereby the participants are seen to go along with the festivities, paying public honor to corporate games but do so only in anticipation of ultimately being rewarded. Inwardly, participants supposedly recognize that there are stakes to be claimed by appearing to be dedicated and loyal employees of Tandem Computers and are willing to appear in foolish guise when it is expedient to do so. The *Believer*, however, might argue that there are real emotions being expressed here and that these merrymakers from Tandem Computer grasp a good deal of their personal identity from their ability to identify with the firm. A sort of consensus theory obtains whereby participants are thought to be swept away by feelings of good cheer and harmony, collectively affirming the values offered by corporate membership. The singing from the corporate songbook is seen as an authentic gesture of social support and companionship, in tune with inner feelings of self-worth, pride in the company, and respect among colleagues.[2]

Both Cynic and Believer have their points. Surely there are many reasons why one might run the three-legged race with furious effort or applaud a company slogan with wild abandon. Some may be doing so to strike a pose, cut a deal, or further their own careers; others may be doing so merely to enjoy one another's presence while unleashed from customary work roles and restraints; still others may be doing so in a bemused, if bewildered, way, to simply go along with the crowd. All are attending to the matters at hand with a degree of enthusiasm, but the meaning such participation holds for them is no doubt highly variable. Whether the observed fealty, affection, intensity, and warmth generated by occasions like Tandem's cultural workout are more apparent than real is, as we shall see, a rather difficult question to answer.

For the moment, however, we are concerned less with the authenticity of emotion than with its display. In particular, we are concerned with the nature and range of occasions that call out emotional displays on the part of organizational members. The argument we will develop throughout this paper is that the rules governing the expression of emotions at work are an important part of the culture carried by organizational members. Any attempt to manage culture is therefore also an attempt to manage emotion. Culture influences not only what people think, say, and do but also what they feel. We begin our analysis of culture and emotion with a few examples.

Consider, first, the celebrated case of Tupperware. Here is a firm whose worldwide organization seemingly rests squarely on the management of collective emotion. Tupperware's cell-like structure is maintained (and enhanced) by the regularized use of ceremony designed to reward, individually and collectively, party-hosting sales representatives during elaborately orchestrated weekly and monthly sales meetings. These emotional little assemblies are evangelic in style, wherein good cheer is virtually mandated on the part of the participants. The "Tupperware Way" is promoted as a design for living, as well as a rapid route to financial gain. It is hard to imagine any more explicit or vigorous efforts to mobilize employee emotions (and efforts) than those designed by Tupperware officials.[3]

Consider, next, the legendary efforts of IBM to direct employee activities by providing the form and substance of a corporate state to which all are expected to honor and to contribute. Statements of employee rights, highly structured promotional and relocation policies, extensive and continual training programs, benevolent fringe benefit packages, and the provision of an elaborate social calendar all presumably contribute toward the loyalty and camaraderie apparently felt by at least some, if not most, of the membership. Cohesion is seemingly so strong that IBM personnel who leave the firm talk about "emigrating" and sorely missing banquets, office parties, summertime picnics, and IBM-maintained country clubs used by corporate members to mix business with pleasure. One observer of the IBM scene quotes a senior executive saying: "The firm instills a belief that you don't work for IBM, you are a citizen of IBM" (Kaible, 1983). Another suggests that some IBM employees report feeling more comfort and pride in seeing their corporate flag waving over an office building than they do when seeing their national flag (Seidenberg, 1975).

Perhaps less diffuse than the warm glow that sometimes results from corporate membership are those sharper, more apparent, and often more animated emotional expressions brought forth in many of the social gatherings associated with work life. Tandem in Paradise is, of course, an example of one such gathering. But consider other types of gatherings, such as the less formal ones that take place whenever and wherever organizational members cluster together to partake of food, drink, and mutual sociability. Playtime is hardly unknown in the work world. In some organizations, it seems almost a daily routine. For example, Van Maanen (1986) reports on the drinking episodes of Scotland Yard detectives, episodes notable for their regularity, full participation, ritualized forms, and distinct emotional tones. Some drinking occasions simply celebrate membership in this somewhat exclusive occupational club through the civility and respect displayed by members toward one another. Other occasions serve to vent hostility and anger across the ranks in the organization. All occasions have consequences, however, beyond the immediate pleasures of drinking, talking, and feeling good or "stroppy" (aggressive). One consequence involves what many take to be the disclosure of "real feelings" on matters considered too hot or sensitive to be discussed during ordinary and sober working time. The point of interest here is not so much the content and form of these pub crawls, shared meals, refreshment breaks, office parties, or other alcoholic rendezvous but the fact that so much of the emotional expression of members in this organization is channeled into these institutionalized and high predictable forms. Observers of Japanese organizations report similar sorts of extracurricular routines on the part of the membership (Rohlen, 1974; Christopher, 1983).

Another example of how feelings emerge and are patterned in organizational life is provided by Rosen's (1985) graphic description of the annual corporate breakfast held by a large Philadelphia advertising firm. Unlike previous illustrations, here is an occasion that is attended by most of the management personnel in the organization, planned down to the last detail, and serves chiefly to generate a sense of identification and belongingness among those present as well as provide those attending with a relatively clear perspective of just where they currently sit within the pecking order of the firm. By seating arrangement, closeness to the podium, invitation (or lack thereof) to be one of the presenters in a long series of spirited talks, those who attend this earnest, if not unctious, convocation leave with a better sense of just what the company means to them and, presumably, they to the company.

In a similar vein, Bob Slocum, the fictional protagonist of Joseph Heller's (1966) *Something Happened*, begins his narrative by informing the reader:

> In the office in which I work there are five people of whom I am afraid. Each of these five people is afraid of four people (excluding overlaps), for a total of twenty, and each of these twenty people is afraid of six people, making a total of. . . . (p. 13).

Despite this wicked contextual setup where the lines of company control determine just who fears whom, where risk is everywhere, and avoiding responsibility seems as important to success as claiming it, the distressed narrator longs to give the presentation on his department's performance at this year's corporate meetings. In his words:

> I want very much to be allowed to take my place on the rostrum at the next company convention in Puerto Rico (if it will be Puerto Rico again this year) . . . It was downright humiliating to be the only one of Green's managers left out. The omission was conspicuous,

the rebuff intentionally public, and for the following four days, while others had a great, robust time golfing and boozing it up, I was the object of expressions of pity and solemn, perfunctory commiseration from many people I hate and wanted to hit and scream at. It was
jealousy and pure, petty spite that made Green decide at the last minute to push me off the
schedule . . . after I had worked so long and nervously (I worked at home just about every
night—to the wonder and consternation of my family) on my speech for the three-minute
segment of the program allotted to me and had prepared a very good and witty demonstration
of eighteen color slides (p. 35).

Examples of the mobilization of emotions in organizational life could be
multiplied many times over. From the inculcation of ''Service Ideals'' at Boston
Gas & Electric, to the whipping up of excitement for Ivory Soap or Spic 'n Span
at Procter & Gamble, corporate life seems not to lack instances that are intended
to generate emotional ups and downs. What these various examples have in common, however, are several features not often discussed in academic circles devoted to the study of organizations.

First, the occasions cited above have a slight to obvious time-out character.[4]
That is, they are episodes closely associated with work but placed outside the
everyday working context. They may occur in off-site training, around a lunch or
dinner table, in a bar, or at the office at mid-afternoon. The point is that time-
outs occur at some remove from the usual pace, place, or routine of the workplace. Second, there are strong symbols in the performance of these disparate
ceremonial activities. Such symbols serve to signal relative power and status of
participants, as well as signify collective membership by drawing attention to
objects, people, ideas, and programs that members are to give their allegiance.
Third, these occasions are markedly collective. They bring together similarly sit-
uated individuals for the purpose of sharing experiences allowing for emotional
expressions somewhat distinct from those typically sponsored in the everyday
working environment.

Finally, these occasions have a planful design and an orchestrated character.
The thoughts and feelings that flow from participants can be assessed, therefore,
in terms of their appropriateness; generally, participants learn quickly and know
well the roles they are expected to play. Improvisation of conduct is always required, of course, but such improvisation is limited to the fine nuances of assuming a stance to be read grossly as cheerful and enthusiastic, serious and somber,
sentimental and blue, troubled and sad, and so forth. Sustaining an appropriate
collective (or gross) emotion is at stake on these occasions, and normally most
participants can bring themselves to feel or at least feign the mood in line with
what organizers regard as expected.[5]

In short, collective emotions and ritual seem essential to the little gatherings
we are discussing. This is not to say that these gatherings are in any way
unappreciated or unwelcome intrusions in the workplace. Indeed, rituals and the
collective emotions associated with them are sometimes among the most satisfying and rewarding events for members of an organization. The way such matters
work, however, deserves more attention. We will begin with a definition.

Ritual is a rule-governed activity of a symbolic character that draws the attention of participants to objects of thought and feeling they are expected to hold in special significance (Lukes, 1975). There are both positive and negative rituals, as well as the highly dramatic and drawn-out sort discussed above, and the perfunctory, mundane, thoroughly conventionalized type such as a hurriedly muttered "how'ryah" might initiate with an acquaintance one meets in the supermarket. Whatever the type, however, participants suffer a degree of normative pressure to honor at least outwardly the occasion by playing by the rules.

From this perspective, rituals (and their absence or abuse) can provide an emotional charge (of, no doubt, varying voltage) for participants. More pointedly, as Durkheim first suggested, there can be no group worthy of the name not needing at regular intervals the reaffirmation of collective sentiments and ideals. Ritual, of all sorts, can provide a sense of unity and perceived character. The moral order of a collective is displayed through ritual of a public sort, and members are more or less pressed by others on the scene to disclose their adherence to or distance from such an order through their presence and participation. Thus, gatherings such as meetings, parties, conventions, shared meals, assemblies, and so forth provide opportunities for participants to express their allegiance to the collective.

It should also be apparent that rituals provide, for those in charge of them, a marvelous opportunity to define as authoritative certain ways of seeing the world. Ritual, in addition to whatever revitalization function it may serve in organizations, offers its managers a mode of exercising (or, at least, seeking to exercise) power along the cognitive and affective planes. Ritual occasions can then be seen as mechanisms through which certain organizational members influence how other members are to think and feel—what they want, what they fear, what they should regard as proper and possible, and ultimately, perhaps, who they are. Since culture can usefully be defined in terms of those things a group member in good standing must think, feel, and do (Goodenough, 1970; Spradley, 1979), rituals offer penetrating examples of just what constitutes such thinking, feeling, and doing.[6]

The variety of ritual and cultural forms appearing in organizational settings is of special interest to us in this essay. We are struck by what seems to be a systematic bias among organizational researchers to examine only the positive and dramatic forms while ignoring the negative ones and the far more frequent mundane forms (e g , Trice, 1984; Trice & Beyer, 1984). This highly selective choice of cultural materials (whether ritual, story, myth, rite, symbol, totem, etc.) overemphasizes the integrative and cohesion-producing side of culture. Yet the problem of organizational order is exceedingly complex, and the participation of members in, for example, an organizational ritual is not necessarily an index of value consensus or shared belief. Compliance may also be explained because, for participants, no realistic alternatives are perceived.

When alternatives are perceived, however, rituals of resistance may be observed (Ditton, 1975; Willis, 1977). Alternative and nonofficial values are expressed in many ways in organizations (Martin & Siehl, 1983; Martin, Sitkin, & Boehm, 1985). Strikes may symbolize worker willingness to stand up to their bosses; office parties may be marked by displays of overt defiance by subordinates toward their superiors (although perhaps excusable later because the defiant ones were "clearly out of their minds"); marketing people may systematically be degraded by sales personnel whenever they come together; or sacred operating norms may be done away with by night shift workers who do not have to contend with supervisory surveillance. In short, many organizational activities are ritualized, but they are not always of an integrative kind nor can we assume that rituals, by their mere existence, serve the strategic intent so glibly attributed to them by interested observers. These are always empirical questions.

The study of ritual forms and culture as enacted in work settings does have, however, an intriguing, if paradoxical, history. It is worth quickly reviewing the broad outlines of this history in order to grasp what we consider essential for understanding the recent growth of a sort of culture cult among managers of large organizations and among those who, for fun and profit, study them.

THE CULTURE CULT

Social theorists and critics help define the world we live in by providing arresting images of society based on their presumably rich and timely understanding of current events and social trends. One such image, sketched out some thirty to forty years ago, pictured those working in large American companies as members of a buttoned-down, homogeneous, male marching society, each rallying around their respective organizational flags with honor and pride. The organization men of William Whyte (1956) were, for example, a sizable chunk of David Riesman's (1950) lonely crowd of conformists who, in their identical gray flannel suits, shuffled off each day to work in some stifling crystal palace of bureaucracy. America, it seemed, was a highly organized, individually repressive society, whose business institutions were mostly intolerant of personal or cultural diversity. More to the point, people were thought to like it this way, for there was said to be little discomfort among the timid masses faithfully filling corporate slots without query or complaint.

Vestiges of such views remain, of course, but most of us would regard this simplified portrait of corporate America rather misleading if not downright archaic by today's standards. Organizational life, from the late 1960s on, seems a far cry from the conforming and placid "Father Knows Best" days of uncomplaining compliance to managerial standards of performance and demeanor. Most corporate managers in our supposed zero-sum society might well experience something akin to vertigo when reading about the alleged good old days when legions of organizational soldiers obeyed administrative commands without grumble and shared in a valued business culture centered around putting one foot after another up the magic ladder of success. If anything, what was once a worry about the tyranny of organizational culture has been replaced by serious doubt as to whether there is any culture at all. The midcentury corporation of "yes men" united by shared images, similar values, strong attachments, and personal identities etched by affection and loyalty to employers has been turned upside down into a corporation of male and female nay sayers wherein no more than one person seems to agree on anything and whatever emotions are generated through work experience are of the negative, competitive, distancing, and alienative variety.

Evidence for this latter image of corporate life seems virtually omnipresent. Turnover, in the form of job hopping for certain highly prized categories of organizational members (notably the managerial and professional classes), has become so common that a profitable industry called "headhunting" is thriving. Lipset and Schneider (1983) report a dramatic drop in confidence in our major institutions. Apparently the public does not believe government, big business, educational establishments, or the churches are performing very well. Scholars describe organizations as anarchies, garbage cans, and loosely coupled places of distrust, misunderstanding, mutual ignorance, and displaced goals. Cynicism, pessimism, and suspicion seem hallmarks of managerial thought as described in the popular press. Newly minted MBAs from the best schools are no longer rather fondly thought of as naive or gullible but are attacked from many sides for their scheming, self-interested, money-hungry ways. Perhaps most telling is the comparison of American corporate life with images rendered of corporate life in Japan. American managers, it seems, are astonished and awestruck at the descriptions of obedient, loyal, hard-working, patient managers of Japan, so accustomed have they become to rivalry within the firm, internecine squabbling between departments, and excessive (to them) self-concern of others (Vogel, 1979).

Enter now the current glut of prescriptive writings, addressed to American managers, about the tender benefits of hearty organizational cultures where pride, craftsmanship, fealty, honor, and lasting emotional attachments can be forged. Organizational culture has become something of a commodity that those who run our large organizations deeply believe they must possess. Once an academic pastime engaged in by a few errant anthropologists and sociologists who looked for manifestations of culture in mundane work contexts close to home (as opposed to the sacred headwaters of the Amazon, deviant and criminal enclaves of large cities, or the institutionalized traits of national character), virtually everyone now has something to say about organizational culture, and the formal study of such beasts is clearly on the make (Fine, 1984; Ouchi & Wilkins, 1985).[7]

How are we to interpret such turnabouts in social imagination? Our basic premise here is simply that the current gnashing of teeth and outpouring of concern for organizational culture reflects at least two interrelated matters. First, nostalgia and the waxing romantic over previous periods in American life is involved. This no doubt reflects the accelerated rate of social and technological change in the society, as well as the heightened competition in international marketplaces. Second, organizational culture is a hot topic because in many organizations there is seemingly so little of it (at least of the sort that managers prefer). Following what appears to be a universal social law, we become conscious of things only byperceived absence (i.e., the "golden age" or "good old days") or by contrast (i.e., Japan). So it is with organizational culture, although there now are numerous prophets for profit to tell us just how we can restore it.

We argue throughout the remainder of this paper that attempts to build, strengthen, deepen, or thicken organizational culture often involve the subtle (or not so subtle) control of employee emotions—or at least those emotions expressed in the workplace. In essence, we think that much of the organizational culture discourse inside organizations masks managerial attempts to control not only what employees say and do but also what they feel. Whether this is good or bad depends surely on one's point of view, but it is high time to pull the attention of the culture cult toward those emotional or feeling domains within which ritualized activities are central.

"REAL FEELINGS"

Emotion, according to T. S. Eliot's much-quoted definition, is the "objective correlate" of art. A set of objects, a situation, a melody, a chain of events, a patch of color are the raw elements to be combined into a formula to evoke a particular emotion. When the (inspired) external facts are given, the particular emotion is immediately brought forth. In Eliot's view, symbolic mediation may be instantaneous and pass unnoticed, but such mediation is nonetheless required.[8] The analytic experts of emotion are then the artists able to imagine and bring forth feeling. While we all have direct knowledge of feeling through experience and mood, we have little knowledge of feeling derived from descriptions of its form and content except by those rendered by artists (Langer, 1967, pp. 64–65).

Other sets of social actors, however, have practical interests in emotion. Consider the advertisers, the politicians, the lifeguards, the labor organizers, the nurses, the police officers who, in various ways, must constantly deal with "human nature." Those concerned with public rituals have also occupational interests in the nuances of emotion—the funeral director, the wedding coordinator, the divorce or PI (personal injury) attorney, and so forth. In organizations, persons concerned with the public image of the firm (in economic terms, "corporate goodwill") or in charge of ceremonial occasions such as retirement dinners or in-house training have special interest in managing appearances and events such that desired emotional responses from others may be generated. Exemplary managers might also be included on this list when they make, sustain, and model meanings and values for others. In brief, there is something of a division of emotional labor at work in the world in which some people are trusted with more of such blessed responsibilities than others and, moreover, some people and organizations are demonstrably better at the job of emotional management than others. Before considering where and why this might be so, let us first consider what we mean by emotion.

Emotions are ineffable feelings of the self-referential sort. They index or signal our current involvements and evaluations. Like sight and hearing, emotion provides a communication channel between the world and its moments and our assessments of just how we are gearing in and out of this perceptual world. Emotions build up and melt down. They may be intense or subtle, fluctuate wildly or show stability within a narrow band. What is certain, however, is the fact that we have no scientific or otherwise privileged access to feelings as either states or processes beyond that provided us by self-reports. The validity of an emotion for those who feel it is a given, is subject to no known truth test, and is neither right nor wrong.

Emotions are, however, subject to interpretation of all sorts. Their study lies somewhere between biology and ethnology. But since the Schacter and Singer (1962) experiments documenting the plasticity of reported emotion to identical physiological arousal, studies of emotion cluster closer to the latter pole than the former—even psychological ones (Zajonc, 1980; Averrill, 1980; Izard, 1972). Sociologists, too, have carved out a domain in the area (Shott, 1979; Kemper, 1978; Denzin, 1984; Scheff, 1977). Much of the sociological work examines the labels certain groups of people use to describe emotions and the situations that call out such labels. In general conversation, a term may fit a very large class of emotions and provide little detail. Anger, for instance, may mean the speaker is mad, hostile, frustrated, hateful, nauseated, anxious, excited, or jealous—all distinctions a listener or observer may or may not readily grasp. In understanding the words someone uses to describe a feeling, sociologists argue that we typically note only the attitude it projects (and whether the available clues surrounding the speaker support such a projection) rather than what the speaker "really" feels (Goffman, 1959, 1969). Feelings, then, are intensely personal, including those commonly thought to be sympathetic or empathetic.

Following the logic of interactionist theory, we will define emotions as self-referential feelings an actor experiences or, at least, claims to experience in regard to the performances he or she brings off in the social world.[9] Some performances have precious little self-referential value, of course, for we couldn't care less—within certain limits—just how we are judged in such a capacity. Other performances will matter a great deal, and, thus, the anticipation, doing, and remembering of such performances will be engaging emotionally. What Goffman (1955) calls "face-work" is central to this definition because when we are involved in direct interpersonal relations with others, we are virtually always at some emotional risk. Whatever sterling or flawed qualities we possess are subject to communication, observation, confirmation, or denial. "Feeling good," then, is in large measure attributable to our skill in making sure others have the same charitable view of ourselves as we ourselves have. This requires a considerable degree of impression management, much of which will reflect well or poorly on whatever self-concepts we hold dear.

Hochschild (1977, 1983) has written brilliantly on the nature of felt emotion, and we will follow her lead here. She argues that emotional responses vary considerably between and among categories of people. Feelings stem from interaction but are not simply triggered by external cues. Emotional response is part institutive (emerging as action brought forth by the actor) and part interpretive (alive to the situation and context calling out an appropriate response). The most vital feature of Hochschild's imagery is her instructive notion of "emotional work." Labor in the feeling world consists of learning and maintaining the proper affective tone (by proper management, gesture, appearance, words, and deeds). Moods are contextually appropriate matters, and we have the ability to manage them willfully. Consequently, there are, in Hochschild's model, "feeling rules" of the situational sort known to us and available for judging emotional presentations—our own and others.

Moving to the wonderful world of work, it takes little effort to see just how emotional labor operates. The "friendly greeting" of the salesman, the "happy face" on the hamburger clerk, the "worried look" worn by the boss are all superficial, though common, examples of emotion work. In most cases, the cost to the performer is little (and the gains slight) and are taken for granted that whatever effort they entail is unnoticed and regarded as "natural." Matters become more problematic, however, when the "worried look" is carried by the self-imagined office cut-up, or when the "friendly greeting" is a gift to the noxious and personally detested customer, or when the "happy face" must be screwed on tight by the clerk who has been on his feet for twelve hours in a crowded, steaming, hot service gallery.

When occupations, careers, and organizations specifically are considered, things become meatier for, again, as sociologists are quick to point out, what we do for a living is perhaps the best clue available for determining our social (attributed) and personal (felt) identities (Hughes, 1958). In these domains, valued attributes may well be on the line because not only are our emotional repertoires involved, a form of what Mills (1956) called "personality capital" (a commodity that can be bought and sold in the marketplace), but also because we profoundly care about what this capital good represents to us.

The upshot of this discussion is a proposition: The more emotional labor involved in a particular work role, the more troublesome work identity becomes to the role holder. Because emotions are involved, at least on the surface, the more difficult it is for individuals to distance themselves from the tasks at hand. Emotional labor inevitably calls for some self-investment in the role. As such, the ability to "psych one's self up (or down)," "to put one's heart into it," "to get tough," "to have an iron gut," "to be warm (or cold)," "to show concern for the misfortunes of others" become artful performances that over time may become self-defining.

Examples are plentiful in this domain. Consider the cheerful cocktail waitress in an upscale watering hole who must continually appear exuberant and friendly if tips are to be forthcoming (Spradley and Mann, 1975), or the sour urban schoolteacher who must continually attend to matters of student discipline (Lortie, 1975). Consider also the foreman on the shop floor charged with enforcing work rules he personally thinks inane (Dunkerley, 1975), or the policewoman who is required to be calm and dispassionate in the face of human misery (Martin, 1980). In each of these settings, managing one's emotions is crucial to successful role performance, yet such self-control raises questions as to what feelings are one's own and what feelings go with the job. Keeping the two separate is, for many, no easy task (Van Maanen, 1979).

There is always the problem at work about just where to draw the line between the real person who presumably stands behind the occupational mask. Just how much to invest of ourselves in our work settings is a matter of considerable uncertainty, showing, no doubt, much variance over time with multiple, often conflicting goals in mind. Yet there is also a structural peculiarity to contend with because some jobs ask more of us than others. An emotional division of labor attaches itself to organizations wherein the management of emotions for some categories of employees is of more concern than it is for others in the organization. Perhaps only the dominant and the doormat in organizational life have a relative freedom from emotional constraint. Those proverbial tycoons or founders of organizations can more or less feel and express what they want, as can the (equally proverbial) day laborers or temps who have little or nothing to risk in the workplace. The vast middle are less free, however, for in many ways, their continuance on the job depends on at least the display of proper emotion. Such display is made far easier if the emotions expressed are genuinely felt rather than feigned, although we think even the best actors will have difficulty at times knowing what is genuinely felt and what is not.

Where might emotional management be most prevalent in organizational life? A number of rather self-evident propositions can be suggested. A few will suffice as samples. Wherever face-to-face contacts—with customers, suppliers, subordinates, consultants, superiors—dominate the workday, we would expect considerable emotional management. Supervisors are expected to keep their feelings in check more so than workers for whom behavior, not mood, is usually at issue. Managers, because they are noticed and regarded by most as important, must be accorded a certain amount of deference for their well-being. This requires, for those reporting to them, a cultivated amount of mood management. Service workers, whose style of delivery may be as important to the customer as the product delivered, must constantly monitor their performance ("service with a smile") more so than, say, manufacturing workers where style is unseen and only the product counts. We would expect emotional labor to be higher in the complaint department than in the stockroom or warehouse; higher in a commercial bank than in an auto parts business; higher in a small luxury goods boutique where customer sensibilities are catered to than in a discount store where masses of customers are dealt with impersonally.

Relatedly, the more emotional labor is performed in an occupational role, the more "feeling rules" there are to be learned and, probably, the more training and surveillance would be expected to go with the role. In terms of particular "feeling rules," we would expect that the longer persons are employed and the greater are their perceived rewards—in terms of pay, advancement, status, honor—the more likely they are to support and advance the feeling rules that go with and surround the job. Professionals, also, by virtue of long training and high status, are normally bound by a greater variety of specific feeling rules than are nonprofessionals (although the context—self versus organizationally employed—may affect the degree such rules are regarded as appropriate). Finally, individuals working on interdependent tasks involving coordination, harmony, and perhaps group bonuses are subject to more emotional demands than persons working in quasi-isolation on piece rates. Teamwork is, from this standpoint, more emotionally trying than solo performance.

These are, of course, relative and probabilistic matters, not universal and deterministic ones. Propositions such as these are, however, useful for suggesting where the fault lines of emotional work might fall. Of more interest to us are the ties between culture of an organizational sort and the kinds of feelings expressed by members of such cultures. The proposition of merit in this regard is rather simple and direct: Organizations (and segments within organizations) displaying pronounced concern for culture are precisely those organizations where member adherence to a set of feeling rules is considered by management crucial to the success of the enterprise. Culture, from this standpoint is, then, a control device that when fully embraced acts to inform, guide, and discipline the emotions of organizational members. In varying ways, therefore, such things as ritual, myth, stories, espoused values, special language, and prescribed norms index the way members are expected by others in the organization to feel.

In this regard, the form that organizational culture takes is of some practical interest. We assume that the more explicit, codified, and monitored the codes of emotional conduct are, the less effective (and more costly) such regulation is. Rituals enacted on a highly proscribed and mandated basis seem to have, for example, less force than those that emerge more or less spontaneously from the membership. Witness the fate of national revitalization holidays, such as presidential birthdays, when moved from their historical calendar date to that of a humble third day of the weekend. These new convenient holidays may celebrate the value of gaining a day off from work perhaps, but lost in the transition is the day's societal significance.

This suggests that to the degree culture is of an imposed or calculated sort, the less likely organizational members are to be swept away by its force. Put in mind, for example, the hollow, awkward, and thoroughly mechanical ways telephone operators handle the ritual requirement to utter "Thank you for using AT&T" when assisting each and every long-distance caller. There is apparent emotional labor in carrying out such job requirements, but, for many, it is very clearly not a labor of love.

As with all other things social, we expect variance here too. Over time, distance from organizational rituals and claims may slacken as members self-select in and out of the organization, with those remaining finding it perhaps easier to identify more closely with the organization, and, in the end, coming to regard its rites, symbols, and codes of conduct as appropriate, if not natural. Such is seemingly the case with many of the airline attendants studied by Hochschild (1983) who, following company commandments, were eventually able to treat certain bothersome and obnoxious passengers as "nervous fliers" or "unruly children" rather than the "drunken louts" they initially thought them to be. Emotional control, in this case, owes much to the rather explicit corporate culture adhered to by the attendants within which each customer is to be valued and treated well even in the face of considerable abuse.

Closer to the core of the emotional life of organizational members is the immediate work group to which they are assigned. Here is where emotional control is probably the most effective, for it is stage managed by those with whom members must spend most of their time. Roy's (1959) work here is exemplary when discussing the ritualized ways emotional release is built into the workplace, as is Kanter's (1977) work on secretaries. Presumably colleagues and close companions at work provide a good deal of the emotional supervision that occurs in organizations.[10] Take, for example, the newly hired engineer who finds it difficult to hold back on his enthusiasm or check and channel his perceived mastery of new techniques in ways approved by the old hands with whom he may work. In no uncertain ways, he will be reminded of the proper emotional stance to be enacted at work, which, for this mythical fountain of ideas, might be the tried and true "shut up and listen." Eventually the bubbling may stop as our engineer learns appropriate working ways and levels out his moods. Such feeling rules will not always be discovered in the procedural manuals or training classrooms, but we can be reasonably sure they will exist. As Goffman (1956) tells us, when we break the rules of interaction—including, most assuredly, the emotional ones—our immediate neighbors will be the first to let us know.

Our interests in the remainder of the paper are with those aspects of organizational cultures that are rather explicit and sometimes codified. Of most concern are those cultural matters that play on the emotional life of organizational members. We take as axiomatic that organizational culture is managed and, in many respects, managed actively. This work is not always undertaken consciously, nor it is always successful. There are a vast number of tiny filigrees that operate as tripwires in this domain. Organizational members do, after all, have conflicting sources of attachment and, when it comes to deciding what rules are to govern action, thought, and feeling, organizational ones will not always suffice or win out (Van Maanen & Barley, 1984, 1985). Sometimes they do, however, and when these rules bear down on the emotions expressed by organizational members (both heartfelt and faked), we have perhaps the clearest instance of cultural management possible.

One method of approaching the role culture plays in the management of emotion is to look closely at a few organizations that place great emphasis on their culture and are rather widely admired for doing so. To this end, two brief (and very partial) ethnographies—of Disneyland and High Technology, Inc. (a pseudonym)—are offered as a way of detailing how organizational life can be structured to channel, mold, enhance, sustain, or otherwise influence the feelings organizational members assume toward the organization itself, others in the organization, customers of the organization, and, crucially, themselves. These organizations are quite different, but both require from their membership a good deal of emotional labor and both manage to sustain rather remarkable levels of hard work and goodwill. We turn first to examine how culture and emotion are joined together at Disneyland.

LIFE WITH TINKERBELL

Part of Walt Disney Enterprises is the theme park Disneyland.[11] In its pioneering form in Anaheim, California, this amusement center has been a consistent moneymaker since the gates were first opened on July 17, 1955. Apart from its semiotic and sociological charm, it has of late become something of a prototype for culture vultures and has been held up for public acclaim in several best-selling publications as one of America's top companies, most notably by Peters and Waterman (1982). To outsiders, the fierce loyalty of its long-time employees, the seemingly inexhaustible repeat business it generates from its customers, the immaculate condition of park grounds, and, more generally, the intricate and largely conscious physical and social design of the business itself appear wondrous. For those who have worked in the Magic Kingdom, however, disenchantment with the Disney Way is not unknown, however subtle and muted its expression.

Our focus is mainly on the largest category of workers at Disneyland, ride operators, who during the busy summer months number close to four thousand. When applying for a position at Disneyland, "wannabe" operators are subject to at least two personal interviews with park representatives. Each successful applicant must conform to certain highly particularistic standards of appearance; complexion, height and weight, straightness and color of teeth, or disfigurement of any sort are all grounds for flunking the Disneyland body test. In times past, race, sex, nationality, age, and accent operated openly as a basis for hiring and staffing, both with the advent of affirmative action and equal employment opportunity legislation, such matters are no longer open, although, to a large degree, they still operate. Voice auditions also used to be required of new employees but now serve primarily as an internal labor market device, helping to filter and distribute operators across the seventy or so rides in the park.

Despite the apparent standardization and considered rationality of what is a very lengthy hiring process (taking sometimes up to six months to complete), ride operator myth has it that one must know someone already working in the organization in order to be hired. As in many other, if not most, organizations, selection from the employee's standpoint is friendship and kin dependent, and the higher up one's contacts, the better. In this view, formal selection criteria operate as claimed by the company but do so only as a necessary, not sufficient, condition of employment. Virtually every ride operator has a tale to relate regarding how he or she obtained the Disneyland employee card and just how crucial some personal link—remote or intimate—turned out to be. Competition for jobs in the park is, according to public and employee lore, intense, and having the right attributes must be coupled with knowing the right people if the ride operator job is to be secured. The effect of such a mechanism, if operating as employees claim, reduces the social variability of the new hire pool and provides at least some, if small, insurance that newcomers are properly motivated, for sponsors have no wish to be embarrassed by the sponsored.[12]

There is, among insiders and outsiders alike, a rather common view on the social attributes of the common denominator or standard-make Disneyland ride operator. Single, white males and females, in their early twenties, of healthy appearance, possibly radiating good testimony of a recent history of sports, without facial blemish, of above-average height (and below-average weight), with conservative grooming standards ("punk" appearances and accoutrements are apparently as taboo among current employees as "hippie" appearances and accoutrements were in the late 1960s and early 1970s) are typical of these social identifiers.[13] There are representative minorities on the payroll, but since ethnicity displays are sternly discouraged by management, minority employees are rather close copies of the standard model, albeit in different colors.

College students, mostly local, are given preference in hiring. Personnel needs peak during the summer months (and other school holidays), which nicely complements the employment patterns of students. Relevant ride operator categories are part time, permanent part time, and permanent. Everyone must begin their careers as part-timers or "seasonals" where pay and benefits are set at minimal levels.[14] Most operators play out their careers in the park at the part-time level, working anywhere from 8 to 35 hours a week during the summer. Permanent part time is a label reserved for those selected to continue their work part time during the slower off-season months, returning, with the heat, to near full-time employment. Most ride operators retire after several seasons saying, without apparent irony or malice, that they are ready for a "real job." There are, however, a few ride operators who, by Disney standards, are ripe veterans, having been with the park seemingly since creation. Without exception, they fall into the small permanent category, although there are some other "lifers," mostly local schoolteachers who are in the permanent part-time category. Old-timers are regarded with both curiosity and suspicion by the college-age seasonals, and considerable social distance is the rule between obvious age cohorts. Disneyland, at the ride operator level, is a distinctly youthful organization.

Among ride operators, rewards and status are partly attributable to the number of hours one draws each week. Seniority is the main correlate here, but it is far from a perfect one, for there are few guarantees that one will automatically be granted increases with time on the job. Post-training work ordinarily begins with weekend work, coupled with the lowly regarded (by employees) all-night graduation parties hosted at Disneyland each year for a number of southern California high schools. Starting at perhaps ten hours per week, the ride operator gains more through the favors of his or her immediate boss, the ride foreman, who handles the employee schedules on each attraction. The available work hours are methodically determined at administrative levels and are based on what appear to be happy attendance estimates.[15] Just who among a group of part-timers on a given ride will be offered these hours is, however, a constant source of uncertainty and of obvious interest to all. Disneyland rides are notoriously "overstaffed," thus giving considerable leeway and reward power to foremen.

In everyday practice, operators build up credits and personal relations (or lack thereof) with particular foremen and can therefore predict with some accuracy the number of hours they are likely to work from week to week. Nonetheless, operators know well just how vulnerable and dispensable they are to the organization. Not only are they repeatedly told of the hordes clamoring at the personnel gates to take their place, they know that errors in their conduct (however slight), when detected, can be costly in terms of next week's hours. Only a few rides in the park require specific operational skill (e.g., the jungle cruise with its "live spiel"; the submarine ride with its massive people-processing demands and delicate docking maneuvers; the monorail with its subway-like requirements of drivers and loaders; and some the thrill, or "white knuckle," rides with intricate traffic and customer control procedures). Overwhelmingly, then, generalized skills such as getting along with others on the work teams, unruffled demeanor, cheerfulness, and the ability to forge mutual regard with the foreman become criteria for increasing one's hourly involvement in the park.

Employees bring with them personal badges of status that operate among peers in the park; in very rough order, they are: "good looks," college affiliation; for males, involvement in college sports; career aspirations; past achievements and reputation locally (if any); age (directly related to status up to about age 25 or 26 and inversely related thereafter); and assorted other particularistic matters. Nested closely alongside these imported identity badges are organizational ones.

For example, where one is assigned to work in the park carries social weight. Assignments are mysterious to employees when there are no apparent social links involved. Postings are consequential, however, for the ride and area (Tomorrowland, Fantasyland, Frontierland, Adventureland, and Main Street) a person is assigned carries its own little rewards beyond those of wages, which are fixed for each category of ride operator regardless of station. Regarding inside-the-park stature, whether unique skills are required appears crucial. Disneyland neatly complements Williamson's (1979) economic theorizing in this matter because those employees with the most occupational skill find themselves at the top of the internal status ladder, making their loyalties to the organization, perhaps by virtue of intensified social gratuities, more predictable.

Ride operators, as an undifferentiated but distinctly middle-class group of employees, compete for status with other employee groupings who are hired on a similar basis. Notable among these groups are: (1) the prestigious tour guides (bilingual young women in charge of ushering—some say rushing—little bands of tourists through the park); (2) the recently reorganized WED group, now merged into the general ride operator category but nonetheless still in possession of a distinct and somewhat immodest employee identity (operators who symbolically control customer access to the park and drive the costly entry vehicles such as the antique trains, horse-drawn carriages, and monorail); (3) the proletarian sweepers (keepers of the concrete grounds); and (4) the subprole or peasant status food and concession workers (whose park sobriquets reflect their lowly social worth—"pancake ladies," "peanut pushers," "Coke blokes," "suds divers," and the seemingly irreplaceable "soda jerks").

Pay differentials are slight among these employee groupings; thus collective status adheres, as it does internally for ride operators, to assignment or functional distinctions. Most employee status goes to those allowed to exhibit higher degrees of special skill, relative freedom from constant and direct supervisory monitoring, and whatever prerogatives exist (or can be carved out) to organize and direct customer desires and behavior rather than merely respond to them as spontaneously expressed.

Uniforms provide instant communication about the social merits and demerits of the wearer within the little world of Disneyland workers. Uniforms also correspond to a wider status ranking that casts a significant shadow on employees of all types. Male ride operators on the autopia (miniature car rides) wear, for example, untailored jumpsuits similar to pit mechanics and consequently generate about as much respect from peers as the grease-stained outfits worn by pump jockeys generate from real motorists. The ill-fitting and homogeneous whites worn by sweepers signifies lowly institutional work tinged, perhaps, with a remainder of hospital orderlies rather than street cleanup crews. On the other hand, for males, the crisp, officer-like monorail operator stands alongside the swashbuckling Pirate of the Caribbean, the casual cowpoke of Big Thunder Mountain, or the smartly vested Riverboat pilot as carriers of valued symbols in and outside the park. Employees lust for these higher-status positions and the rights to small advantages such uniforms provide. A lively internal labor market exists, with much scheming for mobility.[16]

For women, a similar market exists, although the perceived sexiness of uniforms, rather than social rank, seems to play a larger role, as shown by the rather heated antagonisms that developed years ago when the ride "It's a Small World" first opened and began outfitting the ride operators with what were felt to be the shortest skirts and most revealing blouses in the park. Tour guides, who traditionally headed the fashion vanguard at Disneyland in their above-the-knee kilts, knee socks, tailored vests, black berets, and smart walking stick, were apparently appalled at being upstaged by their social inferiors and lobbied actively (and, judging by the results, successfully) to lower the skirts, raise the necklines, and generally remake their Small World rivals.

Important, also, to ride operators are the break schedules followed on the various rides: the more the better. Work teams develop inventive ways to increase the time-outs during the workday. Most rides are organized on a rotational basis (the operator moving from a break, to queue monitor, to turnstyle overseer, to unit loader, to traffic switcher, to driver, and, again, to a break). The number of break men or women on a rotation (or ride) varies by the number of employees on duty and by the number of units on-line. Supervisors, foremen, and operators also vary as to what they regard as appropriate break standards (and, more important, as to the value of the many situational factors that can enter the calculation of break rituals). Self-monitoring teams with sleepy supervisors and lax (or savvy) foremen can sometimes manage a shift comprised of 15-minute-on and 45-minute-off periods. They are envied by others, and rides that have such a potential are eyed hungrily by other operators who feel trapped by their more structured (and observed) circumstances.

These examples are precious, perhaps, but they are also important. There is an intricate pecking order among very similar categories of employees. Attributes of reward and status tend to cluster, and there is intense concern about the cluster to which one belongs (or would like to belong). Form follows function, to a degree, because the rides requiring the most skill typically offer the most status and reward. Interaction patterns reflect and sustain this order. Few tour guides, for instance, will stoop to speak at length with sweepers, who speak mostly among themselves or to food workers. Ride operators, between these poles, line up in ways referred to above with only ride proximity (i.e., sharing a break area) representing a potentially significant intervening variable in the interaction equation. These interaction patterns are of more than slight concern because Disneyland during the summer, can be compared quite usefully to a college mixer where across-sex pairing is of vital concern (Schwartz and Lever, 1976). More to the point, what Waller (1937) so accurately called the "rating and dating complex" is in full bloom among park employees. The various modern forms of mating games are valued pastimes among Disneyland employees and are often played with corporate status markers in mind.

Even when not strictly devoted to pairing-off objectives, employee pastimes usually involve other employees. Disneyland's softball and volleyball leagues, its official picnics, employee nights at the park, and beach parties provide a busy social scene for those interested. Areas and rides, too, offer social excitement and bonus as kegs of beer are rolled out when work crews break turnstyle records ("We put 33,147 on the mountain today").[17] During the summer, some night crews routinely party in the early morning while day shifts party at night. Sleep is a commodity not greatly valued by many employees caught up in a valued social whirl.

The so-called youth culture is indeed celebrated in and out of the park. Many employees, for example, live together in the large and cheap (by Los Angeles standards) apartment complexes that surround Disneyland. Employees refer to these sprawling, pastel structures as "the projects" or "worker housing." Yet the lively attractiveness of the collective, low-rent life-style for those living it is easily grasped by some landlords in the area who refuse to rent to Disneyland employees during the summer as a matter of principle and, maybe, sorry experience since these rentals often serve as amusement centers for off-duty Disneylanders who, as they claim, "know how to party."

A fusion of work and play is notable, however, even when play seems to be the master goal. Certainly no Disneyland get-together would be complete without ride operators launching into their special spiel practiced at work ("Before we depart, folks, take another look at the jungle boat dock; it may be the last time you ever see it"). The figurative parallel here is, of course, the atmosphere of a most collegial college. It has a literal parallel as well.

Paid employment at Disneyland begins with the much renowned University of Disneyland whose faculty runs a day-long orientation program followed by classes held during a recruit's 40 hours of apprenticeship training on park grounds. Newly hired ride operators are given a thorough introduction to matters of managerial concern and are repeatedly tested on their absorption of famous Disneyland fact, lore, and procedure. Language is a central feature of university life, and new employees are schooled on its proper use. Customers at Disneyland, for instance, are never referred to as such; they are "guests." There are no rides at Disneyland, only "attractions." Disneyland itself is a "park," not an amusement center, and it is divided into "backstage," "staging," and "onstage" regions. Law enforcement personnel hired by the park are not policemen but "security hosts." Employees do not wear uniforms but check out fresh "costumes" each working day from "Wardrobe." And, of course, there are no accidents at Disneyland, only "incidents."

The university curriculum also anticipates probable questions ride operators may someday face from customers and are taught the approved public response. A sample:

Question (posed by trainer): "What do you tell a guest who requests a rain check?"

Answer (in three parts):   "We don't offer rain checks at Disneyland because (1) the main attractions are all indoors;
(2) we would go broke if we offered passes;
and (3) sunny days would be more crowded if
we gave passes."

Shrewd trainees readily note that such an answer blissfully disregards the fact
that waiting areas of Disneyland rides are mostly outdoors and that there are no
subways in the park to whisk guests from land to land. Nor do they miss the
economic assumption concerning the apparent frequency of Southern California
rains. They discuss such matters together, of course, but rarely raise them in the
classroom. In most respects, these are recruits who take easily the role of good
student.

Classes are taught by professional Disneyland trainers who concentrate on
those aspects of park procedure thought highly general—matters to be learned by
all employees. Particularistic skill training (and "reality shock") is reserved for
the second wave of socialization occurring on the rides themselves as operators
are taught, for example, how and when to send a mock bobsled caroming down
the track; or, more delicately, the proper ways to stuff an obese adult customer
into the midst of children riding the monkey car on a miniature circus train; or,
most problematically, what exactly to tell an irate customer standing in the rain
who, in no uncertain terms, wants his money back and wants it back now.

During orientation, considerable concern is placed on particular values the
Disney organization considers central to its operations. These values range from
the "customer is king" verities to the more or less unique kind, of which "everyone is a child at heart when at Disneyland" is a decent example. This latter
piety is one few employees fail to recognize as also attaching to everyone's mind
as well after a few months of work experience. Elaborate checklists of appearance standards are memorized and recited in the training classroom, and great
efforts are spent trying to bring employee emotional responses in line with such
standards. Employees are told repeatedly that if they are happy and cheerful at
work, so too will be the guests at play. Inspirational films, hearty pep talks, family imagery, and exemplars of corporate performance are all representative of the
strong symbolic stuff of these training rituals.

Another example, perhaps extreme, concerns the symbolic role the founder,
Walt Disney, plays in such matters. When Disney was alive, newcomers and
veterans alike were told how much he enjoyed coming to the park and just how
exacting he was about the conditions he observed. For employees, the cautionary
whoop, "Walt's in the park" could often bring forth additional energy and care
for one's part in the production. Upon his death, trainers at the university were
commonly said to be telling recruits to mind their manners because "Walt's in
the park all the time now."

Yet like employees everywhere, there is a limit to which such overt company propaganda can be effective. Students and trainers alike seem to agree on where the line is drawn, for there is much satirical banter, mischievous winkings, and playful exaggeration in the classroom. All are aware that the label "Disneyland" has both an unserious and artificial connotation and that a full embrace of the Disneyland role would be as deviant as its full rejection. It does seem, however, because of the corporate imagery, the recruiting and selection procedures, the goodwill trainees hold toward the organization at entry, the peer-based employment context, and the smooth fit with real student calendars, the job is considered by most to be a good one. The University of Disneyland, it appears, graduates students with a modest amount of pride and a considerable amount of fact and faith firmly ingrained as important things to know (and accept).

Matters become slightly more complicated as the new hires move into the various realms of Disneyland enterprise. There are real customers, and employees soon learn that these good folks do not always measure up to the typically mannered and grateful guest of the training classroom. Moreover, ride operators may find it difficult to utter the proscribed "Welcome Voyageur" (or its equivalent) when it is to be given to the twenty-thousandth human being passing through the Space Mountain turnstyle on a crowded day in July. Other difficulties present themselves, but as operators learned in training, there are others onstage to assist them.

Employees learn, however, that supervisors and, to a lesser degree, foremen are not only on the premises to help them; they are also there to catch them when they slip over or blatantly violate procedure or policy. Since most rides are tightly designed to eliminate human judgment and minimize operational disasters, much of the supervisory monitoring is directed at activities ride operators consider trivial: taking too long a break; not wearing parts of one's official uniform such as a hat, standard-issue belt, or correct shoes; rushing the ride (although more frequent violations seem to be detected for the provision of longer-than-usual rides for lucky customers);[18] fraternizing with guests beyond the call of duty; talking back to quarrelsome or sometimes merely querisome customers; and so forth. All are matters covered quite explicitly in the hefty codebooks ride operators are to be familiar with, and violations of such codes are often subject to instant and harsh discipline. The firing of what to supervisors are "malcontents," "troublemakers," "bumblers," "attitude problems," or simply "jerks" is a frequent occasion at Disneyland, and, among part-timers who are the most subject to degradation and being fired, the threat is omnipresent. There are few workers who have not witnessed first-hand the rapid disappearance of a coworker for offenses they would regard as "Mickey Mouse." Moreover, there are few employees who themselves have not violated a good number of operational and demeanor standards and anticipate, with just cause, the violation of more in the future.[19]

In part because of the punitive and what are widely held to be capricious supervisory practices in the park, foremen and ride operators are usually drawn close and shield one another from suspicious area supervisors. Throughout the year, each land is assigned a number of supervisors who, dressed alike in short-sleeved white shirts and ties with walkie-talkies hitched to their belts, wander about their territory on the lookout for deviations from park procedures (and other signs of disorder). Occasionally supervisors pose in tourist garb and ghost-ride the various attractions to be sure everything is up to snuff. Supervisors are well known among park employees for the variety of surreptitious techniques they employ when going about their monitoring duties. Blind observation posts are legendary, almost sacred, sites within the park ("this is where Old Man Weston hangs out. He can see Dumbo, Story Book, the Carousel, and the Tea Cups from here"). Supervisors in Tomorrowland are, for example, famous for their penchant of hiding in the bushes above the submarine caves, timing the arrivals and departures of the supposedly fully loaded boats making their 8 ½ minute cruise under the polar icecaps. That they might also catch a submarine captain furtively enjoying a smoke (or worse) while inside the conning tower (his upper body out of view of the crowd on the vessel) might just make a supervisor's day—and unmake the employee's. In short, supervisors, if not foremen, are regarded by ride operators as sneaks and tricksters, out to get them and representative of the dark side of park life. Their presence is, of course, an orchestrated one and does more than merely watch over the ride operators. It also draws operators together as cohesive units who must look out for one another while they work (and shirk).

Supervisors are not the only villains who appear in the park. The treachery of co-workers, while rare, has its moments. Pointing out the code violations of colleagues to foremen and supervisor—usually in secret—provides one avenue of collegial duplicity. Finks of all sorts can be found among the peer ranks at Disneyland and, while their dirty deeds are uncommon, work teams on all rides go to some effort to determine just who they might be and, if possible, drive them from their midst. Newcomers are carefully appraised on these matters, and those who fail the inventive tests of "member in good standing" are subject to some uncomfortable treatment. Innuendo and gossip are the primary tools in this regard, with ridicule and ostracism providing the backup. Since perhaps the greatest rewards working at Disneyland offers its ride operator personnel are those of belonging to a tight little network of like-minded and sociable peers where off-duty interaction is at least as vital and pleasurable as the on-duty sort, such mechanisms are quite effective. Here is some of the most powerful and focused emotion work found in the park, and those subject to such attention, rightly or wrongly, will grieve, but grieve alone.

Another candidate for ride operator attention and scorn is the unruly or ill-mannered guest. Such characters offer amusement, consternation, and the occasional job challenge that occurs when remedies are deemed necessary to restore employee dignity in the face of some real or imagined slight from a customer. By and large, the people-processing tasks of ride operators pass smoothly, with operators hardly noticing much more than the bodies passing in front of view (special bodies, however, generate special attention). Sometimes more than a body becomes visible, as happens when customers overstep their roles, challenge employee authority, or otherwise disrupt the daily routines of operators. In the process, guests become "ducks," one of many derisive terms used by ride operators to label those customers they believe beyond the pale. Normally these characters are brought to the attention of park security officers, ride foremen, or area supervisors who decide how the ducks are to be disciplined.[20]

Sometimes, however, the alleged slight is too personal or too extraordinary for a ride operator to let it pass unnoticed or merely by informing others. Restoration of one's respect is called for, and routine practices have been developed for these circumstances. Common remedies include the "seatbelt squeeze," a small token of appreciation given a deviant customer consisting of the rapid cinching up of a required seatbelt such that the passenger is doubled over at the point of departure and left gasping for the duration of a ride; the "break-toss," an acrobatic gesture of the autopia trade whereby operators jump on the outside of a norm violator's car, stealthily unhitching the safety belt, then slamming on the brakes and bringing the vehicle to an almost instantaneous stop while the driver flies on to the hood of the car (or beyond); the "seatbelt slap," an equally distinguished gesture by which an offending customer receives a sharp, quick snap of a hard plastic belt across the face (or other parts of the body) when entering or exiting a seatbelted ride; the "break-up-the-party" gambit, a queuing device put to use in officious fashion whereby bothersome pairs are separated at the last minute into different units, thus forcing on them the pain of strange companions for the duration of the Trip to the Moon or a ramble on Mr. Toad's Wild Ride; the "hatch-cover ploy," a much beloved practice of submarine pilots who, in collusion with mates on the loading dock, are able to drench offensive guests with water as their units pass under an artificial waterfall; and the rather ignoble variants of the "sorry-I-didn't-see-your-hand" tactic, a savage move designed to crunch a particularly irksome customer's hand (foot, finger, arm, leg, etc.) by bringing a piece of Disneyland property to bear on the appendage, such as a Mine Train door or the starboard side of a Jungle Cruise boat. This last remedy is most often a "near miss" designed to startle the little criminals of Disneyland. They usually get the message. All of these unofficial procedures (and many more) are learned on the job, and, although they are used sparingly, they are used. Occasions of use provide a continual stream of sweet revenge talk to enliven and enrich colleague conversation at break-time or after work.

Too much, of course, can be made of these subversive practices. By and large, Disneyland employees are remarkable for their forbearance and polite good manners even under the most trying conditions. They are taught, and some come to believe, they are really "onstage" while working. Surveillance by supervisory personnel certainly fades in the light of the glances the employee receives from perhaps 50,000 or 60,000 paying guests who tromp daily through the park in the summer. Disneyland employees know well that they themselves are part and parcel of the product being sold and learn to check their more discriminating manners in favor of the generalized countenance of cheerful lad or lassie whose enthusiasm and dedication are obvious to all.

At times, the emotional resources of employees appear awesome. When the going gets tough and the park is jammed, the nerves of all employees are frayed and sorely tested by the crowd, din, sweltering sun, and eye-burning smog. Customers wait in what employees call "bullpens" (and park officials call "reception areas") for up to several hours for a 3 ½ minute ride that operators are sometimes hell-bent on cutting to 2 ½ minutes. Surely a monument to the human ability to suppress feelings has been created when both users and providers can maintain their composure and seeming regard for one another when in such a fix.

It is in this domain where corporate culture must be given its due. Perhaps the depth of a culture is visible only when its members are under the gun. The orderliness—a good part of the Disney formula for financial success—is an accomplishment based not only on physical design and elaborate procedures; it rests also on the low-level, part-time employees who must be willing, even eager, to keep the show afloat. The ease with which employees glide into their user-friendly roles and the everyday acting skill they display in bringing off these roles are, in large measure, feats of social engineering. Disneyland does not pay well, supervision is arbitrary and skin close, its working conditions are chaotic, its jobs require minimal amounts of intelligence or judgment, and it asks of its employees a kind of loyalty that is almost fanatical. Yet it attracts a particularly able work force whose personal backgrounds suggest potential and talents far exceeding those required of traffic cop, people stuffer, queue or line manager, and button pusher. As we have suggested, not all of Disneyland is covered by the culture. There are small pockets of resistance, and various degrees of autonomy are maintained by employees. But, nonetheless, the adherence and support for the "Disney Way" is remarkable. And, like swallows returning to Capistrano, part-timers look forward to their seasonal migrations.

Four features alluded to in this shotgun description can be pointed out as a way of closing our discussion. First, socialization, while costly, is of a most selective, collective, intensive, serial, sequential, and closed sort. These tactics are notable for their penetration into the private spheres of individual thought and feeling (Van Maanen and Schein, 1979).[21] Incoming identities are not so much dismantled as they are set aside as employees are schooled in the use of new identities of a situational sort. These identities are symbolically powerful and, for some, laden with social approval. It is hardly surprising that the most problematic ride in terms of employee turnover during a summer is the Autopia, where ride operators apparently find little to identify with on the job. Distinguished Mountaineers, Jet Pilots, Storybook Princesses, Western Sheriffs, or

Southern Belles (of New Orleans Square) have less difficulty on this score even though they owe their particular work role far more to chance than merit since they all come from the same pool. Disneyland, by design, bestows identity by systematically putting newcomers through a process carefully set up to strip away the job relevance of other sources of identity and learned response and replace them with others of organizational relevance. It works.

Second, this is a culture whose designers have left little room for individual experimentation. Supervisors, as noted by their focused strolls and attentive looks, keep very close tabs on what is going on at any moment in all the lands. Discretion of a personal sort is very limited while employees are "onstage." Even the "backstage" and certain "offstage" domains have their corporate monitors. Employees are indeed aware that their offstage life beyond the picnics, parties, and softball games is subject to some scrutiny, for police checks are made on potential and current employees. Nor do all employees discount the rumors that park officials make periodic inquiries as to a person's habits concerning sex and drugs. Moreover, the sheer number of rules and regulations are striking, thus making the grounds for dismissal a matter of multiple choice for those supervisors who discover a use for such grounds. The feeling of being watched is a rather prevalent complaint among Disneyland people, and it is one that a person must learn to live with, however disturbing it may seem. The culture is apparently one where the managers do not trust the employees to carry on without their able assistance. The management of this culture is a very active one.

Third, emotion management occurs at Disneyland in a number of quite distinct ways. From the instructors at the orientation center who beseech recruits to "wish every guest a pleasant day," to the foremen who plead with their charges to "at least say thank you when you herd them through the gate," appearance, demeanor, and etiquette have special meanings at Disneyland. Since these are prized personal attributes over which we normally feel in control, making them commodities can be unnerving. Much self-monitoring is involved, of course, but even here, self-management has an organizational side. Consider those ride operators who may complain of being "too tired to smile" but at the same time may feel a little guilty for having uttered such a confession. Consider too the pressure of being onstage and the cumulative annoyance of having children and adults asking whether the water in the lagoon is real, or where the well-marked toilets might be, or where Walt Disney's tomb is to be found, or the real clincher—whether one is "really real." The mere fact that so much operator discourse concerns the handling of "ducks" suggests that these emotional disturbances have costs. There are, for example, times in all employee careers when they put themselves on "automatic pilot," "go robot," "can't feel a thing," "lapse into a dream," "go into a trance," or otherwise "check out" while still on duty. Despite the crafty supervisors' attempts to measure the glimmer in an employee's eye, this sort of willed emotional numbness is common to many of the onstage Disneyland personnel. In a sense, it is a contracultural form of passive resistance, suggesting that there still is a sacred preserve of individuality among employees in the park.[22]

Finally, taking the three above points together, it seems that even when people are paid to be nice, it is hard for them to do so all the time. When such efforts succeed to the degree that Disney officials have succeeded, it appears a rather towering achievement (if not always admirable). It works at the collective level by virtue of elaborate direction. Employees at all levels are stage managed by higher-ranking employees who, having come up through the ranks themselves, hire, train, and closely supervise their replacements on the bottom rungs. Expression rules are laid out in corporate manuals. Employee time-outs intensify work experiences. Social exchanges are forced into narrow channels. Training and retraining (whenever one moves to a new ride) programs are continual. Hiding places are few. It is difficult to imagine work roles being more defined than those at Disneyland. If the deskilling of work in manufacturing moved control of the worker's thought processes into the manager's office, the routine ways Disneyland controls emotional expression in the park has brought the worker's heart into the office as well. Subtasks seem infinitely broken down: "Did you smile?" "Did you say thank you?" "Was it a sincere thank you?" Here is organizational culture worthy of the name.

We now move to examine another much heralded company culture, High Technology Inc. (Tech), whose outlines are perhaps a little less explicit than Disneyland but are nonetheless visible. Here is a deadly serious organization that designs, manufactures, and services a line of technically sophisticated products and is well in the mainstream of American corporate life. The valued employees at Tech are, most assuredly, not college students whimsically playing at work but are instead highly trained, competitive "professionals" for whom corporate success may quite literally be a life-and-death matter. Here is also a company that apparently takes to heart many of the academic and popular pronouncements on the consequences of corporate culture and has tried rather hard to sustain, if not build, what is regarded, at least by most outsiders, as a very good one.

LIFE IN (AND AROUND) THE TRENCHES

High Technology Incorporated is a large and successful corporation.[23] It was founded some years ago by a small group of ambitious engineers with timely ideas and the abilities to design and produce a (then) revolutionary product. The firm began its operations in a site located well within what is now known as technology region, one of the several well-known high-tech centers that have sprung up around large urban and academic centers. Tech has grown into a worldwide organization with close to 100,000 employees who in various roles develop, manufacture, sell, and service products that are said to be "on the cutting edge of high technology."

Engineering is the heart of this organization. Tech is headed by one of its founders, an engineer who thinks nothing of personally redesigning products before they are shipped or intervening in the most nitty-gritty details of product development. More crucially, Tech is built around people who have emerged from engineering backgrounds. These are people who seemingly relish telling others of the time they spent doing product design, delivering deliverables and shipping steel, of the infinite number of meals they have eaten served to them by vending machines, and of the various addictions and obsessions they have developed for their work. Persons of repute and status at Tech will invariably launch into stories about their "time in the trenches" when conversational openings are presented to them.

At Tech, "technical sophistication," "practical experience," and "knowing what it takes to get a product out the door" are the honorable claims for status. However, as in all other organizations, there are pressures for change. The growing size, changing markets, several embarrassing failures of recent vintage, and a sort of managerial *zeitgeist* have generated insider calls for more professional management and the development of a business perspective to challenge what some in the organization regard as an overly technical one. The response to these calls has not yet been overwhelming. Certainly most old-timers are more bemused than threatened when suggestions are made that Tech is now ready for the "day of the MBA."

The materials we present focus on the engineering division of the company and are based in particular on one engineering group. Managed by a vice-president, members of this group are responsible for developing a set of products that many in the company see as part of a technological new wave and therefore critical to the future success of the firm.[24] This group has high visibility. Senior management pays close attention to its affairs, and its successes and failures are closely noted and discussed frequently and widely within management circles of the organization. Like many other groups at Tech, this one is marked by frequent reorganizations. "Change is the only thing constant around here," is a common remark among members of this group who believe, generally, "Tech never encourages stable groups." In this view, managerial habits also contribute to such fluidity. As put by one engineer: "The managers move from project to project every year or two, trying to capitalize on short-term gains or bail out of failing projects with their reputation intact when things look bad."

The group of interest here is a quasi-independent division of the company. Top management and staff of the group are located at corporate headquarters— the hub of corporate activity and center of politics at Tech—but the bulk of engineering work is carried on at other local facilities. A few outposts of the group are found across the Atlantic (the notorious "Brits") or on the far side of the

Rockies. These distant facilities sometimes offer refuge for those who have tired of "the corporate puzzle palace." But the heart and soul of the company as a whole, as many "Tech watchers" claim, is in the much mythologized technology region and, in particular, at "corporate."

Organizational charts at Tech are not easy to come by. Although they exist in various subgroups, collected through the painstaking piecing together of information, gossip, and frequent organizational announcements flashed across the Technet, members of engineering groups appear to frown on such charts ("simple mappings of a complex network").[25] Many employees are vague about reporting relations and proclaim an antistructure attitude, a stance that is somewhat fashionable at Tech. This posture is realistic to a degree, for it is indeed difficult to display the structure or relations at Tech. But it is also a key element of the explicit and often discussed "Tech culture." Phrases such as "matrix management," "multiple dotted lines," "dense networks," and "structural ambiguity" are frequently used by members of the organization to describe the engineering division. In this view, the difference between formal and informal organization is not readily distinguishable. For many, "culture" replaces "structure" as an organizing principle and is used both to explain and guide action. Depending on the context, this is either celebrated as a source of creativity or seen as a pain in the neck.

Despite this stylized rendition of lack of structure, there are recognizable segments of the organization that serve to order member knowledge of where people are located and what they might do—even if particular people are hard to pin down. The engineering division consists of several thousand engineers, managers, and support staff divided into a number of groups. Each group is responsible for a variety of products or would-be products lumped together as a system, wherein each unit of the group is thought to have something in common with the other units of the system. Units within a group can be either staff or line, with the status edge, as is true in most other industrial organizations, going to the line, where "real things" get managed and "value added" is clear to all. A fundamental distinction exists in all groups between "technical" and "business" areas, although in practice it is sometimes difficult to determine which side of the distinction a given unit or individual emphasizes. Most clarity, however, is ordinarily obtained on the technical side where development teams work on highly specific engineering projects. These domains are regarded as the "guts of Tech." Here is where the "trenches" are located, representing, to those who occupy them, the "firing lines" of the organization.[26]

Projects vary in size and expected length, but there is an order, known to insiders, that gives status to some projects and denies it to others. The rough correlates are the resources devoted to a project, the reputation of the team members, and the state-of-the-art technical problems they tackle. Project teams are headed by development managers who, with the help of supervisors (on the management side) and project leaders (experienced technical people), direct the various engineers, technicians, technical writers, and support staff assigned to the team. Above the project level, business areas play more of a role, and personnel shifts are thought to be as frequent as reorganizations. While projects are relatively more stable, their members report an ever-present concern with the possibility of being "unfunded" or "killed" (cancelled on short notice).

Managers throughout the organization typically possess technical backgrounds. The majority have formal engineering training or at least engineering experience at Tech. Without such credentials, managers are unlikely to gain much respect from others in the organization.[27] Respect is also gained by a manager's reputation as an aggressive and successful promoter of projects within the company. The top of the pecking order is, then, occupied by technically trained "entrepreneurs," the bottom by nontechnical "bureaucrats." The contrast is felt to reflect, among other things, managerial savvy, wit, energy, and imagination. In short, whatever the "entrepreneur" is, the "bureaucrat" is not.

Managers have moved out of "hands-on" engineering by virtue of promotion. Reasons for "opting out" are attributed to personal factors. Common accounts include "getting burned out on engineering," "bored with technical work," or "becoming too ambitious." Some refer to their move into management as "getting the disease," while others call it "a sign of growing up." Most appear committed to managerial careers, aspiring to reach the higher ranks at Tech or elsewhere in the industry. To this end, they attempt to complement their assumed technical sophistication by acquiring new forms of knowledge: "people skills," "political know-how," and "business sense." A few will sometimes speak of wanting to retire early and assume a quieter life. All would concur that the manger's life at Tech is a hectic one.

Engineers not making the transition into management can progress also—from an entry-level position involving lowly and boring "shitwork," one can move to principal engineer, to consulting engineer, to senior engineer (those at the pinnacle are the "technical gurus" of the company). As one moves up the technical ladder, responsibilities for more elements of a product (or even system) are added to the role. Engineering domains are highly competitive, populated by individuals who are either winners or losers. The winners are the wizards or geniuses of Tech whose status is sometimes debated ("the only way he'll make the list of 100 brightest scientists in *Technology Times* is if he mails coupons from the back of cereal boxes") and sometimes acknowledged ("Peter is brilliant, no question about that, a crackerjack engineer"). The losers are the journeymen (and the occasional woman) often treated in word and deed as "bodies" ("They were short on the project so they brought down a body from the Lyndsville group; the body's name was Bill").

Engineers also sort themselves out by the kind of work they do. Of most interest is the contrast between hardware and software engineers. The former are described by the latter as narrow, concrete, speak "technologese" rather than English, undereducated, hard drinking, interested only in the blood and guts of the machine. The latter are seen by the former as undisciplined, loose, airy-fairy types, dreamers, talkers not doers. In both camps, however, these Tech engineers enjoy presenting themselves to others as artists with big egos, addictive personalities, few social graces, a propensity for hard work (supposedly at the expense of their families, said to be headed by "Tech widows"), and doomed to "burn out" at some point, the scars of which can then be carried about and displayed like a purple heart.

Project engineers in the trenches are reputed to be interested in "neat things" (roughly translated as personally challenging design tasks, interesting problems, and complicated technologies). If these "neat things" are not available during regular working hours, they can feed the "midnight projects" engaged in by some at Tech. "Art is what you do for yourself; work is what you do for others," says a prominently displayed slogan on the wall of an engineering cubicle.

Engineering work is felt by most in the organization to be "flexible," and Tech engineering facilities are designed as open office space. On a typical day, engineers are in their cubicles, in front of their terminals, in the labs, or in various meetings. When working alone, some wear earplugs to keep out the unending background noise of high-tech squeaks and whirs. They are also worn to minimize the chance of interruption and interaction. Every engineer also has a terminal at home, where much work is said to take place.

In the common spaces of Tech facilities (usually in or around the cafeteria), many informal meetings take place where engineers huddle over computer output or paper-and-pencil designs. Meeting rooms off the central office area provide space for the more private or formal design meetings, status reports, staff meetings, and other gatherings in which time is spent or misspent. Since engineers largely control their own schedules at Tech, perceptions of who's working and who's shirking (at home or in the office) are matters of constant concern. Gossip levels rise and perceptions of inequality increase at "crunch time" (when deadlines draw near) when reputations are on the line.

It is the engineering manager's job to squeeze the most out of these self-proclaimed artists. Managers are to create the "right environment" so that engineers will be able to work to the limits of their abilities. Managers are also keepers of organizational time, and thus scheduling represents the eternal bone of contention between engineers and managers. Engineers typically want more time than managers are willing to grant. And managers themselves often believe they are committed to unrealistic schedules. As one manager put it: "Let's face it. If you want the project, you have to lie! And your engineers? Well, they're lying to you." Since most engineering managers are assessed by their bosses on their ability to "ship on time" and their bosses are judged on similar grounds ("time to market"), they evaluate their engineers by their ability to "drive a stake in the ground" (to settle on a well-defined piece of work and to produce it in reasonable time). Time thus becomes the grand criterion of organizational assessment. The balance between art and business or "neat things" and revenue is, in large measure, worked out by managers trying to keep a project on schedule by curbing the engineers' predilection for "creeping featuritis" and "bells and whistles" or their urge to move what is a "midnight project" to high noon.

The "business perspective" at Tech is carried by senior managers and certain staff groups such as marketing, strategy, and product management. The business of business is, of course, profit. Making money is regarded as both a necessity and an ideal. Promoters of the business perspective are not bashful or subtle on this matter. As one senior manager claims in an often-repeated phrase: "We are here to make gobs and gobs and gobs of money." Some of those who hold this perspective see themselves as out to reform the company by introducing more businesslike attitudes and procedures. These managers also regard engineers and the "engineering mentality" in a critical light: "They are know-it-alls with a one-way-only mentality who want to just throw the product over the wall without any conception of the customer or the market."

Engineers return these compliments. They see their business counterparts as "overhead," "do nothings," or, the worst curse of all, "product preventers." Thus, the battle lines are drawn, and each skirmish is seen as being hard and merciless. To some, Tech is a "primordial soup" where everyone is out to get everyone else and only the fit survive.

Evaluations at Tech are thought by the membership to be quick and firm. Managers and engineers are said to have a "press" (a reputation regarding their past performance that determine their current credibility). A central myth proclaims people are assessed on the basis of their most recent project. One manager summed up his view of Tech's assessment practices with an analogy: "[It's like] you are a violinist and if the string breaks, you've had it, and you're as good as lost."

While there is usually ongoing debate as to just who is winning among managers, there is often consensus on just who is losing. Association with a failed project is the key, and it is the subject of much discussion. For example, one manager, briefing his staff, refers to a peer in the following way: "He's dead. He can't be highly successful anymore. We'll help him out but keep our distance. . . . If he goes down, he might drag us down too. He's got no credibility anymore. A lot of unspoken stuff around him . . . I heard that the strategy is to make him such a bastard that everything goes around him."

The "walking wounded" are those losers who suffered through failure and are either "burned out," "stuck," or "recuperating." There are a number of relatively ill-defined jobs at Tech apparently designed to allow the company to live up to its public commitment to take care of its employees. Among managers, this means taking care of the casualties. Most are sent away from the center of Tech to make what they can of their now-stigmatized careers. More serious casualties are also discussed by managers. Stories of alcoholism, psychiatric breakdown, work-related family troubles, and suicide are favorite tales of this genre.

Literal interpretations of this talk must be viewed with caution. By talking of the misfortunes of others, the combat-like character of life at Tech, or the apparently bitter struggles for organizational success, the talkers are also making implicit statements about their own polished, noble, and true-grit selves. By depicting the organization and its members in these ways, the storytellers give dramatic form to what may well be mundane and general organizational events. In choosing these forms of description, tellers of the tales not only position themselves onstage at Tech but also imply what strong characters they are themselves, able to play "hardball" with the best of them. Grains of salt must be cast on these tales; they may well reveal more of what is a culturally appropriate presentation than what is a factual one.

Given such frequently encountered and publicly acknowledged presentations of life in the Tech trenches, what are we to make of the company culture? In answering this interpretive question, the first thing that strikes the Tech watcher is that he is not the only one posing the question. Within the organization, there are many lay and a few professional culture vultures. This is of consequence to understanding the subject matter itself. What kinds of descriptions do these inside analysts divine?

Consider, first, the codified versions of Tech culture. There are numerous written materials available to employees claiming to describe what Tech and its people are like. One category consists of polished and published documents that put forth top management views. Such documents are openly prescriptive, seeking to define what is proper at Tech and what is not. For example, there is the Tech handbook, an internal document listing all the groupings in the organization. It is issued yearly and is considered to be of some interest because it contains the closest thing to an organizational chart that is officially distributed by the company. It is found in most managers' offices.

The introduction to the handbook of 1985 offers a glimpse into the prescribed culture. A reader finds first an article by W. J. King, an engineering educator, reprinted from a 1944 edition of an engineering journal. Titled, "The Unwritten Laws of Engineering," the article is a moralistic exhortation. It quotes liberally from Emerson's essay on self-reliance and offers aphoristic advice to the enterprising organizational engineer. It is essentially a call for initiative, responsibility, individualism, self-control, honesty, and fairness. Rules for emotional control are also made explicit:

> Do not harbor grudges. . . . Form the habit of considering the feelings of others. . . . Help the other fellow when the opportunity arises. Even if you are mean-spirited enough to derive no satisfaction from accommodating others, it is a good investment.

King's article is interesting not for its dated tone but for its no-nonsense laying out of an ideological position. In essence, a role is outlined for members who are, presumably, expected to embrace it. Thus, in this view, to be "successful" requires management of feelings and self-presentations; moreover, management must be done sincerely. Placing this article at the front end of a book many employees value (although, no doubt, for other reasons) is perhaps indicative of the importance top management places on such matters. And if the lazy reader skipped over King's earthy advice, an updated version is available in the next selection of the handbook called "Tech Culture" (no author listed). It begins with a descriptive tone suggesting that the role is an integral part of the culture:

> Honesty, hard work, moral and ethical conduct, a high level of professionalism, and team work are qualities that are an integral part of employment at High Technology. These qualities are considered part of the Tech culture. Employees conduct themselves in an informal manner and are on a first-name basis with everyone at all levels. . . . The opportunity for self direction and self determination is always present.

Then it shifts to an elaboration of management expectations:

> Management expects hard work and a high level of achievement. . . . A great deal of trust is placed in employees and employees are expected to act in a mature manner at all times. The organization depends on trust, communication, and team work.

Another form of presenting Tech culture derives from organizationally sponsored research. Studies conducted by outside researchers circulate throughout the firm, particularly in upper-management, training, and personnel circles. Consultants too are called in occasionally to formulate their version of Tech culture. More interesting perhaps are the internal studies members of the organization conduct on their own culture. In the engineering group studied here, there is a full-time culture expert charged with unearthing, documenting, and, presumably, preserving the culture of Tech engineers.

The output of this corporate anthropology is a variety of materials: management reports, memos, summaries of popular books, and reprints of the published popular and academic articles dealing with Tech (unmasking pseudonyms when required); slide presentations and talks given throughout the company by self-proclaimed cultural experts; and videorecordings of top managers talking about the culture.

In many of these products, an attempt is made to describe the culture and its role requirements in informal terms as expressed by the words of celebrated "old-timers" in the company. For example, an internal paper, "Talking Values: Heroes of Engineering Speak," consists of excerpts from interviews with senior Tech managers. One is asked to describe the "Tech type":

> A lot of people we hire into this company, at least the ones that stick around, have basically the same mind set. Someone who is innovative, enthusiastic, willing to work hard, who isn't hung up on structure, and who has absolutely no concern with educational background. They demand an awful lot from themselves. The harshest critic in the system is yourself and that drives you to do some terribly difficult things. You have to be a self-starter, an individual who takes chances and risks and moves ahead. The expectation is that everyone is going to work hard, not for hard work's sake, but for the fun of it, and enjoy doing what they are doing, and show commitment no matter what it takes. A core of the environment is individual commitment, a lot of integrity, and a very high level of expectations from yourself. Hassle is the price

of the organizational structure. For those who don't like it, it's very frustrating. You can wrap those three or four things together (openness, honesty, success, fairness) and you can sum it all up in one word and that is caring. Caring about your job, the people who work for you, yourself.

Another internal paper, "*A Cultural Operating Manual* (Version II)," offers a formalization of what its anonymous author calls the "assumptions that support the culture":

> WE ARE ALL ONE FAMILY. . . . Subcultural differences are encouraged, failure among members is tolerated to some extent, people are encouraged to express their feelings and to give candid feedback, all doors are open.
>
> PEOPLE ARE CREATIVE, HARD WORKING, SELF GOVERNING AND CAN LEARN. . . . People are encouraged to learn from experience by the sink or swim method with some support. Be a self-starter, push at the system from your position (bottom up), respect the differences of others, find a way to enjoy work, take ownership, do the right thing.

In a later section, the "*Cultural Operating Manual*" describes the "typical" experiences of new employees in the form of a narrative titled "The Valley of the Shadow of Tech." An excerpt conveys this tale:

> They have just been hired into a new group or are going to try out a new task. They receive a lot of encouragement. This is called the walk-on-water point of entry. For a while, they vacillate and finally they reach decision point B. Feedback is given but it is not positive. The employees may even be beat up. . . . [For some] the experience is not so good. . . . The employee falls into the Valley. . . . The passage of time will cause some better feelings. Other employees will console the injured person. Some people do not risk again. Some choose to update their resumes and leave the company. Most people get to Point E, fully recovered, and find better ways to interact with the system, a wiser employee.

The tone here is perhaps less moralistic than other versions of Tech culture, but, nevertheless, guidance is again provided the reader, and the benefits of cultural learning and self-control are preached. As with other representations of the Tech Culture spread through the company in managerially approved form, this little story provides a version of the good (and, by implication, the bad) Tech employee.

Two themes are apparent in all these renditions of Tech culture. One speaks to the individual's proper relationship to the organization and the other to the individual's proper relationship to work. The message of the first involves the pride and loyalty an employee is to feel at membership in what is to be regarded by all as a successful and caring community. The language suggests employees should experience something of a communion with the company, a sense of we-ness and belongingness. The second theme establishes the attitudes an employee is to bring to the job—enthusiasm, dedication, willingness to learn, high standards, initiative, and so on. In both cases, a member role consisting of appropriate beliefs, emotions, and behaviors is outlined and offered as a condition of local success.

Employees learn about Tech culture in the flesh as well as from the printed page. Public events are an opportunity to transmit and recreate the prescribed culture. Cultural transmission might be explicit, as in training and educational programs. The orientation workshop provides a good example in this regard. This program, also called "bootcamp," is a two-day affair, offered several times a year and designed for the newly hired engineer with only a few months on the job. The materials covered concern the history, products, markets, and culture of Tech. The workshop has a reputation for providing valuable information, and many employees sign up for more than one session. Even experienced Tech managers and engineers are known to put in an appearance. Understanding Tech is thought by most managers and engineers to give one an edge over the less knowledgeable. How such understanding is achieved can be glimpsed in the following excerpt from fieldnotes describing a workshop session on Tech culture.

The instructor is standing in front of the group, magic marker in hand, ready to kick off the "culture module." "What are the characteristics of people at Tech?" she asks with a warm, eager-looking smile. Her question remains hanging. No answer from the class. "You feel like you've all been chosen, right?" Still no reply. She persists. "What else? What are people like at Tech?" Some volunteers finally speak up: "Friendly" . . . "Amicable" . . . She writes it all on the flip chart. "Individuals" . . . "Team oriented" . . . "I'm expected to be a good corporate citizen" . . . "Strong customer orientation" . . . Still writing, the instructor, her back to the group, adds: "In other places you're incompetent 'til proven otherwise; here it's the other way around. Right?" And not waiting for confirmation, she writes it down too, and adds: "Confidence in competence; they know what they are doing."

"A little too much," the guy sitting next to me whispers to his neighbor, smiling. But the session is warming up, and many are getting in the act. The instructor says: "People tend to like Tech, no matter how confusing it seems." One of the younger-looking men nods and adds: "I like it. I respect the president a lot. Where I worked before, you'd hope they fail!"

Toward the end of the session, the instructor gives a short, apparently impromptu speech of a personal, almost motherly sort. "Be careful, keep a balance, don't overdo it, don't live off vending machines for a year. I've been there; I lived underground for a year, doing code. Balance your life. Don't say, 'I'll work like crazy for four years then get married.' Who will marry you? Don't let the company suck you dry. After nine or ten hours, your work isn't worth much anyway."

The last bit sounds subversive, but it creates an air of hushed regard in the room. These words are allowed to be spoken. This must be a great place to work. The instructor adds the finishing touch. "What kind of company did you think allows me to be saying these things to you?" I feel moved myself.

Culture is also the explicit concern of certain public presentations made by senior managers to particular groups of employees. For example, one senior manager has a ready-made presentation on Tech culture, a "road show" that he readily and frequently presents to interested employee groups. The theme of the

presentation is avowedly prescriptive, built around his formulation of key elements of the Tech Culture. Consider one such presentation given to a group of
engineers and managers after lunch. The talk is long and accompanied by overhead slides flashed on a screen. On each slide are several "bullets" (key points).
With each exposure of a bullet, a few minutes of elaboration and anecdotes follow. Again, from fieldnotes:

> He reveals the first bullet: RESPECT. "Treat others with the respect and the consideration you
> expect, the way they want to be treated. I get *very* upset when I hear someone say 'that tur-
> key.' It says you don't value people."
>
> I look around. I've heard the expression for more than one person in the room. Heads are
> nodding in agreement, seeming to increase in vigor as the presenter's gaze moves across the
> audience. "Build on what others have done. Avoid the NIH (Not Invented Here) syndrome.
> Nothing is more fun than making; but if others have done it, for god's sake, use it!"
>
> Another bullet is revealed: TRUST. "Cooperate with other groups. Hell, it's not Lyndsville
> and Middletown [two sites of Tech engineering groups] that are our enemies; it's Chiptech,
> it's Silicon Technologies."
>
> More vigorous nodding and another bullet: HONESTY. "Say what you intend. Make it
> public at Tech. Avoid situations where you can't be honest."
>
> At the end, there is a burst of applause, and a number of people ask for copies of the slides.

Even within playful periods, "time-outs," cultural allusions are present. One
development manager, for example, having organized a sports day for his group,
uses the opening ceremonies to make a few special points. All are gathered in a
conference room that usually serves for senior staff meetings. The manager-
promoter enters the room carrying a torch of rolled-up computer output and
wearing a crown of leaves. In slow-motion running movements, he assumes his
place at the head of the table and, with a practiced motion, switches on the
viewgraph. He also switches from parody to dead seriousness for his introduc-
tory speech (complete with slides and the ever-present bullets):

> It's good we are doing this. I'm glad you could come. It will give you people an opportunity
> to relax and take your minds off things, work off your excess energy, feel a little better about
> things, get a little more motivated. Also, you'll get to know each other, improve your morale.
> But, remember, nobody is watching you. This in not a Tech event. So don't take off company
> time too blatantly. There is enough of that anyway. And don't get hurt.

The prescribed culture also appears to pervade the company in the form of
aphorisms, quick formulations, words of conventional wisdom, and slogans.
Most employees are relatively familiar with these phrases and will go to some
lengths to explain them if asked. Familiar pieties include: "Do the right thing";
"The engineering sandbox where you get paid to play and call it work"; "It's
not work; it's a celebration"; "There are no problems, only opportunities";
"Engineering is a bottoms-up organization."

Tech culture, as expressed repeatedly in the words of so many, offers employees a seductive, imposing presence. One response is to join the communion and become part of the "we." Another response is to seek distance and detachment. Members display both of these responses and frequently seem to oscillate between these poles.

Communion is expressed in a number of ways. Privately, one manager puts it this way:

> You know, I like Tech. I don't think of leaving. Maybe the culture swallowed me. But there really is a feeling of loyalty I have. We have a lot of that in the culture. We like working for Tech. It is a positive company. You get really involved. I get a real charge when Tech gets a good press. Or when people I knew from this other company were dumping on Tech, I was offended. I didn't like hearing it. They made millions with us! Because of us they got rich! They get all this free knowledge from us and say it with impunity! My husband works for Tech, and he feels the same way. We spend time with friends talking about work; we're worse than doctors. I guess you can call me a Techie.

In the same vein, an engineer remarks:

> People might say I've swallowed slogans, the party line. But I *do* believe that Tech does the right thing. We don't lay off, even though some people deserve to be laid off. So you feel loyalty back. The boss believes in taking care of people, and he gets paid back with loyalty. I trust the man. He means well. There is a lot of honesty at the top and the bottom of the company. I don't know about the middle. But he really means it when he says it's the company's duty to take care of employees and customers. I've never met him, but I've seen the videotapes. He can be very powerful. I got excited when I heard him say it's our moral duty to give the customers what they want. Moral duty!

The routine use of language in the organization is indicative of communion. The use of *we* when referring to the company is an example. Many members use the terms *super* and *terrific* in enthusiastic tones after relatively banal statements, a custom that seems to have worked its way down the hierarchy. The use of overworked clichés in earnest ways also suggests a merging of the individual with the organization. ("He works hard, and he always want to do the right thing.") Some cars and doors around the facility are armed with bumper stickers claiming "I LOVE TECH" (complete with the familiar red heart).

Communion is also accomplished, in its most familiar form, through participation in the various ceremonial rituals of organizational life. Formal presentations invariably call for some sort of affirmation on the part of the audience. Consider the closing lines of a speech given by a group manager and the kind of response it elicits, as described in fieldnotes:

> Each of us needs this undying quest for excellence. We set tough goals and seldom meet them but feel good if we are close. That is good, but in tough times we might be tempted to back off, accept only partial fulfillment. My real goal is to pull together in tough times and "go do things!"

The speech is over. The first question comes from a man sitting in the front row where the head nodding during the speech was most noticeable. Flushed with excitement, half turned to face both presenter and audience, and emphasizing the pronouns, he says: "Eric, given what *you've* said about finances, from where *we* are sitting, what single thing could *we* do to help *you* fulfill *your* needs?"

There is an air of excitement and expectation in the room. The questions follow in a like manner. The mutuality seems contagious.

There are limits, however, to communion and its implied merging of the individual and collective. Indications of individual distancing from the culturally prescribed role demands are abundant. They often take the form of a professed attitude suggestive of emotional labor given off as confession during private conversations. A veteran engineering manager says:

> I've learned here that you can do your own job, but you've got to let the waves roll over you. Ignore most of the other people around here, or you'll go crazy. There is a lot of shit coming down, people wandering around, consultants, studies. That's the way it is, but it isn't too bad a place. On a scale of ten, maybe a six or a seven. But they really know how to stuff ten pounds of shit into five-pound bags. I have a Russian immigrant friend who says it reminds him of the USSR: all this shit about Big Brother.

Emotional distancing is also expressed in time and space. The words of a project manager, ordinarily one of the most harried of organizational roles at Tech, are illustrative:

> I don't work too hard. I drive home 35 miles a day, real slow on the right-hand side of the road. I play Mozart on the stereo, that sort of buffers me from the stuff here. I don't smoke or abuse stuff, and I do a lot of sports. I want to retire at 40. In the meanwhile, it's a good place to work if you keep in mind that it is a large company. So you have to put up with all the shit, all the talk about Tech and Tech culture.

Momentary separation is also achieved by assuming an unserious stance toward the organization. Humor is one way of making public criticism of Tech that most members find tolerable. It plays its part: the ubiquitous comic strip segments pasted on office doors that speak of the stupidity of organizations; the ironic twists given to well-known Tech sayings (e.g., "There is unlimited opportunity—for inflicting and receiving pain"); and the posting of company materials in public places with commentary attached (e.g., To a personalized form letter from a Tech vice-president thanking the recipient for contributing to the success of a sales event, the recipient, an engineer, adds in scrawl: "What kind of nerds run this company? I was only there for a few hours. No wonder Tech stock is down. ")

Distancing of this sort occurs even in the midst of rituals that call for the expression and experience of communion. Routine business, it seems, can not be conducted without allowing form some humorous expression of distaste, dissent, mockery, or absurdity. Skillfully balancing the public expression of communion and separation is a part of the day's work. Take, for example, the company-related chatter that occurs among staff members waiting the arrival of a tardy colleague.

> "Who owns the T-675? You, Pete?"
>
> "No. Derek Smith does, but he reports to Cranston, so now he's got that monkey on his back, or some other animal."
>
> "I hear he's hanging out the window by his shoelaces and could slip any minute."
>
> [laughter, followed by silence]
>
> "Ahhaaa. . . . It's such a nice day outside. I just want to be a beach bum. But I'm trying for the big bucks now."
>
> "We all had the same reason to come . . ."
>
> [John walks in the room, all business. The mood shifts rapidly into the breathless, curt, clipped, pragmatic language of action and commitment.]
>
> "OK. Who has some action items? No time for the intergalactic stuff today."

There are boundaries beyond which negative displays and signs of detachment are not tolerated by many organizational members. One incident taking place during an off-site meeting of an engineering group is instructive. The manager of the group is holding forth on what he calls "Tech trauma," a state of affairs he deems deplorable. To this manager, the essence of Tech trauma is the self-fulfilling danger of corporate criticism. "We think we're in terrible shape," he says to the group, "but, in fact, we're in great shape, and still we love to beat ourselves up and then wind up losing a lot of good people."

An engineer, Bob, quietly leaning back in his chair, taking all of this in, suddenly pushes forward and bursts out with the angry remark: "What all this talk about Tech? I don't see any Tech. What is this we? I haven't met a Tech."

There is a brief but very tense silence. The manager swivels in his chair and turns back to the flip chart, saying with cocked eyebrow, "Moving right along . . ." Others in the room exchange glances, and a few titter and whisper to one another. The next time Bob starts to speak, another engineer takes out a dollar bill and says: "I'll buy you a beer if you stop talking, Bob." Everyone laughs, and Bob is silent for quite a while.

The tension between communion and distancing apparently can build swiftly, tightening stomach muscles and drying throats. It can also be released just as swiftly. In all organizations, perhaps, but in Tech specifically, episodes of spreading nervous tension and its containment are quite familiar and sometimes extreme.

As a final example, consider the presentation given by a project manager about to leave her group for another assignment. In the middle of her talk, she mentions in a cracking voice the coming transfer and begins to sob. It is all quite unexpected. The scene freezes momentarily as she tries to regain her composure.

All eyes are on her. The emotional intensity is released, however, when Ted, an old-timer facing retirement, shouts out from the back of the room, "C'mon, Jean, you said you couldn't wait to get the hell outta this group anyway!" Those present relax, Jean smiles, shrugs, and continues her talk. The interlude is soon forgotten as the situation returns to normal.

Let us now close this quick look at Tech by submitting what seem to be the key points. First, there is a recognized culture at Tech promoted by top management and pushed, with considerable self-consciousness and effort, down through the ranks. Most members, at least those close to engineering, are quite familiar with a good part of this culture and often invoke it for a variety of reasons. Much of the time the culture is used to justify actions, excuse them, or simply try to understand them as something other than capricious, desperate, or random. It serves also to create an aura of uniqueness about the organization, useful as a way of generating pride in many employees and as a way of differentiating for them the organization (and its products) from other similar organizations (and products).

Second, Tech is a massive complex of shifting people, programs, projects, and plans. We have examined only a tiny part of this firm, the presumed technical heart of the organization. But even at the most visible and apparently crucial domains of operation, cliché and aphorism provide the mainstay organizing principles. Perhaps anything more concrete or precise could not stand up to much continual use across segments of the organization. Moreover, many of the everyday activities that obtain in the studied segments (particularly for managers) are highly ritualized (e.g., meetings, pep talks, Technet messages, conferences, project reviews, etc.), thus allowing the appearance, if not substance, of order to prevail. Ritual, if only by its repetition and familiarity, allows some members of the organization a modest degree of predictability. From this perspective, antistructure is itself an organizing device.

Third, top management at Tech appears to take quite seriously its role of installing the "right attitude" among those below them. Much of their time is spent rallying the troops, prowling the trench lines, and generally trying to drum up enthusiasm and support of various projects they believe crucial to the organization. This reflects the somewhat suspicious stance top management takes toward those filling technical and specialist roles—particularly engineers—in the organization. Affection is present, but so is distrust. The phrase, "You have to be one to know one," works in senior management's favor, allowing them the conceit that they know what those in the trenches really do, want, and need. A similar distrust (and a different sort of conceit) is also characteristic of engineers toward their bosses. An uneasy truce is maintained through the constant attention both groups give to working out limited, turf-specific, temporary, and contingent agreements in a seemingly endless series of formal and informal meetings (negotiations) that bring members of each camp together.[28]

Finally, for the employees studied here, organizational life is rich, conflictual, and challenging. Emotional investments are deep, and many participants are more than occasionally bothered by a felt merging of the self into the organizational role. But, perhaps more important, they are equally troubled when their spirits are low, when their motivation seems to sag, and when they can find little to appreciate in the organization. Too much separation is as discomforting as too much communion. Culture is, then, both a cause and consequence of these very real feelings.

THE DARK SIDE OF CULTURE

We began this paper with a quick description of a back-slapping episode of culture work in paradise. The emotions unleashed during this exotic time-out were of a loose, cheerful, and spirited sort. Indeed, the unashamed enthusiasm of some participants may well be what the sponsors of the afternoon want to see more of back in the office as a way of spurring Tandem Computer on to greater heights (and increased sales). But, as we suggested in the following sections, the formula for producing and sustaining such warm feelings is complicated by a number of matters, most of them social and persistent. People and groups vary in their response to corporate direction. Guardedness, suspicion, and outright rejection are certainly among the many stances possible when organized efforts are made to whip up the proper mood or ''right attitude.'' Members may play their respective parts in the various cultural workouts of organizations, but they may not like the parts they play.

The ethnographic portions of this paper were given over to descriptions of two organizations reputed to have very strong cultures. As presented, these cultures contain images of the basic concerns of the organization; the principles and bodies of manners, rituals, ethics, and ideologies of which members are aware (and, to a degree, accept), including the crucial notions of just what is considered good and bad work; various legends and bits of folklore; and, importantly, a set of ideals around which the efforts of members can be judged (by themselves and others). One consequence of working in a culturally self-conscious context is that apparently most members come to know relatively well just what is expected of them by others (impossible as it may be to live up to such expectations unambiguously, continually, and without conflict).

At Tech, it appears that those in the trenches have little doubt of the intelligence, zeal, care, self-reliance, independence, and technical imagination they are to bring to the job. Disneylanders, too, know rather precisely what it is they are to do and how they are to go about it. Their prideful composure, sunny disposition, scrubbed appearance, and mannerly way toward customers, peers, and superiors are requirements of working in the park.

These simple expectations key some rather complex understandings shared by members of these organizations. Such understandings do not emerge by fiat or reasoned decree. They are understandings built up over a lengthy period of time during which considerable negotiation and interaction among members is mandatory. Nor can they be transmitted instantly because their meanings are multiple and always modified by the context in which they are used. To know what "keeping your balance" means at Tech is to know what "losing it" means, and this, in turn, requires a relatively detailed knowledge of situations where "balance" is likely to be an issue.

These understandings are, in short, cultural ones, made, remade, and sometimes changed in a vast number of ways. Their stylized expression is apparent in both the positive and negative, dramatic and mundane rituals of organizational life. They appear as thematic elements in the frequently told stories and jokes of the membership. They serve as the focus for much of the celebratory activity that goes on in organizations, as well as many of the more somber ceremonies. In essence, these understandings are the result of people appraising their more or less shared situations by talking about them and, through such talk, coming to modest agreements about what they mean.

To a degree, these agreements or understandings, beyond their self-fulfilling character, are validated retrospectively, largely through the success the organization is seen to have by its members (Schein, 1985). Disneyland, for instance, depends a great deal on the clean-cut boy- or girl-next-door imagery conveyed by its ride operators to customers. Respectful and alert college students are thought to give the park a distinctive edge over its competitors. Disneyland management has no desire to staff its attractions with transient roustabouts who, in the eyes of management, might threaten the show by reminding paying guests of sleazy carnival attendants with tattoos of MOTHER on their arms. Nor does management at Tech have much interest in imposing clear lines of authority on its engineering personnel who are thought to be too creative to respond well to such structure.[29] The acceptable view among managers is that dedicated, aggressive, in-demand engineers are attracted to Tech because of the autonomy and challenge the organization offers them. The problem from top management's perspective is how to keep and direct such people after they have been brought abroad.

In both organizations, this is no easy task. Valued employees have many options, interests, and sources of loyalty beyond working for Tech or Disneyland. Ride operators know they could be making better money by lifeguarding, slinging hash in the college fraternity house, or driving a pickup van for the local cleaning service. Tech engineers are convinced they are only a phone call away from another job that might in fact be less emotionally demanding and more financially rewarding. Status competition enters the picture here, for employees of both organizations are kept in place partly because many of them regard their workplace as the very best of its kind, offering them something more than just a job with its expected economic returns. This is clearly a cultural matter and suggests why public displays of cynicism and disbelief are among the greatest crimes employees at Disneyland and Tech can commit.

How do organizations or, more properly, senior managers of organizations, influence the work culture surrounding key employees (and themselves)? We have already offered a long list of some concrete practices and will only summarize the list here under some general headings. First, the codification of values and beliefs is important as a means of promoting a sort of culture-consciousness among organization members. Moreover, Disneyland and Tech have gone to great lengths to reach selectively into their respective histories and make public the kinds of exemplary performances highly regarded employees are to demonstrate. Operating principles are derived from these formal and informal histories, and efforts are made to make them as explicit as possible. The culture manuals at Tech provide an example, as do the University of Disneyland materials.[30]

Second, considerable interaction and close ties among employees in both organizations are promoted. Retreats, social events, parties, gossip sessions, official ceremonies, meetings, and the physical design of the workplace are illustrative in this regard. Teamwork and block loyalties, with their intensive face-to-face relations, are important organizing features. These tactics of collective organization decrease self-regarding actions on the part of teammates since the interests of each become linked to those of others, and, equally crucial, all can police instances of self-pursuit and discourage them. Cross-loyalties may be developed, but in both organizations mobility across units (projects and rides) is the rule. Upscale and downscale careers are possible (and of constant concern) for employees who are in motion, though their particular job titles and external status markers may appear unchanged.

Third, great care is taken when newcomers enter these cultural enclaves. Homogeneity of recruit backgrounds, intensive peer socialization, continuous exposure to the apparently always risky business of creating and maintaining acceptable, if not harmonious, relations with colleagues and supervisors, tales of corporate heroism (and cowardice), and numerous occasions (mundane and dramatic) to test one's standing in the group are key elements contributing to the maintenance and support of the culture. Learning of various out-groups, internal and external, also sharpens the culture consciousness of members on the make. Perhaps nothing is quite as effective in drawing people into a cultural net than suggesting what a terrible fate awaits them if they miss or all through.

Finally, considerable attention and effort goes into monitoring the extent corporate values, norms, and practices are being received and put into use by employees. Virtually all managers at Disneyland demonstrate, for example, a "hands-on," intimate, obtrusive, and highly visible style of supervision, with considerable attention placed on the personal, private, and sometimes sacred preserves of the employee. At Tech, the roles are often reversed, for it is the supervised who display a lively interest in the thoughts and feelings of their avowedly "hands-off" supervisors. Expressions of emotion are encouraged in both organi-

zations since all members are taught the (sometimes questionable) virtue of saying precisely what is on their minds. Judgments tend to be quick, frank, and
often harsh; neither Tech nor Disneyland would be viewed by insiders as organizations whose members are particularly sensitive or tactful when it comes to the
feelings of other members.

In sum, these heralded corporate cultures are of a very conscious sort. They
are organized and fine-tuned with considerable attention to detail. Emotions are
involved because employees attach themselves to these organizations and their
respective parts in many ways—through the establishment of close friendships;
the acceptance of company standards for proper performance and attitude; the
willingness to draw values and a sense of what is important in the world in line
with corporate objectives and working principles; the ability to enjoy and support
the ritual occasions that go with membership; and the ever-present desire to talk
with other members and come to collective assessments of just what is going on
in the organization.

All of these emotionally relevant aspects of membership are learned. Some of
them are, no doubt, learned in a cold sweat. The humiliation of a faulty presentation and being "beat up" by peers and superiors is an occasion few members of
Tech can forget (or wish to repeat). Nor can the tardy ride operators easily dismiss being chewed out by a sharp-tongued foreman in front of the crew. Certain
standards are not to be profaned in these organizations, and, although members
have little to do with their invention and may privately regard some of them as
thoroughly inappropriate, they learn to honor them as best they can. Some members, normally the more experienced, centrally placed, better rewarded ones,
come to regard such standards as both vital and natural, standards laced with
moral certitude. Needless to say, among such figures, the culture penetrates most
deeply.[31]

The implicit argument we are using to close this paper can now be made explicit. In essence, we regard conscious managerial attempts to build, sustain, and
elaborate culture in organizations as a relatively subtle yet powerful form of organizational control. It is subtle because culture is typically regarded as something people can do little about, something that flows from the ordinary problems
people face and the characteristic ways they solve them. Culture is seldom
regarded—except in the case of conquest—as something deliberately imposed
on people.[32] It is powerful because it seemingly aims at a deeper level of employee compliance (i.e., emotional) than other forms of control. On this last
claim, a hasty justification is required.

Broadly conceived, managerial control of the workplace operates in a number
of ways that extend from the simple, explicit, contractual, and individually centered varieties to the complex, implicit, assumptive, and collective varieties.[33]
There are at least three generally recognized forms of control, and we will add a
fourth. The first is what might be called the market control of labor. Each individual, working to self-imposed or craft-guild standards, is free to sell the fruits

of his or her labor to the highest bidder. The light but guiding touch of the invisible hand operates here as the elementary control device. At issue in market control are the demands for products or services that are exchanged for a fee and not the producers or servers themselves.

The second form of control corresponds to the mechanization available in society, the presence of large organizations and the national markets they serve, and whatever general dissatisfaction is felt among managers and owners with the workings of the invisible hand as a means of matching people and jobs. Control in this form is technical in the sense that workers are subject to the authority of the production process itself. This is the hallmark of scientific management with its systematic job analysis methods, time and motion studies, homogeneous skill levels among certain categories of workers, and, in general, its ability to make employees as interchangeable as the parts, services, or products they produce.

The third form of control corresponds to bureaucratic devices. Such devices enable managers to stem resistance to technical control (and, perhaps, increase efficiency) by emphasizing "neutral" rules and procedures in the workplace, thus lending greater rationality to the organization of work. Technical control, standing alone, represents, in part, something of a catalyst whose consequence, it seems, is to encourage worker class consciousness and collective opposition to managerial authority (e.g., informal organization, "the fix," unionization, strikes, industrial sabotage). Bureaucratic control deals directly with such disruption and, to managers, disorder by tying individual interests to those of the organization itself. True, too, as Max Weber taught, bureaucratic control has its own logic independent of the presence or absence of technical control. Such logic is most clearly visible in the formalized personnel systems, long-term employment practices, and highly differentiated hierarchies of pay and status based presumably on merit, that are the defining features of bureaucratic control.

In review, market control focuses only on the outcome of labor (*object control*), whereas technical control acts primarily on the overt behavior of contracted employees (*body control*). Both forms have little or no regard for the thoughts or feelings of workers. Bureaucratic control, however, with its intricate administrative procedures designed to justify and direct individual contributions to the organization, focuses on the calculations of self-interest made by employees (*mind control*). Bureaucracy is a means of harnessing (perhaps harmonizing) the efforts of many by welding the interests of each to the collective. Career systems, performance appraisals, universal selection and recruitment standards, rewards for seniority, pension plans, and the ever-present rule books are all devices that help stabilize and make predictable organization work.

We think this scheme concerning the control of object, body, and mind can be pushed to one more level, the control of the heart.[34] *Culture control* is the label we use. Its aim is to influence and spark the felt involvement and attachment of organizational members (*emotion control*). The tools of the trade in this domain are highly symbolic and include the self-conscious use of ritual, myth, and ceremony. Such devices are intended to act on the values, loyalties, sentiments, and desires of employees. Where such control seems most advanced, it is no longer sufficient to design jobs as explicitly as possible and then provide the appropriate short- and long-term incentives to lure and bind qualified employees, but moral commitments to the ends of the organization must also be developed among key segments of the work force in order to combat the presumed negative and deadening effects of market, technical, and bureaucratic controls.

This is a very simplified model. But if there is a measure of truth in the tale, several implications follow. First, control systems build on top of one another rather than servicing as substitutes. Forms of control do not replace other forms but, for the most part, stand alongside each other.[35] Disneyland is a superb example of social engineering (technical control) on the ride operator level, coupled with a good deal of formalized rules and regulations that employees are contractually bound to honor (bureaucratic control). It is also a superb example of the extent to which an explicitly formulated company culture helps to make palatable other control mechanisms and further corporate ends by providing employees valued images of what they do. Tech pushes object control perhaps more so than technical or bureaucratic control, but they are nonetheless all present to a degree. The point here is that both organizations utilize a number of control devices beyond the overlay of cultural control.

Second, culture controls used by some organizations have not gone unnoticed by other organizations. Like the spread of bureaucratic devices in industrial organizations, the shadow-like culture controls such as intensive and continual training, busy ritual calendars, focus on special vocabularies and symbols, team-building efforts and cell-like organizations, widespread and ceremonial dissemination of top management goals, plans, and values, attention to the nonwork affairs of employees, and sponsored forms of intraorganizational networks also spread. Media attention on high-flying U.S. firms seems to devote considerable space to matters we have considered cultural in this paper. This is the case because, for some organizations, certain of these culture controls seem relatively new and are therefore newsworthy but also partly because these forms help to differentiate firms that on market, technical, and bureaucratic grounds might look quite similar.[36]

Third, there is probably a good deal of interaction and hence shifting of emphasis on differing control forms within organizations over time. Object control creates an anxious work force compelled to look ahead continually to an uncertain and perhaps too capricious market. Body control fuels resistance because it dehumanizes employees when it asks them to become mere cogs in an industrial machine. Mind control leaves many members feeling tapped in cold and calculating organizations where it seems they are merely numbers shoved about by impersonal rules, regulations, and objectives. Emotion control appears ludicrous to many employees who may have difficulty working up any warmth or affection for an organization that produces missiles or toilet paper or for an organization whose managers seem to be forever waving pompoms and banners.

Control, it would seem, is a many-splintered thing. It operates in a variety of ways in any organization, on a diverse work force, few of whom are fully predisposed to submit fully to any one form. The mix of control forms is forever changing and the relative emphasis of one form rather than on the others depends, no doubt, on a vast array of contextual matters, some internal and some external to the organization. Scarce resources may quickly gobble up culture controls, whereas munificence may lead to their expansion. As bureaucratic devices multiply, whatever logic they once possessed may become incomprehensible and difficult to discern, and, thus, technical or market or cultural controls may receive a boost from management looking for ways to cut red tape or produce cheaper products of higher quality.[37] There is, in short, no message here as to the most effective, demeaning, liberating, or efficient control form. All have their proverbial costs and benefits to be assessed in line with what one deems important and proper. It is indeed difficult to say more.

Where it is less difficult to say more is in the culture-praising and culture-bashing domain. State-of-the-art culture management seems aimed at creating organizations full of members sharing values and holding a strong sense of belongingness. We have dealt with many of the ways these influence attempts are dealt with by Disneyland and Tech employees and have suggested that there are some very real limits at just how effective these attempts can be. While culture is managed, sometimes very actively, it does not always accomplish what its advocates would prefer. Managers may define what is given, but the managed will define what is taken. The limits of state-of-the-art culture management and its attempts at emotion control are matters with which we will close this discussion.

We have linked culture and control in this final section because we believe the two are tightly connected. But as the ethnographies suggest, organizational life is complicated. Employees bring with them (and develop during their tenure) affiliations and loyalties other than the managerially approved and designated. The so-called Tech underground that delights in the flaunting of convention is an example in this regard, as are those social desperadoes at Disneyland who take every opportunity, while they last, to express their independence from overseers. The power to induce shared values, pride, affection, fealty, and ''we-ness'' seems as constrained as the power to induce strict behavioral compliance to the logic of a machine or produce grateful displays of respect for bureaucratic authority. The common dilemma here is simply that all of us experience uncertainty, conflict, doubt, and fluctuation when it comes to deciding how much to invest of ourselves in our work roles and organizations.

It seems true also that the more those at the top of organizations offer tips to those below, the more those at the top wish to dictate to others the precise kinds of meanings they are to attach to their work experience. Employees often rightly regard this as a form of social molestation. Cultural control, from this perspective, may turn people off rather than on. Even for those who are not put off by such forms, there may be costs. Burn-out at Tech apparently occurs as a result of too much dedication, identification, and enthusiasm. "Phoneyness" and a sort of emotional numbness is what ride operators at Disneyland often talk about when they feel they are overacting and their onstage work begins to take a personal toll.

In both organizations, a degree of what Hochschild (1983) calls emotional dissonance exists among many employees. It is marked by the curious claim of having to make a display of affection (or disdain) toward something the claimant does not apparently feel. Dissonance theorists would predict that such a state is unstable. Yet if the feeling gives way and comes into line with the display, authenticity and singularity may suffer, for the employee's sense of self begins to move to the rhythms of corporate ups and downs, matters the employee may have very little control over. If the display gives way, however, inappropriate passions may be released that may cost the wayward worker a job.

Probably most of us live in a somewhat emotionally dissonant state within our work organizations. Viewed as a control device, corporate culture asks us to put our heart and soul into our work. There is, however, surely a limit to which we are willing to sell our hearts and souls for the production and sale of soap, aspirin, entertainment, research, or computers. The culture movement is heartening to the extent that by focusing on symbolic matters, people are viewed as more than mere producers, bodies, or calculating machines. The movement is frightening to the extent that people are expected to fall in line with a culture organized for the commercial purposes of others and over which they have little influence.

The prescription addressed to researchers in this area is to examine cultural features of organization critically, keeping in mind always the multiple meanings and intentions such features may signify. Member claims in this regard must be treated skeptically because culture and the symbolic work that goes on under this label are always matters requiring interpretation (and there may be many interpretations). If rituals are studied, for example, we must see them not only as promoting or celebrating cohesion and collective goodwill, we must also examine what may be their weasel-like character by asking: (1) who prescribes them; (2) who holds them up as significant (and, in just what ways); and (3) how such rituals are used strategically by those who organize, participate in, or observe them. Rituals, words, symbols, stories, gestures, myths, and other cultural means of communication are also modes of exercising power over cognitive and emotional dimensions of member life, as well as over the behavioral. They are methods of influencing what members love or fear, regard as possible or impossible, and take to be good or bad. Their use raises primal questions.[38]

One final irony, however, offers grounds for optimism. It is true that a good deal of our social identity comes from the organizational affiliations we manage to carve out and maintain. The better we think these affiliations are, the better we are likely to feel about ourselves and perhaps the more confident we are in the world at large. But our personal sense of identity, who we think we "really are," probably derives far more from the various ways we influence these affiliations or even react negatively to their perceived demands than from any or all of the ways we go along. Our individuality seems to depend most on those moments when we move in different directions from the crowd, modify the calls of others, or experience emotions seemingly deviant from those around us. An organization is, in this light, something of a foil against which we shape our identities and sharpen our emotional wits. Goffman (1961, p. 320) puts it best: "Our sense of being a person can come from being drawn into a wider social unit; our sense of selfhood can arise through the little ways in which we resist the pull. Our status is backed by the solid buildings of the world, while our sense of personal identity often resides in the cracks."

ACKNOWLEDGMENTS

A draft of this paper was originally presented at the American Academy of Management Annual Meeting in San Diego, August 13, 1985, at a symposium organized by Stan Harris and titled "Emotion: Exploring a Neglected Organizational Issue." Many readers have helped us in redrafting this paper and encouraging our emotional pursuit. At various times and in various ways, aid and comfort on this project were provided by Lotte Bailyn, Steve Barley, Larry Cummings, Joel Cutcher-Gershenfeld, Bob Gephart, Debbie Kolb, Arlie Hochschild, Peter Manning, Joanne Martin, Ed Schein, Don Schon, Barry Staw, and Bob Sutton. We are grateful.

NOTES

1. Paradise, to be precise, is Poipu Beach, Kauai (Hawaii). The company is real, as are the merry materials gathered in July 1985 from a beach chair observation post close to the action. The description is pursued here not as serious science or a send-up but as a tale designed to titillate and bring the reader aboard. Decontextualized elements of this happy occasion are covered analytically in various portions of the paper.

2. We are reminded here of Goffman's (1967) celebrated analysis of adults squirming on the wooden horses of merry-go-rounds. Goffman suggests two extremes between which most riders fall. One mode of horsemanship consists of trying to establish as much distance between the person being displayed and the display itself. Using gestures intended to convey that one is fully aware of his odd appearance, the horseman lets others know that his body, not his soul, is along for the ride. The other mode, rare it seems, catches those galloping away on the cockhorse body and soul. Little or no distance operates here since the rider is apparently carried away by the occasion.

The responses of those with Tandem in paradise are similar. Some, by their bemused expressions, their exaggerated gestures, falsetto response cries to the action in the park, and sly little nods to co-conspirators, signal to others (and perhaps themselves): "Hey, this isn't the real me, you know." Other Tandem revelers appear fully engaged in the games at hand and apparently moved by the spirit of the occasion. Uncontrolled gales of laughter, eager embraces of teammates, singing of songs in deep voice and delight, and the display of a sort of terminal glee when winning an event.

To the possible embarrassment of both Cynic and Believer, however, these response categories do not sort people per se but rather sort responses to different situations, with people falling in and out of given categories depending on what was going on at the moment. The lively ghost of Goffman (1967, p. 3) makes the point well: ''The proper study of interaction is not the individual and his psychology, but rather the syntactical relations among acts of different persons mutually present to one another. . . . Not, then, men and their moments. Rather, moments and their men.''

3.   Tupperware has been well covered by the popular press. It also occupies a good number of pages in Peters and Waterman (1982). There is also a marvelous Stanford Business School case written on the company by Kaible and Paddock (1983), as well as a dry but informative sociological analysis by Peven (1968).

4.   The notion of an ''organizational time-out'' is addressed in some depth in Van Maanen (1985). Broadly conceived, it represents a gathering of organizational members during which some of the ordinary social relations and norms of the workplace are situationally redefined. These periods are patterned and involve pressure on participants to conduct themselves in particular ways. key definitional elements include: (1) discourse on nonwork topics; (2) behavioral patterns that deviate from those in the office or generally at work; and (3) expression of sentiments often hushed or inappropriate elsewhere. In most ways, time-outs denote autonomy for participants (at least of a collective sort) and a general feeling of freedom from organizational constraint. Norms of common types of social drinking occasions, similar to organizational time-outs and subtype among them, are well covered by Cavan (1966), MacAndrews and Edgerton (1969), LeMasters (1975), and Lithman (1979).

5.   Our language here may seem unnecessarily fussy. We have, nonetheless, a modest blow to strike by its use. By *gross control* we mean that fully furnished settings (with props, people, and definitions) ordinarily provide more than a few clues as to what stance an individual is to assume if he or she is to play a part in the setting. But, crucially, the individual necessarily exercises ''fine control'' over just how (or, even, if) he or she is to do so. There are, in brief, many ways to mourn appropriately at the funeral or celebrate at the wedding. The limits are broad and allow for the polishing of personal character. Yet there are limits, and that is the point. Langer (1967, pp. 25–29) provides helpful hints.

6.   Ritual has long been the centerpiece of Durkheimian social theory. Lukes (1975) provides the revisionist touch by suggesting just how much ambiguity often surrounds rituals of the official sort. Sometimes, as Zurcher (1982) neatly demonstrates, official rituals can be too intense, leading participants to question the appropriateness of their membership in the group from which the ritual is derived. The standard version of ritual—as revitalization and collective dues paying—is, however, well entrenched in the organizational studies literature and is best represented by Ouchi's (1981) version of the clan.

7.   Ouchi and Wilkins (1985) suggest that the study of organizational culture is best seen as a continuation of mainline organizational sociology, which has always been concerned with the normative bases and shared understands that regulate social life in organizations. They also argue that the subfield is the fastest-growing and perhaps most lively one within the organization field. Self-enhancement is involved here, as it is when any of us review fields with which we have more than passing concerns. But Ouchi and Wilkins provide an impressive count of recent publications to substantiate their claim. Schein (1985) performs some of the same service for psychologists by usefully linking present interests in organizational culture to a rich body of psychological thought appropriate to the topic. Fine's (1984) review does much the same thing but, is more tightly focused on interactionist theory and research, which, in our view, has been doggedly pursuing the relevance of culture in organizational (and occupational) studies for a very long time. Fine's worry (and ours) is that much current theorizing is uninformed by classic interactionist studies.

8.   This definition is to be found in Eliot (1932, pp. 124–125).

9.   This is a central tenet of Meadian social psychology and is addressed directly in Van Maanen (1979). All we can do here is wave the flag since the literature representing this position is voluminous.

10.   There are literally hundreds of small group studies done in various work settings from a natu-
ralistic perspective that document such a remark. Among the most relevant to organization theorists
are those of Burns (1955, 1961, 1977); Manning (1977, 1980); Dalton (1959); and Roy (1959). One
that strikes a responsive chord in regard to the essay here is Katz (1966), where the argument is made
that workers are often allowed to import their working-class culture into the workplace, while managers are expected to export their organizational culture to groups outside the workplace. The upshot of
this argument is simply that managers are more tied to their employers than are workers and, as such,
are expected to be organizational ambassadors wherever they may go. It is a small jump to suggest
that the emotional labor they perform is likely to be greater than that of the worker who must provide
the organization with his or her body but little else for a limited amount of time.

11.   This account is based primarily on the lead author's 3 ½ year work experience as a permanent part-time ride operator at Disneyland during the late 1960s. Sporadic contacts have been maintained with a few park employees, and periodic visits, even with children in tow, have always proved
informative. Also, lengthy, repeated interviews of an informal sort were conducted during the sum-
mers of 1985, 1986, and 1987 with three ride operators then employed at the park, so at least some of
the information forthcoming is more or less fresh. But, alas, most of the ethnographic materials are
informed by emotional recall triggered by the immediate pressures of writing this paper. Disneyland
(and the lead author) has, of course, changed over the years, there are strikes now, many rides are
new, and most of them are more automated than in the past, the pay for all categories of ride operators is a little better, there are more minority employees, and women have come to play more parts in
the production. For the most part, however, life for the middle-class ride operators, with their quiet
college student reserve, remains, sociologically, much the same. This description must stand until a
better one comes along. Like all other ethnographies, it is offered as a plausible hypothesis, not
definitive proof (Van Maanen, 1988). Since feelings are at issue in the description, numerical matters
are glossed in favor of response and status taxonomies, which are closer to matters of the heart for
Disneyland workers. The selection of Disneyland as a contextual example is based largely on the
good press bestowed on the institution and the absent or, at best, weak descriptions that accompany
such press.

12.   This point on sponsorship and its dynamics is made by Glaser (1968) and, in business contexts, by Strauss and Martin (1956). Full treatment of the theoretical fine details is provided in Glaser
and Strauss (1971). Kanter (1977) also provides vivid illustrations of its workings in corporate settings. Network theorists provide structural sketches of sponsorship links, which apparently are far
more common than personnel officers or equal opportunity advocates would like. Grannovetter
(1974) provides the informative text.

13.   Control of public face extends to the Disneyland gates as well. Although standards for customer appearance have relaxed in response to several lawsuits over the past ten years, Disneyland
border guards still patrol the entrance portals in search of those who would slip through security
inappropriately adorned. Up to the mid-1970s, long hair on men was verboten and enforced, no matter what the likely tab a so-called freak might run up when in the park. Radical styles of all types are
still viewed suspiciously by park officials, and those who choose such styles for a visit to Disneyland
still risk being turned away at the gate. The Disney image is said, by park officials, to be at stake in
these fashion wars, for apparently they are worried lest they offend the sensibilities of the middle-
class customer to whom they cater. Most ride operators regard such policing as making good sense—
except, of course, when similar, although far more conservative, glances are cast on them.

14.   Ride operators, even part-time ones, are also Teamsters. The Disneyland local is, however,
hardly typical of this grim union with the shady past. There was a short strike in 1982, the first of its
kind among ride operators, although contract negotiations had been known to run to the eleventh hour
in times past. Historically, few Disneyland employees participate in union affairs, and those who do
are invariably the old-timers with permanent job classifications. All part-timers grumble about the
initiation dues taken from their initial check. But for the most part, this is one of the last thoughts they
ever have on union matters while working at the park. Very few grievances are ever filed, and most

employees would be puzzled, probably stumped, if asked who their shop steward might be. Virtually no aid is forthcoming from the union when part-timers are fired, as they frequently are during the summer (except in one or two extraordinary cases). More protection is available for the permanent part-time category and most, of course, for the permanent. This is only surprising by virtue of the fact that employees gaining these classifications are hand-picked by the company. Labor relations per se have never been happy topics for Disney management, and there is a long history of virulent antiunion sentiments within the larger Disney organization (Schickel, 1968). Lessons have apparently been learned (or deals struck) at Disneyland because it has been a relatively peaceful place for 30 years. Changes are afoot, it seems, but our information here is quite sketchy.

15.   By "happy," we mean swollen attendance estimates. To the ride operators' delight, official estimates typically overestimate the size of the crowd expected. Whatever the source of these "computer errors," one consequence is that most shifts are marked by considerable shuffling, breaking, and other personnel adjustments. Ride operators who wish to go home early can normally do so, and others who want the hours can usually hustle about and manage to get them. Some griping exists among operators and foremen, but both groups seem to appreciate the added discretion such happy estimates allow. We might note, too, that estimation procedures are based partly on turnstyle figures, as well as money receipts. Like crime statistics, these hard numbers are subject to bias of both a counting and an interpretive sort. Bias in the turnstyle count is promoted by ride operators who, for various reasons, often flick their turnstyles over to admit many phantom riders, thus keeping their particular attraction on the popularity charts. We will have reason to say more about this practice in yet another footnote.

16.   Shrewd insiders would surely challenge this status-only argument, pointing out that some rides provide more opportunity of overtime, freedom from supervision, and, because of their design, less chance of being sent home early when crowds begin to thin late at night or never thicken because of rain or faulty estimates. We would quickly agree with such an argument but would also point out that such particularistic features typically correlate with ride status anyway, hence, putting yet another mark in the ledger for our shortly forthcoming clustering argument in the text.

17.   See note 14.

18.   See footnotes 14 and 16. Rushing the ride is officially taboo, but full professors at the University of Disneyland might well be shocked at just how frequently it occurs during busy periods. Employees and foremen know the realistic demands of crowd control mean moving the herd through the attraction as fast as possible. Supervisors appear to adopt a tolerance policy on this matter and, in effect, encourage operators, by oversight, in their efforts. Little contests between shifts, rides, or previous bests also help push people through the turnstyles at record rates. Submarine operators (and those managing them) know quite well that it is impossible to cram 30,000 people on the subs during regular park operating hours and still observe the 8 ½ minute rule for ride length. The customers may see blurred mermaids or sea serpents, but operators see records. Speed-ups in other industries are common as a management-directed attempt to boost production. At Disneyland, although there is tacit managerial approval, the speed-up is a worker tactic to boost production and cut the boredom surrounding the ride cycle. Whatever the extrinsic reward provided the record-breaking team, typically a keg of beer, there is exhilaration and excitement in the record chase itself. One operator became something of a legend in his own time by remaining on his feet in the Submarine conning tower (an area no bigger than a full-length sports locker) for 12 hours, without a break or rotation, during one attempt at the turnstyle record.

19.   The lead author serves as a case in point. He was indeed fired for what he considered a Mickey Mouse offense. The specific violation—one of many possible—involved hair growing over the ears, an offense he had been warned about more than once before the final cut was made. The form the dismissal took, however, deserves comment, for it is easy to recall and followed a format familiar to an uncountable number of ex-Disneylanders. Dismissal began by being pulled off the ride after the work shift began by an area supervisor in full view of cohorts. A forced march to the admin-

istration building followed, where employee identification cards were turned in and a short statement was given by a personnel officer as to the formal cause of termination. Security officers then walked the former ride operator to the locker room where work uniforms and equipment were collected and personal belongings returned while a locker inspection was made. The next stop was the time shed where the employee's time card was removed from its slot, marked "terminated" across the top in red ink, and replaced in its customary position, presumably for all Disneyland employees to see when clocking on or off the job over the next few days. The dismissed was then escorted to the parking lot where two security officers scraped off the employee parking sticker attached to his car. All these little steps of status degradation in the Magic Kingdom were quite public; as the reader might guess, the process still irks. This may provide the reader with an account for the tone of this narrative, although it shouldn't because the lead author would also claim he was ready to quit anyway. And, as we will note in the concluding section of this paper, the lead author still derives as much a part of his identity from being fired from Disneyland as he derives from being employed there in the first place.

20.   Such figures of disdain are seemingly necessary in all lines of work—perhaps most apparent in service or people-processing vocations. They are, in Skolnick's (1966) classic phrase, "symbolic assailants" out to undermine whatever authority and sanctity workers feel they are due. Doctors have their "crocks" (Friedson, 1970), airline attendants have "irates" (Hochschild, 1983) traffic wardens have "animals" (Richman, 1983) and barmaids have their "stiffs" (Spradley & Mann, 1975). Van Maanen (1978) has written about those who violate norms sacred in occupational cultures, using the technical term *assholes* to guide analysis.

21.   These tactics are covered in some depth in Van Maanen (1976, 1977; Van Maanen & Schein, 1979). When pulled together and used simultaneously, a people-processing system of some force is created that tends to produce a good deal of conformity among recruits who, regardless of background, come to share similar occupational identities, including just how they think and feel on the job. Such socialization practices are common whenever recruits are bunched together and processed as a batch and when role innovation is distinctly unwanted on the part of the agents of such socialization.

22.   On territories of the self and their preservation, see Goffman (1971).

23.   High Technology, Inc. is a pseudonym, and its use follows company request. Other identifying elements are disguised as well. While this situation is not ideal, it is common, and we feel making the materials public is well worth the price of concealment. Moreover, we are convinced that Tech is similar in many respects to other high-tech firms where culture consciousness is promoted by management. The materials presented in this section were gathered by the second author during a year's study of an engineering group in the firm. The methods used were those of the cultural anthropologist, including extensive observation of routine activities at Tech, participation in some of those activities, systematic interviewing across representative samples, document collection and analysis, and intensive work with a few key informants. Several physical sites provided the ground on which the participant observer stood at Tech, including corporate headquarters. All funding for the work came from MIT. For details, see Kunda (forthcoming).

24.   We must note that the terms *member* and *employee* apply, in the main, to only those engineering, staff, and management personnel who are the primary targets of this description. The majority of Tech employees are not, of course, ranking officials, professional engineers, or trained specialists but are production workers, uniformed staff, secretaries, clerks, and service providers of all kinds. The Tech culture may touch these workers also, but if so, we think it a very light touch indeed. For the most part, these employees are extracultural since they are all but invisible to those within the everyday sight and sound of the Tech culture described in this paper. *Management culture* might have been a more descriptive phrase for the matters of our concern, but since its use also raises a good number of questions, we will grudgingly follow conventional practice and use the increasingly suspect phrase *organizational culture*.

25.   The "Technet" mentioned in the text refers to the electronic mail and bulletin board commu-

nication system that allows authorized employees to exchange messages of all sorts with one another. Those in the system regard it as the latest thing in "networking," containing all the "bells and whistles."

26.   Development engineering represents the glamour work at Tech. There are many other engineering groups, but most are involved in lower-status support work (e.g., field service, performance testing, maintenance, etc.). Most young engineers aspire to jobs in development. Some engineers are, however, quite comfortable in the quieter nine-to-five atmosphere of lower-status work, where the "crunches" of the sort mentioned in the text are less distressing and common. Development engineers, then, feel the bulk of the pressure to be creative, productive, and conform to the "I-want-it-yesterday" time demands of management.

27.   Tech seems to add a nice local variation to some of the studies that have explored organizational status elsewhere (Bailyn, 1985; Glaser, 1968; Dalton, 1959). At Tech, the technical-nontechnical and entrepreneur-bureaucrat distinctions create four logical types ordered as suggested in the text. There are also contextual features that enter this status calculation including: how long one has been with the firm (yellow badges versus relative newcomers), where one works, and the particular kind of technical (or nontechnical) and entrepreneurial (or bureaucratic) work one does (e.g., line versus staff). As with Disneyland, these status attributes cluster, and knowing a few allows one to predict others with a fair measure of ease. Surprises are frequent (and informative) enough, however, to make us leery of the merits (or value) of strict formulations.

28.   Those of us who study culture in work settings tend to disattend or dismiss the little, annoying issues like "How did the culture get started in the first place?" Or, "How does it operate and change over time?" Great assistance is to be located in the so-called negotiated order approach to the study of organizations. The framework belongs to Strauss (1963, 1978, 1982), and it is a sadly neglected one, all but ignored by mainstream organizational theorists. See also Maines (1977) and Dingwall and Strong (1985).

29.   Changes are afoot at Tech and what, to some old-timers, represent the insidious, dark powers of bureaucracy are gaining footholds in the organization and tightening up formerly loose operations. True Believers in the "organizational life cycle" approach might regard this as evidence of natural law (Kimberly and Miles, 1980). We see neither dark forces nor inevitable mutation but rather continuous, minor adjustments made by numerous actors and groups in the organization to what they consider changing conditions. Foremost among these conditions are those that reflect directly on particular actor or group's status and clout inside the organization. Recent technical disappointments at Tech have certainly wounded the "techies" and served the "pro-business crowd," but things could just as easily turn around. Organizational structure, from this perspective, is a resource members make use of when furthering their own ends (Bittner, 1965; Silverman, 1971).

30.   We must note that the term *culture*, while frequently used by Tech employees is seldom, if ever, used by Disneyland operators. As suggested throughout the text, no doubt part of the reason for this variation in organizational vocabulary reflects the differing roles (specialized versus general), training (extensive versus slight), regions (East versus West), and career concerns (central and serious versus ephemeral and playful) of the studied employees. More important, however, the culture builders in the two organizations differ markedly in their awareness and openness to current managerial concepts. Disneyland managers are a remarkably closed and introspective group who, having worked their way up through the ranks, are suspicious of others who do not know their specific business. They are quietly confident of the abilities to run a successful operation on their own. In their minds, they are unique (far more unique than a—chortle—high-tech company) and have no need of guidelines developed outside the entertainment industry. Tech managers, on the other hand, demonstrate an equally remarkable readiness to seek aid and comfort wherever they can find it. As noted in the description, consultants, management books, participation in general management programs run outside the company, and previous work experience in other firms provide many Tech managers with a good deal of information on current management thought and fashion. But merely because Disneylanders talk as if culture is something that grows on the walls of swimming pools does not

mean they are not caught up by their organizational membership. In some ways, the rather deceptive talk among Disneyland employees about being in "show business" documents just how deeply the organizational culture has penetrated the ranks, both high and low. Keeping the culture tacit, while no doubt a thoughtless managerial strategy, has its advantages.

31. Those most committed to these organizations have special labels other employees use, in mildly derogatory ways, to refer to them. Tech employees who are thought most devoted to the company are "Technies" (as opposed to those "total engineers" swept away by technical pursuits). Ride operators who are seemingly the most impressed by the need for proper conduct in the park are the "pixies" and "elves" of Disneyland (as opposed to the "trolls," "robots," and "soshes" with different views and interests). Apparently, for these curious employees, the norms, values, and feelings learned in the organization are pushed well back into the recesses of the mind until they are literally taken for granted as fair, just, proper, and natural. Those with the most careful training are, of course, the top managers of organizations, who not only help shape the culture but are often the living embodiments of it.

32. See Van Maanen and Barley (1984, 1985) for a far more intensive treatment of this matter as it pertains to the inherent conflicts between and among occupational communities.

33. We draw extensively on Edwards (1979) in this section. While there is apparent agreement as to the descriptive side of the changes in the workplace, there is heated and instructive debate as to what logic we are to attribute to such changes. The neo-Marxist camp presents a strong case but little direct data for the central role management efforts to control labor plays in the historical drama (Noble, 1982; Braverman, 1974). The neo-Weberian camp presents impressive data but inconsistent and sometimes illogical argument to support the role administrative or organizational rationality and efficiency play in the matter (Blau & Schoenherr, 1971; Williamson, 1979). Baron et al. (1986), working deep in the empirical trenches, present some intriguing data in this regard. Using organizational self-reports over a 40-year period, they found bureaucratization closely linked to governmental guidelines developed during World War II to stabilize the work force in key industries. The bureaucratic devices invented to satisfy government standards remained in place after the war, though the standards were themselves lifted. Not only did they remain in place, they were copied by other organizations, which apparently found such controls attractive. Marx might appreciate the role played by the "oppressive state apparatus" in this regard, but some of his current namesakes may not be so pleased, since there is very little evidence that the capitalists themselves were very willing or conscious actors in the spread of bureaucracy.

34. We should note that we have no Whiggish history in mind to fix these control devices in some linear sequence of development. Control mechanisms of all sorts emerge in no set pattern. Their invention and use varies by historical period, by industry, by organization, by society, and so forth. Governmental and service organizations may lead, for example, in the refinement of bureaucratic devices but lag in technical ones. This is an important qualification to keep in mind as we discuss culture control, for many of its characteristics are indeed ancient.

35. See Gordon et al. (1982), Jacoby (1984) and, again, Baron et al. (1986) for some aggregate data on this matter. The importation of several Japanese management tools provides an interesting parable. Quality control circles, for example, seem to be regarded by American managers as add-ons to current management practices—a little something extra to boost employee involvement and perhaps promote more concern for production standards (Lawler & Mohrman, 1985). Thus, as a late-blooming practice, quality control circles in the United States must operate with far more constraints on them than in Japan. Their relative disappointment to American managers may then have less to do with differences among employees in the United States and Japan than with differences in the overall control systems in the two countries.

36. Meyer and Rowan (1977) provide the underlying rationale for institutionalization theory on which we draw for the point in the text. In brief, they argue that organizational innovations are initially driven by management's desire to improve practice (broadly defined). But such innovations, when seen as successful, soon become infused with values that go well beyond the specific usefulness

of the particular innovation itself. Adoption of new techniques, then, becomes driven by management needs to legitimize their operations and organizations (as perhaps, forward-looking, modern, or state of the art), rather than driven by task requirements. Zucker (1977, 1983) and Tolbert and Zucker (1983) establish this argument and provide fine confirmatory data. DiMaggio and Powell (1983) tie a good deal of this work into a neat theoretical bundle and suggest the logical consequence of the organizational sonar and imitation implied by institutionalization theory: isomorphism among organizations. Martin et al. (1985) provide a useful illustration of how such processes may look in regard to corporate bedtime stories.

37.   The point here is that control systems of any sort seem to decay in effectiveness over time. Bureaucratic controls provide the exemplary case, as first pointed out by Merton (1957). The argument is essentially one of function giving way to form. Thus, in well-defined bureaucratic organizations, employees may carry out their duties, but they do so with little zest or care for what they are doing. Recalcitrance to bureaucratic control is perhaps expressed most often in passive and clandestine ways. Bureaucracy, in its most virulent forms, creates self-regarding organizations wherein employees frequently maintain a lively interest in only their own welfare and have little sense (or concern) for how their own ends complement those of others or complement those of the organization as a whole. Reform in such organizations boils down to managerial attempts to insert any or all alternative control devices—object, technical, and cultural controls.

38.   These methods certainly raise ethical questions too. Schein (1961, 1966, 1985) has been something of a voice in the wilderness on these matters, consistently raising ethical questions in the domains of, first, socialization, and now, culture.

REFERENCES

Averril, J. P. (1980). A constructivist view of emotions. In R. Plutchik & H. Kellerman (eds.), *Emotion theory, research and experience.* New York: Academic Press.

Bailyn, L. (1985). Autonomy in the industrial R&D lab. *Human Resource Management 24,* 129–146.

Baron, J. N., Dobin, F. R., & D. Jennings (1986). War and peace: The evolution of modern personnel management in US industry. *American Journal of Sociology, 92,* 350–383.

Bittner, E. (1965). The concept of organization. *Social Research, 32,* 239–255.

Blau, P. M., & R. Schoenherr (1971). *The structure of organizations.* New York: Basic Books.

Braverman, H. (1974). *Labor and monopoly capital.* New York: Monthly Review Press.

Burns, T. (1961). Micropolitics. *Administrative Science Quarterly, 6,* 257–281.

Burns, T. (1955). The reference of conduct in small groups. *Human Relations, 8,* 467–486.

Burns, T. (1977). *The BBC: Public institution and private world.* London: Macmillan.

Cavan, S. (1966). *Liquor license.* Chicago: Aldine.

Christopher, R. (1983). *The Japanese mind.* New York: Fawcett Columbine.

Dalton, M. (1959). *Men who manage.* New York: Wiley.

Denzin, N. (1984). *On understanding emotion.* San Francisco: Jossey-Bass.

DiMaggio, P. J., & W. W. Powell (1983). The iron-cage revisited: Institutional isomorphism and the collective rationality of organizational fields. *American Sociological Review, 48,* 147–160.

Dingwall, Robert, & Phil M. Strong (1985). The intellectual study of organization. *Urban Life, 14* (2), 205–232.

Ditton, J. (1977). *Part-time crime: An ethnography of fiddling and pilferage.* London: Macmillan.

Dunkerley, D. (1975). *The foreman.* London: Routledge & Kegan Paul.

Edwards, R. (1979). *Contested terrain.* New York: Basic Books.

Eliot, T. S. (1932). *Selected essays, 1917–1930.* New York: Harcourt, Brace and World.

Fine, G. A. (1984). Negotiated order and organizational cultures. In *Annual Review of Sociology, vol. 10,* pp. 239–262, Palo Alto, CA: Annual Reviews.

Friedson, E. (1970). *Professional dominance: The social structure of medical care.* New York: Atherton Press.

Glaser, B. G. (ed.). (1968). *Organizational careers.* Chicago: Aldine.

Glaser, B. G., and Strauss, A. (1971). *Status passage.* Chicago: Aldine.

Goffman, E. (1955) On face work. *Psychiatry, 18,* 215–236.

Goffman, E. (1956). Embarrassment and social organization. *American Journal of Sociology, 62,* 264–274.

Goffman, E. (1959). *The presentation of self in everyday life.* New York: Doubleday Anchor.

Goffman, E. (1961). *Encounters.* Indianapolis: Bobbs-Merrill.

Goffman, E. (1967). *Interaction ritual.* New York: Doubleday Anchor.

Goffman, E. (1969). *Strategic interaction.* Philadelphia: University of Pennsylvania Press.

Goffman, E. (1971). *Relations in public.* New York: Basic Books.

Goodenough, W. (1970) *Description and comparison in cultural anthropology.* Chicago: Aldine.

Gordon, D. M., Edwards, R. E., & M. Reich (1982). *Segmented work, divided workers.* London: University of Cambridge Press.

Gouldner, A. (1954). *Patterns of industrial bureaucracy.* New York: Free Press.

Grannovetter, M. S. (1974). *Getting a job.* Cambridge: Harvard University Press.

Heller, Joseph (1974). *Something happened.* London: Jonathan Cape.

Hochschild, A. R. (1979). Emotion work, feeling rules and social structure. *American Journal of Sociology, 85,* 551–575.

Hochschild, A. R. (1983). *The managed heart.* Berkeley: University of California Press.

Hughes, E. C. (1958). *Men and their work.* Glencoe, Ill.: Free Press.

Izard, C. E. (1972). *Patterns of emotion.* New York: Academic Press.

Jacoby, S. M. (1984). The development of internal labor markets in American manufacturing. In P. Osterman (Ed.), *Internal labor markets.* Cambridge: MIT Press.

Kaible, N. (1983). Recruitment and socialization at IBM. Case written for Stanford Business School, Stanford University.

Kaible, N., and M. Paddock (1983). The Tupperware way. Case written for Stanford Business School, Stanford University.

Kanter, R. M. (1977). *Men and women of the corporation.* New York: Basic Books.

Katz, F. E. (1966). *Autonomy and organizations: The limits of social control.* New York: Random House.

Kemper, T. D. (1978). Toward a sociology of emotions. *American Sociologist, 13,* 30–41.

Kimberly, J. R., & R. H. Miles (1980). *The organizational life cycle.* San Francisco: Jossey-Bass.

Kunda, Gideon (forthcoming). *Engineering culture: Culture and control in a high-tech organization.* Philadelphia: Temple University Press.

Langer, S. (1967). *Mind: An essay on human feeling, Vol. 1.* Baltimore: Johns Hopkins University Press.

Lawler, E. E., & S. A. Mohrman (1985). Quality circles after the fad. *Harvard Business Review* (January–February): 65–71.

LeMasters, E. E. (1975). *Blue collar aristocrats.* Madison: University of Wisconsin Press.

Lipset, S. M. & W. Schneider (1983). *The confidence gap.* New York: Free Press.

Lithman, Y. G. (1979). Feeling good and getting smashed. *Ethnos, 44,* 119–133.

Lortie, D. (1975). *Schoolteacher.* Chicago: University of Chicago Press.

Lukes, S. (1975). Political ritual and social integration. *Sociology, 9,* 289–308.

MacAndrews, C. R., & R. B. Edgerton (1969). *Drunken comportment.* Chicago: Aldine.

Maines, D. R. (1977). Social organization and social structure in symbolic interactionist thought. In *Annual Review of Sociology, Vol. 3,* pp. 235–259, Palo Alto: Annual Reviews.

Manning, P. K. (1977). *Police work.* Cambridge: MIT Press.

Manning, P. K. (1980). *Narc's game.* Cambridge: MIT Press.

Martin, J., and C. Siehl (1983). Organizational culture and counterculture. *Organizational Dynamics 12,* 52–64.

Martin, J., M. S. Feldman, Hatch, M. J., & S. B. Sitkin (1985). The uniqueness paradox in organizational stories. *Administrative Science Quarterly 28*, 438–453.

Martin, S. E. (1980). *Breaking and entering: Policewomen on patrol.* Berkeley: University of California Press.

Merton, R. K. (1957). *Social theory and social structure.* Glencoe, Ill.: Free Press.

Meyer, J. W., and B. Rowan (1977). Institutionalized organizations: Formal structure as myth and ceremony. *American Journal of Sociology, 83*, 340–363.

Mills, C. W. (1956). *White collar.* New York: Oxford University Press.

Noble, D. F. (1982). *America by design.* New York: Oxford University Press.

Ouchi, W. G. (1981). *Theory Z.* Reading, MA: Addison-Wesley.

Ouchi, W. G., and A. L. Wilkins (1985). Organizational culture. In *Annual Review of Sociology, Vol. 11*: pp. 367–412. Palo Alto: Annual Reviews.

Peters, T. J., & R. H. Waterman (1982). *In search of excellence.* New York: Harper & Row.

Peven, Dorothy E. (1968). The use of religious revival techniques to indoctrinate personnel. *Sociological Quarterly, 9*, (1), 97–106.

Richman, J. (1983). *Traffic wardens: An ethnography of street administration.* Manchester: Manchester University Press.

Riesman, D. (1950). *The lonely crowd.* New Haven: Yale University Press.

Rohlen, T. P. (1974). *For harmony and strength.* Berkeley: University of California Press.

Rosen, M. (1985). Breakfast at Spiros. *Journal of Management, 11*, 31–48.

Roy, D. (1959). Bananatime. *Human Organization 18*, 158–168.

Schacter, S., & J. Singer (1962). Cognitive, social and physiological determinants of emotional states. *Psychological Review, 69*, 379–399.

Scheff, T. J. (1977). The distancing of emotion in ritual. *Current Anthropology 18*, 483–491.

Schein, E. H. (1961). *Coercive persuasion.* New York: Norton.

Schein, E. H. (1966). The problem of moral education for the business manager. *Industrial Management Review, 8*, 3–14.

Schein, E. H. (1985). *Organizational culture and leadership.* San Francisco: Jossey-Bass.

Schickel, R. (1968). *The Disney version.* New York: Simon and Schuster.

Schott, S. (1979). Emotion and social life. *American Journal of Sociology, 84*, 1321–1334.

Schwartz, P., & J. Lever (1976). Fear and loathing at the college mixer. *Urban Life 4*, 413–432.

Seidenberg, R. (1975). *Corporate wives—corporate casualities?* New York: Doubleday, Anchor.

Skolnick, J. (1966). *Justice without trial.* New York: Wiley.

Silverman, D. (1971). *The theory of organizatins.* New York: Basic Books.

Spradley, J. P. (1979). *The ethnographic interview.* New York: Holt, Rinehart and Winston.

Spradley, J. P., & B. Mann (1975). *The cocktail waitress.* New York: Wiley.

Strauss, A. (1978). *Negotiations.* San Francisco: Jossey-Bass.

Strauss, A. (1982). Interorganizational negotiations. *Urban Life, 11*, 350–367.

Strauss, A., & N. H. Martin (1956). Patterns of mobility within industrial organization. *Journal of Business 29*, 101–110.

Strauss, A., L. Schtatzman, R. Bucher, D. Elrich, and M. Sabshin (1963). The hospital and its negotiated order. In E. Friedson (Ed.), *The hospital in modern society.* New York: Free Press.

Tolbert, P. S., & L. G. Zucker (1983). Institutional sources of change in the formal structure of organizations. *Administrative Science Quarterly, 30*, 22–39.

Trice, H. M. (1984). Rites and ceremonies in organizational culture. In S. Bacharach and S. M. Mitchell (eds.), *Perspectives on organizational sociology*, vol. 4. Greenwich, Conn.: JAI Press.

Trice, H. M., & J. M. Beyer (1984). Studying organizational cultures through rites and ceremonies. *Academy of Management Review, 9*, 653–669.

Van Maanen, J. (1976). Breaking-in: Socialization to work. In R. Dubin (Ed.), *Handbook of work, organization and society.* Chicago: Rand-McNally.

Van Maanen, J. (1977). Experiencing organization. In J. Van Maanen (Ed.), *Organizational careers.* New York: Wiley.

Van Maanen, J. (1978). The asshole. In P. K. Manning and J. Van Maanen (Eds.), *Policing*. New York: Random House.

Van Maanen, J. (1979). The self, the situation and the rules of interpersonal relations. In W. Bennis, J. Van Maanen, & E. H. Schein, *Essays in interpersonal dynamics*. Homewood, Ill.: Dorsey Press.

Van Maanen, J. (1986). Power in the bottle. In S. Srivasta (Ed.), *Executive power*. San Francisco: Jossey-Bass.

Van Maanen, J. (1988). *Tales of the field*. Chicago: University of Chicago Press.

Van Maanen, J., & S. R. Barley (1984). Occupational communities. In B. Staw and L. L. Cummings (Eds.), *Research in organizational behavior, Vol 6* pp. 287–365, Greenwich, Conn.: JAI Press.

Van Maanen, J. (1985). Cultural organization. In P. Frost, M. Louis, and L. Moore (Eds.), *Organizational culture*. Beverly Hills: Sage.

Van Maanen, J., & E. H. Schein (1979). Toward a theory of organizational socialization. In B. Staw (ed.), *Research in organizational behavior. Vol. 1* pp. 209–269, Greenwich, CT: JAI Press.

Vogel, E. F. (1979). *Japan as number one*. Cambridge: Harvard University Press.

Waller, W. (1937). The rating and dating complex. *American Sociological Review, 2*, 727–734.

Whyte, W. W. (1956). *The organization man*. New York: Simon and Schuster.

Williamson, O. E. (1979). Transaction-cost economics. *Journal of Law and Economics 22*: 233–261.

Willis, P. (1977). *Learning to Labor*. New York: Columbia University Press.

Zajonc, R. (1980). Feeling and thinking. *American psychologist*. February, 13–39.

Zucker, L. (1977). The role of institutionalization in cultural persistence. *American sociological review*, 42, 725–743.

Zucker, L. (1983). Organizations as institutions. In S. B. Bacharach (Ed.), *Research in the sociology of organizations*, Vol. 2. pp. 1–47, Greenwich, Conn.: JAI Press.

Zurcher, L. A. (1982). The staging of emotions. *Symbolic interactionism, 5*, 1–22.

WORK VALUES AND THE CONDUCT
OF ORGANIZATIONAL BEHAVIOR

Walter R. Nord, Arthur P. Brief, Jennifer M. Atieh
and Elizabeth M. Doherty

ABSTRACT

Conventional perspectives on work values are reviewed and critiqued in
the light of historical research. A two-dimensional framework is developed
and used to classify and analyze existing conceptions of work values. Analysis revealed previously unrecognized commonalities, differences and
omissions in existing approaches to work values. Among other things, the
assumed relationship between the Protestant work ethic and the contemporary emphasis on intrinsically interesting work is found to be misconceived.
A scenario to account for this misconception is presented and new directions
for inquiry into work values are proposed.

The study of work values has had a central place in Western intellectual thought for several centuries. At first, philosophers, theologians, poets, and fiction writers played dominant roles; it was not until early in the twentieth century that social scientists began to play an important part. Currently, however, social scientists in general and organizational psychologists in particular have come to be some of the most important contributors on the topic. Even though psychologists have attempted, by couching their efforts in the framework of positive science, to divorce their research from value judgments, their inquiry remains linked in important ways to the intellectual *Zeitgeist*. The most fundamental bonds of organizational psychologists to their predecessors can be seen in the assumptions they make about the evolution of work in modern society.

It is commonly taken as given that at some point in the evolution of modern industrial society the production activities of individuals became severed from other aspects of their daily lives. Implicit in this assumption, of course, is the belief that at some earlier point—usually prior to the industrial revolution—the work of individuals was harmoniously integrated with their total existence, and that after the industrial revolution, work ceased to be meaningfully related to other aspects of life. Often, this change has been assumed to be a source of major social problems. As Zuboff (1983) observed: "The context of meanings that held people together could no longer be counted upon to provide what we now think of as 'intrinsic work motivation' " (p. 153). In this context, the focus on work values has often been motivated by the objective of restoring the earlier idyllic state.

In this chapter, we examine the intellectual assumptions that have guided contemporary organizational psychologists and the larger intellectual tradition of which they are a part. Stimulated by Anthony (1977), Rodgers (1974), and others, we begin with a somewhat radical perspective—one that views the assumed harmonious relations between work and the rest of life as a pre-lapsarian myth, not as accurate history. As a consequence, the intellectual history of the study of work values becomes problematic. Of special interest is the process through which the dominant approach emerged and what alternative views may have been obscured.

We define work values as the end states people desire and feel they ought to be able to realize through working. Such feelings and desires can be acquired in a variety of ways, such as through reading, conversation, observation, actually doing work. However acquired, work values are of great practical importance because they affect the means that can be used to manage a society's economic activities. For example, work values may influence what people believe to be legitimate and hence define what they will tolerate. These outcomes will in turn affect what costs elites must pay in directing various forms of work activity and how easily people can be induced to change their ways to satisfy imperatives of technology. Thus at least indirectly, values affect the flexibility and productivity of a given work force.

Work values have a mutually causal relationship with the meanings that individuals attach to their work. On the one hand, over time work values are a consequence of the meanings that individuals collectively attach to work. On the other hand, at any given point in time, these collective meanings can be viewed as given and hence as causing the meanings that individuals attach to a given activity. This causal role suggests that work values are of considerable practical importance. As shared interpretations of what people want and expect, work values are an important component of social reality that influence, for example, the type of work people design for others to do, how people are socialized for work, and how people can successfully relate work to other aspects of their lives. The latter, the role that work values play in helping people create effective alignments (Culbert & McDonough, 1985), may have a significant impact on overall psychological well-being. For example, the easier it is for individuals to perceive a positive relationship between what they do to earn a living and achieving other valued ends, the better they are apt to feel about the quality of their lives in general. Clearly, social scientists who study work values are dealing with a matter of considerable practical import.

The close relationship between work values and ongoing human experience raises two challenges that need to be addressed in the study of work values. First, inquiry about work values must be historically grounded and sensitive to changes in work over time. Work values represent efforts to come to terms with particular arrangements of work under particular social conditions. As the arrangements and/or the conditions change, so will, in all probability, the work values. Moreover, it is likely that work values of one era will influence the work values, work arrangements, and social conditions of the next era. Consequently, students of work values need to be historically informed.

Second, as Gergen (1982) has argued so persuasively, the close association of applied scientists with practitioners often has dysfunctional effects on the development of science, because often scientists are overly influenced by the perspectives of the practitioners. We know of no reason to expect that the scientific study of work values will be immune to such influence. Students of work values are vulnerable to accepting unconsciously the assumptions, beliefs, goals, and definitions of reality about work that are fashionable among their contemporaries, including various interest groups (Baritz, 1960; Dubin, 1976a; Gordon, Kleiman, & Hanie, 1978; Nord, 1977). For example, as Gordon, et al. noted, industrial-organizational psychology is uncomfortably close to common sense; as Dubin observed, applied scientists often pass a market test where passing is a function of sharing common definitions of problems and symptoms with practitioners. Consequently, conventional approaches in applied social science often ignore a variety of alternative sets of beliefs and social constructions.

We argue that contemporary organizational behavior suffers from the lack of historical perspective on the evolution of work and from an overly close tie to certain aspects of the conventional wisdom. (In fact, if, as we have argued work values are a major component of collective understanding, work values *are* a major part of the conventional wisdom of those who share them.) The purposes of this paper are to analyze the conventional approach to work values, to show the intellectual and practical reasons for organizational behaviorists to reexamine and explain their assumptions about work, and to point to some of the new perspectives that reexamination might produce.

We approach this task in four parts. First, we review the history of work and what we term the conventional view of modern work values. We also suggest that while the conventional view seems to have been built on Max Weber's description of the Protestant ethic, it has ignored important components of his analysis. Second, we present an alternative perspective on the evolution of work values. This alternative view reveals certain latent aspects of the conventional view and highlights distinctions that frequently have gone unrecognized. Third, we present a framework for examining these differences and for classifying various orientations to work values. This framework reveals lacunae in various contemporary treatments of work and important distinctions between what we call the neoconventional view and more traditional perspectives. Finally, we use this framework and the alternative perspective to raise "new" questions and approaches to work—new at least to organizational behavior—and suggest the intellectual and practical value of this broadened perspective.

WORK VALUES: THE CONVENTIONAL VIEW

Although the development and transmission of work values are historical processes (cf. Aldag & Brief, 1979), this history is often ignored or misunderstood. Without careful analysis of the total configuration of forces that shape history, the course that history took often seems inevitable. Interests, values, and ideologies influence the content of what is accepted as historical fact. While a number of distortions result, one that is especially central to the current paper is the tendency of historical accounts to overlook the alternative courses that history may have taken, thereby making the course that history did take appear to be inevitable. For example, as Noble (1984) has demonstrated so well, the evolution of technology could have been very different had certain institutional arrangements been other than they were; the forms of technology that failed to survive have been overlooked in conventional accounts.

We hypothesize, with considerable support from scholars such as Braverman (1974), Clawson (1980), Gutman (1976), Nelson (1975), and others, that a similar process has operated in our understanding of the history of organizations and management. A number of scholars (Dubin, 1976b; George, 1968; Heneman, 1973; Parker & Smith, 1976) have argued that the way historical events have been reported and interpreted in the management literature provides only a partially valid picture. As a result, the "conventional view" is based on an incomplete understanding of history. Here too, what has been accepted as historical fact has been influenced by a complex interaction of values, interests, and desires. However, in retrospect, in the absence of in depth analysis of the historical process, those who hold the conventional view interpret the process in a far more linear fashion than it was and view the outcomes themselves as more inevitable than they really were. Moreover, they fail to see the ideological contents of their perspective and become subject to what Bem and Bem (1970) spoke of as an "unconscious ideology." An unconscious ideology contains attitudes and beliefs that an individual accepts without awareness. These beliefs constrain a person's ability to conceive of alternative possibilities and tend to go unrecognized until confronted by a fundamentally different perspective.

The conventional view of work values is so widely shared by managers, organizational behaviorists, politicians, and even trade union leaders, that it contains elements of an unconscious ideology. Managers frequently respond to problems with workers by lamenting the decay of the work ethic. Organizational behaviorists have built much of their theory, research, and advice to managers on the premise that work is somehow noble and that psychologically engaging work is a necessary condition for human development. Politicians appear to find it useful to attach their comments to an assumed set of work values. In celebrating Labor Day, 1971, for example, the President of the United States saluted "the dignity of work, the value of achievement, and the morality of self-reliance. None of these are going out of style" (Gutman, 1976, p. 4). In fact, the work ethic is assumed to be so widely shared that Rodgers (1974) observed that, in the past, trade unionists, radicals, and conservatives often attempted to rally support for their causes through an appeal to the premises of the work ethic (Rodgers, 1974). Even today, it is popular to appeal to the need to rekindle the work ethic to solve a variety of social and economic problems. Clearly, the conventional view represents a major feature in American society.

In this section we examine the conventional view. We summarize its history, its substance, and its lacunae. We begin with a very cursory look at the concept of work in the history of Western civilization. [For a fuller description see Tilgher (1931); de Grazia (1964); and Neff (1985).]

WORK IN WESTERN CIVILIZATION

Ancient Greek philosophers saw work as a waste of a citizen's time and as a corrupting activity that made the pursuit of truth and virtue more difficult. Leisure time provided the vehicle for the attainment of truth and virtue; it was reserved for the exercise of the mind and spirit. For example, Aristotle (1912) maintained that leisure itself was a source of intrinsic pleasure, happiness, and felicity. In his view, happiness did not arise from an occupation; it was a property of those who had leisure. Through the writings of Aristotle as well as Plato and Epicurus, these work values spread to Rome and were largely embraced. Of course, in both societies this classical ideology of work was dependent on slavery; slaves were viewed more as instruments than as people. As Grant (1960, p. 112) observed, the Roman writer Cato the Elder offered the following advice: "The best principle of management is to treat both slaves and animals well enough to give them the strength to work hard." Thus, work was a curse that could be separated from the good life, but the separation required a class of persons to whom one could assign, without feeling remorse, vulgar or degrading activities.

Ancient Hebrew philosophers and theologians shared the Greco-Roman system of work values, but with one principal exception. They saw work as a product of original sin and valued it as a means of atonement. In other words, to the ancient Hebrews, work was *both* a product of original sin and a way of redeeming oneself in the eyes of God. Work, therefore, as a way of cooperating with God in the world's salvation, began to emerge in a positive light.

These more positive feelings about work became part of the very early Christian teachings and continued to be evident through the Middle Ages. Work was viewed as a route to goodness; it was a path for accumulating a surplus of goods and services to be shared with the needy. The hoarding of riches, however, was considered a transgression of the law of God—the sin of avarice. But, work *itself,* (i.e., the activities of work per se) as seen for example by Thomas Aquinas, was morally neutral—a natural condition of Christian life.

With Luther, the moral neutrality of work itself started to wane. He advocated the concept of a "calling," a life-task set by God. According to Weber (1930, p. 85), Luther believed that a calling was "something which man has to accept as a divine ordinance to which he must adapt himself." Failure to accept one's calling, whatever type of work may constitute it, was seen as immoral. Weber argued that interpretations of Luther's concept of a "calling" by Calvin and his followers symbolized "the Protestant ethic" of work and played a major role in the development of capitalism. Weber's analysis of the role of work values and the Protestant ethic for the development of capitalism is part of the conventional wisdom of modern organizational behavior.

Weber saw the development of Calvinism as adding the value of proving one's faith through "good works" to the ideology of work. Furthermore, he saw other Christian movements contributing to the religious foundations of a worldly asceticism, of a secular belief in the practice of strict self-denial as a measure of personal discipline. For example, in discussing the contributions of Richard Baxter (a writer on Puritan ethics who Weber used to represent the major tenets of the doctrine), Weber (1930) noted that wastage of time became, in principle, "the deadliest of sins" (p. 157) and hard, continuous bodily or mental labour" was "the specific defence against all those temptations that Puritanism united under the name of the unclean life" (p. 158). Although the avoidance of such temptations through the pursuit of a calling to work was viewed as an important contribution to production, Weber argued that the this emphasis was directed towards maximizing activities that would increase the glory of God—a nonsecular motive. In this way, work became "in itself the end of life, ordained as such by God" (Weber, 1930, p. 159). The Protestant ethic of work justified diligence and frugality for nonsecular reasons, but in so doing supported economic growth by motivating hard work and encouraging savings.

Although most of the religious content (serving the glory of God) has been omitted, Weber's analysis of the central importance of work to individuals appears to have shaped the version of the work ethic contained in the conventional view. These views are reflected in statements like those of the President of the United States quoted above. Moreover, they are embedded in the thinking of influential organizational psychologists and managers.

Hulin and Blood (1968), for example, described the work norms of the middle class as follows: "Positive affect for occupational achievement, a belief in the intrinsic value of hard work, a striving for the attainment of responsible positions, and a belief in the work-related aspects of Calvinism and the Protestant ethic" (p. 48). They added that the dominance of these values can be explained by children learning in school and at home those values:

brought by the Anglo-Saxon Protestants from Europe in the 17th and 18th centuries. The values have become the standard in middle-class society. Children are taught these values in school by their middle-class teachers and attempt to reach goals defined in terms of these values by means of behavior consistent with these values. (p. 52)

The potential of this view to influence social policy and managerial action can be seen in Blood's (1969) description of efforts to assimilate hard-core unemployed into the industrial work force. These efforts attempted to instill Protestant work values in members of the targeted under class. Other examples evident in the literature include McClelland's (1961) treatment of the Protestant values and the motives presumed to be required for success in management, and Aldag and Brief's (1975) view that commitment to Protestant ethic values directly moderates the relationships between job characteristics and various outcome measures.

So ingrained is the work ethic as an explanation for the success of the U.S. economy that managers reflexively attribute declines in productivity and increases in worker recalcitrance and discontent to the decline of the work ethic. For example, in analyzing unrest in the workplace in the early 1970s, Deans (1973) observed, "Corporation executives seem no less puzzled than many other Americans as to why young people entering the labor force—even in a time of job scarcity—are less enchanted with the so-called Protestant ethic of hard work and upward striving than their parents and grandparents" (pp. 8–9). Thus, it is evident that the tenets of the Protestant work ethic, as described by Weber, are still taken seriously by managers, scholars, and policy makers. They are viewed as central to the development and functioning of capitalism.

Aspects of Protestantism Not Emphasized in the Conventional View

Weber discussed two other aspects of Protestantism that contributed to the success of capitalism that are often ignored in contemporary discussions. First, the Protestant ethic was like the earlier Christian teachings in treating *all* work as potentially worthy. The nature of work itself was not an issue; it adopted a content free view of work. Second, Weber saw the nature of social relationships promoted by early Protestant thinkers as important in the development of capitalism. The conventional view has not recognized these two points sufficiently.

Content free view of work.   At least two features of an ideological system influence its impact. First, the acceptance of an ideology is influenced by its explicit substance—what issues it is perceived to address and what it appears to say about these matters. Second, dissemination is affected by what the system is silent on—what issues it does not address and what it does not say about those matters it does treat (Gouldner, 1970). These two features are closely related, in the same manner as figure and ground are related to each other. However, like figure and ground, they tend to affect perception and thought in qualitatively different ways. The presence of something (figure) tends to focus attention on it and things associated with it. It heightens awareness about a somewhat finite set of things or ideas. In contrast, when things are not focused on (i.e., they are treated as ground) they tend to be taken as given and their effects unnoticed.

The conventional view has focused mainly on what the Protestant ethic said about work—it has focused on the figure. It has not considered what the ethic did not deal with and how its silence on certain matters influenced its impact on society.

The Protestant ethic was not concerned with either the content of work or the nature of the product/service produced. According to Weber, the spirit of capitalism focused attention on earning and accumulating money as an outward sign of salvation. Although Weber (1930) personally lamented the fact that the ethic's ascetic character spawned modern machine production, his description of the Protestant ethic made no mention of the intrinsic outcomes of work itself. Wealth is what mattered for salvation, and it could be contingent on any type of work. Weber maintained that an individual's calling in early Protestantism was "an obligation which the individual is supposed to feel and does feel towards the content of his professional activity, *no matter in what it consists*" (p. 54, italics added).

This silence on the content and outcomes of work allowed economic activities to proceed free from a variety of traditional concerns, moral issues, and social values that could have retarded economic progress by reducing flexibility. Efficient markets require capital and labor to be highly mobile. If wealth is the end and the means are unimportant, investors and workers can concentrate on their economic activities, unconstrained by noneconomic concerns. For example, as Hirschman (1977) suggested, if lending money in return for interest had not been freed from moral prohibitions, capitalist economic development would have been retarded. Similarly, if workers were unwilling to work in a certain way or produce particular products because of religious or other noneconomic reasons, degrees of freedom would have been removed from economic activity. Had the Protestant ethic emphasized intrinsically meaningful activity or put conditions on the achievement of wealth (e.g., the production of only those goods that are consistent with some narrowly defined moral standard), it would have introduced constraints. Since the Protestant ethic was generally free of such content—all work was equally good—it imposed few limitations on how to gain wealth. In Weber's (1930) words: "the usefulness of a calling, and thus its favour in the sight of God, is measured primarily in moral terms, and thus in terms of the importance of the goods produced in it for the community. But further, and, above all, in practice the most important criterion is found in private profitableness" (p. 162). Thus, although the value of the goods to the community was one constraint, it was subsidiary to larger, nonsecular purposes.

Sometimes the conventional view is used to support efforts to introduce new job designs. For example, the authors of *Work in America* (1973) argued that it was a mistake to assume that the recalcitrance of young people in the workplace during the late 1960s and early 1970s represented any real change in traditional work values; instead, the problem was a decrease in "their willingness to take on meaningless work in authoritarian settings that offers only extrinsic rewards" (p. 47). We, in contrast, suggest that such a change would represent a sharp departure from the traditional values of the Protestant ethic (as described by Weber) in two ways. First, there is no reference to the religious basis for the importance of work. As Pence (1978–1979) observed, the modern notion of a calling is entirely secular. It is very different from the Protestant ethic that saw all work as potentially worthy: the calling came from God, not from the secular world. Likewise, Spence (1985) observed that the modern-day form of the work ethic "has been watered down to the belief that work is inherently good in and of itself. . . . Any sense of a larger purpose has been largely lost" (p. 1292).

A second discontinuity between the traditional work ethic and modern discussions of job design (e.g., Argyris, 1957; 1973) concerns the importance of the content and process of work. These are now assumed to be important in many contemporary discussions; as we have shown, these elements were not part of the ethic described by Weber. The central outcomes advanced in Protestant teachings were extrinsic—they were contingent upon results of work, not work itself. In short, any attempt to view recent efforts by organizational behaviorists and others as being consistent with the tradition of the Protestant ethic is misleading.

Social relations and the Protestant ethic. Users of the conventional perspective have also given too little attention to the nature of social relationships implied in some of the teachings of Protestantism. Although the conventional view does recognize a strong individualism advanced by the Protestant ethic, it tends to emphasize this as a positive doctrine and ignore certain sociological implications of the message. Not only did the Puritan stance against the spontaneous enjoyment of life remove distractions from work and restrain consumption, but, Weber argued, it aided in the standardizing of production because it promoted uniformity through certain prohibitions, such as those against differences in dress. Moreover, Calvinism discouraged social bonds among people and legitimated class differences and economic inequality which, in turn, aided capital investment. Weber (1930) observed that the Calvinist's intercourse with God "was carried on in deep spiritual isolation" (p. 107): focus was on the individual's own salvation. Further, the achievement of worldly success by an individual was conducive to a rather asocial elitism. In Weber's (1930) words:

This consciousness of divine grace of the elect and holy was accompanied by an attitude toward the sin of one's neighbour, not of sympathetic understanding based

on consciousness of one's own weakness, but of hatred and contempt for him as an
enemy of God bearing the sign of eternal damnation. (p. 122)

In fact, the "bourgeois businessman," according to Weber, received
"comforting assurance that the unequal distribution of the goods of this
world was a special dispensation of Divine Providence" (p. 177). More
than just legitimizing and fostering class differences, Weber saw Calvinist
doctrine as splintering social relationships. According to Weber, one of
the major consequences of Calvinism "was a feeling of unprecedented
inner loneliness of the single individual. In what was for the man of the
age of the Reformation the most important thing in life, his eternal salvation, he was forced to follow his path alone . . . No one could help
him" (p. 104). Puritanism, Weber asserted, was a source of "disillusioned
and pessimistically inclined individualism" (p. 105). Its doctrines warned
against trusting in the aid of friendship—"Even the amiable Baxter coun-
sels deep distrust of even one's closest friend, and Bailey directly exhorts
to trust no one and to say nothing compromising to anyone. Only God
should be your confidant" (p. 106).

This doctrine of individual isolation provided little basis for collective
action to change any aspect of social relationships. For example, it contained no basis for organization by workers to advance their collective
interests. In fact, it may well have legitimated the teachings of social institutions such as Protestant churches (Pope, 1942) that discouraged such
organization. In other words, the Protestant doctrine discouraged sociological relationships that would support collective action.

With the major exception of Spence (1985), who pointed to the dangers
of a work ethic that is driven by narrow self-interest in the absence of
further justification, most psychologists and organizational behaviorists
have failed to recognize some of the latent social implications of the work
ethic. The values that tend to have been emphasized pertain mainly to
individuals qua individuals. Little attention has been given to desires for
community and other collective outcomes that are affected by work. As
we will show, alternative views about the role of collective action in and
around the workplace are possible. For example, the Roman Catholic
Church (Pope Leo XIII, 1891) has been explicit about the benefits to be
derived from worker collectivities.

Impact of the Protestant ethic.   So far our discussion has centered on the
formal statements of the Protestant ethic. We have assumed, with Weber
and the conventional view, that somehow these formal statements were
related to the work experiences of individuals. How much these statements
influenced the day-to-day behavior of people is open to question, although
some influence seems likely. For example, such statements undoubtedly
affected the content of social norms and institutions (e.g., churches) and

thus had some impact on behavior. Similarly, a person's feelings about self-worth on earth almost surely influenced behavior. Some leading scholars, however, question whether the work ethic had much influence upon the working classes (Clayre, 1974; Rodgers, 1974). While the ethic undoubtedly had a de facto secular impact, how much and through what processes it influenced the behavior of the bulk of the population remains to be documented.

Summary

We have discussed how work, something despised by the Greeks, took on a positive value when it came to be viewed as a means of atonement by the ancient Hebrew philosophers, a route to goodness in early Christian teachings, and a calling with the rise of Protestantism. We examined Weber's (1930) description of the Protestant ethic and its role in the development of capitalism, and we explored how the conventional view of work (both in society in general and organizational behavior in particular) has ignored significant portions of Weber's analysis.

It was also shown that users of the conventional view misunderstand the relationship between their ideas and Weber's. As will be argued in depth later in this paper, the conventional view focuses on secular outcomes of the process and content of work, whereas the Protestant ethic was content free and concerned with nonsecular matters. Moreover, Calvinism and many of its related Protestant sects promoted sociological patterns that are ignored in the conventional view. Consequently, the conventional view contains a limiting unconscious ideology that induces people to misinterpret the past and present and err in their efforts to predict the future. Finally, clear historical documentation of the impact of the ethic on the day-to-day behavior of the masses was lacking.

We conclude, therefore, that the conventional view is built on an incomplete and problematic understanding of history. It fails to consider contradictory ethical and historical views about the nature of work and its relationship to individuals and society. A deeper understanding of these assertions can be gained from the study of an alternative perspective, which we explore in the next section.

WORK VALUES: AN ALTERNATIVE PERSPECTIVE

During the 1970s, a very different interpretation of the social history of modern work values came into vogue. Major contributors have been Anthony (1977), Bowles and Gintis (1976), Braverman (1974), Burawoy (1979), Clawson (1980), Edwards (1978), Gutman (1976), Jackall (1978), Marglin (1974), Nelson (1975), Rodgers (1974), Stone (1974), and Watson (1977).

Although others had crossed this terrain previously (e.g., Hays, 1957; Pollard, 1963; Thompson, 1963), it was during the 1970s that this very different view of the emergence of work forms and values became prominent. This view, which we call "the alternative perspective," is useful in uncovering the unconscious ideology of the conventional view because it is built on different assumptions. (Of course, the conventional view can serve the same function for the alternative perspective.) One should not be misled by the words "the alternative." In reality, this perspective is a loose collection of ideas; taken together these ideas provide a new perspective.

Among the tenets of the alternative view is that members of the working class did not share in the Protestant ethic work values during the period of industrialization (1850–1920) in the United States. To the degree the alternative view is correct, Weber (1930) may have erred when he described the United States of this period as the highest developed offspring of the wedding of the Protestant ethic and the spirit of capitalism. If Weber was wrong, if during this period strict adherence to Protestant work values by working class Americans was a myth, a number of important questions arise. What, for example, can account for the growth in American productivity during this era? What explains the behavior of the working classes of this time? What explains why the work ethic has received so much attention? Whose interests did it serve? Does the work ethic play any role in contemporary society? These questions have led to a series of challenges to the conventional view.

The alternative perspective is a label we have placed on a complex, diverse, and voluminous body of work that is difficult to summarize. In comparison with the traditional view, the alternative perspective tends to be built more on efforts to understand history by looking at the experiences of the "ordinary" person. Moreover, it tends to stress the coercive aspects of work and to see a greater amount of class conflict in and around the workplace. Given this conflict, the alternative perspective examines how it is managed. Of particular importance to the present discussion, this perspective sees the work ethic as a substitute for more direct forms of coercion.

Since several themes of this perspective are central to the current analysis, a brief characterization of it is needed. To provide this overview, we present a summary of one of the most perceptive contributors to this perspective, Daniel Rodgers. We have chosen Rodgers (1974) because his work has had the greatest impact on us, it has been widely acclaimed by historians, it deals explicitly with the work ethic, it has received so little attention in the organizational behavior literature, and it captures the essence of the alternative perspective.

Rodgers (1974) asserted that "the work ethic as it stood in the middle of the nineteenth century [in the U.S.], at the threshold of industrialization, was not a single conviction but a complex of ideas with roots and branches'' (p. 7). In fact, Rodgers observed that there were serious tensions among its components.

> The clearest of the tensions lie between the idea of work as ascetic exercise and work as art. The one looked toward system, discipline, and the emerging factory order; the other towards spontaneity, self-expression, and a narrowing of the gulf between work and play (pp. 13–14).

Work was supposed to be a creative act, yet it demanded self-repression; it was a social duty, but its payoffs were private rewards. Moreover, Rodgers added, there was the nagging contradiction between the ideals of duty and of success—between the dignity of all labor, even the humblest, and the equally universal counsel to work one's way as quickly as possible out of manual toil (p. 14).

In addition to these contradictions within the Protestant work ethic, Rodgers saw tensions between the classes:

> Praise of work in the mid-nineteenth century was strongest among the middling, largely Protestant, property-owning classes: farmers, merchants, ministers and professional men, independent craftsmen, and nascent industrialists. . . . The ascetic injunctions of Puritanism never penetrated very far into the urban working classes. (pp. 14–15)

In fact, Rodgers suggested that the work ethic became important to the moralists during industrialization in the United States because it helped to paper over some basic social contradictions, ''the unsettling presence of the factories in a society committed to the Free Labor ideal'' (p. 40).

Rodgers began by observing that to many members of the middle class of the post-Civil War North, life in the factory seemed uncomfortably close to slavery. Rodgers argued that the work ethic was in large measure a creation of middle-class writers to reduce this discomfort. A product of middle-class thought, the work ethic became increasingly less related to the realities of most workers as the Industrial Revolution took hold. Wage employment and the mechanization of labor widened the gap between Protestant work ideals and the realities of work. Under wage employment, for example, the assumption of the keepers of the mid-nineteenth century Protestant work ethic that ''the worker owned his own toil—that a man's efforts were his to exert and the successes his to be reaped'' (p. 30) began to crumble. Likewise the growing routinization of work weakened the foundation for the view that work was a creative activity.

The writers who attempted to help the middle class respond to these dilemmas developed a wide array of tactics. In response to the institutionalization of wage employment, for instance, moralists promised upward mobility, launched the cooperative movement, experimented with profit sharing, advocated piecework, and crusaded for worker democracy. In response to the lack of opportunities for advancement through work, writers of children's stories promoted the work ethic in a more abstract form that was not rooted in the realities of the workplace. For example, the Horatio Alger stories that are so widely assumed to be woven into the American work ethic showed success coming not from work, but when the heroes were at leisure, or after they had lost their jobs or they had performed a major act of kindness. In short, Rodgers observed, these success stories were romances, far removed from the realities of the factory.

We have not told all of Rodgers' story. Nevertheless, the theme is evident: prior to the Industrial Revolution, Protestant work values did not represent a wholly consistent statement. The Revolution itself sharpened these inconsistencies and made the differences between the spokespersons for Protestant work values and the masses who were supposed to adhere to them more apparent. As far as the holders of the alternative view are concerned, the work ethic in the United States has functioned to conceal the coercive forces that made people work. As Rodgers (1974) said in concluding his discussion of industrial workers:

> But even for those who chafed at labor, the appeal to the moral centrality of work was too useful to resist. Pitched in the abstract, it turned necessity into pride and servitude into honor; it offered a lever upon the moral sentiments of those whose power mattered (p. 181).

Other creators of the alternative view (e.g., Clawson, 1980; Nelson, 1975) concur with Rodgers about the role of coercion in the workplace. An in depth look at their ideas would show that many elements of modern management (e.g., scientific management, certain aspects of technology, personnel management, and supervisory training) were, in part, a response to the desire by managers to exercise the control needed to operate factories efficiently while preserving the image of the ideal of free labor.

In general, holders of the alternative view have proceeded from a critical, often Marxist, orientation. As a result, rather than finding harmony, they have found struggle. They typically have seen large discrepancies between the actual work values of participants and those assumed in the conventional view.

Scholars of the alternative view have drawn on different sources than those traditionally used by most modern organizational behaviorists. The focus of the alternative view scholars has been on the experiences of the working classes of the past and present. Their descriptions of the concrete experiences of workers have drawn heavily on literature from American history, political science, participant observation and oral history. When these sources are used for study, coercion emerges as a frequent explanation for the "motivation" to work.

Although we have oversimplified, we have presented enough of the alternative view for our purposes in this paper. While we recognize that much work is required to validate this perspective, in our judgment it is already sufficiently documented to be taken seriously.

The alternative view, too, may suffer from an unconscious ideology. By focusing on the urban worker of the Northeast as Rodgers did, opportunities and sentiments of other sectors of the nation are ignored. Similarly, the focus on the coercive aspects of work misses the substantial improvements in working conditions over the last century, and tends to treat those who behaved in ways congruent with tenets of the Protestant ethic and achieved great success as "flukes" and therefore not requiring explanation. Thus, we perceive the alternative view as merely that, another perspective that is useful for stimulating analysis of the blind spots of the conventional view.

It was this stimulation that led us to consider a wide variety of treatments of work values. In doing so, we developed a framework for classifying the perspectives. The framework highlights some of the contradictions observed by Rodgers and makes it even more clear that the Protestant work ethic and contemporary approaches to enriching work, which are often lumped together in the conventional view, are based on very different premises. The framework and some of these implications are developed in the next section.

A FRAMEWORK FOR WORK VALUES

Perspectives on work values can be compared through a two-dimensional framework. One dimension assumes two possible loci of benefits from work, a secular outcome and a nonsecular outcome (e.g., salvation). The second dimension concerns the relationship between work itself and the outcome. On the one hand, outcomes can be intrinsic to work, that is, they occur through work. On the other hand, outcomes can be extrinsic, that is, they follow or are contingent upon work. While the terms intrinsic and extrinsic are difficult to define unambiguously (e.g., Brief & Aldag, 1977; Dyer & Parker, 1975), their use here is rather specific. Intrinsic refers to the content of activities of the work itself (i.e., what people do at work) and extrinsic explicitly denotes independence from the content of work. In Table 1, these two dimensions are used to show four possible ways to classify treatments of work values. We have classified some of the major approaches to work values in the table; our rationale for the classifications is in the text.

Table 1. Possible Stances on Work Values

	Relationship of Preferred State and Work Activity	
	Intrinsic	Extrinsic
Secular	1	2
	Neoconventional view (Argyris, Maslow, McGregor, Herzberg), Classical Marxism	Roman Catholic Church,[a] Economic theory, Maoist China, Organizational behaviorists such as Goldthorpe et al., Fein
Locus of Benefits		
Nonsecular	3	4
	Monastaries/communities (where work develops person spiritually for communion with God), Hindu religion	Protestant ethic (as described by Weber)

Note:
[a] The classification of the Roman Catholic Church as secular is based on the contents of two major papal encyclicals on work. Obviously, the teachings of the Church are linked to nonsecular outcomes. However, the contents of the encyclicals about the role of work have a secular focus.

Extrinsic Values

While most treatments of work give at least some attention to extrinsic outcomes, there is great variation in the type of outcomes considered. One is salvation, others are economic, and still others are social (e.g., equity). These outcomes are extrinsic in that they are contingent upon work, but do not depend on the substance of work itself.

Extrinsic/nonsecular outcomes (cell 4).   Some approaches view outcomes of work as contingent upon work, make no mention of the specific content of the work, and view the outcomes as taking place in a nonsecular arena. The Protestant ethic is the prime example. It stresses the extrinsic outcome of salvation. Moreover, unlike money or status or other extrinsic outcomes that are reaped in this world, salvation is nonsecular.

Extrinsic/secular (cell 2).   Many approaches view outcomes of work as contingent upon work, make no mention of the specific content of work, but view the outcomes as occurring in the secular world. Those who have focused on money and other material rewards obviously belong in this cell, as do the treatments of other major religions and political doctrines.

The Roman Catholic Church, in its teachings about work (see Pope Leo XIII, 1891; Pope John Paul, 1981), has for some time centered on extrinsic/secular outcomes. Although the linkages of worldly activity to salvation are so strong in the teachings of the Catholic Church that perhaps they are assumed to be present in any particular document, the papal encyclicals of 1891 and 1981 focused primarily on secular outcomes of work. This secularism was associated with a quite different sociological stance than early Protestantism.

The worldly focus of the Roman Catholic Church near the end of the industrial revolution can be seen clearly in the papal encyclical of 1891, *Rerum Novarum*. Quality of life, justice, and social harmony were major concerns. As Pope Leo XIII (1891) put it, "some opportune remedy must be found quickly for the misery and wretchedness pressing so unjustly on the majority of the working class" (p. 2). Because work was seen as a major factor in producing social tensions, work relationships needed to be changed to promote social harmony. In the words of Pope Leo XIII, "the church . . . tries to bind class to class in friendliness and good feeling" (p. 13).

This concern contrasts sharply with the views of the early Protestant theologians who justified class differences as part of God's order and who encouraged the individuals to ignore their economic inferiors. As a result, the Catholic Church dealt with a number of issues that were of little explicit concern to the Protestant churches including: a just wage, rights of workers, property rights, an equitable division of property, and workingmen's unions for mutual benefit. Moreover, contrary to the emphasis on the accumulation of wealth and the splintering of social elites from the masses implicit in Protestant theology, Pope Leo XIII had special praise for affluent Catholics who have "cast in their lot with the wage-earners, and who have spent large sums in founding and widely spreading benefit and insurance societies" (pp. 31–32). Similarly, he wrote against greed and thirst for pleasure . . . which too often make a man who is void of self-restraint miserable in the midst of abundance" (p. 17). In short, Pope Leo XIII focused on extrinsic/secular outcomes, including a wide spectrum of social conditions such as justice, harmony, and equality.

Jewish teachings appear to stand ambiguously between those of the Protestants and the Catholics by seemingly emphasizing both secular and nonsecular extrinsic outcomes. Sombart (1913), seeking to exemplify the teachings of the Old Testament and the Talmud on the issue, tells the following story.

> Let us imagine old Amschel Rothschild after having 'earned' a million on the Stock Exchange, turning to his Bible for edification. What will he find there touching his earnings and their effect on the refinement of his soul, an effect which the pious old

Jew most certainly desired on the eve of the Sabbath? Will the million burn his con-
science? Or will he not be able to say, and rightly say, 'God's blessings rested upon
me this week. I thank Thee, Lord, for having graciously rested upon me this week.
I thank Thee, Lord, for having graciously granted the light of Thy countenance to
Thy servant. In order to find favor in Thy sight I shall give much to charity, and
keep Thy commandments even more strictly than hitherto'? Such would be his words
if he knew his Bible, and he did know it (p. 217).

Like at least early Protestantism, traditional Jewish moral theology teaches
that prosperity in work is at one and the same time the outward symbol and guarantee of God's pleasure; it also teaches that prosperity provides the means (through charity) to do God's will on earth. Thus,
Judaism directs the expenditure of economic success towards the less
well-off in a way more consistent with the social emphasis of the Catholic church.

Many organizational behaviorists belong in cell 2, but because often
they have not linked their ideas explicitly to underlying values, classification is speculative. For example, studies of compensation systems (e.g.,
Lawler, 1971) focus on extrinsic/secular outcomes without explicit justification, except for improved performance, which is presumably another
secular/extrinsic outcome.

A growing amount of research has revealed the importance of extrinsic/
secular concerns to workers. Goldthorpe, Lockwood, Bechhofer, and Platt
(1969), for example, reported that work was mainly a means to consumption. Based on an extensive literature review, Fein (1976) concluded
that many people value work primarily as an activity that is instrumental
for their lives outside of work, e.g., consumption and support of one's
family. Jackall (1978) arrived at a similar conclusion. Although it is possible
that these concerns are rooted in some nonsecular outcomes, social scientists have seldom considered such "ultimate" uses.

A variety of other approaches also emphasize extrinsic/secular outcomes. Modern economists, much as the social scientists we have just
discussed, deal mainly with material rewards for work and ignore any
specifics about how they should be consumed. The economists merely
assume that rewards will be spent in ways that maximize individual utility
and eschew any further value judgments. Also in cell 2 is the approach
of Maoist China where, according to Whyte (1973), one works to benefit
the revolutionary cause. Schwartz (1983) proposed yet another set of ex-
trinsic/secular values. Arguing from a psychoanalytic perspective,
Schwartz developed a theory of deontic work motivation in which work
is instrumental for self-esteem through a feeling of moral worthiness that
results from having lived up to one's responsibility to others. In short,
work serves to discharge social obligation.

As diverse as these outlooks are, they all focus on the extrinsic outcomes of work in the secular world. They are silent on the role that the content of work might play.

Some spokespersons for American organized labor, such as Irving Bluestone (Maccoby, 1981), have been concerned with the self-development aspects of work, but for the most part, trade union leaders have focused on extrinsic/secular outcomes. Although, as Rodgers (1974) noted, labor has often felt compelled to state its agenda in ways consistent with the work ethic, the sentiments expressed by William Haywood, a working class leader of the late 1800s, " 'less work the better' " (Zuboff, 1983, p. 164) seems to have been more central to labor's concerns than the intrinsic benefits of work. Recently, Tyler (1983) spoke of a union work ethic that takes "the worker, rather than the work" (p. 209) as the prime concern. In this view, work is a necessity that does not need to be justified "with theologic overtones" (p. 198)—humans work to live, not live to work. The union work ethic is concerned with hours, working conditions, safety, wages and benefits, and psychological and physical safety. It is concerned that leisure be available, not merely as an escape from drudgery or for rejuvenation so that one can work better, but as an opportunity for people to grow and to develop themselves and to participate fully in a democratic society.

A comparison among the extrinsic approaches we have considered reveals an interesting difference among them. The social scientists stop their considerations of what people want from work with the attainment of the rewards; they pay little attention to how the rewards are spent. Similarly, Tyler's union work ethic asserts no ultimate purpose. In contrast, theological approaches are more apt to be concerned with how the fruits of labor are consumed. In general though, the cell 2 writers, like the developers of the Protestant ethic, are not especially concerned about the content of work.

Intrinsic Values

Some organizational behaviorists have drawn attention to the positive outcomes that can be gained through work itself. The content of work and the relationship of that content to human development and/or psychological well-being are central to these treatments. For the most part, social scientists assume that intrinsic values are realized in the secular world; however, other perspectives have introduced nonsecular outcomes.

Intrinsic/nonsecular (cell 3).   Sometimes work is valued as a means to develop the human spirit, and/or to prepare people to communicate with God or some other postworldly experience. Since the nature of work matters, these approaches are intrinsic; because the outcomes occur in an afterlife, they are nonsecular. Such views may characterize certain monastic orders or spiritually oriented communities. Service to the poor, work that requires a special form of discipline, and activities that promote contemplation may be assumed to develop the character of the individual's spirit in some desirable way. For instance, one of the Vedas, the holy books of the Hindu religion, treats working as a process of purifying one's spirit. The ultimate purpose of this process is to transmigrate to nirvana. Overall, however, cell 3 work values have been given little attention in modern organizational behavior and related social sciences.

Intrinsic/secular (cell 1). Most writers who have used secular criteria and who have focused explicitly on values that are achieved through the work itself, have been concerned primarily with human development. Within this category there seem to be two subgroups—writers who treat human development as a collective or social process (e.g., Marx) and writers who treat human development as an individual outcome (e.g., Maslow). Although the similarities that do exist between Marx and modern behavioral scientists have been documented by a variety of writers (viz., Clayre, 1974; Nord, 1974; Anthony, 1977), these views have not drawn on each other.

Marx glorified work. Work was a major way that humans differed from other animals; "as soon as [they] began to produce their means of subsistence, [they] are indirectly producing their material life" (Marx & Engels, 1965, p. 33). Marx's philosophical position was that "man created his world, and therefore himself, through work" (Anthony, 1977, p. 140). Thus, he saw work as an essential human activity. Fromm (1961), interpreted Marx as asserting, "Labor is the self-expression of his individual physical and mental powers. In this process of genuine activity man develops himself, becomes himself; work is not only a means to an end—the product—but an end in itself, the meaningful expression of human energy" (pp. 41–42). Israel (1971) came to a similar conclusion, "Through creative work man achieves self realization, i.e., he realizes the potentialities of the species and at the same time gives expression to his basic social nature" (p. 38).

The emphasis on social nature is important. Marx saw work as a means through which people related to each other; it was a way in which one could help satisfy the needs of others. It thus appears that work content was important in a double sense; both the nature of the process and the product make a difference for human development.

Another intrinsic/secular view assumes that individual psychological development results from specific types of work. This view has been so important in contemporary organizational behavior that we call it the neoconventional view. Most recent treatments of job redesign, quality of work life, worker participation/democracy and organizational development seem to stem from this perspective.

The neoconventional writers share much of Marx's perspective about work content and the nature of control of the workplace, but omit attention to the nature of the product and tend to be more concerned with individual than collective development (Nord, 1977). These values are at the core of the writings of McGregor (1960), Herzberg (1966), and Argyris (1957, 1973). While there are differences among these writers, for the most part there is consensus on the essence of human nature and on the need for "enriched" forms of work to utilize and develop human capacities fully. Such work is necessary both for human growth, productivity, and organizational effectiveness.

We will refer primarily to early and paradigm shaping work of Argyris (1957; 1973) in describing the neoconventional perspective since he has provided one of the most influential and explicit statements about this view. His personality vs. organization theory proposed a model that described the human adult as striving for such things as independence, autonomy, development of many abilities, use of a few abilities in depth, and a longer time perspective than one had in youth. When arrangements at work suppress these ends, conflict and frustration result. According to Argyris, the social scientist needs to take a normative approach which "promulgates certain values" (p. 160). Although the focus has been mainly on individual development, Argyris (1973) noted that the nature of work can affect the social organization of society, including its ability to operate as a democracy. In this sense, Argyris went well beyond most contemporary cell 1 writers who tend to, as their social science colleagues in cell 2, be interested only in the consequences of work *at the workplace*.

When compared to Marx and the Protestant ethic, the neoconventional view is interesting in several respects. First, when classified in terms of Table 1, it is more closely aligned with Marx than with the Protestant ethic. Writers such as Argyris share Marx's focus on the process of work and shared control in the workplace. Second, both Marx and the neoconventional writers are humanistic; they focus on outcomes in this world rather than in an afterlife. If work is a calling to Marx and Argyris, it is because of human nature, not of Divine action (unless, of course, human nature is taken as an expression of Divine action). Third, unlike Marx, the neoconventional view is content free with respect to the product; it seems to make little difference what one produces as long as one does it in the right way (Nord, 1977).

The neoconventional view is widely espoused and has affected policy matters and managerial practices (Zuboff, 1983). Its dominance is apt to make it vulnerable to an unconscious ideology. In particular, as Anthony (1977) and Clayre (1974) have argued, their psychological growth models may lead the neoconventional writers to romantic notions of humanity and of the past and present.

Anthony (1977), in tracing the ideology of work from the Greco-Roman period to the present, observed large costs associated with deficiencies that stem from ignoring historical evidence that contradicts an underlying ideology. Although Anthony may have overstated the case, we believe he was generally correct when he wrote:

> If there are methodological problems concerning the validity of behavioral science theory these problems are multiplied by the time unreliable theories have been vulgarized by consultants and then simplified by teachers in order to transmit them to managers, whose knowledge of basic behavioral science theory may be nil. Perhaps we can understand why there is no controversy. It would be hard to find another field of educational activity in which intelligent, and sometimes educated minds, were so harmoniously disposed. There may be occasional disagreement about educational methods, never about doctrine. (p. 262)

Clayre (1974) raised a related matter. Clayre sought to understand where the view of work as a central life interest, concerned with more than instrumental outcomes, originated. Study of the works of Marx, Ruskin, Morris and others revealed that they shared a desire to return to the type of work available prior to the factory. Clayre asked, "Was work better then"?

The only available clues for answering this question were in the oral history of preindustrial times that he was able to trace. Analysis of these songs and poems revealed concerns over pay, cruelty, and injustice, but no evidence that there was any great pleasure derived from the intrinsic nature of the work. Clayre found that people wanted to combine necessary work with intrinsically rewarding activities. They desired to fuse work and play. Clayre concluded that these people wanted the enjoyment of a fresh landscape, presence of other people, erotic happiness in work, the ability to interrupt their work, rhythmic work, ease of movement, choices of pace and space, and absence of close supervision. Work was seen as a necessity; it was neither fun nor consistent with human rhythms and freedom. Escape from work and the control of one's own relation to work were important. In short, the work values assumed by Marx and the neoconventional writers to have been achieved in preindustrial times may never have existed.

In addition to the critiques by Clayre and Anthony, the neoconventional writers have been severely criticized by Strauss (1963), Fein (1976), and others for representing their own personal values as universal ones and for ignoring material, extrinsic interests. These critiques are similar to Rodgers' (1974) conclusions about the middle-class moralists who wrote on the work ethic nearly a century ago. In essence there are conflicts between certain tenets of our important social values and the realities of workers and the workplace.

To some degree these critiques are unfair—most of the neoconventional writers do deal with the "lower level needs" by explicitly stating the importance of satisfying them or implicitly assuming they are satisfied. Nevertheless, such statements or assumptions do seem to bypass the realities of many members of the workforce. We do, for example, see a tendency for the extrinsic outcomes to get more attention as social scientists base their notions empirically on data collected from workers at lower levels in the organization (e.g., Harris & Locke, 1974; Jackall, 1978; Locke, 1973).

Conclusion

When approaches to work values are classified as they were in Table 1, some significant commonalities, differences, and omissions can be observed. It is important to note that we observed, but did not attempt to discuss fully, the differences among writers within specific cells. Further, it should be recognized that the framework does not permit precise classification in many cases. A number of perspectives such as Judaism and perhaps Clayre's (1974) view of work and play have components that make them difficult to classify within this typology. These ambiguities indicate that there are deficiencies in the framework for which other dimensions are needed for more precise classification. Moreover, the boundaries between the cells should be viewed as permeable. As we will suggest in the next section, this permeability means that it may be very easy for one to be unaware of having moved through the different cells.

The typology, in combination with the alternative view, helps to frame some issues for future inquiry about work values. In addition, this combined perspective aids in our understanding of the practice of modern organizational behavior by calling attention to some subtle and not so subtle similarities and differences among theories and perspectives. Some examples of such benefits will be evident in the following section when we apply this framework to the writings of some key figures in the study of work that underlie much of modern organizational behavior.

IMPLICATIONS FOR ORGANIZATIONAL BEHAVIOR AND THE STUDY OF WORK VALUES

We have suggested a number of problems and omissions in previous perspectives on work values. In this final section we attempt to account for these problems and to explore the practical and intellectual implications of our analysis. First, we explore how organizational behaviorists may have come to misunderstand the relationship between the neoconventional view and the work ethic. Second, we consider how the close ties between applied science and the language and concerns of the layperson have confused the study of work values. Third, we outline the rudiments of an expanded approach to work values.

Misunderstanding of the Work Ethic by Organizational Behaviorists

We have shown that the neoconventional view in cell 1 differs from the Protestant work ethic on two salient dimensions. Yet, it is not unusual for applied social scientists, managers, and policy makers to view the desire of people for intrinsically interesting work as a modern statement of the "calling." How did organizational behaviorists come to tie intrinsically interesting work to the work ethic?

Although a fully defensible answer to this question would require at least another paper, here we sketch a scenario that demonstrates how the framework we have presented might be useful in understanding the development of the neoconventional view in organizational behavior. This scenario draws on two ideas that we developed earlier—Rodgers' (1974) alternative view and the classification of work values summarized in Table 1. In addition, we build our discussion on three assumptions. First, we assume a tendency for organizational behaviorists to be, like psychologists (Sarason, 1981) and other modern American social scientists, ahistorical. Second, we assume that the nature of work and working conditions have changed markedly during the last century. Third, we assume the importance of what Zuboff (1983) described as concept of a "psychologized"[1] work ethic. In our scenario the ahistoricism is a background factor that helps to explain why organizational behaviorists were not aware of the interaction between their enterprise and events in the larger social system. Hence, in developing our scenario, we do not consider the ahistoricism further; the alternative view, Table 1, the changes in the nature of work, and the psychologized work ethic receive most of our attention.

In our simplified story, Rodgers' (1974) account is used to provide evidence that many people were interested in finding some form of ideology to reconcile the irreconcilable—the harsh realities of work and the belief in voluntary, free labor. We suggest that the neoconventional view has come to play this role.[2]

Rodgers' analysis stopped with 1920, a time when social scientists had just begun to examine work. Before stopping, however, he did give us the basis for classifying these early efforts. Rodgers noted the role that industrial psychology had begun to play in focusing attention on the surroundings of work. He observed that the concept of habit from nineteenth century psychology was used to argue that routine work was good for the worker, "routine emancipated the worker by wearing deep comfortable tracks in the nervous system that set his mind free for thought" (p. 88). If monotony was a problem, the answer was to change the worker's mental state, not the work. Thus, a widely advocated solution was to give the worker "something to think about" (p. 89) such as an article for the company newspaper, tasteful surroundings, or friendships made at work. Hugo Munsterberg (1913), of course, focused on individual differences in tolerance for repetitive work and the use of testing to match people to appropriate work. Thus, although born into a culture that still held the work ethic as social doctrine, industrial psychology was essentially secular and did not consider intrinsic benefits from work. Hence, it began in cell 2.

In the 1920s and 1930s, a related but qualitatively different way of resolving the tensions emerged with the Hawthorne studies. Like early industrial psychology, it offered the promise of a scientific base. The findings of such science promised many benefits from enlightened management.

The Hawthorne studies pointed to a new way of reducing conflict over work without introducing major changes in: the nature of work, control of the workplace, and technology. The promise of cooperation made by the Hawthorne studies and Mayo's (1960) book, *The Human Problems of an Industrial Civilization* (first published in 1933) became an important part of the foundation for organizational behavior. Despite disputes over their scientific merit, the Hawthorne studies contributed the credibility of science to the pursuit of cooperation in the workplace. However, when viewed in terms of Table 1, they did more.

Zuboff (1983) observed that the Hawthorne studies psychologized the matter of cooperation. "If managers were to achieve . . . cooperation, they would have to become competent in deciphering the psychological map of the workforce and harnessing worker's sentiments in support of the organization as a whole" (pp. 165–166). Clues for this success could be gained from scientific disciplines, especially psychology. Thus, the way had been paved for managers to take an interest in theories of human motivation and ways to achieve cooperation.

The human relations movement belongs in cell 2. No intrinsic matters were involved—the nature of work itself was not taken as problematic. What was problematic were ways of managing the social relationships in the workplace to increase collaboration. As Miles (1975) summarized so well:

> if management would simply treat people as human beings, acknowledge their needs to belong and to feel important by listening to and heeding their complaints where possible and by involving them in certain decisions . . . then morale would surely improve and workers would cooperate with management in achieving good production. (p. 40)

It is somewhat difficult to be certain about how to classify the human relations writers because they were not fully explicit about exactly what were the consequences of work for individuals. It seems clear that they assumed important individual differences in what people wanted from work—Roethlisberger and Dickson (1939) wrote: "no two individuals are making exactly the same demands of their job" (p. 553). They added that "noneconomic motives, interests, and processes, as well as economic, are fundamental in behavior in business" (p. 557). Although they considered mechanization of work as a possible cause of problems, they concluded that even though most of the jobs they studied were semiautomated, there was little to suggest that repetitive work was a major source of problems. Rather, they suggested modern industry had created many new occupations; few of these had labels that would be recognized in the community outside the plant. The loss of such an outer symbol, they suggest, "may in part account for the worker's preoccupations over wages and wage differentials, and also may account for complaints of monotony in work" (p. 574).

Finally, it is clear that most of the concerns they reported in the interviews in Roethlisberger and Dickson's *Management and the Worker* (1939) related to what we would now call hygiene factors. It seems reasonable to conclude from these observations, interpreted in the context of the well known emphasis that the human relations writers placed on sentiments and needs for social integration, that their view of what people sought and expected from work did not depend on the nature of the work itself. Besides the traditional instrumental value of pay, the important outcomes of work were to be located in social relationships both inside and outside the plant.

So far we have encountered little evidence for the importance of intrinsically interesting work in the general social history we have reviewed or in the human relations movement. Yet, the importance of intrinsically interesting work has for some time been a major theme in organizational behavior. How did this view develop? In short, how did organizational behaviorists move from cell 2 to cell 1?

The move from the portion of cell 2 we have been discussing to cell 1 involved several background developments. First, after the Depression and World War II, working conditions and the economic well-being of most (but not all) of the work force appeared much improved from the past. Second, the managerial, professional, and white-collar components of the work force grew rapidly, and the nature of work and the social relationships surrounding it were different for many of these people than for the factory worker. For example, coercive aspects of mechanized work were less visible and the potential for upward mobility in management appeared to be more realistic. Research on human responses to this type of work could be expected to yield different results than for blue-collar workers.

In this context several key studies and their integration by Argyris (and probably others) provided the path from cell 2 to cell 1. We speculate that the work of Walker (1950), Walker and Guest (1952), and Turner (1955) played a major role in this transition. Certainly they played a key role in Argyris' (1957) influential formulation.

In Walker's (1950) paper he reported a job enlargement effort conducted by IBM in 1943. Although the jobs were indeed enlarged (in fact enriched in modern terminology), the success might equally well have been attributed to changes in status, compensation, patterns of interaction, or a Hawthorne effect as to any intrinsic desire to work. Interestingly, Walker did not interpret these results as evidence of a need for intrinsically interesting work. Although he did lament the "overspecialization" of modern industry, he provided no clear psychological explanation for any problems. Moreover, he explicitly denied the generalizability of the experiment, "in precisely this form at least" (p. 58), to the assembly line.

Walker and Guest's (1952) *Man on the Assembly Line* potentially provided a basis for attributing a desire for intrinsically interesting work to blue collar workers. However, they stopped far short of doing so. In fact, the respondents reported that the extrinsic aspects of pay and security were the most liked things about the job and that social and group relationships were very important. On the other hand, Walker and Guest did begin to emphasize the importance of job content. They pointed to the importance of variety and a relationship to the "*whole* product" (p. 149). Moreover, they noted that the jobs of utility men were more satisfactory because they involved greater variety. In this context their call for job rotation and enlargement is not surprising. However, it is far from clear that either they or the workers were calling for intrinsically meaningful work.

It is important to recognize that Walker and Guest discussed job rotation and enlargement in their treatment of workers' complaints about pacing and repetitiveness. It is clear that workers sought to escape from pacing and repetition and aversive conditions by including rest periods, opportunities to vary the pace, and to have "breathers" through such activities as building "banks" (i.e., accumulating a supply of output or "working up the line"), job rotation and enlargement, and freedom to plan their work and choose their own tools. While all of these alternatives are means to escape repetitiveness and machine pacing, only a few seem to indicate a desire for more intrinsically rewarding work.

Workers' comments on their mental activity at work also provided mixed support for the view that they wanted challenging work. Workers reported disliking the surface mental attention required by their work, but it is important to recognize that this did not necessarily imply they wanted more demanding jobs. Rather, what seemed to bother many of them was having to pay so much attention to their work that they could not day-dream, but not enough to "absorb their mental faculties to any depth" (Walker & Guest, 1952, p. 155). Perhaps either less demanding jobs or more enriching work would have resolved their concerns. In short, the data Walker and Guest reported fell far short of providing a compelling case that the workers sought more meaningful tasks.

In fact, in their final conclusions, Walker and Guest deemphasized even the role of pacing and repetitiveness. They turned to lack of opportunities for promotion as a source of problems. The short progression ladder is, in their words, "one of the most important effects of mass production methods. . . . By all but obliterating job progression among production workers, it strikes at one of the strongest human incentives. It also strikes at a cultural tradition closely interwoven with American ideas and ideals— the belief in the desirability and possibility of 'rising in the world' " (p. 160). Finally, they concluded that the real problem did not stem from either the machine pacing or repetition directly, but rather from the fact that the technology makes people interchangeable. In their view, deper-sonalization was the core of the problem. In fact, they said:

> the sense of becoming *de*-personalized, of becoming anonymous as against remaining one's self, is for those who feel it a psychologically more disturbing result of the work environment than either the boredom or the tension that arise from repetitive and mechanically paced work. This appeared to be the basis of such bitterly critical comments as were made against Company X as such. (p. 161)

The degree to which these matters represent a desire for work characterized by intrinsic aspects that promote human growth or represent extrinsic matters is open to debate. Much like Roethlisberger and Dickson (1939) who saw the lack of clearly defined occupational labels that communicated one's identity to others, Walker and Guest saw machine-paced work as a source of anonymity, an extrinsic and secular consequence. They belong in cell 2.

Similarly, Turner (1955), drawing on research by Walker and Guest, argued that foremen who successfully reduced the negative influence of the assembly line on their people, did so in two ways. First, they reduced the pressures from mechanical pacing. Second, they counteracted the impersonality introduced by repetitiveness and the destruction of the small group by the technology. The measures used to do these included: absorbing pressure themselves, trusting workers' willingness to work, recognizing individual differences, introducing variety, delegating responsibility, developing groups of workers, and establishing a personal relationship with the men as individuals.

Do these measures belong in cell 1 or cell 2? For the most part, they seem to belong in cell 2. Although some are related to job content, even these have a tone of removing negative features of work rather than indicating positive desires for intrinsically interesting work. Finally, impersonality belongs in cell 2.

We described these findings in such depth because, driven by a psychological model, Argyris (1957) gave a cell 1 interpretation to them. For example, Argyris wrote, "These findings are understandable since these requirements [those of assembly line work] run counter to the needs of relatively mature human beings" (p. 73). Later he cited Walker (1950) and Walker and Guest (1952) as reporting "that one way to increase employee satisfaction *or self-actualization* is to increase the number of formal tasks assigned to an employee" [italics added] (p. 178).

What we seem to observe here is a gestalt shift from the introduction of a new paradigm (Kuhn, 1970). From a cell 2 perspective, the comments of the workers in Walker and Guest's research could easily be accommodated, particularly if one included the removal of aversive stimuli (e.g., pressure) introduced by work as extrinsic factors. On the other hand, when the assembly line studies are interpreted through a paradigm of psychological growth, such as Maslow's (1943) hierarchy of needs or White's (1952) competence motive, they appear to belong in cell 1. For example, Argyris (1957), influenced by White's work, interpreted these and a number of other studies on job enlargement as demonstrating the needs of employees to use the abilities of the mature personality "the knowing and feeling abilities" (p. 181).

The great majority of these early studies centered on blue-collar workers and foremen. Although some research has continued to focus on these groups, since the 1950s the study of work increasingly became the study of the work of white-collar and professional employees, if for no other reason than that these groups made up a much higher percentage of the work force than they did before.

The pioneering work of Herzberg, Mausner, and Snyderman (1959), more than any other research, focused attention on the intrinsic aspects of work in the white-collar arena. As Hulin and Blood (1969) and Fein (1976) noted, most of the research that came to support the importance of intrinsic components was based on this segment of the work force. The essence of this perspective appears in many contemporary systems for improving human performance, including QWL, job design, various versions of OD, job enrichment, and human resources management (Miles, 1975). So powerful is the vision embodied in these perspectives that Miles and Rosenberg (1982) concluded, "There is no longer a meaningful debate in the United States about applicability of the human resources approach to management" (p. 40). Zuboff (1983) concluded on a similar note, suggesting that the psychological work ethic may indeed allow employees to achieve their complex psychological needs and fulfill their aspirations at work.

These statements clearly belong in cell 1 and have little in common with cell 4. Contemporary managers and social scientists, while lacking a full understanding of history and the nature of the Protestant ethic, and seemingly unaware of alternative perspectives, have diagnosed problems in the workplace as due to the decay of the traditional work ethic (Bernstein, 1980; Kopelman, 1986) and the loss of the opportunity for craft work (Maccoby, 1981). Cell 1 solutions are advanced to restore both. As we have shown, even if the models in cell 1 do describe the reality of many members of today's professional workforce, their focus on secular outcomes of intrinsically meaningful work bears little logical relationship to the Protestant work ethic as described by Weber. Moreover, in view of the work of Clayre, Anthony, and Rodgers, the assumption that today's emphasis on cell 1 is an effort to restore work to its preindustrial state is suspect as well.

Whether in fact cell 1 even represents current reality is also problematic. It is important to note that Miles and Rosenberg's (1982) conclusion was published at a time when leading contributors to the field (e.g., Salancik & Pfeffer, 1978; White & Mitchell, 1979) were concluding that the actual design of jobs is far less important in determining a worker's satisfaction than is the socially constructed reality of the workplace. Also, at about that time, based on a major survey of a wide spectrum of the American work force, Schiemann and Morgan (1983) concluded that while most employees were satisfied with the work itself, a number of extrinsic matters (e.g., pay, benefits, supervision, security, responsiveness of the company to employee concerns) were of major importance in evaluating a company as a place to work. Moreover, there is still the belief among many psychologists that the failure to find that intrinsically satisfying work is universally desired is due to individual differences such as growth need strength (Hackman & Oldham, 1980), achievement motivation (Steers & Spencer, 1977) and place of early socialization (Martinson & Wilkening, 1984). However, there is a great deal of research evidence (Aldag, Barr, & Brief, 1981; Cummings, 1980; and White, 1978) that runs counter to this view.

In sum, what the neoconventional view and the psychological work ethic appear to share with the Protestant ethic is a result more of process than of substance. Both the traditional and the psychological work ethic are the creations of middle-class writers. Both seem to ignore the concrete experiences of work advanced by the alternative view. Both seem oriented to reducing conflict at the organizational level without considering causes that may be at a more sociological level. Overall, they appear to be linked more by the common social concerns they address than by what they have to say about work.

Problem of Mixing Scientific and Lay Constructs

Because applied social science tends to be tightly coupled with ongoing social processes, it seems more difficult to conduct inquiry and develop constructs without significant contamination from the "real world." The study of work and work values is no exception. Three types of contamination seem most important: bias, overgeneralization, and construct deficiency.

Bias. The problem of bias in organizational behavior has been so widely discussed (e.g., Baritz, 1960; Nord, 1977; Bramel & Friend, 1981) that all we need do here is acknowledge the fact that undoubtedly the interests of those who have controlled resources that are valued by organizational psychologists have affected the conduct of some research and, hence, the content of knowledge in ways favorable to themselves. For instance, such bias can be seen in the choice and framing of research questions, research design decisions and the interpretation of results (e.g., Kaplan, 1964; Weber, 1949). Quite likely the study of work values is biased as a result. For present purposes we are not concerned with the direction or amount of bias; our major objective in mentioning it here is to reemphasize this generic problem in applied social science.

We know of no ways to eliminate the bias; we suggest that at present the best we can do is to recognize the influence of values in interpreting every piece of research. Procedurally, two ways to stimulate this awareness are encouraging disclosure and diversity.

In regards to disclosure, Mills (1959) reasoned that studying society and publishing the results constitutes a political and moral act; researchers who conceal this condition from themselves and from their audiences are morally adrift. Moreover, Keniston (1965) observed that when the writer's biases are disclosed, "the reader is at least allowed to challenge these assumptions as stated and not required to ferret them out as embedded in 'objective' reporting and interpretation" (p. 12). Of course, merely listing biases and values does not guarantee that the researcher is willing and/or able to give his or her true ones. The problems of a truly "reflexive" social science are difficult ones; disclosure is only a start.

Our second suggestion, diversity, merely recognizes that no one set of biases is apt to be the universally best set on which to conduct all inquiry. As Feyerabend (1975) has argued so well, the quest for knowledge may be best advanced when it employs a wide variety of perspectives.

Overgeneralization. Campbell and Pritchard (1976) observed how constructs in organizational behavior, such as performance, subsume such a diverse set of elements that they lack construct validity. The close relation of organizational behavior with applied interests contributes to this problem because it leads us to measure performance in ways that only make sense to a particular organization. When we attempt to combine the various findings, the meaning of performance is lost because it embodies so many different interpretations or definitions. In fact, the construct becomes dysfunctional because it leads users to overlook important distinctions across these studies. We submit that the term "work" raises similar problems that to date have not been considered sufficiently by organizational behaviorists.

Our inquiry into the history of work and work values sensitized us to the changes in work over time. Ultimately, we realized that organizational behaviorists, ourselves included, have a very poor concept of what work really means. Pence (1978–1979) observed:

> A surprisingly common error in thinking about work is to think of it as having some common essence. . . . The basic error is a classic 'category mistake.' An activity which is complex, highly variable, and meaning–dependent on the individual, is erroneously made into a simple, invariable activity of universal meaning. (p. 310)

Does it make sense to use the same word to compare what people did to earn a living in the Middle Ages with what they did in the Industrial Revolution and what they do today? Does the same word apply equally well to what professionals, managers, and laborers do? Okrent (1978–1979), for example, argued it does not. To illustrate his point, he suggested that if we analyze the words "play" and "work" carefully, it makes more sense to characterize members of the managerial class as playing for a living. In short, an outcome of the unconscious ideology is overgeneralization. Our answers to such questions as What should result from work? and What can result from work? may change substantially once we realize how coarse the concept of work is in our thinking. Discussions of work values would benefit from greater attention to the construct of work itself.

Clearly, such discussions require that the nature of work as experienced by members of society at one point in time is not taken as absolute. Finer discriminations about work are required, although how much finer is difficult to say. To date, organizational behaviorists seem to have taken an extreme view—work is work whether it is done in 1600 or 1985; whether it is managerial or blue-collar; whether it is done during a depression or an economic boom. For example, economic conditions appear to be irrelevant to organizational behaviorists. Seldom do they report the economic conditions of the industry and local labor market at the time of data collection or even the dates when they collected their data. We assert that work must be understood in the context of human experience in its full complexity. To do otherwise runs the risk of overgeneralization. A simple first step in this direction would be for journal editors to insist that relevant macro-data be reported.

Construct deficiency.   The constructs that have guided research on work values are deficient in the sense that they do not subsume all the end states people might desire. According to Schwab (1980), a measure is deficient if it omits part of the construct it purports to measure. We suggest that concepts about work values are deficient because they fail to encompass a number of components individuals might want from work. For example, it is somewhat paradoxical, that in view of the religious origins of the work ethic, spiritual dimensions have received so little attention. Likewise, the relationships between producers and customers and the nature of the product relative to its ability to satisfy important human needs have received little attention in the study of work values.

The consequences of deficiency may be more subtle than those of bias. Following Anthony (1977), we believe the consequences of deficiency are negative for all people who seek to use the work of organizational behaviorists, including those we are presumed to favor—managers! Anthony observed that because our assumptions about work are so narrow, we do not provide a body of knowledge rich enough to capture reality. He wrote: "On the very rare occasions when a manager, or come to that one of his teachers, meets someone carrying another set of doctrines based upon different values, he reacts with bewilderment" (p. 262).

Anthony's (1977) observations raise some pragmatic concerns. Organizational behaviorists, as advocates of the solutions they have formulated to a limited set of problems—even if they are biased in the sense that these are the problems managers explicitly seek to have resolved—may not be serving the needs of their constituency. As consultants and educators, because their models and constructs omit a variety of possible inputs and outcomes, they may be perpetuating a false doctrine through deficient knowledge. As a result, when applying the solutions supplied by organizational behaviorists, clients and students will find that workers will not respond as expected. We suggest that solutions predicated on a particular dogma of work, when applied to individuals who do not believe in that dogma, are unlikely to solve the problems to which they were addressed. Broader, alternative perspectives are needed.

PERSPECTIVES FOR THE STUDY OF WORK VALUES IN THE FUTURE

We have suggested that unconscious ideology, ahistoricism, bias, overgeneralization, and construct deficiency have contributed to the misunderstanding of work values in the past and present. Our suggestions for the future are in the spirit of Gergen's (1982) sociorationalism. Among other things, Gergen suggested that social scientists need to recognize the historical embeddedness of knowledge; the social construction of knowledge; the dynamic interaction of social theory and practice; and the roles of values, ideologies, and visions in "knowledge making." The sociorationalist perspective urges investigators to take their own values as a serious component of their professional work. The investigator is to be motivated by "intellectual expression in the service of his or her vision of the good" (p. 208). In light of this framework and our analysis of work values, we suggest a number of directions for future thought.

First, work values must be treated as socially constructed notions. We should not expect to find uniformity across time, place, and people. Instead, effort must be devoted to discovering a rich array of alternative values. Data from a variety of workers and nonworkers are needed. These data must be interpreted in the genres of the providers instead of being quickly transformed into abstract frameworks. This step, more than anything else, would protect us from unconscious ideology, bias, overgeneralization, and construct deficiency.

Second, the question, Why do we hear so much about the work ethic and work values from managers, politicians, unionists, social scientists, and others? needs to be considered repeatedly. Iaffaldano and Muchinsky (1985), for example, speculated that the incessant research on the relationship between job satisfaction and performance, in the face of a body of evidence that the two are only slightly correlated, reveals an illusory correlation in the minds of organizational behaviorists. Such an account is closely aligned with our view of the role of an unconscious ideology in the study of work values: we continue in the intellectual tradition of the moralists, the writers and the intellectuals described by Rodgers (1974) and our predecessors in social science to find a way to think of work so that it appears to be a less coercive activity than it is for many people.

The alternative perspective suggests a related reason for the concern with work values. Rodgers (1974) and others have suggested that the reason work values have received so much attention is that they reduced the need to deal with the realities of work or what people believed about work.

This observation suggests a third matter—the need to emphasize the distinction between work beliefs and work values, and to give more attention to the former than we have to date. Beliefs refer to what people view as possible; values refer to desires or wants (Scheibe, 1970). While there has been considerable discussion of work values and also of what people find in their particular jobs, to our knowledge little has been done between the extreme abstraction of values and the extreme concreteness of daily experiences. We suggest that there be greater inquiry into what people believe is possible from work and what their expectations are of the costs, benefits, and probabilities of such work. The relationship between beliefs and concrete experience may exert a greater influence on the quality of experience than do the end-states one desires. Thus, more knowledge about what people believe work can realistically provide may supply useful guidance in contemplating work redesign. Among other things, knowledge of these beliefs may make it possible to provide people with accurate information about what is possible, what the necessary trade-offs are, and the accuracy of their beliefs.

Fourth, organizational behaviorists need to consider the relationship between work and other social institutions and investigate the philosophical and religious aspects of work values. We have suggested some of the alternative values that organizational behaviorists have focused on and others that they have ignored without solid intellectual justification for either. More inquiry such as Keeley's (1978; 1983), which reveals how social, ethical, and scientific interests complement each other in the study of organizations, is an example of what we have in mind.

Analysis of work only within the confines of the workplace represents an arbitrary decision common to both cell 1 and cell 2 writers. If work is viewed as instrumental for some other outcome (cell 2), the value of that other outcome ought to influence the assessment of the instrumental activity. For example, the value of working for money is likely to be affected by the attractiveness of what one can buy with money. Likewise, the value of psychological growth from work (cell 1) will be affected by the value of the payoffs for psychological growth both inside and outside the workplace.

Similarly, perhaps it is useful to reintroduce nonsecular values into our study of work. As Cox (1984) has noted, religion is playing an increasingly important role in the secular world. What, for example, are the implications of the heightened influence of Fundamentalist Protestantism for work? Also, the recent encyclical of Pope John Paul II (1981) *Laborem Exercens* raises many important issues about work values in modern society. Perhaps our scientific positivism and the humanistic orientations embedded in our treatments of work values have led us to ignore an important part of human experience—the association of spiritual values and work. The most recent effort in the organizational behavior literature to attempt such a linkage that we know of is Purcell's (1967) discussion of an industrial theology. Perhaps it is time for a deeper consideration of the relationship between work and nonsecular concerns. Many people seem to be seeking some framework for relating their existence to some larger purpose. Since work is such a major part of the existence of most of us, some attention to the existing perceptions and possible alternatives that might foster such a linkage would seem to be an essential part of understanding the human condition.

Fifth, we need to consider work values of other cultures seriously and prudently. If the rapid growth of the global economy continues, increasingly we will be dealing with work values of other cultures. On the one hand, the contrasts between these cultures and our own may help us understand ourselves better. On the other hand, we may need a much richer framework for understanding their work values. Such an understanding of work, both in our own and other cultures, will require serious attention to the history of work and of work and society. Inquiry into the origins, functions, nonfunctions, and dysfunctions of particular work values in individual cultures is needed. Indeed, we are apt to find that stated values about work in other cultures may be equally misleading about reality as they appear to be in our own.

Finally, we suggest the need to recognize that espoused work values in society may often be a result of work activity rather than a cause of it. Rodgers' (1974) argument about the work ethic seems to show this quite well. We suggest the same approach be considered at the individual level. Jackall's (1978) research suggests, for example, that what might appear as statements about work values are responses by individuals to legitimize to themselves the ambiguities and tensions about work and its relationship to the rest of their lives. Clearly, this perspective has much in common with the retrospective sense-making view championed by Weick (1979) and the work of the political scientist Edelman (1977). An extension to the study of work values promises the same revelations that have enlightened other areas, such as organizational symbolism (Pondy, Frost, Morgan, & Dandridge, 1983), to which the retrospective view has been applied. Viewing work values as personal and social constructions may be more productive than viewing them as ideals to achieve. Among other things, this would make the study of work values part of the process of understanding how contemporary individuals come to terms with an important aspect of their total lives.

CONCLUDING REMARKS

Our critique has been sweeping, although probably we have been hardest on the neoconventional writers. Because we share so much with them, however, we cannot conclude without acknowledging their important contributions. Argyris and the other neoconventional writers have done much of what Gergen's (1982) sociorationalist view asks. They have had the courage to step beyond "normal science" and to ask What *should* and what *can* work be? Long before it was fashionable, they did what

Howard (1985) suggested; they explicitly incorporated nonepistemic values in their work to envision what is possible, instead of merely reporting what is.

Our quarrel with the neoconventional writers is their tendency to treat work values as psychological phenomena only while often ignoring major historical, sociological, philosophical, and economic processes. We suggest that this inattention is embedded in an unconscious ideology and that the nature of the unconscious ideology is revealed by consideration of alternative perspectives. What people desire and expect from work is relative to particular historical and social conditions. There has been and will continue to be great variation in work values. Study of them demands an intellectual framework sufficiently rich to capture this variety.

ACKNOWLEDGMENTS

This paper has benefitted from conversations with many people including: John Clancy, Steven Feldman, Peter Frost, Stanley Mellish, Ann Nord, Russell Johnson, Howard Schwartz, Sterling Schoen, Ralph Stablein, John Zipp, and the editors. Their thoughts and criticisms are gratefully acknowledged.

NOTES

1.   It is interesting to note that the work became psychologized rather than physiologized. This shift would of course support Rodgers' (1974) thesis that work values have played a primary role by turning attention away from the concrete towards the abstract. Of course, organizational and other types of psychologists have given some attention to the physiological aspects of work. The reasons for and consequences of the lack of integration among these various approaches is also worthy of investigation.

2.   Most likely the notion of free choice in a free labor market provided by liberal economics played a parallel role, but this is a subject for another time.

REFERENCES

Aldag, R., Barr, S., & Brief, A.P. (1981). Measurement of perceived task characteristics. *Psychological Bulletin, 90*, 415–431.

Aldag, R.J., & Brief, A.P. (1979). *Task design and employee motivation*. Glenview, IL: Scott, Foresman and Co.

Anthony, P.D. (1977). *The ideology of work*. United Kingdom: Tavistock.

Argyris, C. (1957). *Personality and organization*. New York: Harper and Row.

Argyris, C. (1973). Personality and organization theory revisited. *Administrative Science Quarterly, 18*, 141–167.

Aristotle (1912). *Politics*. London: J. M. Dent and Sons.

Baritz, L. (1960). *The servants of power*. New York: John Wiley.

Bem, S.L., & Bem, D.J. (1970). Case study of a nonconscious ideology: Training the woman to know her place. In D.J. Bem (Ed.), *Beliefs, attitudes, and human affairs* (pp. 89–99). Belmont, CA: Brooks/Cole.

Bernstein, P. (1980). The work ethic that never was. *Wharton Magazine, 4*(3), 19–25.

Blood, M.R. (1969). Work values and job satisfaction. *Journal of Applied Psychology, 53,* 456–459.

Bowles, S., & Gintis, H. (1976). *Schooling in capitalist America.* New York: Basic Books.

Bramel, D., & Friend, R. (1981). Hawthorne, the myth of the docile worker, and class bias in psychology. *American Psychologist, 36,* 867–878.

Braverman, H. (1974). *Labor and monopoly capital.* New York: Monthly Review Press.

Brief, A.P., & Aldag, R.J. (1975). Employee reactions to job characteristics: A constructive replication. *Journal of Applied Psychology, 60,* 182–186.

Brief, A.P., & Aldag, R.J. (1977). The intrinsic-extrinsic dichotomy: Toward conceptual clarity. *Academy of Management Review, 2,* 496–499.

Burawoy, M. (1979). *Manufacturing consent: Changes in the labor process under monopoly capitalism.* Chicago: University of Chicago Press.

Campbell, J.P., & Pritchard, R.D. (1976). Motivation theory in industrial and organizational psychology. In M.D. Dunnette (Ed.), *Handbook of industrial and organizational psychology* (pp. 60–130). Chicago: Rand-McNally.

Clawson, D. (1980). *Bureaucracy and the labor process: The transformation of U.S. industry, 1860–1920.* New York: Monthly Review Press.

Clayre, A. (1974). Work and play. *Ideas and experience of work and leisure.* New York: Harper & Row.

Cox, H. (1984). *Religion in the secular city: Toward a postmodern theology.* New York: Simon and Schuster.

Culbert, S.A., & McDonough, J.J. (1985). *Radical management: Power politics and the pursuit of trust.* New York: The Free Press.

Cummings, L.L. (1980). Task design. In B. Karmel (Ed.), *Point and counterpoint in organizational behavior.* Hinsdale, IL: Dryden Press.

Deans, R.C. (1973). Productivity and the new work ethic. In Editorial research reports on the American work ethic (pp. 1–20). Washington, DC: Congressional Quarterly, Inc.

de Grazia, S. (1964). *Of time, work and leisure.* Garden City, NY: Anchor Books.

Dubin, R. (1976a). Theory building in applied areas. In M.D. Dunnette (Ed.), *Handbook of industrial and organizational psychology* (pp. 17–39). Chicago: Rand McNally.

Dubin, R. (1976b). Work in modern society. In R. Dubin (Ed.), *Handbook of work, organization, and society* (pp. 5–35). Chicago: Rand McNally.

Dyer, L., & Parker, D.F. (1975). Classifying outcomes in work motivation research: An examination of the intrinsic-extrinsic dichotomy. *Journal of Applied Psychology, 60,* 455–458.

Edelman, M. (1977). *Political language: Words that succeed and policies that fail.* New York: Academic Press.

Edwards, R.C. (1978). Who fares well in the welfare state? In R.C. Edwards, M. Reich, & T. Weisskopf (Eds.), *The capitalist system* (2nd ed.) (pp. 244–251). Englewood Cliffs, NJ: Prentice-Hall.

Fein, M. (1976). Motivation for work. In R. Dubin (Ed.), *Handbook of work, organization, and society* (pp. 465–530). Chicago: Rand McNally.

Feyerabend, P. (1975). *Against method.* London: Verso.

Fromm, E. (1961). *Marx's concept of man.* New York: Frederick Ungar.

George, C.S. (1968). *The history of management thought.* Englewood Cliffs, NJ: Prentice-Hall.

Gergen, K.J. (1982). *Toward transformation in social knowledge.* New York: Springer-Verlag.

Goldthorpe, J.H., Lockwood, D., Bechhofer, F., & Platt, J. (1969). *The affluent worker in the class structure.* Cambridge, England: Cambridge University Press.

Gordon, M.E., Kleiman, L.S., & Hanic, C.A. (1978). Industrial-organizational psychology: Open thy ears O house of Israel. *American Psychologist, 33,* 893–905.

Gouldner, A.W. (1970). *The coming crisis of western sociology.* New York: Basic Books.

Grant, M. (1960). *The world of Rome.* London: Weidenfeld and Nocolson.

Gutman, H.G. (1976). *Work culture, and society in industrializing America: Essays in American working-class and social history.* New York: Alfred A. Knopf.

Hackman, J.R., & Oldham, G.R. (1980). *Work redesign.* Reading, MA: Addison-Wesley.

Harris, T.C., & Locke, E.A. (1974). A replication of white-collar differences in sources of satisfaction and dissatisfaction. *Journal of Applied Psychology, 59,* 369–370.

Hays, S.P. (1957). *The response to industrialism 1885–1914.* Chicago: University of Chicago Press.

Heneman, H.G., Jr. (1973). Work and nonwork: Historical perspectives. In M.D. Dunnette (Ed.), *Work and nonwork in the year 2000* (pp. 12–27). Monterey, CA: Brooks/Cole.

Herzberg, F. (1966). *Work and the nature of man.* Cleveland: World Publishing Co.

Herzberg, F., Mausner, B., & Snyderman, B.B. (1959). *The motivation to work.* New York: John Wiley and Sons.

Hirschman, A.O. (1977). *The passions and the interests.* Princeton, NJ: Princeton University Press.

Howard, G.S. (1985). The role of values in the science of psychology. *American Psychologist, 40,* 255–265.

Hulin, C.L., & Blood, M.R. (1968). Job enlargement, individual differences and worker responses. *Psychological Bulletin, 69,* 41–55.

Iaffaldano, M.T., & Muchinsky, P.M. (1985). Job satisfaction and job performance: A meta-analysis. *Psychological Bulletin, 97,* 251–273.

Israel, J. (1971). *Alienation: From Marx to modern sociology.* Boston: Allyn and Bacon.

Jackall, R. (1978). *Workers in a labyrinth.* New York: Universe Books.

Kaplan, A. (1964). *The conduct of inquiry.* Scranton, PA: Chandler Publishing Company.

Keeley, M. (1978). A social-justice approach to job attitudes and task design. *Administrative Science Quarterly, 23,* 272–292.

Keeley, M. (1983). Values in organizational theory and management education. *Academy of Management Review, 8,* 376–386.

Keniston, K. (1965). *The uncommitted: alienated youth in American society.* New York: Dell.

Kopelman, R.E. (1986). *Managing productivity in organizations.* New York: McGraw-Hill.

Kuhn, T.S. (1970). *The structure of scientific revolutions.* (2nd Edition). Chicago: University of Chicago Press.

Lawler, E.E. (1971). *Pay and organizational effectiveness.* New York: McGraw-Hill.

Locke, E.A. (1973). Satisfiers and dissatisfiers among white-collar differences in sources of satisfaction and dissatisfaction. *Journal of Applied Psychology, 59,* 369–370.

Maccoby, M. (1981). *The leader.* New York: Ballantine Books.

Marglin, S.A. (1974). What do bosses do?: The origins and function of hierarchy in capitalist production. *Review of Radical Political Economics, 6,* 60–112.

Martinson, O.B., & Wilkening, E.A. (1984). Rural-urban differences in job satisfaction: Further evidence. *Academy of Management Journal, 27,* 199–206.

Marx, K., & Engels, F. (1965). *The German ideology.* London: Lawrence & Wishart.

Maslow, A.H. (1943). A theory of human motivation. *Psychological Review, 50,* 370–396.

Mayo, E. (1960). *The human problems of an industrial civilization.* New York: Viking Press.

McClelland, P.C. (1961). *The achieving society.* Princeton, NJ: Van Nostrand.

McGregor, D. (1960). *The human side of enterprise.* New York: McGraw-Hill.

Miles, R.E. (1975). *Theories of management: Implications for organizational behavior and development.* New York: McGraw-Hill.

Miles, R.E., & Rosenberg, H.R. (1982). The human resources approach to management: Second-generation issues. *Organizational Dynamics, 10,* (Winter), 26–41.

Mills, C.W. (1959). *The sociological imagination*. New York: Oxford University Press.
Munsterberg, H. (1913). *Psychology and industrial efficiency*. Boston: Houghton Mifflin.
Neff, W.S. (1985). *Work and human behavior*. New York: Aldine.
Nelson, D. (1975). *Managers and workers: Origins of the new factory system in the United States 1880–1920*. Madison, WI: University of Wisconsin Press.
Noble, D.F. (1984). *Forces of production: A social history of industrial automation*. New York: Knopf.
Nord, W.R. (1974). The failure of current applied behavioral science: A Marxian perspective. *Journal of Applied Behavioral Science, 10*, 557–578.
Nord, W.R. (1977). Job satisfaction reconsidered. *American Psychologist, 32*, 1026–1035.
Okrent, M. (1978–1979). Work, play and technology. *Philosophical Forum, 10*, 321–340.
Parker, S.R., & Smith, M.A. (1976). Work and leisure. In R. Dubin (Ed.), *Handbook of work, organization, and society* (pp. 37–62). Chicago: Rand McNally.
Pence, G.E. (1978–1979). Towards a theory of work. *Philosophical Forum, 10*, 306–320.
Pollard, S. (1963). Factory discipline in the industrial revolution. *Economic History Review, 16*, 254–271.
Pondy, L.R., Frost, P.J., Morgan, G., & Dandridge, T. (Eds.). (1983). *Organizational symbolism*. Greenwich, CT: JAI Press.
Pope, L. (1942). *Millhands and preachers: A study of Gastonia*. New Haven: Yale University Press.
Pope John Paul II (1981). Laborem Exercens. In C. Carlen (Ed.), *The Papal Encyclicals 1958* (pp. 299–326). Wilmington, NC: McGrath Publishing Company.
Pope Leo XIII (1936). *On the condition of the working classes*. New York: America Press.
Purcell, T.V. (1967). Work psychology and business values: A triad theory of work motivation. *Personnel Psychology, 20*, 231–257.
Rodgers, D.T. (1974). *The work ethic in industrial America, 1850–1920*. Chicago: University of Chicago Press.
Roethlisberger, F.J., & Dickson, W.J. (1939). *Management and the worker*. Cambridge: Harvard University Press.
Salancik, G.R., & Pfeffer, J. (1978). A social information processing approach to job attitudes and task design. *Administrative Science Quarterly, 23*, 224–253.
Sarason, S.B. (1981). An asocial psychology and a misdirected clinical psychology. *American Psychologist, 36*, 827–836.
Scheibe, K.E. (1970). *Beliefs and values*. New York: Holt, Rinehart and Winston.
Schiemann, W.A., & Morgan, B.S. (1983). *Managing human resources: Employee discontent and declining productivity*. Princeton, NJ: Opinion Research Corporation.
Schwab, D.P. (1980). Construct validity in organizational behavior. In B.M. Staw & L.L. Cummings (Eds.), *Research in organizational behavior*. (Vol. 2) (pp. 3–43). Greenwich, CT: JAI Press.
Schwartz, H.S. (1983). A theory of deontic work motivation. *Journal of Applied Behavioral Science, 19*, 203–214.
Sombart, W. (1913). *The Jews and modern capitalism*. London: T. Fisher Unwin.
Spence, J.T. (1985). Achievement American style: The rewards and costs of individualism. *American Psychologist, 40*, 1285–1295.
Steers, R.M., & Spencer, D.G. (1977). The role of achievement motivation in job design. *Journal of Applied Psychology, 62*(4), 472–479.
Stone, K. (1974). The origins of job structures in the steel industry. *Review of Radical Political Economy, 6*, 113–173.
Strauss, G. (1963). Some notes on power equalization. In H. J. Leavitt (Ed.), *The social science of organizations* (pp. 39–84). Englewood Cliffs, NJ: Prentice-Hall.
Thompson, E.P. (1963). *The making of the English working class*. London: Victor Gollantz.

Tilgher, A. (1931). *Work: What it has meant to man through the ages*. London: Harrap.

Turner, A.N. (1955). Management on the assembly line. *Harvard Business Review, 33*, 40–48.

Tyler, G. (1983). The work ethic: A union view. In J. Barbash, R.J. Lapman, S.A. Levitan, & G. Tyler (Eds.), *The work ethic—a critical analysis* (pp. 197–210). Madison, WI: Industrial Relations Research Association.

Walker, C.R. (1950). The problem of the repetitive job. *Harvard Business Review, 28*, 54–58.

Walker, C.R., & Guest, R.H. (1952). *The man on the assembly line*. Cambridge, MA: Harvard University Press.

Watson, T.J. (1977). *The personnel managers: A study in the sociology of work and employment*. London: Routledge & Kegan Paul.

Weber, M. (1930). *The Protestant Ethic and the spirit of capitalism* (T. Parsons, Trans.). New York: Charles Scribner's Sons.

Weber, M. (1949). *The methodology of the social sciences*. Glenco, IL: Free Press.

Weick, K.E. (1979). *The social psychology of organizing* (2nd Ed.). Reading, MA: Addison-Wesley.

White, J.K. (1978). Individual differences and the job quality worker response relationship: Review, integration, and comments. *The Academy of Management, 3*, 267–280.

White, R.W. (1952). *Lives in progress*. New York: Dryden.

White, S.E., & Mitchell, T.R. (1979). Job enrichment versus social cues: A comparison and competitive test. *Journal of Applied Psychology, 64(1)*, 1–9.

Whyte, M.K. (1973). Bureaucracy and modernization in China: The Maoist critique. *American Sociological Review, 38*, 149–163.

Work in America. (1973). Cambridge: The MIT Press.

Zuboff, S. (1983). The work ethic and work organization. In J. Barbash, R.J. Lampman, S.A. Levitan, & G. Tyler (Eds.), *The work ethic—a critical analysis* (pp. 153–181). Madison, WI: Industrial Relations Research Association.

The Evolution and Adaptation of Organizations

Edited by **Barry M. Staw** and **L.L. Cummings**

CONTENTS: Organizational Life Cycles and Natural Selection, *John Freeman.* **Even Dwarfs Started Small: Liabilities of Age and Size and Their Strategic Implications,** *Howard Aldrich and Ellen R. Auster.* **The Political Environments of Organizations: An Ecological View,** *Glenn R. Carroll, Jacques Delacroix, and Jerry Goodstein.* **Managerial Discretion: A Bridge Between Polar Views of Organizational Outcomes,** *Donald C. Hambrick and Sidney Finkelstein.* **Organizational Evolution: A Metamorphosis Model of Convergence and Reorientation,** *Michael L. Tushman and Elaine Romanelli.* **Behavior in Escalation Situations: Antecedents, Prototypes, and Solutions,** *Barry M. Staw.* **A Model of Creativity and Innovation in Organizations,** *Teresa M. Amabileand Jerry Ross.* **When a Thousand Flowers Bloom: Structural, Collective, and Social Conditions for Innovation in Organization,** *Rosabeth Moss Kanter.*

1990   320 pp.   LC 90-4525   Paper $19.50
ISBN 1-55938-221-X

All articles are reprinted from: **Research in Organizational Behavior,** Edited by **Barry M. Staw,** *School of Business Administration, University of California, Berkeley* and **L.L. Cummings,** *Carlson School of Management, University of Minnesota*

JAI PRESS INC.

55 Old Post Road - No. 2
P.O. Box 1678
Greenwich, Connecticut 06836-1678
Tel: 203-661-7602

JAI PRESS

Information and Cognition in Organizations

Edited by **L.L. Cummings** and **Barry M. Staw**

CONTENTS: Management as Symbolic Action: The Creation and Maintenance of Organizational Paradigms, *Jeffrey Pfeffer.* **Rationality and Justification in Organizational Life,** *Barry M. Staw.* **The Use of Information in Organizational Decision Making: A Model and Some Propositions,** *Charles A. O'Reilly, III.* **Negotiator Cognition,** *Max H. Bazerman and John S. Carroll.* **Accountability: The Neglected Social Context of Judgment and Choice,** *Philip E. Tetlock.* **An Attributional Model of Leadership and the Poor Performing Subordinate: Development and Validation,** *Terence R. Mitchell, Steven G. Green, and Robert E. Wood.* **Information Richness: A New Approach to Managerial Behavior and Organization Design,** *Richard L. Daft and Robert H. Lengel.* **Cognitive Processes in Organizations,** *Karl E. Weick.*

1990   320pp.   LC 90-4523   Paper $19.50
ISBN 1-55938-218-X

All articles are reprinted from: **Research in Organizational Behavior,** Edited by **Barry M. Staw,** *School of Business Administration, University of California, Berkeley* and **L.L. Cummings,** *Carlson School of Management, University of Minnesota*

JAI PRESS INC.

55 Old Post Road - No. 2
P.O. Box 1678
Greenwich, Connecticut 06836-1678
Tel: 203-661-7602

Evaluation and Employment in Organizations

Edited by **L.L. Cummings** and **Barry M. Staw**

CONTENTS: Performance Appraisal: A Process Focus, *Daniel R. Ilgen and Jack M. Feldman.* **Self-Assessments in Organizations: A Literature Review and Integrative Model. A Process Analysis of the Assessment Center Method,** *Sheldon Zedeck.* **Sex Bias in Work Settings: The Lack of Fit Model,** *Madaline E. Heilman.* **Understanding Comparable Worth: A Societal and Political Perspective,** *Thomas A. Mahoney.* **The Meanings of Absence: New Strategies for Theory and Research. Employee Turnover and Post Decision Accommodation,** *Richard M. Steers and Richard T. Mowday.* **The Effects of Work Layoffs in Survivors: Research Theory and Practice,** *Joel Brockner.*

1990   256 pp.   LC 90-4533   Paper $19.50
ISBN 1-55938-219-8

All articles are reprinted from: **Research in Organizational Behavior,** Edited by **Barry M. Staw,** *School of Business Administration, University of California, Berkeley* and **L.L. Cummings,** *Carlson School of Management, University of Minnesota*

JAI PRESS INC.
55 Old Post Road - No. 2
P.O. Box 1678
Greenwich, Connecticut 06836-1678
Tel: 203-661-7602

Personality and Organizational Influence

Edited by **Barry M. Staw** and **L.L. Cummings**

CONTENTS: Personality and Organizational Behavior, *Howard M. Weiss and Seymour Adler.* **Interactional Psychology and Organizational Behavior,** *Benjamin Schneider.* **Toward a Theory of Organizational Socialization,** *John Van Maanen and Edgar T. Schein.* **The Politics of Upward Influence in Organizations,** *Lyman W. Porter, Robert W. Allen, and Harold L. Angle.* **Principled Organizational Dissent: A Theoretical Essay,** *Jill W. Graham.* **Power and Personality in Complex Organizations,** *Robert J. House.* **Organizational Structure, Attitudes, and Behaviors,** *Chris J. Berger and L.L. Cummings.*

1990   326 pp.   LC 90-4524   Paper $19.50
ISBN 1-55938-217-1

All articles are reprinted from: **Research in Organizational Behavior,** Edited by **Barry M. Staw,** *School of Business Administration, University of California, Berkeley* and **L.L. Cummings,** *Carlson School of Management, University of Minnesota*

JAI PRESS INC.

55 Old Post Road - No. 2
P.O. Box 1678
Greenwich, Connecticut 06836-1678
Tel: 203-661-7602

Leadership, Participation, and Group Behavior

Edited by **L.L. Cummings** and **Barry M. Staw**

**CONTENTS: Leadership: Some Empirical Generaliza-
tions and New Research Directions,** *Robert House and Mary
Baetz. Charisma and its Routinization in Two Social Movement
Organizations, Harrison Trice and Janice M. Beyer.* **Participa-
tion in Decision-Making: One More Look,** *Edwin A. Locke
and David M. Schweiger.* **Workers Participation in
Management: An International Perspective,** *George
Strauss.* **The Meeting as a Neglected Social Form in
Organizational Studies,** *Helen B. Schwartzman.* **Under-
standing Groups in Organizations,** *Paul S. Goodman,
Elizabeth Ravlin, and Marshall Schminke.*

1990   386 pp.   LC 90-4529   Paper $22.50
ISBN 1-55938-220-1

All articles are reprinted from: **Research in Organizational
Behavior,** Edited by **Barry M. Staw,** *School of Business
Administration, University of California, Berkeley* and **L.L.
Cummings,** *Carlson School of Management, University of
Minnesota*

JAI PRESS INC.

55 Old Post Road - No. 2
P.O. Box 1678
Greenwich, Connecticut 06836-1678
Tel: 203-661-7602

J A I   P R E S S

Also Available !

Theoretical and Methodological Issues in Human Resources Research

Edited by **Gerald R. Ferris** and **Kendrith M. Rowland**
1990   236 pp.   LC 90-4568   Paper $18.95
ISBN 1-55938-227-9

Career and Human Resources Development

Edited by **Gerald R. Ferris** and **Kendrith M. Rowland**
1990   268 pp.   LC 90-4480,   Paper $18.95
ISBN 1-55938-229-5

Performance Evaluation, Goal Setting, and Feedback

Edited by **Gerald R. Ferris** and **Kendrith M. Rowland**
1990   296 pp.   LC 90-5947   Paper $18.95
ISBN 1-55938-230-9

Organizational Entry

Edited by **Gerald R. Ferris** and **Kendrith M. Rowland**
1990   320 pp.   LC 90-4582   Paper $19.50
ISBN 1-55938-228-7

All articles reprinted from: **Research in Personnel and Human Resources Management,** Edited by **Gerald R. Ferris** and **Kendrith M. Rowland,** *University of Illinois, Urbana-Champaign*